The Soar Cognitive Architecture

The Soar Cognitive Architecture

John E. Laird

The MIT Press
Cambridge, Massachusetts
London, England

Set in Stone Sans and Stone Serif by Toppan Best-set Premedia Limited.

Library of Congress Cataloging-in-Publication Data

Laird, John, 1954–
The Soar cognitive architecture / John E. Laird.
    p.   cm.
"A Bradford Book."
Includes bibliographical references and index.
ISBN 978-0-262-12296-2 (hardcover : alk. paper), 978-0-262-53853-4 (pb.)
1. Artificial intelligence. 2. Software architecture. I. Title.
Q335.L329   2012
006.3—dc23

                                                                    2011030567

to my parents, Margaret L. and John R. Laird; my wife, Ann Alpern; and my daughters, Emily, Jessica, and Valerie

The secret of success is constancy of purpose.
—Benjamin Disraeli

In the computer field, the moment of truth is a running program; all else is prophecy.
—Herbert Simon

Contents

Preface

The primary goal of this book is to provide a comprehensive description of the design of Soar, addressing both how it works and why it is designed as it is. Cognitive architectures are complex. In view of the numerous extensions my students and I have made to Soar in recent years, it became clear that the best way to communicate what Soar is was through a book. The hope is that the book provides sufficient detail so that readers can understand the rational for its design and the details of its operation, and can appreciate not only what Soar can achieve today but also its potential for the future.

The book's secondary goal is to provide an example of a methodology for describing a cognitive architecture, beginning with a list of requirements based on a set of assumptions about environments, tasks, and agent structures. The requirements are followed by an abstract description of the computational model. The remainder of the book presents the architecture in simple, implemented, end-to-end examples so that the underlying operational details of architecture are clear. It is hoped that this book will encourage others doing research in cognitive architecture to compile similarly comprehensive descriptions and evaluations of their systems.

The third goal is to evaluate Soar as a cognitive architecture for the support of human-level agents. Throughout our examination and evaluation of Soar, we identify strengths as well as shortcomings and areas requiring future work, which we expect will lead to extensions and redesigns of existing components and the addition of new components. Although many of the research issues are challenging, and promise to engage us for many years, we have yet to identify any that appear to be insurmountable. Our experience in research over the last 30 years makes us extremely cautious about predicting how fast advances can be achieved, but no matter how long it takes, we are placing our bets for achieving human-level artificial intelligence on cognitive architecture in general, and on Soar in particular.

For those who wish to pursue Soar further, it is available (free) at http://sitemaker .umich.edu/soar/home. Source code, manuals, tutorials, an editor, a debugger, and many task environments are included. Soar runs on all standard operating systems, including Windows, Mac OS, Linux, and iOS. We maintain a mailing list (soar-group @lists.sourceforge.net), and we hold yearly workshops on Soar research.

Acknowledgments

I thank all my co-authors: Nate Derbinsky, Nicholas Gorski, Scott Lathrop, Robert P. Marinier III, Andrew M. Nuxoll, Yongjia Wang, Samuel Wintermute, Robert E. Wray III, and Joseph Xu. Without their hard work, this book would not have been possible. Special thanks to Robert E. Wray III, who worked with me on the overall structure of the book and some of the most difficult chapters, and to Nate Derbinsky, who is responsible for developing the current versions of reinforcement learning, semantic memory, and episodic memory in Soar 9. I am also deeply grateful to Jonathan Voigt, who has maintained and extended Soar and many of the task environments used in the book. I thank the many members of the Soar community who contributed material or comments: Mitchell Bloch, Ronald Chong, Karen Coulter, Jacob Crossman, Jakub Czyz, Randolph Jones, Justin Li, Deryle Lonsdale, Brian Magerko, Shiwali Mohan, Kate Pierro, Dave Ray, Paul Rosenbloom, Brian Stensrud, Glenn Taylor, Miller Tinkerhess, and Scott Wallace. I also thank Shelley Nason and Douglas Pearson, who have made major contributions to the development of Soar 9. I thank all of the program managers of funding agencies who have supported our research on Soar throughout the years, including those at AFOSR, DARPA, NASA, NSF, ONR, and TARDEC. Not only have they provided financial support; they have provided inspiration and challenges that have led to major advances in our research. I thank Paul Bethge of the MIT Press for his editing and assistance with the publication process.

Finally, my thanks to Paul S. Rosenbloom and Allen Newell, who started with me on this journey more than thirty years ago.

1 Introduction

Although research in artificial intelligence (AI) has been under way for more than 50 years, we still are far from achieving human-level artificial intelligence. We humans draw effortlessly on many different cognitive capabilities for any given task, and we pursue a seemingly infinite variety of tasks. For a task as simple as cooking, we can read from a cookbook, follow the instructions, plan how to interleave different preparation activities, respond to interruptions such as phone calls, and then easily return to the task. When we have difficulties, we don't freeze up; we muddle through. Sometimes that entails planning and problem solving, but we also can ask for help—for example, we can borrow a missing ingredient from a neighbor, or we can ask a friend how to perform a particularly tricky step. We also learn from experience, becoming expert at tasks we perform repeatedly. And once we have asked for help, we usually don't have to ask again.

In contrast, most AI systems are designed to solve problems of one type by taking one specific approach, and to solve problems of that type very well. AI has been successful in developing systems that perform better than humans on many problems, such as playing checkers or chess, searching through credit card transactions to discover fraud, helping us search the Internet, or scheduling departures at airports. However, we do not yet have computational systems that seamlessly integrate the many capabilities we associate with human intelligence. These capabilities include interacting with dynamic complex environments, pursuing a wide variety of tasks, using large bodies of knowledge, planning, and continually learning from experience.

This book is about one research effort to develop general computational systems that have the same cognitive abilities as humans. As shorthand, my colleagues and I call these systems *human-level agents*. Our approach to developing human-level agents is to study the *cognitive architecture* underlying general intelligence (Langley, Laird, and Rogers 2009; Newell 1990). A cognitive architecture provides the fixed computational structures that form the building blocks for creating generally intelligent systems. A cognitive architecture is not a single algorithm or method for solving a problem; rather, it is the task-independent infrastructure that brings an agent's knowledge to bear on a problem in order to produce behavior. Thus, the goal of our research—to discover the fundamental computational mechanisms that lead to human-level agents—is ambitious if not audacious.

Over the last 30 years, my colleagues and I have been developing Soar, a general cognitive architecture that integrates knowledge-intensive reasoning, reactive execution, hierarchical reasoning, planning, and learning (Laird 1991a, 2008; Laird and Newell 1983; Laird, Newell, and Rosenbloom 1987; Laird and Rosenbloom 1996; Newell 1990; Rosenbloom et al. 1991; Rosenbloom, Laird, and Newell 1993). Soar is distinguished by its ability to use a wide variety of types and levels of knowledge for solving problems and subproblems, so that behavior in Soar agents arises through the dynamic combination of available knowledge whether the knowledge was programmed or was learned from experience. With Soar, we have developed agents that use a wide variety of methods to work on a wide range of tasks, including mental arithmetic, reasoning tasks, configuring computers, algorithm design, medical diagnosis, natural-language processing, robotic control, simulating pilots for military training, and controlling non-player characters in computer games. In addition to being a software system for agent development, Soar is a theory of what computational structures are necessary to support human-level agents. Over the years, both the software system and the theory have evolved, having been infused with new ideas and cognitive functionality as we have expanded the range of environments, tasks, and knowledge to which we have applied them. On the one hand, Soar is a long-term research project in which we continually attempt to extend the human-level capabilities we can achieve in a computer; on the other hand, Soar is a specific architecture that you can use today for developing AI agents.

Recently we have extended Soar by adding reinforcement learning, semantic memory, episodic memory, mental imagery, and an appraisal-based model of emotion. With these additions, the current version (Soar 9) takes important steps toward providing a comprehensive theory and architecture for human-level agents, with a unique combination of capabilities not found in other cognitive architectures. Not only do these extensions provide significant new capabilities; they also represent a major departure from some of our original hypotheses for Soar that emphasized uniformity and simplicity. Among those hypotheses were that all long-term knowledge should be represented uniformly as rules, that a single learning mechanism (chunking) is sufficient for all learning, and that symbolic representations are sufficient for all short-term and long-term knowledge. In contrast, Soar 9 supports multiple long-term memory systems (procedural, episodic, and semantic), multiple learning mechanisms, and multiple representations of short-term knowledge (symbolic, diagrammatic, and imagery-based representations).

This book provides a comprehensive description of the new version of Soar, including the essential aspects that have defined Soar since its inception, as well as the new components. It describes the details of Soar's component memories and processes, and it explores how they contribute to meeting the requirements of a human-level agent. In developing the new components, my students and I have emphasized basic functionality and efficiency so that the components will be useful and usable for problems requiring large bodies of knowledge. Possibly more important than the individual components is how the components work together to support the problem-space computational model (Newell 1991). Even with these extensions, Soar is still a work in progress. It is continually evolving. This book captures its progress at a specific point in time.

The book's primary goal is to describe how and why Soar works the way it does. A secondary goal is to provide an example of how we think a cognitive architecture should be described and evaluated, which includes proposing requirements for general cognitive architectures. The final goal is to evaluate how well Soar achieves those requirements. The presentation emphasizes the functionality of Soar for building human-level agents, in contrast with Allen Newell's seminal book *Unified Theories of Cognition* (1990). In that book, Newell used an earlier version of Soar to model a broad range of human behavior. I have not abandoned research in cognitive modeling; however, this book concentrates on the functionality that can be achieved by creating a complete cognitive architecture *inspired* by the human mind.

1.1 Background

Soar is an outgrowth of the groundbreaking work done by Allen Newell and Herbert Simon from the mid 1950s through the mid 1970s, including their pioneering work on LT (Newell and Simon 1956), on the "General Problem Solver" (Ernst and Newell 1969), on heuristic problem solving (Simon and Newell 1958), on production systems (Newell 1973), and on problem spaces (Newell 1991; Newell and Simon 1972). The "General Problem Solver," created by George Ernst and Newell, used a single, general method called *means-ends analysis* to solve many different puzzle-style problems. Means-ends analysis uses knowledge about how operators (the means) reduce the difference between states and goals (the ends), and it requires that there be an explicit representation of the goal being pursued. Thus, the "General Problem Solver" was limited in the types of knowledge it could use and the problems it could solve, but it was the first AI system that could solve multiple problems.

Although attempting to develop generally intelligent systems was a hallmark of some of the earliest AI systems, over the last 30 years the field of AI has concentrated on developing specialized algorithms for specific problems. It has come to be the case that most research in AI is either problem driven (such that researchers attempt to find the best algorithms for a class of problems) or algorithm driven (such that researchers attempt to discover the class of problems to which a given algorithm and its variants are most applicable). AI has worked across the range of task complexity, from simple to complex; however, for most AI systems the environment and the tasks are fixed and the system is structured to use knowledge for a limited set of tasks and to use specific algorithms and data structures. A good example of specialization is the chess-playing program Deep Blue (Campbell, Hoane, and Hsu 2002). Deep Blue "knows" a great deal about chess and uses specialized knowledge (and hardware) to play chess at the highest levels, but that is all it can do. Following this approach, AI has seen significant scientific and commercial success for many specific problems, but research on more general systems has languished.

In the early 1980s, Allen Newell and I attempted to take a step beyond the "General Problem Solver" by creating a general cognitive architecture that could use not just a single method, such as means-ends analysis, but whatever method was appropriate to the knowledge it had about a task. Our goal was to make it possible for knowledge about problem solving to be decomposed into primitive computational components that dynamically combine during problem solving, so that algorithms arise from the interaction of the characteristics of the task and the available knowledge. Our approach, which led to the creation of the first version of Soar, combined the idea of using *problem spaces* to organize behavior in solving a problem with the use of *production systems* to represent the knowledge used to control behavior. In problem spaces, behavior is decomposed into selection of *operators* and their application to *states* to make progress toward a goal. States are representations of the current situations; operators are the means by which a system can make deliberate changes in the situation. Soar is named for this basic cycle of *state, operator, and result*. In production systems, long-term knowledge is encoded as rules in procedural memory; short-term knowledge is encoded as declarative symbolic structures in working memory.

Many classic AI systems, including LT, the "General Problem Solver," and STRIPS (Fikes and Nilsson 1971), use a single problem space for each task. With Soar, however, different problem spaces are available for different tasks, and multiple problem spaces can be used for different aspects of a single task. This step alone provides a significant increase in generality and flexibility. And by casting all activity within problem spaces, Soar uses a uniform approach for control of internal reasoning and external action. Similarly, although Soar wasn't the first system to use production rules, it was the first one to use them to independently represent different functional aspects of operators: proposal, evaluation, and application. Traditionally, the locus of decision making in a production system is the selection of the next rule to fire. In Soar, in contrast with trying to select the best rule, all matching rules fire in parallel, and the locus of decision making is selecting the next *operator*. Knowledge about which operator to select is encoded in production rules.

In making a decision, the rules relevant to the current situation control behavior, so that, instead of following a monolithic method, the method emerges from a combination of the knowledge and the structure of the task. Thus, as knowledge is added, the behavior of the system changes and often corresponds to general methods, such as the weak methods (Newell 1968). Weak methods include generate-and-test, depth-first search, best-first search, means-ends analysis, mini-max, and A*—that is, all the basic search methods found in AI. The first version of Soar provided the underlying computational engine for representing the primitive components of weak methods, and it dynamically combined them during problem solving, which led to a *universal weak method* (Laird and Newell 1983). A weak method emerges from a combination of task control knowledge and problem structure.

The second version of Soar was extended to include an automatic subgoaling mechanism. That was followed by the addition of *chunking* (Laird, Rosenbloom, and Newell 1986b), which was an adaptation of ideas from Paul Rosenbloom's thesis work (Laird, Rosenbloom, and Newell 1986a). We then decided to re-implement an existing expert system, called R1, that was used to configure VAX computers for the Digital Equipment Corporation (McDermott 1980). At the time, R1 was one of the largest expert systems in existence. Our project, spearheaded by Paul Rosenbloom, successfully re-coded a substantial fraction of R1 into Soar (Rosenbloom et al. 1985). As R1-Soar demonstrated, not only was Soar sufficient for developing systems with individual bits of knowledge; it also could encode very large bodies of knowledge, so that Soar agents could achieve expert performance on a specific task, in addition to having broad competence across a wide range of problems. Although many aspects of Soar have changed over the years, its synthesis of problem spaces and productions systems and its ability to support a spectrum of knowledge, from the universal weak method to expert performance, have been maintained.

1.2 Cognitive Architectures

One of the fundamental challenges in developing human-level agents is defining the primitive computational structures that store, retrieve, and process knowledge. Equally important is defining the organization of those computational structures. In a standard computer, the architecture includes the overall design of the memories, the processing and control components, representations of data, and input/output devices. The memories hold data and programs; the processing components execute the program's instructions, performing primitive operations, moving data between memories, and determining which instruction is executed next. Thus, the architecture defines the language for specifying and controlling computation. The language should be general and flexible so it is easy to specify and control computation, but it must be constrained so that it can be implemented efficiently and reliably.

Cognitive architectures are close cousins to computer architectures. They have memories, processing and control components, representations of data, and input/

output devices, but instead of needing to support general computation they must support the representation, acquisition, and use of knowledge to pursue goals. There is an important distinction between the architecture, which is fixed and task independent, and the agent's knowledge, which is task dependent and grows through learning. Although learning modifies and adds knowledge, it doesn't modify the architecture, and it is the architecture, via its learning mechanisms, that defines how knowledge changes. Architectures can change through development, but the time scales of those changes are much larger than those of individual tasks. Even though one can program a cognitive architecture to solve a specific problem, a cognitive architecture is designed to be the basis for creating general, autonomous agents that can solve (and learn from) a wide variety of problems, using a wide variety of knowledge. One of the primary challenges for a cognitive architecture is coordinating the many capabilities we associate with intelligent systems, such as perception, reasoning, planning, language processing, and learning.

Research on cognitive architectures is distinguished from research on classifying, categorizing, and encoding vast bodies of knowledge for their own right, such as in systems like Cyc (Lenat 1995; Lenat and Guha 1990) and Watson (Ferrucci et al. 2010), which has its own intriguing research problems. The focus of cognitive architecture research is on creating the structures that support learning, encoding, and using knowledge to perform tasks in dynamic environments. Thus, a cognitive architecture must support decision making and interaction with an environment. Although a cognitive architecture might use a system such as Cyc or Watson to store and access knowledge, it must have additional components for encoding procedural knowledge and supporting environmental interaction.

Cognitive architectures are also distinguished from AI languages, toolkits, and general frameworks that provide tools and some guidance in developing agents and AI systems. AI languages, such as Lisp, do not make specific commitments as to the primitive memories, knowledge representations, control mechanisms, or learning mechanisms used in developing agents. Instead, they can be used to build architectures. (Early versions of Soar were implemented in Lisp, as is ACT-R; see Anderson 2007.) Frameworks often distinguish between different types of processing or storage systems in an agent, but they do not have a single implementation with associated languages for representing knowledge. Popular frameworks include rule-based systems (Brownston et al. 1985; Friedman-Hill 2003), blackboard systems (Corkill 1991), logic (Pollock 1999), behavior-based systems (Brooks 1999), finite-state machines (FSMs), BDI (Belief, Desires, and Intention; Bratman 1987), and GOMs (Goals, Operators, and Methods; Card, Moran, and Newell 1987). Jones and Wray (2006) discuss frameworks and a comparative analysis of FSMs, BDI, GOMS, and Soar. Agents developed according to these frameworks share a general approach to agent development, often using a common system organization, and a commitment to general classes of knowledge representations, but without a commitment to specific representations. Some agent architectures are closer to frameworks, such as Polyscheme (Cassimatis 2002, 2006) and 4D/RCS (Albus 2002). Frameworks provide a common base of code and some representational schemes for knowledge, but they do not provide a comprehensive set of memories and processing elements that are sufficient for development of general agents. Developers must fill in many details using some other programming language, such as Lisp, Java, or C++. This makes it difficult to determine the theoretical commitments of a framework, as there is usually little constraint on how an agent is developed. AI toolkits, or middleware systems, are usually collections of different mechanisms, such as neural networks, fuzzy logic, genetic algorithms, rule-based systems, search algorithms, path planners, and semantic networks. Usually they don't provide overall control mechanisms; instead they are a collection of components that a developer can use with a standard programming language.

1.2.1   Levels of Architecture

A computational system can be viewed across multiple levels of abstraction. (See figure 1.1.) Cognitive architectures are one part of one level in a computational processing hierarchy (Newell 1990). The physical level is the lowest level. It provides the physical implementation of computation for the cognitive level. The cognitive level supports the knowledge level. This analysis assumes that there are sufficient regularities so that each level can be productively studied independently of the details of the levels below. As one progresses up the hierarchy, the behavior that is studied is at progressively longer time scales, such that the range of times at the physical level could be between nanoseconds and microseconds, the cognitive level between milliseconds and tens of seconds, and the knowledge level between minutes and hours.

The physical layer itself is usually a series of layers of silicon, digital circuits, computer architecture, virtual machines, and software that provide a set of fixed structures

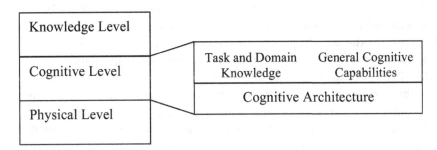

Figure 1.1
Levels of analysis of an agent.

for supporting general computation. Cognitive architectures sit at the interface between the physical level and the cognitive level, providing the structures for encoding knowledge. In theory, a cognitive architecture could be directly implemented in hardware (silicon or brain structures) without the intermediate layers of computer architecture and software that are used today. However, the possible gains in efficiency are greatly outweighed by the flexibility of conventional computers, which is necessary to support an iterative research and development process for current cognitive architectures.

The variability and the adaptability of cognition comes from the knowledge that is encoded in a cognitive architecture. Thus, a cognitive architecture provides the fixed processes and memories and their associated algorithms and data structures to acquire, represent, and process knowledge about the environment and tasks for moment-to-moment reasoning, problem solving, and goal-oriented behavior. This leads to a simple equation: architecture + knowledge = behavior. Throughout this book, I use the term "knowledge" more broadly than it is commonly used in philosophy, where it is often restricted to verified beliefs. I use it to refer to information a system uses to make decisions and produce behavior, even if the information is incorrect. I also use it to refer to the representations of knowledge in an agent—where "knowledge" is technically something that is ascribed to an agent by an observer (Newell 1990). The knowledge encoded in a cognitive architecture includes general knowledge (which supports general cognitive capabilities, such as language processing, planning, and retrospective reasoning) and task knowledge (which is specific to problems and domains).

Although the use of "cognitive" in "cognitive architecture" often evokes a connection to human psychology, the emphasis is on the level of processing. Cognitive architectures vary. Though some attempt to model human behavior, many do not.

The top level is the knowledge level, which abstracts away from the processing of the cognitive level. At the knowledge level, an agent is not described using specific data structures, representations of knowledge, and algorithms; it is described using the content of the knowledge and the principle of rationality (Newell 1982, 1990), whereby an agent selects actions to achieve its goals on the basis of the available knowledge. Achieving the knowledge level requires perfect rationality, which is computationally infeasible except when an agent has simple goals or limited bodies of knowledge. The challenge for a cognitive architecture is to provide structures to approximate the knowledge level under the constraint of being physically realized with limited computational resources. One of the hypotheses underlying research on cognitive architectures is that approximations to rational behavior, and thus intelligence, arise from the combination of large bodies of knowledge and the underlying set of fixed processes that manipulate that knowledge—the underlying cognitive architecture.

1.2.2 History of the Development of Cognitive Architectures

There is a long history of research in cognitive architecture. ACT (Anderson 1976, 1983, 1990, 1993, 2007) and Soar are two of the oldest, most developed, and most studied architectures. Many others have been developed. Figure 1.2 is a time line listing some of the cognitive architectures that have been developed over the years. (For a comprehensive review of pre-1992 cognitive architectures, see Wray et al. 1992.)

Cognitive architectures often emphasize a specific capability to distinguish them from earlier systems, such as multi-method problem solving (which was introduced in the first version of Soar) and declarative memory (which was introduced in ACT). Figure 1.2 includes with each architecture its initial focus. Often the focus is a mix of a knowledge representation (such as semantic networks, production rules, or a blackboard architecture) and some cognitive capability that is emphasized (e.g., planning, problem solving, or meta-reasoning). This emphasis doesn't imply that the specified architecture was the first to consider that focus. As the field has matured, newer architectures have attempted to cover more of the cognitive landscape from their inception, often incorporating multiple approaches for knowledge representation and reasoning.

Moreover, existing architectures are rarely static. Succeeding versions attempt to meet more of the requirements of a complete, general architecture, thereby making it appropriate to a wider range of environments, tasks, and agents. For some architectures, there are radical reconceptualizations in which new versions have only a passing similarity to older versions (e.g., Icarus); other architectures undergo general evolution. For Soar, it has been a combination of evolution and revolution. Soar went through major changes when my colleagues and I began to work in dynamic external environments, and recently it has undergone major extensions to expand the types of learning and knowledge representations it supports while maintaining many of the features that have existed since its inception.

1.2.3 Approaches to Cognitive Architectures

There is great diversity in cognitive architectures, but they fall into three general categories corresponding to different long-term research goals:

• Cognitive modeling, the goal of which is to support the development of models of human behavior that match behavioral data such as reaction times, error rates, and even fMRI results. One of the advantages of using a cognitive architecture for creating a model of human behavior is that the architecture provides processes and structures that have been found to be consistent with human behavior for other tasks, possibly providing a *Unified Theory of Cognition*, as Newell (1990) proposed. ACT-R—an example of an architecture in which cognitive modeling is the primary goal—has been applied to a wide variety of tasks and psychological phenomena.

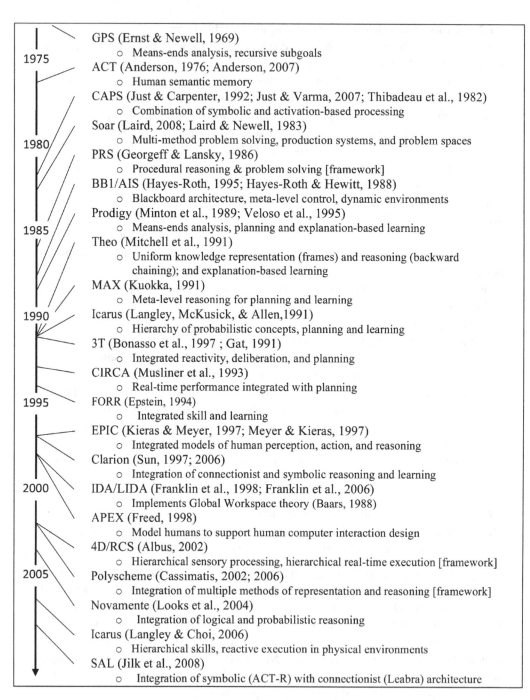

Figure 1.2
Cognitive architectures and their original foci.

• Agent development, the goal of which is to support the development of AI agents that interact with dynamic environments and employ a combination of AI techniques, including reactivity, goal-driven behavior, and planning. *Agent architectures* emphasize the integration of multiple techniques as well as programmability and flexibility. They do not attempt to incorporate all of the cognitive capabilities normally associated with humans, such as large knowledge bases, natural language, or ubiquitous learning. Fine-grained procedural knowledge is often specified using a traditional programming language outside the knowledge-representation schemes supported by the architecture. CIRCA (Musliner, Durfee, and Shin 1993) is an example of an early agent architecture that emphasized guaranteed real-time reactivity.

• Human-level agent development, the goal of which is to support the development of AI systems that support a broad range of behavior and cognitive capabilities and create complete, integrated intelligent agents that have many, if not most, of the capabilities associated with humans. As with agent architectures, these architectures emphasize functionality, but are distinguished in that the goal is to develop agents that can work on a wide variety of problems. These architectures emphasize knowledge-rich behavior, multiple long-term memories, and learning.

We have used Soar to pursue each of these three goals at different times during its development.

1.2.4 Commonalities across Multiple Cognitive Architectures

Although there are many differences between cognitive architectures, there are also many similarities. All the architectures illustrated in figure 1.2 use symbolic representations for descriptions of the current situation, long-term facts, and memories of events (if those structures are supported). In AI more broadly, symbol structures are the building blocks for problem solving, planning, language understanding, meta-level reasoning, and similar activities. Many cognitive architectures rely on non-symbolic processing to aid decision making, knowledge retrieval, and perceptual processing, and some include non-symbolic reasoning (e.g., probabilistic inference). Although there has been a wealth of research on connectionist and neural computation, to date there are no pure neural or connectionist architectures that support the broad range of knowledge and behavior that is possible with today's cognitive architectures. Some architectures, such as Clarion, CAPS4, and SAL, include both symbolic and connectionist representations.

Although there is diversity, the commonalities between some of these cognitive architectures go much deeper. Figure 1.3 is an abstract block diagram of a prototypical cognitive architecture that has memories and processing units common to Soar, ACT-R, Icarus, LIDA, and Clarion. EPIC also shares many of these structures, although it doesn't include learning mechanisms or declarative long-term memories. These architectures also have additional distinctive memories and processing units not

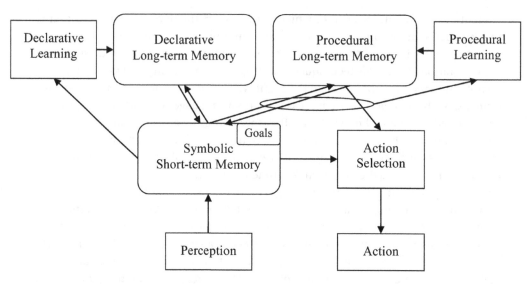

Figure 1.3
A prototypical cognitive architecture.

represented in the figure, and the details of how they implement these common structures are quite varied. The commonality in structure is not a complete surprise—ACT-R, LIDA, Clarion, EPIC are designed to model human behavior, and Soar and Icarus are inspired by it. However, many agent architectures differ significantly in structure from the prototypical cognitive architecture illustrated in figure 1.3.

In this prototypical architecture, sensory information is processed by perception and added to short-term memory. Short-term memory can cue retrieval from a long-term declarative memory to retrieve facts relevant to the situation. Associated with declarative memory is a learning module that uses activity in short-term memory to add facts to this memory. Procedural memory stores knowledge about what to do and when to do it. Retrieval from procedural memory is also cued by short-term memory, and it has an associated learning component. Data from procedural memory and from working memory are used by the action-selection component to choose the next action, which can involve either motor actions in an external environment or deliberate changes in short-term memory.

In addition to these common structures, behavioral control in these architectures has many commonalities. In order to support flexible and reactive behavior, behavior is generated through a sequence of decisions over potential internal and/or external actions. Complex behavior, which can include internal planning, arises in the form of actions that create and interpret internally generated structures and respond to the dynamics of the environment.

These architectures usually assume asynchronous execution of the modules as well as parallel execution (at least in theory) within many of the modules. However, they have limited external parallelism, so action selection chooses a single action (though perhaps a complex one) or a small number of actions to execute. When used to model human behavior, the execution cycle of accessing procedural knowledge and selecting an action corresponds to between 50 and 200 milliseconds in human performance, with Soar, EPIC, and ACT-R all assuming 50 msec. Soar's real-time performance is hundreds to thousands of times as fast.

Many of the design decisions are influenced by the need for a cognitive architecture to support reactive behavior in a dynamic environment as well as more purposeful, knowledge-mediated behavior. Thus, the learning mechanisms are incremental (adding small units of knowledge, one at a time) and online (learning occurs during performance). As new knowledge is experienced and acquired, it is immediately available. Moreover, learning doesn't require extensive analysis of past behavior or previously acquired knowledge.

The need to maintain reactivity in a learning system is challenging because as an agent's knowledge increases, the time needed to find knowledge that is relevant to the current situation usually increases, slowing the response time of the agent. To date, there seems to be great faith that Moore's Law or massively parallel implementations will solve the problem underlying this assumption. As a result, research in cognitive architectures has rarely taken this issue seriously, and the number of agents developed in cognitive architectures with large knowledge bases is small. Although we haven't "solved" this problem, concern about it has had a direct effect on the design and evaluation of Soar during the development of TacAir-Soar and NL-Soar, which had 8,500 and 3,500 rules respectively, and during our exploration of agents that have episodic and semantic memories that contain millions of elements.

Although there are many commonalities between these architectures, there are also many differences. Some of the differences arise from differences in the goals of the researchers, such as that between cognitive modeling and agent development; others arise from differences in the phenomena being studied, especially in systems used to model human behaviors that occur at different time scales. Even with the differences, the commonalities are compelling, suggesting that we should see even more convergence as researchers begin to study similar behavioral phenomena.

1.2.5 The Role of Cognitive Architectures

By providing a fixed computational infrastructure for developing intelligent agents, a successful cognitive architecture provides sufficient structure so that only knowledge about the task (both general and specific) must be added. Inherent to the architecture are solutions to difficult problems of agent design, such as how to integrate reactivity with deliberation, how to integrate learning with performance, and how to represent knowledge so that it can be retrieved effectively and efficiently. By using a cognitive architecture, an agent developer avoids having to figure out how to develop these complex cognitive capabilities from scratch with a programming language such as Lisp, C++, or Java, and can concentrate on encoding knowledge.

For cognitive modeling, a cognitive architecture also provides pre-existing theories of how much of cognition works. An architecture rarely includes all the details, but it provides the overarching structure in which models can be developed, building on years of research. For example, if researchers wish to model human behavior data related to estimating the passage of time, they can avoid starting from scratch by using models in an existing cognitive architecture of how people observe changes in the environment, interpret instructions, retrieve instructions from memory, convert instructions to actions, and so on.

Since it is well known that a Turing machine can mimic the behavior of any other computational system by simulating the primitive steps of that system, and any Turing-equivalent system can do the same, one might question the value of research on cognitive architectures. This might suggest that the details of different cognitive architectures are irrelevant because any architecture can "solve" any problem another architecture can "solve." However, in "solving" the same problem, one architecture can require significantly more time than another architecture—in some cases, exponentially more time. As Pylyshyn (1986) observed, different architectures have different complexity profiles, so a problem that might require N computational steps in one architecture might require a fixed number of time steps in a second architecture and N^3 steps in a third architecture. Thus, the details of architectures matter. One of the reasons we extended Soar with mental imagery was because there are important classes of problems (for example, those involving spatial or visual reasoning) in which the processing afforded by mental imagery can have a different complexity profile and can be orders of magnitude faster than is possible with pure symbol processing (Lathrop 2008).

Although it might be possible to rank or compare alternative architectures by their complexity profiles across a set of problems, it is not clear which problems belong in that set. What is clear is that it would have to be a large set of diverse tasks. Some progress on the characteristics of such tasks and environments will be attempted in chapter 2, but to date there are no accepted benchmarks or test problems, such as there are for evaluating the performance of standard computers.

Another differentiator of cognitive architectures is whether they support specific capabilities, such as specific knowledge representations, reasoning, and learning processes through architectural mechanisms or whether those capabilities are implemented through knowledge interacting with other general architectural mechanisms.

For example, though some have argued for special-purpose representations for language processing, others have argued that language processing is similar to many other types of reasoning. Designers of computer architectures face similar decisions, two extremes being RISC systems (reduced-instruction-set computers), which have simpler architectures but can run at higher speeds, and CISC systems (complex instruction set computers), which have more complex architectures that usually require fewer instructions to perform a given calculation, although each instruction might be executed more slowly.

The choice between realizing a capability in the architecture and realizing it in knowledge using other architectural mechanisms is one of the most important decisions faced by a designer of a cognitive architecture. Below we examine the tradeoffs between the two options, first considering the advantages of including a mechanism in the architecture.

Advantages of Architecture-Based Capabilities

• An architecture-based capability can usually be implemented more efficiently, because it doesn't require the additional cycle of retrieving and interpreting knowledge to produce behavior. In many cases, an architectural implementation can be orders of magnitude faster and can even have a different complexity profile. For example, basic arithmetic, such as multi-column addition, can be done using knowledge in Soar through pure symbolic operations in which individual numbers are represented as individual digits, which are then added together, with carrying and so forth. The time required to add two numbers is linear in the number digits, and requires using the agent's knowledge about arithmetic. If these operations are done in the architecture, with appropriate technology, they can be done in constant time as part of a single operation, independent of the number of digits, up to a very large number of digits.

• An architecture-based capability is available for all tasks, from the beginning of an agent's existence. No additional knowledge or learning is required to enable it, although knowledge may be required to use it.

• An architecture-based capability can have access to information that isn't available to knowledge that is encoded in the agent. For example, many learning mechanisms use historical traces of behavior. A pure knowledge-based approach to learning may be restricted to accessing only the information flowing from perception through an agent's working memory. In contrast, the architecture has direct access to its own internal processing. For example, in reinforcement learning, the architecture can maintain a memory of past decisions that it can update on the basis of the current decisions. These sources of information usually aren't available to a knowledge-based agent, and cannot be made available without significant computational overhead.

• An architecture-based capability is stable, and the designs of other architectural mechanisms can be based on the details of its implementation. In contrast, if a component is open to learning, its behavior may be unpredictable.

• An architecture-based capability doesn't compete with task processing. A mechanism that is implemented indirectly with knowledge could interfere with the agent's normal task processing. Early work on concept learning in Soar didn't include an architectural mechanism; instead it relied on knowledge-based processing and on Soar's chunking mechanism. Although this approach was effective for learning, the agent had to interrupt its task processing in order to learn new associations.

Advantages of Knowledge-Based Capabilities

The advantages of using knowledge to implement a capability are essentially the converse of the advantages for architectural approaches.

• A knowledge-based capability doesn't require additional structure in the architecture, so the architecture can be simpler, which often means that overall the architecture can be implemented more efficiently (and is usually easier to debug and maintain).

• A knowledge-based capability usually is open to some introspection because intermediate representations of the processing are available. Thus, the agent can monitor, and possibly even report, its progress in using the capability. In an architecture-based capability, the processing usually isn't available to the agent, and the agent may even be unaware that it is occurring.

• A knowledge-based capability is usually under control of the agent. The agent can decide whether or not to use it.

• A knowledge-based capability is open to learning. Additional knowledge can be learned (or programmed) that modifies or refines the capability, specializing, and improving it for specific situations and tasks.

Overall, there is a tension between efficiency, availability, and stability versus control, accessibility, flexibility, and adaptability. As in biological systems, the right mix of architecture-based and knowledge-based capabilities for artificial agents can differ from agent to agent, as it does from species to species, depending on a specific ecological niche (McCarthy 2004). Although there are many reasons to incorporate mechanisms in an architecture, the flexibility and adaptability afforded through control and learning are very compelling when one is attempting to create human-level agents. Architectures with the structure illustrated in figure 1.3 tend to minimize architectural mechanisms, adding them only when it is clear that they provide a functional advantage that cannot be achieved through knowledge alone, while also being designed so that the knowledge can be used efficiently. Thus, in these architectures, there are no architectural planning mechanisms or language-processing mechanisms. Instead, the accepted theory is that these capabilities have the same architectural mechanisms as the rest of cognition, and are realized through specialized knowledge.

1.3 Soar

Our current understanding and hypotheses concerning cognitive architectures are embodied in Soar 9. Soar has been under development for more than 30 years and has gradually evolved to include more and more capabilities. Soar's general theory of computation is based on goals, problem spaces, states, and operators. This problem-space computational model (PSCM) is presented in detail in chapter 3. Figure 1.4 presents a structural view of Soar, with its primitive memories represented by square-edged modules, its processes by round-edged modules, and their connections by arrows. Input comes in through the perception module and is held in the perceptual short-term memory. Symbolic structures are extracted from perceptual short-term memory and added to Soar's working memory. Working memory acts as a

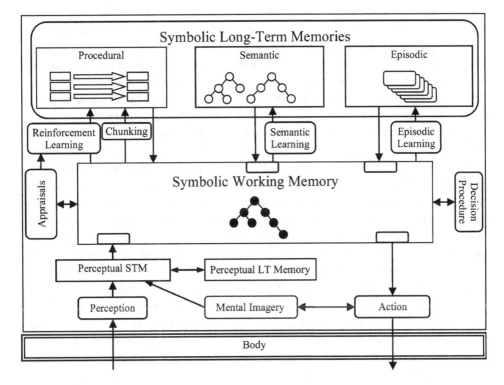

Figure 1.4
Block diagram of Soar 9.

global short-term memory that cues the retrieval of knowledge from Soar's symbolic long-term memories, as well as being the basis for initiating action. The three long-term symbolic memories are independent, with separate learning mechanisms. Procedural long-term memory is responsible for retrieving the knowledge that controls the processing. Soar's procedural knowledge is represented as production rules, which match conditions against the contents of working memory and perform their actions in parallel.

Production rules can modify working memory. To control behavior, they generate *preferences*, which are used by the decision procedure to select an *operator*. Operators are the locus of decision making and action in Soar. Once an operator is selected, it is applied, causing persistent changes in working memory. Working memory has reserved areas that are monitored by other memories and processes, so changes in working memory can initiate retrievals from semantic or episodic memory or can initiate actions in the environment. Soar has two learning mechanisms associated with procedural memory: chunking and reinforcement learning. Chunking learns new production rules. Reinforcement learning tunes the actions of rules that create preferences for operator selection.

Semantic memory stores general facts, whereas episodic memory stores snapshots of working memory. Both memories are accessed by the creation of cues in working memory. Actions can effect change in the external environment, or they can modify Soar's short-term perceptual-based memories through mental imagery.

The knowledge in these modules works together to generate behavior, with procedural knowledge providing control and with working memory acting as a global workspace. For example, if Soar is controlling a simple mobile robot, it may have episodic memories of the places it has visited and the objects that it has seen. It may also have been programmed with semantic knowledge that certain objects (electrical outlets) provide energy for it. It also may have procedural knowledge that, in combination with mental imagery, can navigate around its environment to go to a specific location. And it may also have procedural knowledge that attempts to retrieve knowledge related to the current situation and set goals. When the robot gets low on energy, the general procedural knowledge can query the semantic memory by creating a cue in working memory that retrieves knowledge for determining that the robot needs to be at an electrical outlet to recharge. It can then query episodic memory in a similar fashion for the location of the electrical outlet, which it has previously seen, and then use its procedural memory and mental imagery to navigate to that location and recharge. Thus, behavior is *enabled* by the architecture, but *determined* by knowledge. A cognitive architecture provides a framework for encoding knowledge, but on its own it doesn't generate behavior. Moreover, representations of knowledge without an architecture are like programs without a computer—they do nothing. Representations of knowledge need the architecture to retrieve them and combine them with other representations, whereas an architecture without content is like a computer without software—it is an empty shell. It is the combination of knowledge and the architecture that leads to purposeful behavior.

Originally, Soar consisted of working memory, the decision procedure, procedural memory, and chunking. Although new modules have been added through the years, many of the important properties of Soar were established at its inception in the early 1980s. Many of these properties are not unique to Soar, but are shared with other architectures:

• Knowledge is stored in long-term memories and retrieved from those memories into a shared short-term working memory. Working memory contains declarative symbolic structures that can trigger additional retrievals from multiple long-term memories.

• Behavior arises from a sequence of individual decisions. Soar generates each step of behavior through a processing loop that accesses long-term memories to retrieve knowledge with which to make a decision. There is a declarative representation of alternatives in short-term memory, and the choice from among the alternatives is based on knowledge retrieved from long-term memory. There is never a fixed, uninterruptable sequence of behavior. Purposeful behavior, as well as complex methods and algorithms, arises dynamically from context-dependent control knowledge that influences successive decisions.

• Procedural knowledge is accessed via associative retrieval. All long-term knowledge for directly controlling behavior is encoded as situation-action rules (production rules). Rules provide an efficient and scalable representation of procedural knowledge, and are used by many other cognitive architectures, including ACT-R, 4CAPS, and EPIC. Although production rules have been used throughout Soar's existence, the theoretical commitment is to a set of functional capabilities, including associative retrieval and fine-grain representation of independent units of knowledge.

• The decision procedure is fixed. All decisions for both internal and external actions are made by a fixed decision procedure that interprets preferences created by rules. Thus, decisions are based on a combination of what is sensed from the environment, what is maintained in working memory, and what is retrieved from long-term memory.

• Complex reasoning arises in response to impasses. Soar detects when an agent's available knowledge for decision making is incomplete, uncertain, or inconsistent, which signals an impasse. In response to an impasse, it creates a substate in which the agent can attempt to resolve the impasse. This capability, together with Soar's commitment to problem spaces, supports *universal subgoaling* (Laird, Rosenbloom, and Newell 1986a), planning, reflection, and more advanced types of reasoning (including anticipation and perspective taking).

• Learning is incremental and driven by experience. Learning is a side effect of experience and doesn't require deliberate engagement (although it can be aided by specific strategies, such as rehearsal).
• All modules are task independent. There are no task-specific or method-specific modules in Soar, such as a language module or a planning module. Instead, task-specific or method-specific knowledge representations are encoded in long-term memory.

Although the current version of Soar shares the above properties with earlier versions of Soar, it includes significant departures, which are listed below.

• Multiple long-term memories with associated learning mechanisms. The current version of Soar supports multiple representations of long-term memory and multiple learning mechanisms, whereas the original version of Soar was committed to representing all knowledge as rules and to using a single learning mechanism (chunking). We introduced reinforcement learning (RL) and semantic and episodic memories after we recognized that different types of knowledge can be most efficiently learned and accessed with different learning mechanisms. Attempting to use chunking to learn semantic and episodic knowledge was cumbersome and interfered with task processing. Encoding semantic and episodic knowledge as rules limited how the knowledge could be retrieved. Table 1.1 summarizes the current memories in Soar.
• Modality-specific processing and memory. Originally, all representations of the current situation were symbolic and stored in working memory. However, general,

Table 1.1
Memories and learning systems in Soar.

Memory and learning system	Source of knowledge	Representation of knowledge	Retrieval of knowledge
Procedural memory via chunking	Traces of rule firings in substates	Production rules	Exactly matches rule conditions, retrieves actions
Procedural memory via reinforcement learning	Reward and numeric preferences	Numeric preferences in rules	Exactly matches rule conditions, retrieves preference
Semantic memory	Working memory	Mirror of working-memory object structures	Exactly matches cue, retrieves object
Episodic memory	Working memory	Episodes: snapshots of working memory	Partially matches cue, retrieves episode
Perceptual memory	Perceptual short-term memories	Quantitative spatial and visual depictions	Deliberately recalls based on symbolic referent

symbolic representations are not as efficient for many spatial and visual imagery-based tasks. The introduction of short-term and long-term perceptual memories is a recognition that certain computations can be carried out more efficiently and accurately in non-symbolic representations. Although mental imagery introduces a new representation, the control of the processing is still vested in procedural knowledge encoded as rules.

• Multiple uses of non-symbolic processing. At its inception, all processing in Soar was purely symbolic. All knowledge retrieval was based on exact matches, and all decision making was based on symbolic preferences. Soar now uses non-symbolic processing in many different ways. We distinguish between two types of non-symbolic processing. In *subsymbolic* processing, the underlying non-symbolic processing gives rise to symbol structures. SAL (Jilk et al. 2008) uses a non-symbolic architecture (Leabra, O'Reilly, and Munakata 2000) in place of some of the symbolic memories of ACT-R. The second type of non-symbolic processing is *co-symbolic* processing, in which non-symbolic processing controls symbolic processing or (in the case of mental imagery) provides an alternative to symbolic processing. All non-symbolic processing in Soar is co-symbolic. Table 1.2 summarizes the different forms of non-symbolic representations and processing in Soar.

Missing from the current version of Soar are general modules for perception and action (although the processing of mental imagery is an important step in that direction). Soar has a task-independent approach to accept new sensory data and initiate motor actions, but new perception and action modules must be created for new task environments. This shortcoming reflects the absence of a consensus among environments in terms of common interfaces for sensory information and motor actions. Soar has been integrated with many custom environments and robots and with many independently developed simulation environments and computer games, including ModSAF/OneSAF/JSAF, Descent III, Unreal Tournament, Unreal 3, Quake 2, Quake 3, ORTS, Microsoft Robotics Studio, USARSIM, and Player/Stage. Unfortunately, none of these environments share common perceptual or motor interfaces (including the

Table 1.2

Non-symbolic representations and associated processes in Soar.

Non-symbolic representations	Processes
Numeric preferences	Influence decision making to select operators
Numeric preferences	Learn operator-selection knowledge
Activation of working memory	Bias long-term memory retrieval
Mental imagery	Support spatial reasoning
Appraisals	Compute intrinsic reward for reinforcement learning

multiple versions of Unreal and Quake). One approach could be to create a common interface that corresponds to how humans sense these environments using vision, touch, and audition. However, rendering and then extracting general visual information is computationally burdensome and in general is beyond the current state of the art in machine vision. For now, we are left with custom perception and action modules.

1.4   Research Strategy

As was mentioned earlier, research in cognitive architectures has multiple goals. One of the distinguishing characteristics of Soar is that researchers have used it to build complex integrated AI agents, and to create detailed models of human behavior. Allen Newell, in his 1990 book *Unified Theories of Cognition*, explored using Soar as a model of human behavior across a variety of time scales, from milliseconds to minutes. Such research continues in Soar, which (as has already been noted) has much in common with other architectures that focus on cognitive modeling. This is not surprising, insofar as for 30 years our research on Soar has been informed by human behavior and by the functional requirements and constraints that arise in building actual architectures and agents. We have found that combining what is known in psychology, in neuroscience, and in AI is an effective approach to building a comprehensive cognitive architecture.

An alternative approach is to ignore psychology and to assume that natural selection has gone down one idiosyncratic path, and that there may be many other approaches to developing generally intelligent systems. There are many AI systems that diverge from human approaches and exceed human behavior in areas such as planning and scheduling, chess, and data mining. Yet such successes have occurred in limited domains, and this alternative approach has yet to succeed in creating agents with the breadth and robustness of behavior that is the hallmark of humans.

Although it might be possible to develop a new approach to intelligence, our strategy is to learn what we can from psychology and neuroscience—something that makes good engineering sense. It seems unlikely (although not impossible) that artificial human-level intelligence will arise from one or two breakthroughs in science and engineering. Maybe someday a crucial equation will be written on a whiteboard and then encoded in software or hardware, and that after the flick of a switch (or after much development and training) artificial human-level intelligence will emerge. Our bet is that achieving human-level intelligence is a long path of incremental experiments, discoveries, tests, reformulations and refinements. If that is so, we need to accumulate knowledge about the foundations of intelligence.

Where better to look for guidance than to humans? We know a lot about which kinds of problems are easy, hard, and impossible for humans to solve. If we ignore humans, we risk developing systems that work on one class of problems but fail utterly when we try to extend them to the next level of capability. We might have to start over as new constraints conflict with earlier design decisions. In contrast, if we successfully capture a subset of the mechanisms and approaches that humans use, those mechanisms and approaches are likely to be compatible with achieving broader, general intelligence. Invariably our implementations incorporate assumptions that require redesign, but the corrections may be smaller than if we ignored human intelligence. This path doesn't guarantee success, but it mitigates some of the risks.

The recent extensions to Soar were motivated by the desired to replicate capabilities that are inherent to humans but missing from Soar (and other cognitive architectures). Our work on episodic memory was inspired in part by the movie *Memento*, directed by Christopher Nolan and released in 2000. Though it isn't a scientific study of the effect of the loss of the ability to form new episodic memories, *Memento* is a relatively accurate depiction of the cognitive deficits faced by a human with anterograde amnesia. It dramatizes the effect of this loss, which prevents the protagonist from pursuing a productive life. Most AI systems are crippled in exactly the same way (see Vere and Bickmore 1980 for an early exception), so they don't know what they have done or what they have experienced. Similar observations about the role of emotion and mental imagery have led us to consider how they interact with cognition to provide new functionality. Although these extensions required the addition of major modules to Soar, they didn't require the redesign of existing modules in Soar, such as the decision procedure, working memory, production memory, or chunking.

Although its design is inspired by psychology, Soar also has been designed for functionality—to scale up to problems that require large bodies of knowledge, to respond quickly to changes in the environment, and to use a variety of problem-solving and reasoning strategies. Clearly humans are functional and efficient, but we lack an understanding of how to achieve that functionality efficiently with today's computational systems. Moreover, the behavior we are interested in occurs at time scales of tenths of seconds and above, much above the range of neurons and neural circuits. Soar, and especially ACT-R and EPIC, have demonstrated that it is possible to model a significant range of overt human behaviors without resorting to modeling the details of individual neurons. Our strategy is to use the best computational algorithms for achieving architectural functionality, even if they aren't supported by psychological or neurophysiological data. For example, Soar matches rules using the Rete algorithm (Doorenbos 1994; Forgy 1982), which has no known basis in human psychology or neural anatomy but which performs very well on standard computer architectures. That said, there is still much to be learned from the structure of the brain: what are the major modules, what processing is performed and what knowledge is represented in different modules, how the modules are connected.

The final distinguishing characteristics of our research methodology are that we build agents in order to understand the various demands that complex environments and tasks make on cognitive architectures, and that we build them to span a wide range of tasks. Chapter 13 provides a list of representative tasks that have been implemented in Soar. Some examples are toy AI tasks (Laird, Rosenbloom, and Newell 1986a), knowledge-rich expert systems (Rosenbloom et al. 1985), algorithm design (Steier 1987; Steier and Newell 1988), mobile robot control (Benjamin, Lyons, and Lonsdale 2004; 2006; Laird 2009; Laird and Rosenbloom 1990), natural-language processing (Lehman, Lewis, and Newell 1991; Lewis 1996), modeling the NASA test director (Nelson, Lehman, and John 1994), synthetic pilots for military training simulations (Hill et al. 1997; Jones et al. 1999; Tambe et al. 1995), and characters in computer games (Laird 2001a; Magerko et al. 2004). These tasks have stressed Soar along many dimensions, and our evaluations of Soar's ability to meet the demands of a general cognitive architecture (described in more detail in chapter 2) have led to both major and minor changes in the architecture. Many of these changes have arisen from the challenges of supporting learning and knowledge-mediated performance in highly dynamic interactions with external environments, but some have arisen from careful observations of where *ad hoc* or complex sets of knowledge are required.

1.5   Preview of Chapters 2–14

Chapter 2 presents the characteristics of environments and tasks that appear most relevant to developing general cognitive architectures and presents a set of requirements for the design of a cognitive architecture that we use to evaluate Soar throughout the remainder of the book.

Chapter 3 presents the problem-space computational model of behavior that underlies Soar. The fundamental components of problem spaces (including states and operators) are defined, and the distinction between problem-space search and knowledge search is introduced. A significant portion of the chapter is devoted to the derivation of increasingly complex problem-space computational models, culminating in the model used by Soar.

Chapters 4–11 present the details of Soar, starting with the processing cycle, and then adding mechanisms for generating complex behavior, learning, mental imagery, and emotion. These chapters first present the architectural mechanisms, then offer demonstrations of those mechanisms across a variety of domains, and then discuss the mechanisms relative to the requirements for a cognitive architecture introduced in chapter 2. These chapters describe both the strengths and weaknesses of Soar's mechanisms, highlighting where additional research is required to satisfy the requirements set forth in chapter 2.

Chapter 4 describes how the basics of the problem-space model of computation presented in chapter 3 are realized in Soar and brings problem spaces and production systems together in a computational cognitive architecture that provides the infrastructure for developing simple agents. Chapter 5 describes how Soar deals with incomplete or conflicting knowledge by automatically generating substates in which it can reason about how to select or apply operators. Substates enable agents developed in Soar to use complex strategies, including hierarchical task decomposition, planning, and perspective taking, for problem solving and for learning. Chapter 6 presents Soar's original learning mechanism, chunking, which compiles the processing of substates into rules. Chapter 7 describes how reinforcement learning is integrated in Soar and how it automatically tunes knowledge for operator selection. Chapter 8 describes semantic memory, Soar's repository for long-term factual knowledge. Chapter 9 presents Soar's implementation of episodic memory and learning, which captures an agent's experience and provides a mechanism for recalling it. Chapter 10 describes Soar's module (SVS) that supports mental imagery and spatial reasoning. Chapter 11 presents our implementation of an appraisal theory of emotion in Soar.

Chapter 12 presents three agents that achieve novel cognitive capabilities by employing different collections of the new architecture modules. Chapter 13 presents applications and agents implemented in Soar. Chapter 14 examines Soar as a cognitive architecture from both structural and functional perspectives, evaluates Soar relative to the requirements laid out in chapter 2, and speculates on the future of research on Soar, cognitive architecture, and human-level agents.

Chapter 3, chapter 4, and the first three sections of chapter 5 are recommended as a general introduction to Soar. Chapters 6–12 discuss specific components of Soar, including chunking, reinforcement learning, semantic memory, episodic memory, mental imagery, or emotion. Chapter 13, which can be read independently of chapters 3–12, reviews many of the applications and agents that have been developed using Soar. Chapters 2, 3, and 14 are recommended to readers interested in cognitive architectures more broadly.

2 Requirements for Cognitive Architectures

with Robert E. Wray III

The previous chapter introduced cognitive architectures, using Soar as an exemplar of an approach for creating the cognitive component of human-level agents. This chapter analyzes characteristics of tasks, environments, and agent structures as they relate to cognitive architectures. The goal of the analysis is to determine the requirements for cognitive architectures that support the full range of human-level intelligent behavior. Although many different architectures have been proposed, understanding the relative strengths and weaknesses of these architectures and their unique contributions to the pursuit of human-level intelligence has proved elusive, whether via analytic (Anderson and Lebiere 2003; Jones and Wray 2006; Sun 2004) or empirical comparisons of task performance (Gluck and Pew 2005).

For architectures developed for the purpose of modeling psychological phenomena, such as ACT-R and EPIC, matching human data is "the coin of the realm"; however, because those architectures broaden the tasks they model and eventually attempt to cover the full range of human behavior, requirements related to functionality are increasingly important. The requirements explored here are most relevant to comparing and evaluating cognitive architectures designed to support human-level agents, independent of their relationship to human behavior. We have not included criteria related to how easy or hard it is for human developers to design, develop, debug, maintain, or extend agents developed in cognitive architectures, nor have we included criteria related to properties of the theory underlying the architecture, such as parsimony (Cassimatis, Bello, and Langley 2008).

A cognitive architecture by itself is not a complete agent. A complete agent includes interfaces to its environment (sensors and effectors), the cognitive architecture, and knowledge. To determine requirements for human-level agents, we begin with the observation that an agent's structure supports interaction with an environment as it attempts to perform tasks. Thus, as Cohen (1995) suggests, three influences determine an agent's behavior: the agent's structure, its environment, and the tasks it pursues. We use "task" throughout this chapter as a placeholder for any type of problem, goal, drive, or reward that provides direction to an agent's behavior.

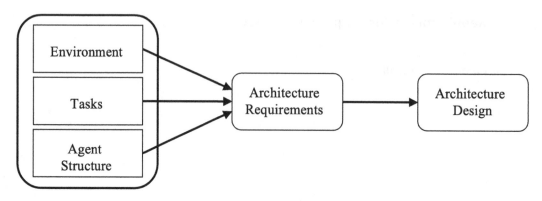

Figure 2.1
Influences on architecture design.

In view of the diversity of environments and tasks, we are not attempting to create architectures that are necessarily the best or even sufficient for *all* possible environments and *all* possible tasks. We assume that agents exist in an environment and that they pursue tasks similar to those we find in the world we inhabit. The challenge in designing an architecture is to take advantage of the structure of the environment and the tasks while avoiding optimizations that apply to only a subset of tasks. For specific problems, specialized architectures can be more appropriate (e.g., Deep Blue for chess; see Campbell, Hoane, and Hsu 2002).

In figure 2.1, the characteristics of the environment, the tasks, and the agent's structure determine a set of requirements for a cognitive architecture. These requirements, in turn, are the basis for the design of a specific architecture. Cognitive architectures must provide a comprehensive computational story that puts all the components of intelligence together from perception, through reasoning, problem solving, and learning, to action. In later chapters, we motivate design decisions made for Soar using these requirements and base our evaluation and comparison of Soar and similar architectures on their ability to satisfy these requirements.

In practice, researchers have typically focused on communicating an architecture's design and its performance on specific tasks. We propose to also include the requirements that motivate the design. There are two immediate benefits to this approach. First, it makes little sense to compare architectures (as works in progress) when they share few requirements. If one architecture attempts to satisfy a requirement that all decisions must be made in bounded time but another architecture is developed independent of that requirement, we expect to see very different approaches that would be difficult if not meaningless to compare. Being explicit about requirements makes it easier to see what "spaces" architectures are attempting to occupy—that is, for what environments and problems they are appropriate. Second, because human-level intelligence is broad, there is no existing list of necessary and sufficient requirements. This chapter, drawing from our experience, proposes an initial list of these requirements. We expect it to be refined, extended, and corrected via interaction with other researchers.

We recognize that this attempt is not novel. John Anderson (1990) took a step in this direction with the design of specific components of ACT-R using a rational analysis. He determined optimal methods for primitive architectural functions, such as retrieving an item from declarative memory, given the expected use of that memory in the future. This revolutionized his design process and led to significant advances in ACT, including the development of a new process for retrieving items from long-term declarative memory. Although rational analysis is useful for designing the performance of specific components, it is difficult to apply to the specification of a complete cognitive architecture, because it doesn't specify what components there should be or how they combine together to provide general intelligent behavior. To determine those aspects of an architecture, we fall back on a more qualitative analysis of the dependencies between general characteristics and architectural requirements. We do not use our analysis to determine the setting of specific architectural parameters (as was possible in ACT-R), but we do use our analysis to determine the primitive processing and memory modules and general characteristics of their performance. Thus, our goal is to determine the most important characteristics of environments, tasks, and agent structure, and their effect on architecture design.

Our analysis also builds on previous descriptions of evaluation criteria for cognitive architectures (Laird 1991b; Laird et al. 1996; Laird et al. 2009; Langley, Laird, and Rogers 2009) and on previous theories of cognition (Anderson and Lebiere 2003; Newell 1990). Previously identified criteria include constraints on behavior (flexible behavior, real-time performance), on architecture (support vast knowledge bases), and on underlying technology (brain realization; see Newell 1990, Anderson and Lebiere 2003). Our effort is distinguished by the separation of characteristics of the environment, tasks, and agent structure, and the behavior of an agent (described in section 2.1) and the derivation of the requirements for cognitive architectures from those characteristics (described in section 2.2).

2.1   Characteristics of Environments, Tasks, and Agents

In this section we list characteristics of environments, tasks, and agents that lead to requirements for architectures that support human-level intelligent agents. Some of these characteristics, such as the existence of regularities at different time scales in the environment, are obvious, or are so ingrained in the literature that they are rarely made explicit. Some of them are characteristics of one of the three components, independent of the others, but many of them are characteristics of interactions between two components or even all three. The interactions are important because the characteristics of an environment are only important to the extent they influence the agent's ability to pursue its tasks.

C1:   The environment is complex, with diverse interacting objects.
The world is large and complex. Agents can usefully interpret the environment as if it consists of independent objects, together with other materials that do not have object-like structure (e.g., air, water, and sand). There are many objects, and the objects interact with each other via physics. Objects have numerous and diverse properties. In order to comprehend and reason about these objects, an agent must be able to manipulate internal combinatorial representations of objects, their properties, and their relations. Because the environment is rich, there is much to be learned.

C2:   The environment is dynamic.
The agent's environment can change independent of the agent in such a way that the agent doesn't determine the state of the environment and the agent must respond to the dynamics of the world. Because the world can change while an agent is computing, the agent must respond relative to the dynamics of the environment (in real time). Moreover, the dynamics of the environment are complex enough so that the agent cannot always predict future states of the world in detail.

C3:   Task-relevant regularities exist at multiple time scales.
An environment, though it may be complex and dynamic, is not arbitrary. The laws of interaction that govern the environment are constant, often are predictable, and lead to recurrence and regularity that affect the agent's ability to achieve its goals. There are different regularities at different time scales, which makes it possible and useful to organize knowledge about tasks, actions, and the environment hierarchically.

C4:   Other agents affect task performance.
The agent is not alone, and must interact with other agents in pursuit of its goals. Other agents may help or hinder the agent's achievement of its tasks. The agent can communicate with other agents to share knowledge or to indicate intent. In addition, if some other agents are similar to it in structure and in capabilities (for example, have similar perception, action, and mental capabilities), the agent may be able to learn from them by observing the methods they use to solve problems. This characteristic is a special case of C1, C2, and C3, but it has enough of an effect on the structure of agents (both natural and artificial) to warrant its own item here.

C5: Tasks can be complex, diverse, and novel.

A general, intelligent agent must be able to work on a diverse set of novel, complex tasks. Tasks can interact so that in some cases achieving one task aids in achieving another but in other cases achieving one task makes achieving another more difficult. Tasks can also vary in the time required to achieve them: some must be performed at a time scale close to that of relevant changes in the environment, but others require many orders of magnitude longer to complete.

C6: Agent-environment-task interactions are complex and limited.

There may be many regularities in the environment, but they are relevant only if they can be detected and only if they influence the agent's ability to perform its tasks. Thus, an agent must have sufficient sensory capabilities that it can detect (possibly only through extensive learning) task-relevant regularities in the environment. An agent also must have mechanisms for acting in the environment in order to pursue a task. Although sensing and action modalities can be extensive, they are limited. The environment is partially observable, both from inherent physical limits in the sensors and from the size of the environment. Sensors are noisy, can be occluded by objects, and have limited range, making the agent's perception of its environment incomplete and uncertain. The agent's actions must obey the physical limitations of the environment. For example, actions usually take time to execute and are limited in extent.

C7: An agent's resources are limited.

An agent has physical limits on its resources relative to the dynamics of the environment. Here, we focus on energy and computation resources. Energy resources are finite and are consumed by movement and computation, and thus must be replenished. Computation resources are limited so that an agent cannot perform arbitrary computation in the time it has available to respond to the dynamics of the environment. Thus, an agent has *bounded rationality* (Simon 1969) and cannot achieve perfect rationality (or universal intelligence; see Legg and Hutter 2007) in sufficiently complex environments and tasks when it has a large body of knowledge.

C8: An agent's existence is long-term and continual.

The agent is always present in its environment, and it must actively pursue tasks (such as self-protection) related to its survival. The agent may act to position itself so that the dynamics of the environment have little effect on it for extended times (e.g., it may hide in a protected area), but it has no guarantee that those efforts will be successful. Further, the agent has a long-term existence relative to its primitive interactions with its environment. Its activity extends indefinitely across multiple tasks, and possibly across multiple instances of the same task.

2.2   Architectural Requirements

The overall purpose of a cognitive architecture is to make it possible for an agent to bring to bear all of its available knowledge to select actions in pursuit of its goals within the constraints of the environment and its own structure. This is the essence of Newell's principle of rationality (Newell 1982, 1990). Newell defines intelligence as an agent's ability to use its knowledge to select actions to achieve its goals.

Looking at this from the other side, the inability to achieve a goal because of lack of available knowledge *is not* a failure of the underlying architecture to support intelligence. However, the inability to achieve a goal when the knowledge is available can be a failure of the architecture. Such a failure can arise if the agent never acquired the knowledge when it was available, or it can arise if the agent acquired the knowledge but fails to apply it to relevant situations. Thus, a cognitive architecture must not only use available knowledge to support performance on its current tasks; it also must acquire knowledge (through learning) that will support performance on future tasks.

Unfortunately, it is not possible for a knowledge-rich agent embedded in a complex and dynamic environment with non-trivial novel tasks to achieve perfect rationality. There are computational limits that restrict the amount of knowledge that can be accessed and dynamically combined in real time, and there are limits on the amount and complexity of knowledge that can be extracted from the environment in real time. Thus, the design of a cognitive architecture is not simply an exercise in engineering a system that is optimized for one task or situation; it is the task of engineering the system so it performs well across a wide range of tasks in a broad range of situations. These engineering efforts play out against a background of the technology that is available for implementing the architecture. Different technologies have different computational strengths and weaknesses; thus, there are tradeoffs between the amount of knowledge that can be stored about a situation, the accuracy with which it can be stored, and the efficiency and accuracy with which it can be retrieved in the future. All of this must take place within a system that is dynamically expanding its relevant knowledge by learning whatever it can from the environment, so as to improve itself for future tasks.

If it were possible to design an architecture that supported perfect rationality, the architecture would disappear, meaning that the agent's knowledge, tasks, and environment would completely determine optimal behavior for the agent, and the underlying structure of the architecture would not be evident in its behavior. In AI architectures, the architecture usually shows through when an architecture fails to bring relevant knowledge to bear on a decision. Instead, irrelevant knowledge is retrieved, or the architecture doesn't retrieve all the relevant knowledge, or doesn't retrieve it quickly enough (often because of the relentless growth of knowledge). Another possibility is that the relevant knowledge was never learned in the first place, because of shortcomings in learning. Often the shortcomings of an architecture are masked by the inclusion of additional knowledge that would not be necessary in the ideal architecture. Thus, an important metric to use when comparing alternative architectures is the amount of knowledge that is required to achieve a specific level of performance. In humans, our architecture often shows through in the quirky behavior that psychologists love to study (such as the difficulty of remembering a telephone number with more than seven digits); that gives us some confidence that intelligent systems are possible even with imperfect underlying architectures.

Using the characteristics of environments, tasks, and agents presented in the previous section, we derive the following requirements for cognitive architectures related to knowledge acquisition, representation, and use. Our goal is to generate a list of what is necessary, such that all human-level agents must meet these requirements, and what is sufficient, such that meeting these requirements guarantees human-level behavior. Architectures that don't support all of these requirements can lead to useful, non-human-level agents, as is evidenced by non-human animals that meet only a subset of these requirements. Although we attempt to be complete, some requirements may be missing; we will return to that possibility in subsection 13.3.2.

R0: Fixed for all tasks.

An individual agent adapts to its environment not through changes in its architecture but through changes in knowledge. The rationale for this requirement is that regularities exist (C3) at time scales that approach or exceed the life of the agent (C8), and these regularities are worth capturing in a fixed architecture, which then provides a stable platform for acquiring and using knowledge. There can be some changes in an architecture, such as occurs in humans through development, but those changes occur at time scales of years. Fixing the architecture's structure extends to disallowing manually tuned parameters.

R1: Realize a symbol system.

The consensus in AI and in cognitive science is that in order to achieve human-level behavior a system must support universal computation. Newell (1990) makes the case that symbol systems provide both sufficient and necessary means for achieving universal computation; that is, a symbol system is capable of producing a response for every computable function. Possibly most important, symbol systems provide flexibility. In particular, they provide the ability to manipulate a description of some object in the world "in the head" without having to manipulate the object in the real world. Symbol structures also provide arbitrary composability to match the combinatoric complexity and regularity of the environment (C1, C3). Thus, structures encountered independently can be combined later to create novel structures never experienced together (C5). We use this generative capability when we combine letters or sounds to make new words, and when we combine words to make new sentences. Symbol systems also allow us to accept instructions from another agent and then use those instructions later to influence behavior; thus, symbol systems provide additional flexibility and more generality, so that not everything must be programmed into a symbol system beforehand. In addition, symbols are required for communication that doesn't cause the meaning to be directly experienced by the agent (C4). For example, striking someone directly causes an experience in another agent, whereas a verbal threat involves the transmission of symbols that require interpretation.

Requiring that the agent realize a symbol system doesn't imply that symbolic processing must be implemented directly via some symbolic knowledge representation. Neural and connectionist models obviously can support human-level behavior. Rather, this requirement posits that such approaches must implement symbol systems to some degree (Barsalou 2005).

R2: *Represent and effectively use modality-specific knowledge.*
Although pure symbol systems support universal computation, they rely on modality-independent methods for representing and reasoning to achieve universality and complete composability. However, complete composability isn't always necessary. For many problems, modality-specific representations can support more efficient processing through regularities (C3) in sensory processing (C6) (Funt 1976; Glasgow and Papadias 1992; Huffman and Laird 1992; Kurup and Chandrasekaran 2006; Larkin and Simon 1987; Lathrop 2008; Tabachneck-Schijf, Leonardo, and Simon 1997). For example, some representations and associated processes for visual input have qualitatively different computational properties for image operations. Examples include rotation, inversion, and detecting and reasoning about spatial relations. For tasks (C5) where the agent has limited computational resources (C7), modality-specific representations are necessary for achieving maximal efficiency; this is especially true of tasks that require real-time performance (C2). Modality-specific representations can also provide precision and accuracy for reasoning and motor control that is difficult to achieve with purely symbolic representations, especially when using task-independent transformations from sensory data to symbolic representations (Wintermute 2010).

R3: *Represent, effectively use, and efficiently access large bodies of diverse knowledge.*
The agent must be able to represent and use large bodies of knowledge, because of the wealth of available knowledge that arises from the complexity of the environment (C1) and its associated regularities (C3), the variety of tasks the agent must pursue (C5), the agent's complex interaction with the environment (C6), and the agent's continual existence (C8). Not only are large bodies of knowledge available; the

knowledge is diverse, including memories of experiences, facts of the world, skills, and knowledge about other agents (C4). As knowledge grows with experience, access to the knowledge must continue to be fast enough to be useful relative to the dynamics of the environment (C2).

R4: Represent and effectively use knowledge with different levels of generality.

The agent must represent and use general knowledge that takes advantage of environmental regularities (C3). The agent must also be sensitive to details of its current situation and be sensitive to its relationship to its tasks. These details are ubiquitous in complex (C1), dynamic (C2) environments in which an agent can have many tasks (C5).

R5: Represent and effectively use diverse amounts of knowledge.

An agent must be able to take advantage of whatever knowledge is available. For novel tasks and environments, its knowledge is limited. Even for familiar tasks and environments, its knowledge may be incomplete, inconsistent, or incorrect. If there is extensive knowledge available for a task, the agent must be able to represent it and to use it effectively. This is due in part to the combination of the fact that there are regularities in the environment worth knowing (C3), the complexity of an agent's limited sensing of its environment (C6), the complexity of its environment and tasks (C5), and limits on its computational resources (C7). Planning systems often fail this requirement. They often have a required and fixed set of input knowledge (the task operators and a declarative description of the goal). Without this knowledge, they cannot even attempt the problem. Further, if additional knowledge (such as knowledge about the likelihood of an operator leading to the goal) is available, the planner is often unable to use it to improve behavior.

R6: Represent and effectively use beliefs independent of perception.

The agent must be able to represent and reason about situations and beliefs that differ from its current perception. Perceptual information is insufficient because perception is limited (C6), the environment is dynamic (C2), and there are regularities in the environment worth remembering (C3) for task completion (C5). Thus, the agent must be able to maintain a history of situations as well as the ability to represent and reason about hypothetical situations, a necessary component of planning. Symbol systems provide the means for representing novel combinations of previously sensed information. Meeting this requirement makes it possible for an agent to make a decision based not just on its current situation but also on its memory of previous situations and its predictions of future situations. This capability is also necessary for perspective taking, in which an agent can reason about what other agents will do in different situations.

R7:   Represent and effectively use rich, hierarchical control knowledge.

The agent must have a rich representation for control, because the actions it can perform are complex (C6). Because of the dynamics of the environment (C2) and the multiplicity of the tasks playing out at multiple time scales (C5), some actions may have to occur in rapid sequence whereas others may have to occur in parallel. To keep up with a rapidly changing environment (C2) with limited computational resources (C7), the agent must take advantage of the structure of regularities of the environment (C3), maximizing the generality of the knowledge it encodes because of the complexity and variability of the environment and the agent's tasks (C1, C5). In many cases, this means organizing knowledge about actions hierarchically. With such an organization, the agent can decompose some of its actions into sequences of simpler actions, using the context of higher-level actions to constrain the choices and thereby reducing the knowledge required to generate action.

R8:   Incorporate innate utilities.

In view of the agent's long-term existence (C8), the accompanying regularities at long time scales (C3), and the agent's limited resources (C7), there are states of the world that either favor or impede the agent's ability to survive and pursue its long-term tasks (C5). The exact value of states for the agent depends on the details of the structure of the agent, the environment, and the agent's long-term tasks. Some of these may be contingent on interactions with other agents (C4).

R9:   Initiate, represent, and manage goals at multiple time scales.

An agent must be able to initiate tasks on the basis of interaction with other agents (C4) or on the basis of its own situational analysis (R8). Many tasks cannot be achieved immediately; others are ongoing and must be continually pursued. Thus, an agent must maintain an internal representation of the task it is attempting to achieve so as to direct its behavior in service of the task (Wooldridge 2000). We call such an internal representation of a task a *goal*. Different tasks, and thus different goals, can have different temporal extents (C3), some lasting over significant portions of an agent's lifetime (C8). Goals can be complex, diverse, and novel (C5), and interactions among goals can require that the agent actively manage them by, for example, determining when it is appropriate to pursue a goal, interrupting pursuit of a goal, or even abandoning unachievable goals.

R10:   Access, represent, and effectively use meta-cognitive knowledge.

In addition to the different types of knowledge discussed above, it is sometimes necessary for an agent to represent and use knowledge about itself and knowledge about its own knowledge (meta-knowledge). An agent invariably faces novel tasks (C5) in which its task knowledge and/or its computational resources (C7) are not sufficient to determine the appropriate behavior, owing to environmental complexity (C1), but in which there are regularities of which the agent can take advantage (C3). In these situations, an intelligent agent can detect its lack of task knowledge and then use meta-knowledge to acquire new task knowledge. An agent can use other types of meta-cognitive knowledge to set its own goals and to direct future behavior in preparation for tasks, events, and situations that it expects to arise. This is done in response to the characteristics listed above and in response to the fact that the agent exists beyond a single task or problem (C8). The exact range of necessary meta-cognitive knowledge isn't clear—some appears to be necessary, but complete meta-cognitive knowledge isn't required (at least, not in humans). We humans don't always know exactly what we know, and often we discover what we know only when put in a situation where that knowledge is useful.

R11: *Support a spectrum of bounded and unbounded deliberation.*
At one extreme, in tasks with time constraints close to those of the dynamics of the environment (C2), the agent must respond using bounded computation (C5). Because of inherent limits to its computational resources (C7), it cannot reason or plan from first principles for all tasks. At the most primitive level, the absolute time to respond is bounded by the environmental dynamics for some subclass of responses. Reactive behavior is possible if the agent's knowledge of the environment and other agents is complete, correct, and encoded for bounded access below the level of dynamics of the environment. However, because of the complexity of the environment (C1), the diversity of tasks (C5), and the limitations on environmental interaction (C6), that generally isn't possible. Moreover, at the other extreme, when there are sufficient computational resources available relative to the dynamics of the environment and task, the agent should have the ability to compose novel responses using its knowledge to take advantage of regularities in the tasks and environment (C3). This composition is the basis for planning. It takes time, but it allows the agent to integrate its diverse and potentially large bodies of knowledge for novel situations (R1–R10). In between these two extremes, the agent must use its knowledge of the situation to balance between reaction and deliberation.

R12: *Support diverse, comprehensive learning.*
An agent with long-term existence (C8) requires different learning mechanisms when exposed to diverse environments (C1) and tasks (C5) involving complex interactions (C6). Learning takes advantage of regularities (C3), some of which can be extracted from a single situation in which all of the information is available at the same time, whereas in other cases the information may be spread across time. Although general learning mechanisms exist, they are invariably biased toward specific regularities and types of knowledge that are available to the agent in different ways and often at

different time scales. Moreover, a general cognitive architecture should be able to learn all the types of task-specific knowledge it represents and uses—a property we call the *learning completeness principle*. A significant component of our research is exploring what types of regularities are available to an agent and what types of knowledge and associated learning mechanisms are required to extract and later retrieve those regularities and achieve complete learning.

R13:   Support incremental, online learning.
An agent with long-term existence (C8) in a complex active environment (C1, C2) with regularities (C3) must learn and modify its knowledge base so as to take advantage of environmental regularities (C3) when they are available. Once the experience has happened, it is gone. Only the information that the agent itself stores while it is behaving is available to guide its future behavior. This is not to suggest that an agent cannot recall situations and perform additional analysis at some future time (R6); however, some primitive learning mechanism must store the experience for that more deliberative future learning. Moreover, the mechanisms for storing and retrieving those experiences must operate in real time even as more and more experiences are captured. Incremental learning incorporates experiences when they are experienced.

One of the more challenging aspects of architecture design arises from a combination of requirements. An agent must maintain reactivity (R11) as it acquires large bodies of knowledge (R3) through learning (R12). Thus, over the lifetime on an agent, there must be bounds on the time it takes to access and use knowledge relative to demands of the environment even as the amount of knowledge grows. An agent that initially takes milliseconds to generate a sentence in response to a question from a human but later takes many minutes to respond as it gains knowledge isn't useful in many applications. One of the great challenges of developing a cognitive architecture is not only developing the processing and memories modules that support all the other requirements and capabilities we desire for our agents, but also developing the data structures and algorithms that support bounded access to large bodies of knowledge. Sometimes our dreams for capabilities must meet the reality of computational complexity, so that we must find ways to reduce the expressiveness of our representations and processes. This requires both complexity analysis of our supporting algorithms and empirical evaluation of the time it takes to perform architectural functions as knowledge grows across a range of tasks.

Our table of the interactions between the environmental, task, and agent characteristics and the induced agent requirements (table 2.1) highlights the dense connectivity between characteristics and requirements—no single characteristic is responsible for any requirement, and no characteristic influences only a single requirement.

Table 2.1

Connections between environment, task, and agent characteristics and architectural requirements.

	C1 (complex environment)	C2 (dynamic environment)	C3 (task regularities)	C4 (social environment)	C5 (complex tasks)	C6 (limited interaction)	C7 (limited resources)	C8 (long-term existence)
R0 (fixed structure)			X					X
R1 (symbol system)	X		X	X	X			
R2 (modality-specific knowledge)		X	X		X	X	X	
R3 (large bodies of knowledge)	X	X	X	X	X	X		X
R4 (levels of generality)	X	X	X		X			
R5 (amount of knowledge)			X		X	X	X	
R6 (non-perceptual representations)		X	X		X	X		
R7 (rich action representations)	X	X	X		X	X	X	
R8 (innate utilities)			X	X	X		X	X
R9 (goals across multiple time scales)			X	X	X		X	X
R10 (meta-cognitive knowledge)	X	X	X		X		X	X
R11 (spectrum of deliberation)	X	X	X		X	X	X	
R12 (comprehensive learning)	X		X		X	X		X
R13 (incremental learning)	X	X	X				X	X

Many characteristics contribute to each requirement, because eliminating a characteristic allows for extreme simplification. Simple environments (eliminating C1) require only simple agents. There is no need to have large bodies of knowledge, no need for rich representations of action, and limited need to learn. An agent that pursues only simple well-known tasks (eliminating C5), or one that has unlimited computation (eliminating C7), can be much simpler than one that supports agents and tasks, in an environment with these characteristics. At the extreme is the requirement for task-relevant regularities (C3), which has universal impact because knowledge, reasoning, learning, and architecture are useless if there are no environmental regularities.

In contrast, the absence of C4 or C8 doesn't eliminate the need for their associated requirements. As was mentioned earlier, C4 (interaction with other agents) is a specialization of C1, C2, and C3, and thus the requirements associated with C4 would still exist in its absence. The requirements for C8 (long-term and continual existence) would similarly still be required if the task, the environment, and the interactions are sufficiently complex, but clearly long-term existence adds to the demand for the ability to store and use large bodies of knowledge in a learning agent.

The requirements derived above (R0–R13) define a rough design envelope for underlying architectures. However, the role of knowledge in agent development complicates attempts to match the achievement of specific requirements with specific architectural components. Behavior in an agent is the result of the interaction between knowledge and architecture; some requirements may be achieved through a combination of general knowledge and multiple architectural components. For example, many cognitive architectures lack explicit architectural support for planning. Not including such architectural support simplifies these architectures, but requires the encoding of knowledge representations and algorithms for planning using architectural primitives. Achieving a requirement directly with the architecture allows for a more efficient implementation. Achieving a requirement in knowledge usually leads to a simpler architecture while providing more flexibility and the possibility of improving the capability through learning. This tension is analogous to tradeoffs between RISC and CISC in traditional computer architectures.

Our own hypothesis is that significant bodies of knowledge in combination with architecture are required for many of the cognitive capabilities needed to achieve human-level performance. Examples include natural-language processing, logical thinking, qualitative reasoning, and multi-agent coordination. However, the requirements listed above don't address what knowledge is necessary to support such capabilities, or how that knowledge is acquired and encoded. Thus, even if we create architectures that satisfy all the listed requirements, we will still fall short of creating human-level agents until we encode, or until the systems learn on their own, the content required for higher-level knowledge-intensive capabilities.

Even when we restrict ourselves to considering the requirements within the context of cognitive architecture independent of knowledge, it is difficult to evaluate the sufficiency of these requirements by examination alone. Many of the requirements are qualitative and vague, and thus difficult to apply to existing architectures. For example, how do we judge whether an architecture supports sufficient levels of generality in its knowledge representations, or sufficient representations of meta-cognitive knowledge, or sufficiently comprehensive learning mechanisms? Thus, an important goal for future research in human-level agents is to refine these requirements as we learn more about the capabilities that are necessary for human-level behavior. We discuss of the sufficiency of these requirements in the final chapter, where we evaluate Soar's overall ability to satisfy the complete set of requirements.

3 The Problem-Space Computational Model

The problem-space computational model (Newell et al. 1991) is the general theory of decision making and problem solving on which Soar is based. Soar and the problem-space computational model (PSCM) both originated from the need for a scheme for organizing knowledge and behavior for general intelligent agents, and they were developed contemporaneously in the early 1980s. The evolution and refinement of the PSCM captures much of the progress in our research on Soar. Fundamental to the PSCM is that behavior arises as a series of decisions as an agent attempts to use its available knowledge to select actions to make progress toward its goals. This chapter reviews the fundamentals of problem spaces and describes how they form the basis of a general and flexible approach to computation.

In the 1960s and the early 1970s, Allen Newell and Herbert Simon studied how people solve a variety of tasks and developed a framework for describing human performance, summarized in *Human Problem Solving* (Newell and Simon 1972). They observed that a task puts limits on behavior in an environment and coined the term *task environment* to refer to the aspects of the environment (the objects and their relations) that are relevant to the task. Consider the game of chess. It can take place in many environments: a park, a home, a school, even a ballroom. However, the task of playing chess limits the relevant environment to the board, the pieces, and the opponents. The lighting, the type of table, and the materials of which the pieces and the board are made can be abstracted away when we focus on the task. If a new task arises, such as cleaning up after the game, the relevant aspects of the environment (and thus the task environment) change to include dirt on the table, the type of material the board is made of, the placement of chairs, and so on. Characteristics C1–C6 (set forth in chapter 2 above) emphasize the interaction of the task, the environment, and the agent.

Newell and Simon took their analysis of task environments one step further by considering the possible behaviors of an agent (human or artificial) within a task environment. What is the space of possible actions available, and how do these combine to generate behavior? This led to the concept of a *problem space*, and later to the *problem-space hypothesis*—that problem spaces are fundamental to reasoning, problem solving, and decision making (Newell 1991). The PSCM attempts to refine the basics of problem spaces so that they can be the basis of a cognitive architecture.

The PSCM engages a subset of the requirements set forth in chapter 2 by providing a fixed framework (R0) in which knowledge can be used to control behavior (R5, R4), internal representations can be maintained independent of perception (R6), and rich, hierarchical representations are supported (R7), along with goals (R9), meta-cognitive knowledge (R10), and multiple levels of deliberation (R11). The PSCM is silent on the representations used for reasoning (R1, R2), although one important feature is that it can support a variety of representations. The current PSCM is also silent on innate desires (R8) and learning (R12, R13), as the PSCM is a theory of performance, although it provides a decomposition of behavior that clarifies what an architecture must do to support bounded response in the light of increasing knowledge by introducing the distinction between problem search and knowledge search. We address these requirements in chapters 4–11, where we discuss the implementation of the PSCM in Soar.

3.1 Task Environments

Early AI systems, including early versions of Soar, worked on tasks in *internal* environments, where the states and operators are represented within the agent and do not involve interaction with an external environment. For the internal version of the Blocks World, the agent has an internal representation of the blocks and the tables, the properties of the blocks (names, sizes, colors, and so on), the relations between the objects (such as whether a block was on top of another block), and operators that directly manipulate these representations. Many complex problems can be represented and solved internally, and much of the research on planning is on how to solve problems internally and then use the solution to control behavior in an external environment. Internal problems are usually characterized by well-defined state descriptions and operators with localized effects, where the "physics" of the environment is under the agent's control. The first versions of Soar solved internal problems that included puzzles (Laird and Newell 1983), computer configuration (Rosenbloom et al. 1985), algorithm design (Steier 1987; Steier and Newell 1988), medical diagnosis (Washington and Rosenbloom 1993), production scheduling (Hsu, Prietula, and Steier 1989), and natural-language processing (Lehman, Lewis, and Newell 1991; Lehman, Dyke, and Rubinoff 1995; Lewis 1996).

An agent working in an *external* environment must perceive its state through sensors and must act on the world through a motor system. The external environment might be the real world, a simulation, or even the Internet. External environments are usually more challenging, because the agent may have only limited and possibly imperfect perception of the environment and the agent may not be the only source of change in the environment. Since the early 1990s, Soar has supported problem solving in both internal and external environments.

Throughout this book, a variety of environments are used to illustrate important properties of problem spaces and how knowledge is encoded, used, and learned in Soar. Most of these environments are not representative of the complexity of environment normally tackled by Soar agents; they were selected because their simplicity makes it easy to provide detailed descriptions of how a Soar agent can solve problems in them without distracting the reader with the details of the task. (Chapter 13 describes agents developed in Soar for more complex environments and tasks.)

One of the environments is the classic Blocks World, where there are blocks on a table that can be stacked on top of each other. The environment abstracts away from many details of real blocks; for example, a block can only be placed directly on top of another block, and the actions to move a block from one position to another are atomic and instantaneous. Thus, in this version of Blocks World, both time and space are discrete. In general, we use an external version of this task, where the agent perceives the blocks and manipulates them through external actions. However, for some discussions, we also consider internal versions, where all aspects of the task are represented within the agent. Although this is a trivial task, it is useful for describing Soar—it is well known, and its simplicity makes it possible to present the exact details of how it is encoded and solved in Soar under different conditions and when different architectural mechanisms are used. All of the mechanisms we demonstrate in Blocks World are general and scale up to much more complex tasks as described in chapters 12 and 13.

A second environment is Rooms World, in which a Soar agent controls a mobile robot in a simulated indoor environment consisting of a set of interconnected rooms. Figure 3.1 is a top-down depiction of an exemplary environment in Rooms World. The map consists of rooms and doorways, ultimately decomposed into rectangles. The robot is depicted as in room 12, moving to the right to pick up a gray block in the room. There are other blocks in rooms 0, 1, and 4, and an additional block in room 12. The robot moves continuously through the world, restricted only by walls. There can also be other agents that move through the world, so that this world is continuous in time and space, and has dynamics independent of the robot. For simplicity, the robot can sense the walls and doorways in its current room, but it cannot see into adjoining rooms. It has restricted sensing of objects and other agents: it is able to detect them only if they are in front of it. The robot's actions include moving forward, turning left or right, stopping, picking up an object in front of it, and putting down an object it is holding. The Soar-controlled robot plans a path through its environment to move from room to room; follows that path, avoiding unexpected obstacles; and

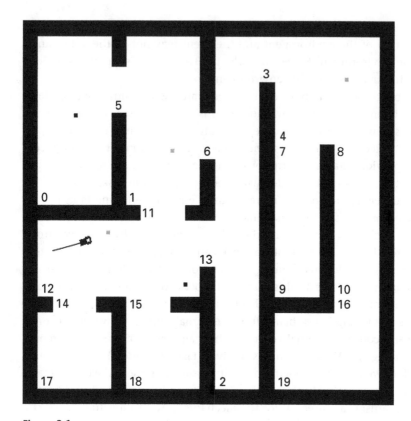

Figure 3.1
Example of a Rooms World environment.

revises its plan if its path is blocked (Laird 2009). The agent can perform simple tasks (e.g., chasing another agent or moving to an object and picking it up), and more complex tasks, such as cleaning its world by exploring and finding certain types of objects and moving them into a storage room.

We have both simulation and a mixed/real-world versions of Rooms World. In the mixed version, the agent moves in the real world and the robot's position in the simulated environment is updated on the basis of that movement. The agent senses its real-world movement and the distances to real-world objects (via a laser rangefinder). The sensing in the real world is dynamically combined with its sensing of walls and objects in the simulated environment. With this approach, the agent has more complex sensing and manipulation of the environment (such as identifying and picking up blocks) than is possible with the real robot, while the movement of the robot is faithful to the complexities of the real world. The experiments reported in the book were run in the simulation version for speed and repeatability.

3.2 The Problem-Space Framework

In the problem-space framework, an agent is always in some situation and confronted with having to select its next action, using whatever knowledge it has available, as it attempts to solve a problem. In problem-space terminology, the agent is in a *state* and its alternative actions are *operators*. Once an operator has been selected, it is applied. That changes the situation, moving the agent to a new state. The application of an operator may involve action in the world, or it may involve changes in state structures that are internal to the agent.

A *problem space* is the space of states through which the agent can move using its available operators, and a *problem* consists of an initial state and a set of desired states to achieve or maintain. Throughout this chapter, we use the term "problem" instead of "task" in deference to its relationship to problem spaces. To solve a problem, the agent, by selecting and applying operators, must move from the initial state to succeeding states in search of a desired state. This is called *problem-space search*, or just *problem search*.

Consider the Blocks World configuration illustrated in figure 3.2, where the problem is to move blocks from the initial state shown on the left to the desired state shown on the right. Each state is a configuration of blocks on the table or stacked on top of each other. In this simplified environment, there is a single operator, move-block, that moves a single block from one location to the top of another block or onto the table. The external environment defines external states—the objects and possible relationships between them that are available via perception—and the actions that an agent can use to transition from one situation to another in the environment. The problem defines the set of desired states to achieve or maintain.

The effort required to solve a problem is determined by properties of the problem space, such as the number of operators required to reach a solution and the number

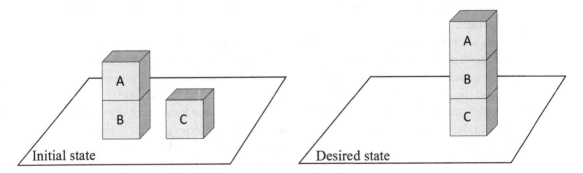

Figure 3.2
Example of Blocks World initial and desired states.

of operators that are available at each state, as well as the agent's available knowledge to direct the selection of operators toward a desired state. With little knowledge, the agent is forced to search through the problem space by applying operators and moving through states by trial and error, until it achieves a desired state, or possibly abandons the problem. However, if the agent has appropriate knowledge, it can select the correct operator to apply in every state and move directly to a desired state. This is still problem search because operators must be selected and applied to solve the problem. It is just that all of the missteps and backtracking commonly associated with search have been eliminated. However, even with large bodies of knowledge, it is possible that the agent's problem space doesn't contain the desired state or a path from the initial state to the desired state. For example, using the Blocks World problem space we defined, it impossible to achieve a state where both A and B are directly on top of C. If the desired state isn't in the agent's problem space, the agent is unable to solve the problem, and it has to either abandon the problem or change the problem space.

Problem spaces provide a way for an agent to organize knowledge independent of a specific problem. Knowledge learned about the problem space, such as invalid sequences of operators, or sequences of operators that maintains some invariant property, can potentially aid problem solving in any problem in that problem space (or in other problem spaces that share the same operators).

3.2.1 States

In the problem-space framework, the agent is always in a state. For internal problems, the state is completely under the control of the agent. For external problems, the agent's state is determined by the sensory information it receives from perception, the agent's interpretation of that sensory information, and other internal structures the agent has generated on the basis of internal inferences or retrievals from its memories. For external environments, the state can change independent of the agent, and often the agent's state is only a partial representation of the overall state of the environment.

There are no *a priori* restrictions on the representations used in states, which can include both symbolic and numeric data. In the internal version of the Blocks World, the state consists of symbolic descriptions of the blocks and their relationships to each other and the table. In Rooms World, the state consists of the robot's sensory information, which includes its location, the direction it is facing, the location of objects, the walls, and the doors of the room it is in. It can include memories of what it perceived in other rooms, such as the location of an object. These memories can be incorrect for dynamic aspects of the world, such as the location of another agent. The state also includes inferences the robot makes, such as, that there is an object nearby that it can pick up.

3.2.2 Operators

Operators are the means by which an agent makes persistent changes in the state. Operators have *preconditions* that test for relations and properties of objects in the state that must be true for the operator to apply. For the move-block operator in Blocks World, the object being moved must be a block (it cannot be the table) and must be clear, and the destination must be clear (the table is always clear). In most states, the move-block operator can have multiple instances, each of which is a different combination of a block being moved and a destination. When the blocks are completely stacked in a single tower, there is one operator instance available—moving the top block onto the table. In the initial state in figure 3.1, there are three possible move-block operator instances: move-block(A, C)—which means move block A on top of block C, move-block(A, Table), and move-block(C, A).

For the Rooms World robot, the available operators include move-forward, turn in a direction, turn to a specific heading, stop, pickup object, and putdown object. There are no pre-conditions for the turn operators—the robot can always turn. The operator to turn in a direction is parameterized by the direction (left or right) and by the speed of the turn. The pre-condition for the move-forward operator is that a wall isn't directly in front of the robot, and the operator is parameterized by the speed of linear motion. The pre-condition for the pickup operator is that there is an object in front of the robot, whereas the pre-conditions of the putdown operator are that the robot is holding an object and there is no object or wall in front of the robot.

Once an operator has been selected, it can be applied and its actions performed. A single operator may involve multiple actions. An internal operator changes the internal state. An external operator initiates (possibly multiple) actions in the environment. In Rooms World, in order to move toward an object, the agent can select the move-forward operator to generate a motor command to begin moving, and then when close to the object, select the stop operator that causes the robot to come to a halt.

For an internal problem, there are two general approaches to operator application. In one approach, the operator actions destructively modify the current state: the operator removes structures (such as, that the block being moved was on top of another object) and adds new structures (for example, that the block is now on top another object). In the other approach, a new state is created, and the existing state structures that are not changed by the operator are copied to it; simultaneously, structures created by operator actions are added. Most AI systems that solve only internal problems use the second approach, as did the original version of Soar. The advantage of this approach is that it maintains representations of past visited states, and the agent can backtrack to an earlier state if the current state is undesirable. In the approach based on destructive changes, only the current state is available.

For problems embedded in external environments, maintaining and selecting from among all previous states is impractical. First, the agent is embedded in its environment and it isn't possible to "jump" back to a previous state. Second, the state isn't under the agent's control, as it can change because of the dynamics of the environment. Third, the time to select a state increases as more states are maintained, and can end up becoming the dominate factor in the time it takes an agent to make a decision, threatening the agent's reactivity. This final reason makes state selection in large problem spaces untenable even for internal problem solving. Thus, to support external interaction and guarantee reactivity, Soar maintains only a single state and applies operators by making destructive changes in that state. The state changes either from operator actions or from changes in perception due to changes in its environment.

In the problem-space framework, only a single operator is selected and applied at a time. Thus, the robot cannot simultaneously select two operators such as move-forward and turn to execute in parallel. If multiple operators can be applied at the same time, there can be interactions and conflicts between their actions, requiring some further decision process to resolve the conflicts. Adoption of the problem-space hypothesis presupposes that operator selection is the locus of choice. To avoid an additional decision-making process to resolve conflicting actions, parallel operators are not allowed, and individual operators must be free of conflicting actions. However, there is significant flexibility in the definition of individual operators. A single operator can involve multiple, parallel changes in the state that execute over time, and a requirement when defining or learning parallel actions is that they are conflict free. In Rooms World, a move-turn operator can be defined that bundles both move-forward and turn into a single operator that initiates both move-forward and turn as part of its actions.

As is obvious from the Rooms World example, operators take time to execute, especially those that involve the initiation of action in an external environment. For example, if the robot selects an operator to turn to a specific heading, it takes time for the robot to turn. During that time, the operator remains selected, but it can be interrupted by the selection of another operator. Another operator can be selected because of internal or external changes in state such as perceiving a mouse that the agent prefers to pursue, or because an unexpected obstacle that prevents the turn to continue. If the interrupted operator initiated an action, such as to turn the robot, it might be necessary for the interrupting operator to stop the interrupted action before it performs its own actions.

The problem-space definition of operators doesn't presuppose any specific internal representation of operator, such as the representation used in STRIPS (Fikes and Nilsson 1972). In fact, the Soar implementation of the PSCM as described in chapters 4 and 5 avoids monolithic structures such as used in STRIPS in order to provide maximal flexibility in problem solving and learning.

3.2.3 Problems

Within a problem space, many different problems can be posed and attempted with different initial and desired states. In the Blocks World, we can use any pair of the states in the problem space to define a problem with an initial state and final state. Similarly, we can decompose chess into its problem space, which consists of the pieces and the rules for moving and taking pieces, and the problem, which is to place the opponent's king in checkmate. Different problems can be defined within the chess problem space either by changing the initial configurations of pieces or by changing the desired state, such as making the goal to be taking all of the opponent's pieces, or to put the queen in checkmate instead of the king. In an external environment, the initial state of a problem is usually the agent's current situation. For example, in Rooms World, the initial state consists of the current location and orientation of the robot, as well as the location of walls, doors, and other objects in the rooms. There can be many desired states, such as the robot holding a specific object, or having all the objects placed in one room. Problems can also be defined where the agent must maintain certain aspects of a state, such as keep a room free of objects (Covrigaru and Lindsay 1991).

In defining a problem, the desired states do not have to be explicitly represented. In Blocks World, the desired state is explicit, whereas in chess the set of states where there is a checkmate is not. Having an explicit representation can be useful in choosing which operators to select (such as via means-ends analysis); however, it isn't a requirement.

3.2.4 Problem Spaces

Problem spaces are defined by the set of available operators and the available state information. Sometimes (as in basketball, which has human-defined rules), the problem space is an agreed-upon restriction of possible actions and states; other times, it is the agent's knowledge that limits the possible states and actions, and thus limits the problem space. There is a tradeoff in picking a problem space. A small problem space can make finding the solution easier because there are fewer states to search. But if the problem space is too small, the problem may be impossible to solve. In such cases, the agent must expand beyond the initial problem space and, as the saying goes, think outside the box.

The current problem space can change if the available state information or available operators change. For example, adding a fourth block to the Blocks World increases the number of possible states, with the move-block operator providing the connectivity between them. In contrast, if we add an operator so that a stack of blocks can be moved at the same time (move-stack), the number of states isn't changed, but additional transitions between states are added. In addition, if new information becomes available in the state, along with operators for manipulating that information, the agent is in a different problem space.

Some simple problem-space extensions involve expanding operators and states so they maintain a history of recent moves, which the agent can use to avoid looping or undoing an operator. For example, if an agent is randomly searching the problem space of the Blocks World, it can easily loop by picking up a block from the table, placing it on another block, and then picking up the same block and placing it back on the table. Without a memory of its previous states or actions, it can be difficult to avoid this inefficient behavior. Adding history changes the problem space because now the current state contains not just the information from the task, which we call the *task state*, but it also includes the history of task states and the task operators that applied to generate them. This takes the agent from the original task problem space to a problem space where the *path* that the agent has traveled through the task states determines which problem space state the agent is in. Similarly, if the agent in Rooms World remembers objects it has seen in other rooms, it is in a different state than if it doesn't have such a memory.

Not all changes in the state representations make important changes in the problem space. The state representation can often be extended with entailments of the current situation that do not change the "information content" of the state. In such changes, the set of available operators and the identity of the states are unchanged, but the entailments can simplify selecting operators or detecting that the goal has been achieved. For example, in Blocks World, the state representation can be expanded to include the "above" relation, which specifies that a block is above another, possibly with intervening blocks between them (e.g., (above A C) in figure 3.1). A desired state could be that a block is above another block, so that this feature is useful for detecting the desired state.

Sometimes the problem space is insufficient for solving the problem at hand. Instead, a completely new conception of the problem is necessary, using a different problem space with a different state representation and different operators. A classic example of the importance of changing problem spaces is the mutilated checkerboard problem (Gardner 1994), shown in the left panel of figure 3.3. In this problem, two opposite corners of a checkerboard are missing (the mutilation). The task is to determine whether it is possible to cover the remaining checkerboard with dominos, each of which covers two adjacent squares. The right side of figure 3.3 shows partial progress when using the obvious problem space where the operators involve placing dominos on the board, the states are partial coverings, and the goal is to find a legal covering or prove that one doesn't exist. Trying to solve the problem using this problem space is time consuming— all placements of dominos must be tried because none of the placements work out—you are always left with at least two open squares that cannot be covered with a single domino. However, if you change your "view" of the problem, meaning change the problem space, the problem can be trivial to solve. The change is based on the observation that each domino covers one black and one white square. The original checkerboard

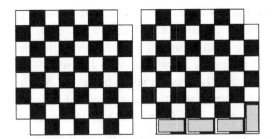

Figure 3.3
The mutilated checkerboard problem.

has an equal number of black and white squares, but the mutilation removes two squares of the same color. Thus, it is not possible to cover the checkerboard with dominos that always cover a single white and a single black square, as there is an unequal number of white and black squares. In the new problem space, the state abstracts away from the original state to include only the number of black and white squares. The new operators count and then compare the number of each colored squares.

An agent can (and should) have many problem spaces. For a given problem, as the example above illustrated, an agent might need to switch to a new problem space that it dynamically creates, although for many problems, an agent can use an existing problem space. Moreover, some problems may involve decomposing a problem into subproblems, and for each of those subproblems, different problem spaces can be used. This ability to use (and reuse) multiple problem spaces across problems and subproblems was one of the early distinguishing characteristics of Soar and it was critical to our ability to create large knowledge based systems, such as R1-Soar (Rosenbloom et al. 1985), TacAir-Soar (Jones et al. 1999), and RWA-Soar (Tambe et al. 1995). Although many, if not most, AI systems work in only a single problem space, there are approaches such as the knowledge sources of blackboard systems (Corkill 1991; Englemore and Morgan 1988) and PRS (Georgeff and Lansky 1986), as well as the micro-theories of Cyc (Lenat and Guha 1990), that are similar in concept to the multiple problem spaces in Soar.

3.3   Knowledge Search

Problem spaces are a natural way to represent any problem where the answer isn't immediately known and the problem must be solved by taking a series of steps. Some of those steps may be internal reasoning steps; others may involve interaction with an external environment. As part of problem-space search, an agent uses *knowledge* to select and apply operators, generating new states until a desired state is reached (or the agent quits). In order to select and apply operators, the agent must solve another problem: determining which of the knowledge it already has is relevant to making these decisions. Even though it already "has" the knowledge stored in a long-term memory, it must search through its memory to find the knowledge relevant to the current situation. In other words, it must perform a *knowledge search* (Newell 1990; Strosnider and Paul 1994). Knowledge search is the way an agent brings its *directly available* long-term knowledge to bear on the current situation to control and perform problem search. Directly available knowledge is knowledge that can be retrieved quickly, without protracted inference. Thus, the "outer" loop of behavior is problem search, where the agent selects and applies operators in order to generate, combine, or derive knowledge that it doesn't already have stored in long-term memory. The "inner" loop of behavior is knowledge search, where the agent retrieves knowledge from long-term memory in order to select and apply the appropriate operator to the current state. Thus, for any problem where the agent doesn't already know the answer, the agent uses problem search, which is variable and controlled by the agent's available knowledge, whereas with knowledge search, there is a fixed architectural process for finding the knowledge relevant to the current situation.

With knowledge search in the inner loop of problem search, an agent's ability to quickly select and apply operators in response to changes in its environment is determined by the computational cost of knowledge search. If knowledge search is unbounded, reactive behavior is lost. Thus, to preserve reactivity, a cognitive architecture must constrain the types of knowledge that can be encoded and/or the types of queries that can be made. The architecture can include fixed methods for organizing its knowledge so that it can be searched quickly (relative to overall temporal scale of the agent), possibly in bounded time, using data structures such as hash tables, heaps, or trees that avoid the exponential explosion inherent to problem-space search. The structures that can be searched in bounded time depend on the underlying computational technology and the representations of knowledge supported. One of the challenges of cognitive architecture development is to discover expressive knowledge representations that can support efficient retrieval (using current computational technology). These efficiencies must be realized even as knowledge increases through learning.

Using the problem/knowledge search approach, complex behavior is spread across multiple decisions, where each individual decision is controlled by knowledge retrieved from memory, but where the processing for knowledge search within the inner loop is limited. Within knowledge search, there cannot be arbitrary cascading and combining of knowledge retrieved from memory. As we shall see later in section 3.5, when knowledge search fails, the search for knowledge can be recast as a problem-space search, so the problem of finding the appropriate knowledge for selecting or applying an operator, can itself be decomposed into selection and application of operators in a problem space.

Even though Soar embraces the problem-space hypothesis more explicitly than other architectures, many architectures share, at least implicitly, the dichotomy between knowledge search and problem search. In subsection 1.2.4, we noted that many cognitive architectures, including Icarus, LIDA, ACT-R, and Clarion, assume that there is a basic processing cycle in which knowledge determines the next action to perform. In Soar, this is selecting an operator. In ACT-R, it is selecting a production rule. Thus, in order to maintain reactivity as the amount of knowledge grows through learning, someday these architectures must also address the issue of bounded knowledge search.

Although the split between problem search and knowledge search is common in many cognitive architectures, many AI systems (e.g. Cyc) take a different approach. These systems tightly integrate a knowledge base and inference engine in the same module. Probably the most important advantage of the integrated approaches is that they can combine the results of multiple knowledge searches within a single search, so that they can derive information beyond specific facts or structures stored in their memories. In contrast, the approach used in Soar requires multiple knowledge searches *combined with* problem search to derive the same information. A second advantage of the integrated approach is that algorithms can be developed that optimize the combination of inference and knowledge—for example, there can be special types of structures in the knowledge base that have specific inference algorithms associated with them, such as for inheritance. Because of the additional processing, the integrated approaches usually take significantly longer to provide results, thereby reducing reactivity; however, time limits can be used to bound the processing.

The main advantage of the combined problem/knowledge space approach is that the reasoning to find, combine, and perform inference over knowledge isn't controlled by fixed algorithms, as it is in the integrated approach. Instead, any inference or combination of knowledge beyond simple associational retrieval from long-term memory is open to improvement through knowledge acquired by any of the agent's learning mechanisms. The problem-space computational model described below is our attempt to specify how that is possible.

3.4 Problem-Space Computational Models

Problem spaces provide an abstract language for characterizing tasks, environments, and the agent's interaction with the environment as it pursues a task. In general, problem spaces also distinguish between information about the current situation (the state), how the agent can change the situation (the operators), and what role knowledge can play in aiding in problem solving (controlling selection of operators, enriching the problem space with additional state information and operators). One can develop a *computational model* on the basis of problem spaces, where states are the primitive forms of data, operators are the primitive actions that manipulate the data, and control of operator selection through knowledge is the primitive deliberative act (Newell et al. 1991).

A problem-space computational model (PSCM) is far from the details of the specific syntax used to specify knowledge and the underlying processes and algorithms that bring the knowledge to bear when appropriate. A cognitive architecture specifies these details. Soar was designed to support a specific PSCM. (The details are described in chapters 4–6.) Although the details of syntax are important for creating Soar programs, and the details of the implementation are critical for efficient performance, they are the trees among which one can easily get lost if one doesn't know much about the forest. The more macro-level forest view of Soar is a theory of how computation should be organized—when and how decisions should be made to make progress in the task, how knowledge contributes to controlling decision making, how learning fits in with reasoning, and so on. That is the PSCM level. The PSCM is also a level where comparison to other architectures is most meaningful. What types of decisions does an architecture allow, what are the possible actions that can be taken in a specific situation, and what knowledge is available to make those decisions?

There is a spectrum of computational models that vary by the primitive functions they have and how open those functions are controlled by knowledge. In this section, we present a series of problem-space computational models that incrementally increase flexibility and conditionality by factoring the processing cycle into the primitive PSCM functions and implementing those functions via knowledge search. We culminate with the PSCM on which Soar is based. These computational models do not directly support complex forms of reasoning such as planning or reflection, which require extensions that are discussed in section 3.5.

3.4.1   Minimal Knowledge Search: von Neumann Computers

We begin with a PSCM that doesn't include knowledge search. To generate behavior, the architecture performs a fixed, task-independent calculation to determine which operator to perform in each situation, and the operator is completely specified, leading to the processing cycle illustrated in figure 3.4. This is the type of processing cycle found in standard von Neumann computer architectures, where operators are organized linearly as statements with explicit conditional branching points. These systems maintain a program counter that determines which operator (line of code) is executed next, and the code completely specifies what actions to take. Once the action is executed, if it isn't a branch operation, the counter to the next line is incremented. There may be choice points with explicit tests, but they are embedded in specific

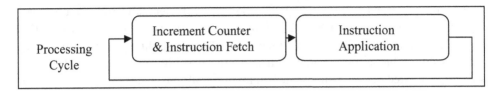

Figure 3.4
Von Neumann architecture processing cycle: no knowledge search.

points in the program. These tests provide conditional behavior, but they do not draw on any global long-term knowledge. By using a fixed calculation to determine the next operator, this type of architecture eliminates any knowledge search, and it requires that all behavior be pre-specified.

Consider the robot in Rooms World. We can encode the knowledge to control its behavior in a standard computer language. In this approach, the programmer must decide where to include explicit tests for dynamic changes in the environment to provide reactivity. Whenever there are non-conditional sequential commands, the agent cannot react to the environment. For example, if the object that the agent was about to pick up is suddenly removed, the robot still tries to pick it up even though it is gone.

To make the agent fully reactive, conditional tests must be made before every action. The hypothesis behind Soar is that it is more straightforward and efficient to provide specific architectural structures to support this conditionality as opposed to requiring programmers to include all the conditionality intertwined with sequential execution. Thus, this first approach isn't viable for a general cognitive architecture because it violates the goal of least commitment reasoning, and the requirements of representing and using situation and goal-directed knowledge (R4) and using a spectrum of bounded and unbounded deliberation (R7).

Although von Neumann architectures fail to meet our requirements for a general cognitive architecture, we use them to build cognitive architectures—Soar is implemented in C and in C++. This is possible because the primitive functions of C and C++ that are useful to *build* a cognitive architecture are different from the primitive functions (such as those provided by Soar) that are useful for creating human-level agents. Soar's ability to meet the requirements of a general cognitive architecture come from the task-independent algorithms and data structures that have been implemented in C to perform Soar's primitive functions, such as efficiently representing, matching, and firing rules. It is appropriate for the implementation of these algorithms to be pre-specified and not open to run-time deliberation because the architecture is meant to be fixed and task independent. It is quite a different issue if we try to directly implement task-dependent knowledge in a standard von Neumann architecture. Soar depends only indirectly on the structure of C to support its algorithms, such as C's ability to support random access to memory, pointers, conditional branching, and content-addressable access through constant-time hashing. As proof, Soar has also been implemented in Java, which differs in many details but shares the critical properties listed above.

3.4.2 Knowledge-Based Operator Proposal

To increase flexibility and responsiveness, AI systems moved away from a fixed list of actions that are executed one after the other, to an approach where the next operator is selected on the basis of the current situation and the goal. Figure 3.5 shows the inner loop of this style of PSCM. Each time through the outer loop, knowledge search is employed to determine which operator should be selected and applied. Within that loop, knowledge search retrieves the operators that are candidates to apply to the current state (Operator Proposal). In our figures, rectangles with square corners and the pair of semi-circular arrows indicate functions performed by knowledge search, whereas rectangles with rounded corners indicate fixed procedures. Remember that, although it is called *knowledge search,* this is a search of existing knowledge and is similar to a look-up or retrieval from memory, finding operators whose conditions match the current situation.

After operators are proposed, the Operator Decision module chooses among those operators using a fixed, task-independent process. The Operator Application module then uses the retrieved description of the selected operator to generate a new state. This approach is essentially the model used in GPS (Ernst and Newell 1969) and STRIPS (Fikes and Nilsson 1971), where the operator representations stored in memory include a complete description of both the preconditions for when the operator is legal to apply as well as the operator's actions. This also is the model of pure rule-based systems such as OPS5 (Forgy 1981) and JESS (Freidman-Hill 2003), or even ACT-R (Anderson 2007). In these systems, rules correspond to operators, working memory

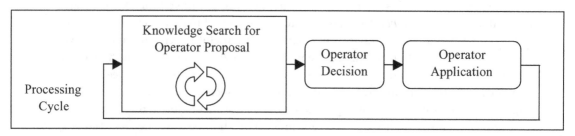

Figure 3.5
Knowledge search for operator selection.

corresponds to the state, and the only PSCM function open to knowledge search is rule selection.

Systems differ on what criteria are used for retrieving operators. Some systems retrieve all operators that legally apply (leading to forward search); others retrieve the operators that have actions that reduce difference between the current state and the goal (leading to means-ends analysis), but in general they are using knowledge about the current situation to retrieve relevant operators from memory. If the result of operator proposal is a set of operators, Operator Decision must make a selection on the basis of fixed task-independent criteria. For example, GPS has a fixed ordering of which operator to try first. In rule-based systems, OPS5 has a list of conflict-resolution strategies that use factors such as the specificity of the rule and the recency of the elements to select from all rules that match, whereas PSG (Newell 1973), an early rule-based system, has a fixed ordering, as in GPS.

3.4.3   Knowledge-Based Proposal, Evaluation, and Application of Operators

Although the previous style of PSCM is more flexible than a von Neumann architecture, knowledge search is still limited to only retrieving operators. It doesn't allow for arbitrary task-specific knowledge to be used in selecting between proposed operators, nor is it possible to have situation-specific implementations of operators. To remedy these shortcomings, we can add knowledge search for operator evaluation and operator application, as illustrated in figure 3.6.

With the addition of knowledge-based operator evaluation, this PSCM allows task-specific knowledge to compare and evaluate the operators that were proposed for the current state. This makes it possible to separately encode general knowledge about when an operator should be considered at all (that it *can* be selected), and specific knowledge about when an operator is desirable (when it *should* be selected). For example, in Rooms World, the agent can have knowledge that it can move forward when it isn't facing a wall. This is general knowledge about proposing an operator that is useful in every task. There can be additional task-specific knowledge that if

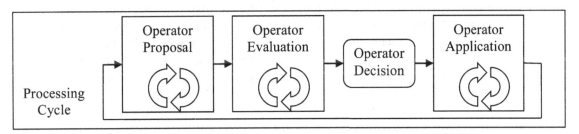

Figure 3.6
Knowledge search for operator selection, evaluation, and application.

there is an object that is to be picked up, and the object is in front of agent, but not directly in front of the agent, then the agent should prefer moving forward.

Knowledge search for operator application makes it possible to have conditional implementation knowledge for operators so that the application of an operator can be specific to details of the current state. Although not evident at this level of description, knowledge search for operator application can also support the implementation of operators that execute overtime and respond to dynamic changes in the environment, such as an operator that keeps an aircraft level and headed in the same direction as it is buffeted by winds (Pearson et al. 1993). Examples of conditional operator execution are included in chapter 4, where we present the Soar implementation of the PSCM.

Decomposing selection knowledge into proposal and evaluation has many advantages over approaches that rely on monolithic representations of operators. First, it allows the system to independently represent and learn when an operator is legal to apply to different situations and when an operator is advantageous to apply to different goals (R4). Operator knowledge need not be learned at once, nor does a single description of an operator have to be modified as more knowledge about an operator is acquired. Instead, the representation of the operator can be learned as independent units that combine together at run time (R5). Second, this approach naturally supports disjunctive preconditions so that an operator can be proposed in different situations, and can be applied as the details of the situation require. Third, the possible combinations of these different types of knowledge do not have to be represented explicitly because they combine dynamically for the current situation and task. Thus, if there are three independent situations in which the operator can be selected, and there are four independent ways in which certain details of it are applied, it isn't necessary to define twelve different operators. Fourth, each aspect of an operator can be learned independently and incrementally (R12). The actions (or pre-conditions) of an operator are not set in stone when the operator is first defined.

3.4.4 Interacting with an External Environment

At this point, we expand the PSCM further to support interaction with an external environment. To interact with an environment, the agent must receive input from its perceptual system and send output commands to its motor system. As depicted in figure 3.7, we have added two modules. During the input phase, changes from perception are converted to changes in the state, and during the output phase, motor commands are delivered to the motor system for execution in the environment. Thus, when the robot in Rooms World selects an operator to move forward, a command is sent to the output system that causes the robot to move to a new location. During input, changes are made to the robot's internal state to reflect the changes in the robot's senses. These changes then influence which operators are proposed, the

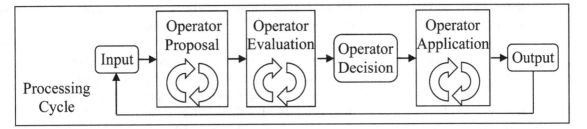

Figure 3.7
Processing cycle with input and output.

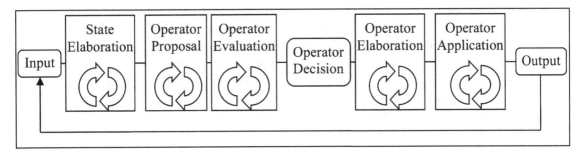

Figure 3.8
Processing cycle with elaborations.

evaluation of proposed operators, leading to the selection of another operator, a new motor action, and so on. At this level of description, the PSCM makes no commitments as to the details of what type of input or output is available to the agent.

3.4.5 Knowledge-Based Elaboration

The final extensions to the PSCM arise from the observation that many of the data structures associated with the state are direct entailments of other state structures, especially those created via input. These entailments do not require deliberation—they are always computed when the necessary data are available and they do not involve changing or removing existing structures, but are monotonic additions that enrich the agent's understanding of the current situations. We call these structures *elaborations*, which are similar to *secondary relations* in planning systems (Ghallab, Nau, and Traverso 2004). The addition of elaborations is illustrated in figure 3.8, which includes the complete set of PSCM functions: state elaboration, operator proposal, operator evaluation, operator elaboration, and operator application. Although operator elaboration is a PSCM function, in our experience it is of minimal importance as any structures created during operator elaboration can be created during operator proposal. Thus, in presentations of the PSCM in future chapters, it will rarely be included, and we will focus on state elaboration, operator proposal, operator evaluation, and operator application.

A simple example of state elaboration from Rooms World can arise when the robot's goal is to catch another agent. For that task, the robot can elaborate the state with information as to whether it is in a room with a single door or multiple doors (because it can possibly trap another agent in a room with a single door). If the robot and the other agent are in a room with a single door, the robot can elaborate the state with information as to whether it is between the other agent and the door. These elaborations simplify the determination of which operator should be selected.

Part of the semantics of a state elaboration is that when the structures on which it is based are removed from the state, the elaboration is no longer valid and is removed (or recomputed). Thus, elaborations provide the functionality of reason maintenance (Doyle 1979). For example, when the robot chases the other agent to a new room, the number of doors in the current area is recalculated. As the robot and other agent move, the relative position of the robot and agent are recalculated. Without state elaborations, a separate operator would be required to compute such structures, and a second operator would be required to remove the structure when it was no longer valid.

3.4.6 An Alternative View of the PSCM Processing Cycle

Another way to look at the processing cycle is in terms of a duality of non-persistent (elaborations) and persistent changes. The persistent changes are those that persist independent of other changes in the state. In the processing cycle, these include input, where new structures are added to the state; operator decision, where the current operator is selected; and operator application, where deliberate changes are made to the state on the basis of the current operator. The non-persistent changes include entailments of the current state and include elaborations of the state that are independent of the operator, as well as operator proposals, evaluations, and elaborations. For compactness, we combine elaborate state, propose operator, and evaluate operator into a single phase called *proposal* (which is how they are implemented in Soar). In addition, there is an elaboration phase for computing entailments of the current operator, once it has been selected.

In order to ensure that persistent changes are based on a complete understanding of the current situations, entailments of one set of persistent changes must be computed before the next set of persistent changes are made. This leads to slightly expanded processing, with an elaboration phase added after operator application (figure 3.9). This elaboration phase allows entailments from operator applications to be computed before output. This is useful in cases where the structures created by operator application need to be translated into output commands. Shading indicates

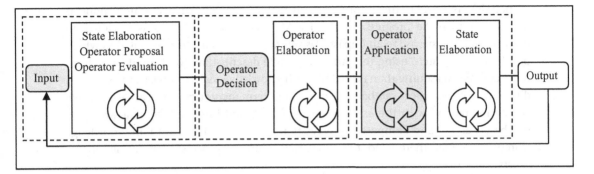

Figure 3.9
Alternative view of final PSCM processing cycle.

phases that create persistent changes; dotted boxes indicate pairs of persistent and non-persistent phases.

This view provides a slightly different perspective on the components of the processing cycle and gives some insight as to which components are necessary for three different classes of problems:

• For purely internal problems, output and input are not needed. Once input and output are removed, the two state-elaboration modules can be combined, giving two pairs of modules: operator decision/operator elaboration and operator application/ state elaboration. In this scheme, operator proposal occurs immediately after operator application in parallel with state elaboration.

• For agents that do not maintain any internal state, only the first two pairs would be necessary (input/state elaboration and decision/operator elaboration). Input would be processed by the first pair, followed by the deciding which operator to apply. The actions of the operator would not modify any internal structures, so that the actions could be passed directly to the Output module, making the operator application phase unnecessary.

• For a simple reactive system whose knowledge is organized so that only a single operator is suggested for any situation, there is no need for the operator decision module and the ensuing elaboration. Operator proposal suggests only a single operator, and that operator is always selected.

3.5 Impasses and Substates

The processing described up to this point involves solving problems in a single problem space and assumes that there is sufficient knowledge directly available to perform all PSCM functions. In this section, we describe how the PSCM is extended to handle cases when the information available from knowledge search alone is insufficient to make progress. In the PSCM, such a lack of progress is called an *impasse,* and in response to an impasse, as *substate* is automatically generated in which problem-space search, using the processing cycle described above, is used to perform more complex reasoning than is possible with knowledge search alone. In the substate, different problem spaces can be used, other long-term memories can be accessed, there can be interaction with the external environment, and intermediate data structures can be generated and composed in ways that are not possible with pure knowledge search. In general, there is no *a priori* restriction on the processing performed in the substate.

For impasses that arise because the agent has insufficient knowledge to select the next operator, the reasoning in the substate corresponds to deliberation, where the agent explicitly considers each alternative operator proposed in the original state. In these cases, the agent can internally simulate those operators to determine which operator leads to a better situation.

For impasses that arise because a selected operator isn't immediately applied, one possibility is that the agent has initiated actions in the external environment and is waiting for feedback that the operator has applied successfully. In this case, the reasoning in the substate consists of monitoring the execution of the operator in the environment. In other cases, the operator may be complex and the agent may not be able to apply it directly. In these cases, the reasoning in the substate corresponds to reasoning in a different problem space using more primitive operators that implement the original operator. Thus, the original operator becomes a goal to be achieved in the substate. Thus, in the PSCM, the proposal and selection of goals is recast as the proposal and the selection of abstract operators that are implemented in substates, and in the PSCM, the same decision procedure is used uniformly for all types of reasoning, including primitive operator selection, goal selection, or internal planning.

For all impasses, independent of the type, the substate includes structures that represent the type of impasse and that allow access to the state in which the impasse occurs. Figure 3.10 illustrates how the substate subsumes the original state, including information about the impasse, as well as additional structures local to the substate. In the substate, operators can be selected that create structures and perform reasoning without disrupting the original state. Thus, as the system takes steps in the problem space of the substate, it creates and modifies structures local to its state; although it can also make changes in the original state if that is necessary to make progress.

During processing in the substate, additional impasses can arise, leading to a stack of substates. This sets up the possibility of an alternating recursion where problem search and knowledge search are intermixed throughout the recursion. Thus, knowledge search controls problem search, and when knowledge search fails, it invokes problem search to deliberately search for knowledge. Conceptually, processing

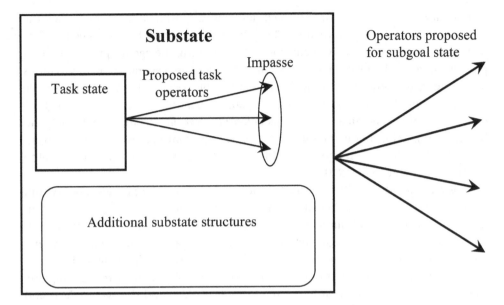

Figure 3.10
Substate structure of an operator tie.

continues across all states concurrently, though because there are impasses for all but the most recent substate the majority of the processing usually occurs in the most recently created substate. However, if there are changes in input or results are returned from substates, those new structures can lead to new retrievals from knowledge searches at other levels—possibly changing the proposed operators and their evaluations, which in turn resolves an impasse. There is no need for an explicit signal to terminate the substate; instead, when the impasse resolves, processing resumes, and the substate and its associated structures are removed.

Extending the PSCM to include substates provides the portal for accessing additional sources of knowledge and integrating complex deliberate cognitive functions with reactive reasoning. Examples include planning (in which the agent internally simulates the effects of actions to determine which are most likely to make progress on the current task), perspective taking (in which the agent creates a representation of another agent's situation and attempts to predict which actions it will take), and hierarchical goals (in which an operator is applied by decomposing it into simpler, more primitive operators that are from a different problem space). (These examples are explored in more detail in chapter 5.)

Creating substates in response to impasses has two important implications. First, substates and thus subgoals are generated automatically, which we call *automatic subgoaling*. Substates arise when needed because knowledge is inadequate, but if additional knowledge is acquired through learning, a substate doesn't arise when the agent encounters the same situation. This provides a transition from deliberate reflective behavior, to faster reactive behavior by transitioning the agent's processing from problem search to knowledge search. Second, substates are generated for *all* situations where the agent cannot make progress. This is possible because the PSCM has a simple model of computation: propose, select, and apply operators. Whenever one of those fails, a substate is generated. We call this *universal subgoaling* (Laird, Rosenbloom, and Newell 1986). Achieving universal subgoaling is important because it gives the agent the ability to reflect on all knowledge-driven aspects of its behavior. This is critical to meeting requirements R5–R10.

Substates provide a limited form of on-demand *meta-reasoning* or *reflection*. Within a substate, the agent can deliberately reason about why it isn't making progress, consider the implications of alternative actions, or decompose complex operators into simpler operators. It can imagine hypothetical situations and determine what it would do in those situations and use that knowledge to aid in decision making or the execution of an action. These forms of meta-reasoning arise only when there is an impasse; when the agent "knows" what to do, reflection is avoided and the agent selects and applies operators without impasses.

Although an agent can reflect on its knowledge-based processing, it cannot directly reflect on architectural components such as the decision procedure and learning mechanisms (described in chapters 7–10). Opening architectural components to direct reflection requires representing architectural data and processes in a way that the agent's knowledge can understand and process. Usually architectural processes and data can be implemented more efficiently using a different computational model than the one used by the agent. For example, it would be extremely cumbersome to represent the backpropagation algorithm used in neural network learning in a way that a neural network could reason about it. Although not as extreme, standard programming languages are more appropriate for representing the fixed processes of the inner workings of a cognitive architecture than declarative structures represented in working memory that are interpreted by operators. Moreover, because the architectural processes are fixed, complete reflection isn't necessary, as the agent's knowledge can adapt to the operation of the architecture without understanding its details.

3.6   Using Multiple Sources of Knowledge

In the PSCM cycle, knowledge is used to propose, evaluate, and apply operators, which is commonly called *procedural* knowledge, and it encodes long-term knowledge for directly generating behavior. It is knowledge about how to do things. An agent can also have other types of long-term knowledge such as *semantic knowledge* (described in chapter 8), which includes knowledge of general facts about the world independent of how they are used, and *episodic knowledge* (described in chapter 9), which encodes an agent's experiences. Both of these types of knowledge can be useful in an agent but they do not directly influence the selection and the application of operators. That is, these other types of knowledge must be *interpreted* by procedural knowledge in order for them to influence behavior. In general, these other forms of knowledge are accessed and interpreted in substates, in service of performing a PSCM function when the processing at a level has stalled because of an impasse. For example, if an agent is trying to apply an operator to open a child-proof container, it could use an operator to query semantic memory for facts related to child-proof containers and might retrieve "push down on the lid while turning." Once the memory is retrieved, additional operators could be selected in the substate to carry out the suggested action. One characteristic of Soar is that one of its learning mechanisms, called *chunking,* can convert access and interpretation of structures in semantic and episodic memory into procedural knowledge, greatly speeding future access and use of that knowledge.

Access to procedural, semantic, and episodic knowledge all involve knowledge search, where the agent accesses them to retrieve what it already about the current situation. However, it is only procedural knowledge that must be within the inner loop of processing. Semantic and episodic knowledge are not as tightly tied to directly generating and controlling behavior and can be thought of as being accessed asynchronously from the processing cycle, and thus no longer in the critical path of the processing cycle. One implication of this structure is that accesses to semantic and episodic memories don't necessarily have temporal constraints as tight as those on accesses to procedural memory.

3.7   Acquiring Knowledge

Learning provides the ability to acquire knowledge that is stored in long-term memory and later accessed via knowledge search to influence behavior. Cognitive architectures are unique in their integration of learning and behavior. Not only do the learning mechanisms in a cognitive architecture use an agent's behavior on a task as input, but also the learning occurs during behavior and can immediately improve behavior. In the PSCM, learning can improve state elaboration, operator proposal, operator evaluation, operator elaboration, and operator application through the acquisition of procedural knowledge for each of those functions, and it can indirectly improve behavior through the acquisition of semantic and episodic knowledge. Some learning mechanisms, such as reinforcement learning, described in chapter 7, use experience to directly tune procedural knowledge. Some learning mechanisms capture knowledge from the agent's experiences, such as episodic memory, described in chapter 9; others save general facts about the world, such as semantic knowledge, described in chapter 8. Learning is also the means by which a cognitive architecture converts problem search to knowledge search, by compiling problem solving using other types of knowledge into procedural knowledge, which is done in Soar via chunking, a learning mechanism described in chapter 6.

3.8 Alternative PSCMs

The PSCM described above includes explicit representations of states and operators, but doesn't have explicit representations of goals or problem spaces. Goals are implicit in the description of substates created as a result of an impasse, and there is no explicit representation of long-term agent goals. Furthermore, there is no explicit representation of the current problem space. Goals and problem spaces can be represented in the state, and operators can be included that change goals and problem spaces, but they are not inherent to the PSCM. Thus, the locus of all decision making is in the selection of the current operator; there is no required selection of the current goal, or problem space. The advantage of explicitly representing only states and operators is that all decision making is unified into selecting, evaluating, and applying operators, simplifying the PSCM.

Soar has not always been this way. Early versions of Soar included the selection of a current problem space, and a current state (Laird, Rosenbloom, and Newell 1986; Laird, Rosenbloom 1996). The need to support external interaction led to the elimination of maintenance of multiple states and the selection of a current state. Instead, the current situation is the current state of a problem space, and it is the only state. There can be multiple states that arise through impasses, but they are not states open to selection.

The elimination of the current problem space arose from a desire to simplify the PSCM, but also from a recognition that the explicit representation of a current problem space leads to a loss of flexibility. In the current PSCM, the problem space is *implicit*—it is determined dynamically on the basis of the operators that are proposed for the current state. The set of available operators, and thus the problem space, changes as structures in the state change, without the agent making an explicit decision. Thus, the agent can "change" problem spaces by selecting operators that modify the state structure so that new operators are proposed, and other operators are no longer considered. For example, in the case of the mutilated checkerboard problem, instead of changing problem spaces by selecting a new problem space, the agent selects operators that add descriptions of the state related to parity and the number of white and black squares. Although problem spaces are implicit, they are an important organizing principle with the PSCM, and most systems developed in Soar maintain state structures that describe some characteristics of the current problem space.

4 Soar as an Implementation of the PSCM

This chapter describes how Soar implements the PSCM described in chapter 3. In order to implement the PSCM, Soar must have data structures for representing states and operators, and it must have mechanisms to support the processing cycle in figure 3.9. As Newell and Simon observed (1972, p. 191–192), "simple, definite algorithms should exist for the component processes for selecting, evaluating and applying operators." Soar must also have processes for input and output, making decisions, and storing knowledge in its long-term memories. The knowledge used to perform PSCM functions is held in *procedural memory*. Procedural memory encodes what an agent can do, possibly what it should do, and how to do it. In contrast, semantic memory (what an agent "knows"—facts about the world) and episodic memory (what an agent "remembers"—memories of experiences) encode knowledge about the world and the agent's experiences in the world. Although these memories are critical for creating a robust and flexible agent, they contribute only indirectly to the basic functions of the PSCM. It is procedural knowledge that drives the PSCM functions, and this chapter focuses on those functions. The other memories and architectural mechanisms for impasse processing, learning, mental imagery, and appraisal processing are covered in later chapters.

Section 4.1 gives background information on the representation Soar uses for long-term procedural knowledge: production systems. Section 4.2 describes how the objects of the PSCM (states and operators) map onto the structures of production systems (working memory and productions). Section 4.3 describes the details of Soar's processing cycle and how it relates to the PSCM functions. Section 4.4 presents demonstrations of Soar. Section 4.5 is a discussion of the implications of Soar's design. Section 4.6 describes how the components of Soar presented in this chapter meet the requirements from chapter 2. This chapter provides an in-depth description of Soar and how it supports the PSCM, but it doesn't contain all of the details of Soar's syntax and operation. For those details, see the Soar Manual (Laird and Congdon 2010) and the Soar Tutorial (Laird 2010).

4.1   Production Systems

The PSCM functions are directly related to procedural knowledge—when and how to perform both internal and external actions. The requirements from chapter 2 demand that any implementation of procedural knowledge must support efficient access to large bodies of knowledge (R3) and the ability to independently encode situation and task knowledge (R4). To satisfy these and other requirements, our implementation of Soar represents long-term procedural knowledge as if-then rules, or *production rules* (Newell and Simon 1972; Post 1943). Throughout this book we use the terms "production rules," "productions," and "rules" interchangeably.

Production systems have been used extensively in AI as the basis for constructing expert systems and agents. For example, OPS5, originally developed at Carnegie Mellon University (Forgy 1981; Brownston et al. 1985), became the basis for many commercial rule-based engines, including OPS83, ART, CLIPS (Giarranto and Riley 2004), and Jess (Friedman-Hall 2003). Production systems are currently used to represent procedural knowledge in other cognitive architectures, including ACT-R (Anderson 2007) and EPIC (Meyer and Kieras 1997).

The left side of figure 4.1 contains a block diagram of the structure of a generic production system. Production memory consists of if-then rules, and the agent's understanding of the current situation is encoded as data structures in *working memory*, and working memory consists of a collection of *working-memory elements*. The "if"

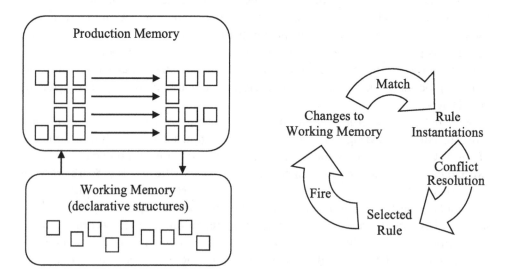

Figure 4.1
Generic production system: structure and process.

part of a rule consists of *conditions* (on the left side of the arrow in the long-term memory block) that must be satisfied by working memory for the rule to match. The "then" parts are *actions* that add, modify, or delete structures in working memory. When used to encode the Blocks World, working memory contains a description of the blocks that the agent can see, as well as a description of the configuration the blocks in the desired state. Working memory can also include additional abstract structures to aid in its problem solving, such as a count of the number of blocks in the world.

The right side of figure 4.1 shows the basic processing cycle of a production system. Starting at the top of the cycle, the conditions of rules are *matched* against the contents of working memory. Matching determines which rules have all of their conditions satisfied by the structures in working memory. For example, if a rule tests that working memory includes a representation of a green block and a red block, and if those structures exist in working memory, the rule matches. Rules can have variables in their conditions that allow them to test for equality and inequality of working-memory elements without testing their exact values. A rule matches only if all instances of a variable consistently match the same value in working memory. For example, a rule can test if a block and a cylinder have the same color, without testing what that color is.

The result of the match process is a set of *rule instantiations*. There is one rule instantiation for each successful match of a rule to working memory. Some rules may match multiple sets of working-memory elements at the same time. For example, if the rule described above is used when there are two blocks, one red and one blue, and two cylinders, one red and one blue, it has two instantiations. The match process can also compute which rules that previously matched no longer match. Although not used in many rule-based systems, this ability to detect when a rule *retracts* is used in Soar.

The next step in most production systems is to choose a single rule instantiation to fire. This process is called *conflict resolution* because the competing rules conflict as to which action should be performed. Conflict-resolution schemes use a variety of criteria, such as preferring rules that match the most recent data in working memory (focusing on the current processing), preferring rules that match more data (using more specific knowledge), or avoiding rule instantiations that have already fired (avoiding repetition). Once a single rule has been selected, it *fires*, which involves executing its actions, which change working memory by adding and removing working-memory elements. The changes in working memory affect which rules match, and the cycle begins again.

The major computational cost of a production system is matching the rules against working memory. The naive approach is to compare all of the conditions of all the rules to all elements of working memory on each cycle. With this approach, the cost of matching rules is $W^{C \cdot R}$, where W is the number of elements in working memory, C is the average number of conditions in each rule, and R is the number of rules. Clearly, as more rules are added, the cost of matching rules can quickly outstrip available computational resources. The Rete algorithm (Forgy 1982) was designed to avoid this problem. Instead of matching all conditions to all of working memory each cycle, Rete processes only the changes in working memory. Rete maintains a memory of all partial matches for all rules and processes the changes in working memory to update the partial matches and determine which rules completely match and which rules no longer match. Together with the fact that usually there are only a small number of changes in working memory during each cycle and that usually those changes affect only a small number of rules, it is possible to create rule matchers that can efficiently process very large numbers of rules (Doorenbos 1994).

Production-rule systems satisfy many of the requirements from chapter 2. They support efficient access to large bodies of knowledge (R3) as described above. They support situation-dependent knowledge (R4) through their conditions which limit when the actions are appropriate. They also provide a representation for knowledge that is modular, which is important when attempting to achieve incremental learning (R13), where it must be possible to add individual units of knowledge, one at a time, without extensive analysis of existing knowledge.

4.2   Mapping Production Systems onto the PSCM

A direct mapping of production systems onto the PSCM would have working memory map to the state and individual rules map to individual operators. This is the approach described in figure 3.5 and is common to many rule-based systems. One problem with mapping individual rules to individual operators is that it is difficult to encode task-specific knowledge to control rule/operator selection. Although knowledge search is used to determine the set of available rules (via the match process), the conflict-resolution phase doesn't involve a knowledge search for rule selection—it uses local knowledge associated with each rule, such as the number of conditions, the recency of the matched data, or a strength associated with the rule. Thus, rule selection isn't conditional on the broader situation outside of those aspects tested in the conditions of individual rules.

In Soar, working memory corresponds to a PSCM state, or, when substates exist, a hierarchy of embedded states. However, individual rules do not correspond to individual operators. Instead, rules encode knowledge for each of the knowledge search phases of the PSCM: state elaboration, operator proposal, operator evaluation, operator elaboration, and operator application (as illustrated in figure 3.8). To support operator evaluation, operator elaboration, and operator application, a Soar agent has separate, but related representations of operators that are created by rules: a declarative representation of the operator, which usually includes its name and any associated parameters; an *acceptable preference*, which indicates that the operator in being considered for selection; and any additional *preferences*, which evaluate a proposed operator for selection; and a working-memory element that indicates that a proposed operator is selected to be the *current* operator.

During the operator-proposal phase, rules can fire and create an acceptable preference for an operator, and a declarative representation of the operator. These structures, together with other state structures, are tested by rules that evaluate the operator and create addition preferences. The preferences are examined by the *decision procedure,* which selects the current operator. The current operator structure provides a declarative representation in working memory which is tested by rules that apply the operator. In summary, Soar has representations for proposed operators (acceptable preferences and declarative structures in working memory), evaluations of operators (additional types of preferences), and the current operator (a special declarative structure in working memory). The knowledge about an operator is spread across rules that propose the operator (which create the proposed operator in working memory), evaluate the operator (which create preferences to select between the proposed operators), and apply the operator (which test the current operator and modify the state). Thus, an operator is represented across multiple rules and across multiple working-memory structures.

Soar's approach makes it possible to independently and incrementally learn new proposal conditions for an operator, new heuristics for when it should be selected (evaluation knowledge), and refinements or extensions to how an operator is applied. These capabilities become important in large, knowledge-rich agents (R3) whose available knowledge increases and changes (R5).

4.2.1 State Representation in Working Memory

Soar's working memory holds the agent's representation of its current state. Figure 4.2 contains three different depictions of working memory. Figure 4.2a shows a picture of the represented blocks and table. Figure 4.2b shows a graphical representation of a subset of working memory. Figure 4.2c shows a text description of the individual working-memory elements as they are represented in Soar; figure 4.2d shows a more compact object-based representation of the same information.

Working memory is organized as a connected graph structure, rooted in a symbol that represents the state (S1 in the figure). In Soar terminology, the non-terminal nodes of the graph are called *identifiers*, the arcs are called *attributes*, and the *values* are other nodes, which can be either identifiers or constants. We often refer to a collection of arcs that share the same node as an *object*, so that an object consists of all the properties and relations of an identifier. A state is an object, and all other objects are substructures of the state, either directly or indirectly.

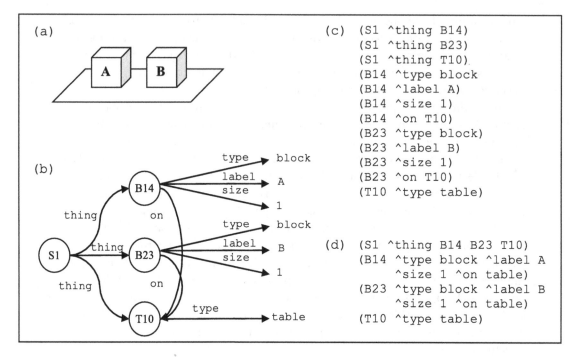

Figure 4.2
Sample working-memory structures for Blocks World.

Each relation or property is represented as an individual working-memory element that consists of the identifier, the attribute, and the value. The identifier is a symbol created by Soar. For example, S1 is an identifier, as are B14, B23, and T10. The attribute is the name of the relation/property and attributes are distinguished by a preceding carat in the text descriptions. Attributes in the figure include: ^thing, ^on, and ^type. Values can be either identifiers or constants, such as "block," "A," or "1." The first three working-memory elements have the same identifier (S1) and attribute ^thing, but different values: B14, B23, and T10. For convenience, we often refer to collections of working-memory elements as *working-memory structures*.

Figure 4.2d shows shorthand for writing the working-memory elements that share the same symbol as their identifier. S1 has three augmentations with the same attribute, the values are written after the attribute. Each of the objects is written as a set of attribute values after the shared identifier symbol.

For the most part, there is no intrinsic meaning in Soar to the symbols used as constants, such as "name," "blocks-world," or "table." These labels are determined by the writer of the Soar rules to aid in understanding the rules and their meaning is ultimately determined by the situations in which they are created by rules and the

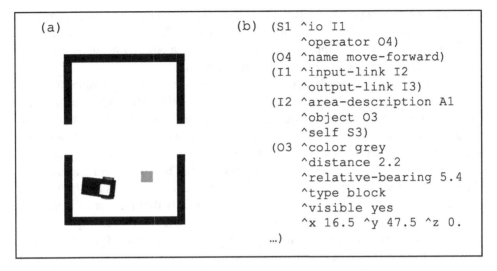

```
(a)                          (b)  (S1 ^io I1
                                      ^operator O4)
                                  (O4 ^name move-forward)
                                  (I1 ^input-link I2
                                      ^output-link I3)
                                  (I2 ^area-description A1
                                      ^object O3
                                      ^self S3)
                                  (O3 ^color grey
                                      ^distance 2.2
                                      ^relative-bearing 5.4
                                      ^type block
                                      ^visible yes
                                      ^x 16.5 ^y 47.5 ^z 0.
                                  …)
```

Figure 4.3
Example working-memory structures for Rooms World.

situations in which they are used by other rules. However, the input and output systems define specific symbols for perceptual data and for initiating action in the environment. In addition, there are a limited number of symbols that are created and maintained by the architecture, such as ^operator for the selected operator; ^io, ^input-link, and ^output-link for communication with the perception and output systems; as well as a small set of other symbols that are created as part of a substate (described in chapter 6).

Figure 4.3b shows a subset of the contents of working memory for an agent in a Rooms World state(figure 4.3a) when an operator has been selected to move forward. The state has augmentations for input/output structures on the ^io attribute, as well as any other structures created by rules (such as closest-object), and the selected operator. The input-link contains everything the agent can sense, organized into information about the room, ^area-description, any object it can sense, ^object, and information about itself, ^self. There are many more working-memory elements that describe each of these, and the figure shows some of the structure of object O3.

As was mentioned earlier, working-memory elements form a connected graph structure, rooted in the state, such that there is always a path from the state symbol through working-memory elements to the identifier of every other working-memory element. If ever an identifier becomes disconnected from the state, all working-memory elements with it in the first position are automatically removed from working memory. For example, if working-memory element (S1 ^object B14) in figure 4.2 is removed from working memory, B14 is no long connected to the state and all working-memory elements with B14 as their identifier are removed. The connectivity of Soar's working memory directly supports organizing working memory into states and sub-states, which are described in more detail in chapter 6.

Associated with each working-memory element is a numeric *activation* (Chong 2003; Nuxoll, Laird, and James 2004; Derbinsky and Laird 2011) reflecting the frequency and recency of its creation and use. The purpose of the activation is to indicate the importance or relevance of a working-memory element. Although Soar supports activation of working memory, its use has not been fully explored in Soar agents to date and was not used in any of the agents described in this book. Its main use is in biasing the retrieval of data from episodic memory (Nuxoll and Laird 2007). It is also used to automatically remove working-memory elements that are not in active use but are stored in semantic memory. The activation in Soar is modeled in part on the activation of declarative structures in ACT-R (Anderson et al. 2004). The activation of a working-memory element increases whenever a rule attempts to create it, or when it is tested in the conditions of a production rule that fires. Activation decays exponentially and when the activation of all the working-memory elements that share a common identifier fall below a fixed threshold, those working-memory elements are removed.

4.2.2 Rule Representation

Production rules in Soar consist of a set of conditions and actions. Figure 4.4 shows an example of a simple state-elaboration rule. An English interpretation of the rule is on the left and the rule in Soar's native syntax is on the right. The rule makes a simple inference—if an object is the table, then it is clear. Throughout the rest of the book, we show only the English versions to make the examples easier to understand. For questions about the details behind the English versions, Soar versions of all rules in the book are available from the Soar website (http://sitemaker.umich.edu/soar).

Every rule in Soar begins with "sp," which stands for "Soar production." This is followed by the body of the rule, demarcated by braces around the body of the rule. In the body, the name of the rule comes first. The name is meaningless to Soar, but

```
If the state has a thing and      sp {elaborate*table*clear
   the thing is a table                (state <s> ^thing <thing>)
then                                    (<thing> ^type table)
   that thing is clear             -->
                                        (<thing> ^clear true) }
```

Figure 4.4
A rule for state elaboration in Blocks World.

can be useful for a Soar programmer to determine the purpose of a rule. The name is followed by a list of conditions, with each condition in parentheses. The conditions are followed by "-->"; then there is the list of actions (in this example there is only one action). The conditions are a conjunctive set of tests, and the actions are a conjunctive set of actions. In the Soar rule, symbols surrounded by angle brackets, such as <s>, are variables. The identifiers in working memory are arbitrary (created by the architecture) so variables must be used to match identifiers, and they can also be used to test for equality of two values (or two identifiers). Limited disjunction can be tested in conditions among constants (such as something can be "red" or "blue"), but in general, disjunction is achieved through multiple rules. In addition, conditions can test for the absence of working-memory elements.

The first condition of a rule must always match a state, and to remind users of that, the first condition includes the word "state," even though that isn't part of a working-memory element. Just as the state defines a graph structure, so must the rule's conditions test a subset of that graph structure rooted in the state. Rule actions add or remove structures within the closure of that graph, ensuring that no unconnected structures are created.

In figure 4.4, the first condition tests for the existence of a working-memory element with ^thing as its attribute, rooted in the state identifier (S1). For the earlier example in figure 4.2, there are three working-memory elements that match that test and there are three values that can bind to variable <thing>: B14, B23, and T10. The second condition tests that the thing is a table, which restricts <thing> to be T10 so there is one instantiation of this rule. The action is to create a new working-memory element that has the symbol bound to <thing> as the identifier. The result is that one working-memory element is created: (T10 ^clear true). Rules can also have actions that create preferences or remove working-memory elements.

4.2.3 Operators Represented in Working Memory

As was mentioned earlier, the definition of an operator is spread across multiple rules that propose, evaluate, and apply it. Examples of these rules are given in section 4.3, where the details of Soar's processing cycle are described. The rules interact via representations of the operator in working memory, an example of which is illustrated in figure 4.5.

The first step in using an operator is to propose it, which involves creating a representation of the operator in working memory so that additional rules can evaluate it for selection. Figure 4.5 shows the structures that are in working memory if an operator is proposed but not yet selected. The first line shows an *acceptable preference* for the operator that signifies that the operator is a candidate for selection. Preferences have a fourth symbol which indicates the type of preference. The symbol for an acceptable preference is a "+" as shown in the figure. The proposed operator also has three

```
(S1  ^operator O45 +)              Operator proposed
(O45 ^name move-block             Operator description in
     ^moving-block B14                working memory
     ^destination B23)
```

Figure 4.5
Working-memory representation of a proposed operator.

```
(S1 ^operator O45)                Operator selected
(S1 ^operator O45 +)              Operator proposed
(O45 ^name move-block             Operator description in
     ^moving-block B14               working memory
     ^destination B23)
```

Figure 4.6
Working-memory representation of a selected operator.

augmentations, one for its name, one that indicates which block is to be moved (B14) and where it is to be moved (on B23).

By representing the proposed operator in working memory, rules can match against the details of the current state, the acceptable preference, and the operator structure and evaluate the operator, creating additional preferences that influence its selection.

Once an operator is selected, an augmentation of the state is created with ^operator as the attribute (without the "+"). An example of the operator from figure 4.5 is illustrated in figure 4.6 after it has been selected. Notice that it has both the augmentation on the state that indicates it has been selected (the top working-memory element) as well as the acceptable preference. To avoid conflict between the actions of multiple operators, only one operator can be the current operator.

Once an operator is selected, additional rules can match and apply the operator. By using multiple rules for proposal, selection, and application, Soar has a flexible representation of operators that makes it possible to have conditional, disjoint sets of preconditions and actions.

4.3   The Soar Processing Cycle

The Soar processing cycle, as illustrated in figure 4.7, is based on the PSCM processing cycle illustrated in figure 3.9. All the processes represented by standard rectangles are

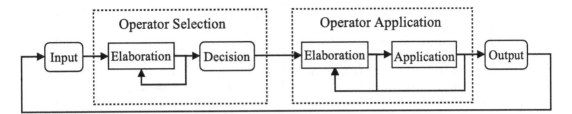

Figure 4.7
The Soar processing cycle.

performed by production rules. The round-cornered rectangles in figure 4.7 are fixed task-independent processes. The Input and Output phases provide Soar's means to interact with an environment; the Decision phase picks the current operator. At an abstract level, the cycle consists of four phases: Input, Operator Selection, Operator Application, and Output.

In Soar, there are two types of rule-firing phases. Rules that test the selected operator and modify the state are operator application rules and fire during the Application subphase. All other rules fire in the Elaboration phases whenever they match. Within the Elaboration phase, rules fire for the State Elaboration, Operator Proposal, Operator Evaluation, and Operator Elaboration subphases in figure 3.9.

Soar supports repeated waves of elaboration until there are no more rules to fire or retract, as shown by the return of processing to elaboration. By continuing to fire (and retract) elaboration rules, all available procedural knowledge is retrieved before the ensuing persistent changes (operator decision, application or output) are made. Soar also supports the application of operators requiring multiple sequential rule firings, through a cycle of elaboration and application.

In the rest of this section, we describe the operation of each phase of the Soar processing cycle, illustrated with an example from an external Blocks World task. In this example, the Soar agent perceives the current configuration of blocks via input and performs actions to modify the world via output. We assume that the goal is block A on top of block B, block B on top of block C, and block C on the table—the same desired state that was described in chapter 3. The description of the processing cycle is divided into four sections: Input, Operator Selection, Operator Application, and Output.

4.3.1 Input
During the Input phase, new working-memory elements are added to reflect changes in perception. If there are no changes or if there is no perceptual module at all (for purely internal problems), the Input phase is skipped. To extract appropriate sensory information from the environment (such as via simulated vision, audition, smell,

```
(S1 ^io I1)
(I1 ^input-link I2)
(I2 ^thing B1 ^thing B2 ^thing B3 ^thing T1)
(B1 ^type block ^label A ^size 1 ^color red ^on B2)
(B2 ^type block ^label B ^size 1 ^color blue ^on T1)
(B3 ^type block ^label C ^size 1 ^color green ^on T1)
(T1 ^type table ^label Table)
```

Figure 4.8
Sample working-memory structures for Blocks World input.

touch, or interaction with other programs) and transfer it to working memory, a perception module must be written in a language that interfaces to Soar, such as C++, C#, Java, or Python. Similarly, to initiate commands in an environment, an output module must be created. For the environments that Soar already interacts with, the required modules exist.

The interface to perception and output systems is via working memory through the *input-link* and the *output-link* structures, which are substructures of the *io* state structure. The input-link is where new structures are created by the input module; the output-link is where output commands are created by the agent that are sent to the output module for processing. By having a reserved areas for input, Soar can distinguish between structures created by perception and those generated internally by its own reasoning.

The exact information on the input-link depends on the domain and the agent's available perception system. In general, the input-link contains symbolic structures, sometimes with some numeric quantities. Chapter 11 provides more details on the Soar's theory of perception, which includes the use of mental imagery. For simplicity, in this example of the Blocks World, we assume that perception delivers symbolic descriptions of the blocks and the table, including the "on" relation for when a block is on another block or on the table. Figure 4.8 shows an example of the structures that might appear in working memory as a result of the Input phase when block A is on block B and block C is on the table. The ^io and ^input-link structures are created when Soar is initialized and are included in the figure to show the connectivity of the state (S1) to the input working-memory elements. This structure is slightly different from the ones illustrated in figures 4.2 and 4.4, where for simplicity, the ^io or ^input-link structures weren't included.

4.3.2 Operator Selection

Figure 4.9 highlights the Operator Selection phase. Operator Selection consists of the Elaboration subphase and the decision procedure. Elaboration includes three of the

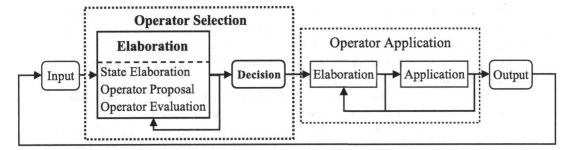

Figure 4.9
Selecting an operator.

original PSCM functional roles: elaborating the state, proposing operators, and evaluating the operators. Soar combines these together so that rules for all of them fire in parallel as a wave, independent of their functional role. Contrary to most rule-based systems, elaboration rules (rules not involved in operator application) *retract* the structures they have created when they no longer match. Thus, their results provide monotonic entailments of the current situation that are removed when they are no longer relevant. For example, if an operator is proposed to move block A on block B, one of the conditions in the proposal rule is that block B is clear. When the operator is selected and applied so that block B is no longer clear, the proposal for moving block A on block B is automatically retracted.

Within Elaboration, additional waves of rule firing and retraction continue until *quiescence*—when no more rules match or retract. The decision procedure then collects all operator preferences and selects the current operator. The data dependencies between rules implicitly maintains the PSCM ordering for individual operators—an operator isn't proposed until the state structures it is dependent upon are created by state elaboration, and an operator isn't evaluated until it is proposed. However, different operators may be processed on different waves, depending on their conditions and interactions among the rules.

State elaboration
During state elaboration, rules create new working-memory elements that are entailments of the existing state. Elaborating the state can simplify later calculations by making concepts explicit that are implicit in the configuration of existing working-memory elements. For example, if there is no block above a block, then it can be concluded that the second block is clear, which can be a condition for moving the block or placing a block on top of it. By creating a working-memory element that explicitly represents that a block is clear, future rules can be simpler (and learning can be more general) because a single structure is tested instead of multiple

working-memory elements. This approach is especially useful if there are multiple, independent ways of deriving a concept. Rules need test only that the derived concept as opposed to all the possible ways of deriving it. In Soar, a state elaboration tests only non-operator structures connected to the state, and creates new state structures but does create any operator preferences.

Figure 4.10 shows an English version of four elaboration rules. P1 detects when a block is clear, and P2 specifies that the table is always clear, which is true in this simple example for the purposes of placing blocks. The next two rules work together to compute whether a block is in its final desired position, where a block is in place if it is on the table in the desired state, or if it is on top of the same block in the desired state and that block is also in place. P3 computes that the table is in-place; P4 detects when a block is in place. P4 fires iteratively as it marks a block above the table that is in-place, and then once that block is marked, the block above can be marked if it is in the correct desired position (and so on). This is useful for detecting that the desired state has been achieved, but it is also useful for some

```
P1*elaborate*block*clear
If there is a block and
    there is nothing on top of that block
then
    that block is clear

P2*elaborate*table*clear
If there is the table
then
    the table is clear

P3*elaborate*table*in-place
If there is the table
then
    the table is in-place

P4*elaborate*block*in-place
If there is an object that is in-place and
    there is a block on that object and
    the block is on the object in the desired state
then
    the block is in-place
```

Figure 4.10
State-elaboration rules for Blocks World.

of the evaluation rules that test whether an operator moves a block into its desired position.

A state-elaboration rule can have multiple instantiations that fire in parallel, creating multiple structures on the state. For example, for the blocks in figures 4.2 and 4.8, P1 matches and fire simultaneously for blocks A and C, but not for block B, which has block A on top of it. Multiple instantiations also arise as a rule matches similar structures created at different times. For example, if block A is moved to the table, P1 fires for block B.

The persistence of working-memory elements is determined by the type of rule that created them. A rule instantiation that doesn't test the current operator and makes changes in the state, removes all working-memory elements it created whenever any of the working-memory elements tested in the conditions are removed from working memory. This is called *instantiation-support*, or *i-support*, as the instantiation provides support for the working-memory elements. For example, if block C is placed on block A, the working-memory element representing that A is clear is retracted. Retractions are processed in parallel with rule firings. The retraction of a rule instantiation can lead to additional retractions or additional rule firings for rules that test for the absence of the removed working-memory elements.

I-support in Soar corresponds to an implementation of the processing provided by a justification-based truth-maintenance system (Doyle 1979). The other class of support, which leads to persistent working-memory elements, is called *operator-support*, or *o-support*. All working-memory elements created by an operator-application rule have o-support and persist until they are removed by the actions of a rule, or when they become disconnected from the state through the removal of other working-memory elements. O-support is discussed in more detail in subsection 4.3.3.

Operator proposal

An operator is proposed by a rule that tests the current state and creates an *acceptable preference* for an operator. An operator-proposal rule usually creates additional working-memory elements that provide a declarative description of the operator, such as its name and parameters, as described in subsection 4.2.3. The acceptable preference indicates that an operator is a candidate for selection and every operator must have an acceptable preference to be considered for selection. The details of the other preferences and how they are interpreted are discussed below.

Figure 4.11 shows the operator-proposal rule for the Blocks World. The first condition of P5 tests for a working-memory element that specifies that there is a problem space named "move-single-unit-block." We assume that during initialization that such a working-memory element was created. For purposes of our example, this problem-space name signifies that the only available operators move one block at a time and that there are only unit-size blocks. By having an explicit representation of

```
P5*propose*operator*move-block
If the state has problem space move-single-unit-block and
    there is a block and
    that block is clear and
    there is a second object that is clear and
    the block is not on the table and being moved to the table
then
    create a move-block operator to
        move the block on to the second object and
    create an acceptable preference for that operator
```

Figure 4.11
A rule for proposing operators for Blocks World.

a problem-space name that implies those restrictions, we can create rules that encode knowledge about state elaboration, operator proposal, and selection that are specific to those restrictions.

Rule P5 proposes an operator to move a clear block on top of a clear object, which can be either another block or the table. The final condition is necessary to avoid attempting to move a block onto the table when it is already on the table. Notice that this rule isn't specific to any task, such as building a tower with A stacked on B, and B stacked on C, but applies to all problems in this problem space.

The preferences and working-memory elements created by operator-proposal rules have i-support and are maintained as long as the rule instantiation match. Thus, the set of available operators is not recomputed from scratch each processing cycle, but only changes in response to changes in the state. On each new cycle, the instantiations that no longer match retract their actions, and new rule instantiations create new operator preferences.

Operator evaluation

Once a candidate operator has been proposed, knowledge encoded as rules can evaluate it and compare it to other candidates. This knowledge is usually dependent on the specific task being performed and can be significantly different from the knowledge used to propose an operator. This type of knowledge is typically called *control knowledge*, because it controls the agent's behavior. Evaluation rules match state structures and proposed operators, and create preferences for the proposed operators. The decision procedure uses the preferences to select the current operator. A single operator can have multiple preferences that influence its selection. Soar has both symbolic and numeric preferences. Soar's symbolic preferences specify absolute or relative orderings of proposed operators, and the numeric preferences specify the expected value of

Table 4.1
Symbolic preferences for selecting operators.

Preference	Meaning
Acceptable	The operator is a candidate for selection. An operator must have an acceptable preference to be considered for selection.
Reject	The operator will not be selected.
Better/Worse	The operator is better/worse than another candidate operator. Allows specification of a partial order.
Best	The operator should be selected if it is not rejected or worse than another operator.
Worst	The operator can be selected, but only if there are no other candidates that are better than this operator.
Indifferent	Two operators are equally good and a random selection can be made between them.

applying the operator to the state, similar to Q values in a reinforcement learning system (Sutton and Barto 1998).

Table 4.1 lists the symbolic preferences along with their meaning. The exact semantics are defined by the processing as described below in the subsection on the decision procedure. There must be an acceptable preference for an operator to be considered a candidate for selection, and the other preferences allow the agent to specify either absolute or relative information about the worth of a candidate. In general, the preferences act as filters on the set of candidate operators. For example, if it is known that a specific operator should never be selected for the current state (it leads to a dead end or a dangerous situation), a rule can create a reject preference for that operator. If an operator is known to be on the path to the goal from the current state, a rule could create a best preference for that operator. The agent might also know that one operator is better than another in some situation and this would be represented by a rule that tests for that situation and then creates a better preference.

To illustrate the use of different symbolic preferences, figure 4.12 contains two rules that determine operator selection in the Blocks World. The first rule (P6) is a simple rule that detects when there is a block not in its desired position and stacked on a second block. It creates a best preference for moving the block to the table. Essentially this rule states that unless there is something better to do, it is a good thing to move a block onto the table that isn't in its desired location. The second rule (P7) encodes standard means-ends knowledge of preferring operators whose actions achieve components of the goal. Thus, rule P7 creates a better preference that prefers an operator that moves a block into its desired position over any other operator. In the initial state, this rule creates a better preference indicating that moving C onto the table is better than any of the other operators proposed. This rule alone isn't sufficient to

```
P6*evaluate*move-block*best*move-block-to-table
If the state has problem space move-single-unit-block and
    an operator is proposed to move a block to the table and
    that block is not in-place and
    that block is not on the table
then
    create a best preference of the operator

P7*evaluate*move-block*better*move-to-goal
If the state has problem space move-single-unit-block and
    an operator is proposed to move a block onto a second block and
    that second block is in-place and
    in the desired state the block is on the second block and
    there is a second operator different from the first operator
then
    create a preference that the first operator is better than the
    second
```

Figure 4.12
Example rules for evaluating operators for Blocks World.

provide optimal behavior as it provides guidance only when blocks can be moved into their final position.

Rules P6 and P7 interact when block B is on block A and block C is on the table. P6 creates a best preference for moving block B to the table. However, P7 creates a preference that moving block B on to block C is better than moving block B on the table. As explained below, the semantics of preferences dictate that moving block B onto block C should be selected. This is a case where an operator "is better than best." (The example problem we have posed is *Sussman's Anomaly* (Sussman 1975), a simple problem where means-ends knowledge alone (P7) is insufficient to find a direct solution to the problem; however, with rule P6, the direct solution is generated. We present results from using rules P6 and P7 for the Blocks World problems in the next section.)

To encode utility-based knowledge about operator selection, especially when there is uncertainty, numeric preferences are used. The numeric portion of a numeric preference specifies the reward that is expected to be obtained by applying an operator. The numeric values of numeric preferences created for the same operator are added together, all contributing to the operator decision, which is described below. When reinforcement learning (chapter 7) is used, the numeric portion of the rules that create numeric preferences are tuned based upon experience.

Soar gives precedence to symbolic preferences, so that numeric preferences are considered only when the symbolic preferences are insufficient to determine a choice.

```
P8*evaluate*move-block*numeric*move-on-table
If the state has problem space move-single-unit-block and
    in the desired state a block is on the table and
        there is an operator proposed to move the block on the table
then
        create a numeric preference for the operator with value 0.9
```

Figure 4.13
A rule for numeric evaluation in Blocks World.

A common approach is to use symbolic preferences to either force the selection of an operator that is known *a priori* to lead to success or eliminate operators that obviously lead to failure. Numeric preferences then specify the expected value of the remaining operators.

There is no need for numeric preferences in our formulation of the Blocks World, but figure 4.13 shows an example of an operator-evaluation rule for selecting an operator on the path to the solution, similar to rule P6, but this time with a numeric value of 0.9. More examples of numeric preferences are included in chapter 7.

The decision procedure

The purpose of the decision procedure is to use the available preferences to select an operator. If there are insufficient or conflicting preferences, an impasse arises, and Soar creates a substate (as described in chapter 6). If the decision procedure chooses a new operator, the selection is made by changing the working-memory element that contains the current operator—the ^operator augmentation of the state. Only the decision procedure can change this working-memory structure, and thus, only the decision procedure can change the current operator.

The set of preferences that Soar provides and their associated semantics provide a rich language for evaluating and comparing operators, also allowing for efficient interpretation of the preferences. Important properties of the preferences and the associated decision procedure are described after the procedure.

The decision procedure evaluates operator preferences in a sequence of seven steps listed below. Each of the seven steps processes a different type of preference. Input to the procedure is the identity of the current operator and the operator preferences. The result of the decision procedure is either the selection of a new operator or an impasse. For each step in the procedure, the name of the preference is listed followed by a description of the preference's effect on selection. Also included is a list of the ways in which the decision procedure can terminate after that step. In general, an impasse can arise if there are no viable candidates or if there are multiple candidates that cannot be distinguished by the remaining preferences.

Acceptable: All operators with acceptable preferences are collected into the *candidate set*. Only operators with an acceptable preference are considered for selection. If the candidate set is empty, a state no-change impasse arises.

Reject: Any operator in the candidate set with a reject preference is removed from the set. Rejection preferences guarantee that an operator isn't selected and can be used to eliminate operators that are useless or dangerous for the current situation. If the candidate set is empty, a state no-change impasse arises. If there is a single operator in the candidate set, it is the selected operator.

Better/worse: All operators in the candidate set that are worse than another operator in the candidate set are removed from the set. Better/worse preferences provide a means of specifying a partial order—that one operator is better than another. If the candidate set is empty, a conflict impasse arises. If there is a single operator in the candidate set, it is the selected operator.

Best: If there are any operators in the candidate set with best preferences, then all operators without best preferences are removed from the candidate set. Best preferences provide a means of specifying that an operator is a good choice that can be selected over those without a best preference. As shown with rules P6 and P7, the semantics of best can be counter intuitive in that when an operator is better than an operator with a best preference, the operator with the best preference is not selected because it would have been removed in step 3. If there is a single operator in the candidate set, it is the selected operator.

Worst: If there are any operators in the candidate set without worst preferences, then all operators with worst preferences are removed from the candidate set. Worst preferences provide a means of specifying that an operator is a fallback choice, one that is avoided if there are alternatives, but if there are no alternatives, it can be selected. An operator can have both best and worst preferences, with the best preference having precedent. If there is a single operator in the candidate set, it is the selected operator.

Symbolic indifferent: Indifferent preferences specify that all operators with indifferent preferences are equally good and a random choice can be made between them. If all operators in the candidate set are mutually indifferent (there is a symbolic indifferent preference for every remaining candidates), and if the current operator is in that set, then the current operator is maintained, otherwise, a random selection from the remaining operators determines the selected operator.

Numeric indifferent: Numeric indifferent preferences specify that a biased random selection can be made between the remaining operators and they provide the means to represent selection knowledge that can be tuned in Soar by reinforcement learning. The values of all indifferent preferences for the same operator are added together, and the operator with the highest numeric values is most likely to be selected. Soar provides users with a choice of three selection procedures for making decisions based on numeric preferences: softmax, epsilon greedy, and Boltzmann. These methods are described in subsection 7.1.3. If all the operators in the candidate set are numerically indifferent (there is a numeric indifferent preference for each operator), and if the current operator is in that set, then it is the selected operator, otherwise, a random selection from the remaining operators using the current selection procedure determines the selected operator. If there are operators in the candidate set that do not have numeric indifferent preferences, then there is a tie impasse.

If the decision is to maintain the current operator, then there is an operator no-change impasse because there has been no progress in applying the operator during the last processing cycle. This type of impasse can be resolved from changes in the environment; however, the impasse arises so that additional knowledge in a substate can respond to it if necessary.

Although agents can rely solely on numeric preferences, symbolic preferences enrich the expressiveness of the architecture, making it possible to eliminate choices (reject and better) but also to indicate that some choices are sufficient so that no further deliberation is necessary (best). Numeric preference schemes can only approximate the semantics of symbolic schemes. Our experience is that expected reward is one of many sources of knowledge an agent has available to inform its decision making, whereas others, such as external instructions, translate more faithfully into symbolic preferences.

At the top of figure 4.14 are the preferences that are generated for operators using the rules from figure 4.12 in the Blocks World where the state has block C on block A, block A on the table, and block B on the table, and where the desired state is block A on block B, block B on block C, and block C on the table.

```
Preferences: Acceptable: O1 (move-block C B)
             Acceptable: O2 (move-block B C)
             Acceptable: O3 (move-block C table)
             Better: O3 > O2 [from rule P7]
             Better: O3 > O1 [from rule P7]
             Best: O3 > [from rule P6]

---Preference Processing by Decision---
Process Acceptable: Candidate set = [O1 O2 O3]
Process Reject:     Candidate set = [O1 O2 O3]
Process Better:     Candidate set = [O3]
Select Operator:    O3 [only operator remaining]
```

Figure 4.14
Example preferences for Blocks World.

There are three operators that have acceptable preferences, and three additional preferences: two betters and a best. When the decision procedure processes the preferences, it goes through the stages described on the previous page. The first step is to create the candidate set with all the operators that have acceptable preferences. Next, reject preferences are processed and remove operators from the candidate set, but in this case there are no rejects so this step is skipped. Next, the better preferences are processed and O2 and O1 are removed from the candidate set because they are worse than O3. At this point, O3 is the only remaining operator and it becomes the current operator, and the best preference is ignored.

Soar's approach to decision making has some important properties:

• Decisions are made only when there is knowledge (in the form of preferences) for a dominant choice. There is no default random selection when there are candidates without differentiating preferences. Rather than assuming alternates are equally valid, Soar creates an impasse arises which allows Soar to deliberate about the decision.

• Soar biases its decision toward the current operator. Knowledge must exist that a different operator should replace the current operator. A different operator is selected if the current operator is retracted or additional preferences are created that prefer an alternative choice, but if the current operator remains the dominant choice, or if it is in the final indifferent set, it stays selected. This helps avoid thrashing between two or more equally good choices.

• Decisions in Soar are based on run-time integration of knowledge. Soar uses *least-commitment* decision making where no *a priori* decision is made ahead of time that commits an agent to a specific course of action in the future. The agent re-evaluates the situation for each decision, biased by the current selection.

• An agent can always change the selection of the current operator in a future decision through the addition of more preferences. This is not an unusual property of decision systems, but it is critical so that any impasse can be resolved with additional preferences and incorrect decision knowledge can be corrected by adding new knowledge that corrects the decision, but not the knowledge (Laird 1988).

• The computational complexity of the decision procedure is linear in the number of preferences; in practice, the decision procedure has minimal effect on a Soar agent's total processing time, which is dominated by rule matching (which is a form of knowledge search) and low-level processing of perceptual data (which is outside or Soar).

These properties are at a level of detail below the requirements from chapter 2, but relate to Soar's ability to represent and effectively use rich control knowledge (part of requirement R7) and support a spectrum of deliberation (part of requirement R9).

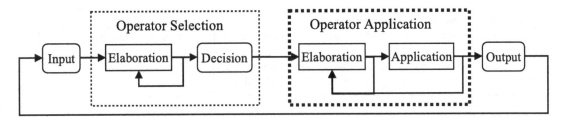

Figure 4.15
The operator application phase.

4.3.3 Operator Application

Operator application is where progress is made in the problem by taking a step in the problem space. During this phase, there are two subphases: Elaboration and Application as highlighted in figure 4.15. Elaboration runs until quiescence, and is followed by a single execution of apply, where persistent changes are made to the state. This sequence continues until there are no more new matches or retractions (or the current operator is removed because it is no longer the dominant choice). The discussion below begins with Elaboration, then Apply, and we then return to Elaboration because of the additional PSCM functions that can be performed after application rules have fired.

Elaboration

The first time Elaboration is entered during operator application, an operator has just been selected. The only new elaborations that could possibly match are those that add structures to the current operator because the previous Elaboration subphase in Select Operator ran until quiescence and the only change in working memory is the selection of the operator. Rules that test the operator and modify the state are held until the Apply subphase so that a complete description of the operator is available before the application rules fire. Operator-elaboration rules test that the operator has been selected and then create additional structures on the operator. These structures can simplify future operator application by associating parameters with the operator. Often there are no operator-elaboration rules, in which case this subphase is skipped.

Application

After operator elaboration, the Application subphase is entered where persistent changes are made to the state via operator-application rules. For operators with external actions, the application rules create commands on the output-link, which are executed by the output system during the Output phase. For operators with internal actions, application rules change the state by creating new structures and removing

```
P9*apply*move-block*external
If an operator is selected for moving a block onto an object
then
    create an output command on the output-link
        to move that block onto that object.
```

Figure 4.16
Rule for applying operators for external Blocks World.

existing structures. A single operator may include both internal and external actions. The changes made by operator application rules involve non-monotonic changes in the state—they are the result of a deliberate choice to take an action and are in contrast to the elaborations, which compute the entailments of the current situation. Thus the actions of operator-application rules are persistent and they do not retract when the operator-application rule no longer matches.

The Apply subphase doesn't fire operator application rules until quiescence. Instead, control returns to elaboration so that the implications of each wave of persistent changes can be computed before taking a next step. This ensures that the operator application steps are based on the agent's complete understanding of the current situation. The important principle is that persistent steps are taken only after all directly accessible knowledge has been asserted (which occurs after quiescence).

Figure 4.16 shows rule P9, an operator-application rule for an external version of the Blocks World. This assumes that the output system can execute a high-level command for moving the block. Once the Application phase is completed, the Output phase executes the command. After execution, perception of the environment changes, leading to changes in the input-link (reflecting the movement of the block) during Input, which then leads to retraction of the operator and selection of a new operator in the next Operator Selection phase. There is no requirement that the action is executed instantaneously—Soar proceeds through the processing cycle (possibly multiple times) until perception changes, at which time it responds to those changes.

Soar agents can create detailed output commands with finer-grained operators that respond to intermediate feedback if that is required by the output system. That approach usually requires operators organized hierarchically, implemented via substates as described in chapter 6.

If the problem is represented internally, without any external environment, the positions of the blocks are represented on the internal state and the operator-application rules modify the internal state directly. Figure 4.17 includes the operator-application rule for an internal version of the Blocks World. Rule P10 matches if the

```
P10*apply*move-block*internal
If an operator is selected for moving a block onto object and
    that block is on a second object
then
    add that the block is on the first object and
    delete that the block is on the second object
```

Figure 4.17
Rules for applying operators for internal Blocks World.

operator is moving a block on to another object. It modifies the block's position so that the block is on the second object.

Some operators require a sequence of operator-application rules, so (as shown in figure 4.15) control cycles back to fire additional operator-application rules until there are no more to fire (or, as explained below, the operator is removed).

Elaboration revisited

If any rules fired during operator application, then there is another Elaboration phase. The purpose of this phase is to allow rules to fire that decode or elaborate output actions that have been created during operator application. For example, as part of application, an operator can create an abstract structure that cannot be directly interpreted by the output system. State-elaboration rules can translate this structure into the detailed commands required by the output system. Although this subphase is included to allow decoding of complex output actions, it allows state-elaboration rules, operator-proposal rules, and operator-evaluation rules to fire, such as when an internal operator directly modifies the state.

As illustrated in figure 4.14, the decision procedure is run only after operator selection. However, during the Elaboration phase, it is possible for changes in working memory to cause proposal and evaluation rules to fire or retract such that the selected operator is no longer the dominant choice. One possible approach would be to leave the current operator selected until the next full decision procedure; however that approach opens up the possibility that some of the actions are inconsistent with what is known about which operator should be selected. To remedy this, whenever the set of preferences change, a reduced version of the decision procedure is run to determine if the current operator is still the dominant choice. If the current operator is no longer the dominant choice, it is removed as the selected operator, but without making a new selection. The new selection occurs when the complete decision procedure runs during the next Operator Selection phase, after input and operator proposal have had a chance to add their knowledge so that the decision is consistent with the agent's available knowledge.

4.3.4 Output

Commands for output are created in working memory by operator-application and/
or state-elaboration rules on the output link. Thus, all output commands are explicitly
represented in working memory before they are sent to the output system. This
approach has the advantage that the agent has a representation in working memory
of the actions it takes, which is useful for the agent to track its own behavior.

When the Output phase is entered, the output system extracts the output commands from the output-link and processes them. In the examples described below,
the output commands are executed directly in the environment. However, Soar also
supports mental imagery, in which the effects of output are "imagined" in the sensory
buffer. (See chapter 10.)

The structure of output commands is dependent on the interface to the external
environment and the available output systems. Soar has no restriction on the types
of output commands and it is possible to support simple single-shot commands, parallel actions, and even complex conditional commands that execute over extended
periods. Whenever there is no new output, Soar skips the Output phase and proceeds
to the Input phase.

4.3.5 Goal Detection

There is no separate phase for goal detection in Soar. The knowledge to detect the
achievement of a goal can be encoded either as state elaborations or as a separate
operator. For simple goals, where it is possible to recognize goal achievement without
extended computation, it is appropriate to use state elaborations; for complex goals,
it can be necessary to include operators that are deliberately selected to check that the
goal has been achieved. For our example, it is possible to extend P3 and P4 and add
one more elaboration rule that detects that the goal has been achieved as illustrated
in figure 4.18.

P11 recognizes when all blocks are in their desired positions. In more general agents
than our Blocks World agent, when one goal is achieved, it is appropriate to retrieve

```
P11*halt*all-blocks-in-desired-position
If block A is in-place and
   block B is in-place and
   block C is in-place
then
   write "Goal Achieved" and
   halt
```

Figure 4.18
Goal-detection rule for Blocks World with three blocks.

or generate another goal and attempt it. In this simple situation, where there is only a single goal, the desired state is recognized and the agent halts.

For more complex agents, that can pursue multiple goals, goals can be created by operators, or operators can act as goals by being selected, but where there are not application rules and the achievement of the operator is pursued in a substate so that the operator becomes a goal (see chapter 5).

4.3.6 Putting it all together

Figure 4.19 shows a partial trace of production rule firings for the example Blocks World task using the rules presented earlier. For this example, we assume that the problem is represented and solved internally, so there are no input and output phases, so that rule P10 is used to apply the current operator instead of rule P9. We also assume that working memory contains a description of the initial state, with the three blocks as well as a separate description of the desired state as shown at the top of the figure. To simplify the figure, the state structures are described as a set of relations and predicates. During the first elaboration phase, rules P1 and P2 fire in parallel and create structures indicating that blocks B and C, and the table are clear. After the creation of the clear predicates, rule P5 fires and creates three operators and their associated acceptable preferences. Once the proposed operators have been created, rules P6 and P7 fire to create preferences. After these rules fire, no additional rules match; the decision procedure interprets the preferences, and an operator is selected as illustrated in figure 4.14. In selecting operator O3, a new working-memory element is created to indicate the current operator and that causes P10 to fire. P10 applies the operator by modifying the state, adding the relation that C is on the table, and removing the relation that C is on A.

After these changes in the state, rule P1 fires to mark that A is now clear. P4 notices that C is now in its desired position on the table. The instantiation of rule P5 that proposed moving C onto the table no longer matches, so the acceptable preference for O3 is removed from working memory along with the operator description. Note that although P10 also no longer matches, it doesn't remove the structures it created because it is an operator application rule; that is, it tests the state and selected operator and makes changes in the state, so the changes it makes have o-support, which persist until removed.

Because of the removal of O3, P6 and P7 retract their preferences. Because of the addition of A being clear, P5 fires four times, creating new operators that can now apply, two for moving block A and one each for moving block B on block A and moving block C on block A. This is followed by more preferences being created, which leads to operator O2 being selected. Figure 4.20 shows a trace of the states and operator selections in generating a complete solution.

```
Initial State: (on C A)  (on A table)  (on B table)
Desired State: (on A B)  (on B C)      (on C table)

--Elaboration Phase--
Fire P1*elaborate*block*clear: (clear C)
Fire P1*elaborate*block*clear: (clear B)
Fire P2*elaborate*table*clear: (clear table)
Fire P3*elaborate*table*in-place (in-place table)
-
Fire P5*propose*move-block: O1 (move C B)
Fire P5*propose*move-block: O2 (move B C)
Fire P5*propose*move-block: O3 (move C table)
-
Fire P6*evaluate*move-block*best*move-to-ground: O3 >
Fire P7*evaluate*move-block*better*move-to-goal: O3 > O1
Fire P7*evaluate*move-block*better*move-to-goal: O3 > O2
--Decision
Select Operator O3

--Apply Operator
Fire P10*apply*move-block*internal: + (on C table), - (on C A)
-
Fire P1*elaborate*block*clear: (clear A)
Fire P4*elaborate*object*in-place (in-place C)
Retract P5*propose*move-block: O3 (move-block C table)
Retract P6*evaluate*move-block*best*move-to-ground: O3 >
-
Fire P7*evaluate*move-block*better*move-to-goal: O2 > O1
Retract P7*evaluate*move-block*better*move-to-goal: O3 > O1
Retract P7*evaluate*move-block*better*move-to-goal: O3 > O2
Fire P5*propose*move-block: O4 (move-block A C)
Fire P5*propose*move-block: O5 (move-block A B)
Fire P5*propose*move-block: O6 (move-block C A)
Fire P5*propose*move-block: O7 (move-block B A)
-
Firing P7*evaluate*move-block*better*move-in-place-lower: O2 > O4
Firing P7*evaluate*move-block*better*move-in-place-lower: O2 > O5
Firing P7*evaluate*move-block*better*move-in-place-lower: O2 > O6
Firing P7*evaluate*move-block*better*move-in-place-lower: O2 > O7

--Decision
Select Operator O2
```

Figure 4.19
Trace of rule firings and operator selections for Blocks World.

```
    ┌─┐
  ┌─┤C│
  │B│A│
  └─┴─┘
1: O: O3 (move-block C table)

  ┌─┬─┬─┐
  │A│B│C│
  └─┴─┴─┘
2: O: O2 (move-block B C)

  ┌─┐
  │B│
  │A│C│
  └─┴─┘
3: O: O5 (move-block A B)

  ┌─┐
  │A│
  │B│
  │C│
  └─┘

Goal Achieved
```

Figure 4.20
Trace of operator selections for complete solution to Blocks World.

4.4 Demonstrations of Basic PSCM

In this section, we present demonstrations of simple agents using Soar as it has been described so far. In the first subsection, we present results from the Blocks World using the rules presented in the previous section that demonstrate the effect of control knowledge on search. In the second subsection, we present behavior of a Soar agent in Rooms World, originally described in subsection 4.2.1., demonstrating interaction with an external continuous dynamic environment and Soar's ability to react to relevant changes.

4.4.1 Blocks World Demonstration

With three blocks, there are a total of thirteen distinct states in the Blocks World, as illustrated in figure 4.21. For a desired state, there can be twelve problems in which the initial state isn't identical to the desired state. The longest solution path for all problems has four steps; the shortest has one. We use variants of this figure to illustrate the effect of the evaluation rules P6 and P7 on problem solving. In the examples presented below, we modified the operator-proposal rule, P5, so that it also creates an indifferent preference for every operator it proposes. With the indifferent preference, a random choice is made between operators when P6 and P7 are not both included.

Without any evaluation knowledge, the indifferent preference leads to a random search, and finding a solution even for the shortest problem can take a large number of steps. Figure 4.22 shows the results of solving the twelve problems that have the final state with A on B, B on C, and C on the table. The vertical axis shows the median number of decision cycles required to solve each problem. In these problems, the

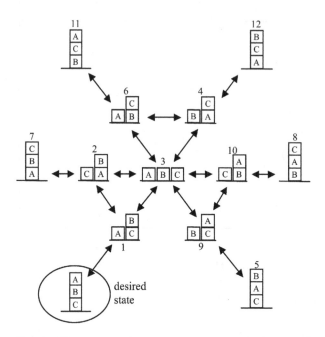

Figure 4.21
The Blocks World problem space.

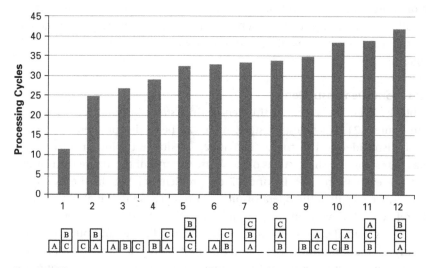

Figure 4.22
Median decision cycles required to solve all Blocks World problems with desired state (block A on block B, block B on block C, block C on the table) via random search.

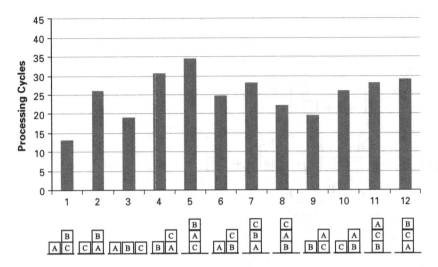

Figure 4.23
Median decision cycles required to solve Blocks World problems using random search constrained by P6.

number of decision cycles corresponds to the number of operator applications. We ran each problem 100 times. All the problems were solved using the rules described above, with P6 and P7 removed and indifferent preferences created for each operator, without any learning. We call this the *base knowledge* level. The problems are ordered from shortest to longest solution. Although not evident from the figure, there is significant variation within a problem. Collectively, the median solution across all problems was 33.5 operators. Although the length of solutions doesn't correspond directly with what might be expected give the distance of the initial states from desired states, such as 5, 7 and 8 being further than 9 and 10, the variance in the results is high so that such orderings are expected.

In succeeding chapters, we show similar results from the Blocks World as we introduce new components of the Soar architecture. Our point is not that these are difficult (or even interesting) problems to solve or that Soar has a unique way of solving them. In general, it is the knowledge about the task that determines how the problem is solved. Our point is that Soar makes it easy to encode and effectively use different types of knowledge. Figure 4.23 shows the effect of adding P6 to the baseline set of knowledge. P6 moves blocks to the table when they are not in their desired position.

P6 reduces the number of cycles compared to the baseline for most of the problems. Figure 4.24 helps explain why by recreating the problem-space diagram and adding in dashed arrows where P6 fires and uniquely selects the operator. P6

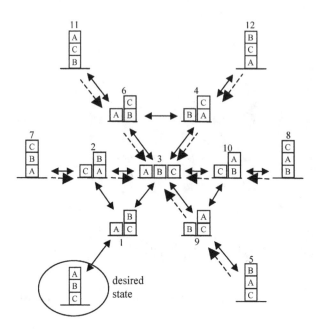

Figure 4.24
Blocks World problem space with P6.

pushes toward state 3, in which all the blocks are on the table, but from there the search can go anywhere. For state 2, P6 cuts off the most direct path to the solution, which is why the performance for problem 2 is marginally worse with P6 than without it.

Figure 4.25 shows the results of including P7, which prefers operators that move blocks into their desired position. For many of the problems, this is sufficient to lead to the optimal solution.

The effect of adding the rule is best understood by looking at figure 4.26, which shows that problems 1, 2, 3, 4, 6, and 7 are solved optimally. What is not as clear is that problems 11 and 12 are also solved optimally, because the first move is predetermined and the first move takes the agent to an optimal path. Thus, only problems 5, 8, 9, and 10 require some search, and it is minimal because once any of the other states are encountered, all remaining operator selections are optimal.

Figure 4.27 shows data from combinations of baseline, P6, and P7. When P6 and P7 are combined together, P6 funnels the outer states to state 3 and P7 then provides direction to the desired state, so that all problems are solved in the minimum number of steps. In state 2, where both rules fire, the better preference created by P7 overrides the best preference created by P6, so that the optimal solution is produced.

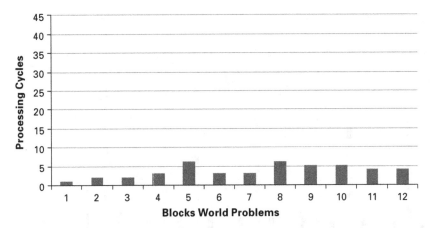

Figure 4.25
Median decision cycles required to solve Blocks World problems using random search and P7.

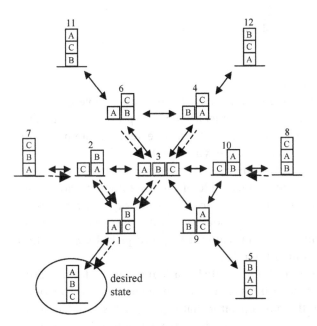

Figure 4.26
Blocks World problem space with rule P7.

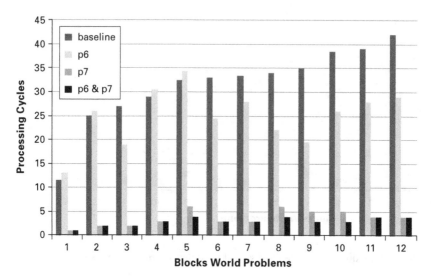

Figure 4.27
Median decision cycles required to solve Blocks World problems using the baseline, P6, P7, P6 + P7.

4.4.2 Rooms World Demonstration

For Rooms World, as described in subsection 4.2.1, we created a simple agent that attempts to pick up a block, but also chases another agent if it appears. This is straightforward to implement in Soar, and it demonstrates that no extensions are needed to support interactions with continuous dynamic environments.

Figure 4.28 shows English versions of the rules encoded for a simple robot agent that moves to a block and picks it up. An example of the resulting behavior is presented in figures 4.29 and 4.30. The rules produce the behavior illustrated in the figures and there are many situations where additional rules are needed for more complete behavior, such as to move the block after it has been picked up, or to find a block that isn't in the same room as the robot.

In figure 4.29, for clarity, the robot is represented as a triangle and is facing north. The robot can perceive anything that is in its cone of vision, including walls and other objects. In its original position, the only operator that is proposed is turn-left, as all the other operator proposals test whether a block is visible. Once turn-left is selected (as shown in position 1 in figure 4.29), the rule to apply it fires and creates an output command for turning left. The output system initiates the turn, and Soar continues in the processing cycle. It takes time to turn, so that during the next processing cycle, there are no significant changes in working memory and turn-left stays selected. This causes an impasse and the generation of a substate (as described in chapter 6); for these examples, however, that aspect of Soar can be ignored.

```
propose*turn-left
if the robot does not have a block and does not see a block,
then propose the turn-left operator

apply*turn-left
if turn-left is selected,
then initiate the turn-left output action

elaborate*facing-block
if the robot's heading is within +/-2 degrees of a block,
then the robot is facing the block.

elaborate*not-facing-block
if the robot's heading is not within +/-2 degrees a block,
then the robot is not facing the block.

propose*face-block
if the robot does not have a block, sees a block, and is not directly
facing the block,
then propose face-block

apply*face-block
if face-block is selected and the block is at given heading,
then initiate turn to that heading

elaborate*block-within-pickup-range
if a block's distance is less than pickup range,
then the block is within pickup range

elaborate*block-not-within-pickup-range
if a block's distance is not less than pickup range,
then the block is not within pickup range

propose*move-to-block
if the robot does not have a block, sees a block, is directly facing
the block, and is not within pickup range of the block,
then propose move-to-block

apply*move-to-block
if move-to-block is selected,
then initiate move-forward and stop all turning

propose*pickup-block
if the robot sees a block, is directly facing the block, and is
within pickup range of the block, and is not already holding a block
then propose pickup-block.

apply*pickup-block
if pickup-block is selected,
then initiate pickup, stop all movement and turning
```

Figure 4.28

Rules for pickup-block agent in Rooms World.

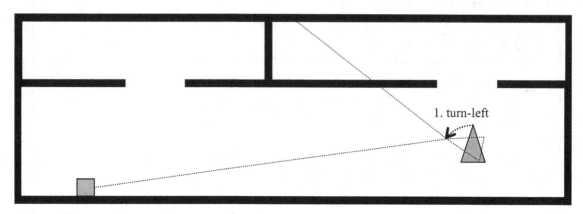

Figure 4.29
Robot turning in Rooms World until it senses the block.

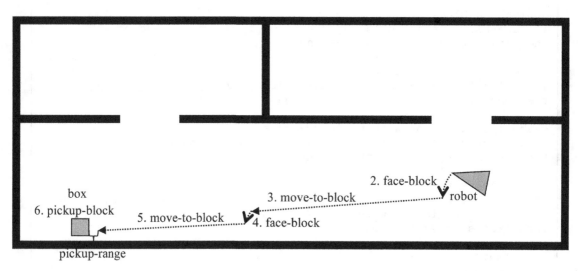

Figure 4.30
Robot turning and moving to block.

When the robot has turned sufficiently to the left, the block comes into view, and the input module adds a representation of the block to working memory on the input-link. This triggers a retraction of the turn-left operator proposal, which in turn causes turn-left to no longer be selected. However, the addition of the block causes elaborate*not-facing-block to fire, which creates a structure in working memory that then leads to propose*face-block to fire and propose the face-block operator, which is then selected as shown by 2 in figure 4.30.

There is no inherent need to include elaborate*not-facing-block (and its pair elaborate*facing-block). The conditions for these rules could be directly included in propose*face-block. However, it is useful to separate the calculation of such concepts from their use to simplify other rules, especially when there are specific parameters being tested or if there are multiple ways of computing them. In this example, we use elaborations to demonstrate their use. Once face-block is selected, apply*face-block fires and initiates an output command to turn toward the block. This assumes that the output system accepts not only commands to turn left or right, but also a command to turn to a specific heading.

Figure 4.30 illustrates selection and application of face-block, which subsequently is replaced by move-to-block (3) when the robot is facing the block. Move-to-block initiates moving to the block and terminates the turn command so that the robot goes straight. The robot then moves toward the block. As shown in the figure, if the robot isn't facing directly toward the block when it initiates move-to-block (because of noise in its sensors or output system), elaborate*facing-block retracts, causing move-to-block to retract. In parallel, elaborate*not-facing-block fires, causing face-block to be selected (4), which initiates a turn. As coded, the robot continues moving forward during the turn, and once the robot is again facing the block, face-block is retracted, followed by the selection of move-to-block (5). When the robot gets within pickup-range of the block, it selects pickup-block (6), which stops all motion and initiates the pickup-block action.

To demonstrate interruption and reactivity, we can add another agent that the robot chases if it sees it. To support this behavior, we add new rules for a chase-agent operator as illustrated in figure 4.31. The first pair of rules mirror the elaboration rules for facing a block. We could write two general rules that work for any type of object the robot might be facing, but in this case we use rules that are specific to blocks and agents. In order to have the robot move toward the other agent as quickly as possible, the chase-agent operator differs from moving toward the block in that it includes both turning and moving together. This is a design choice and here we use both to show that both sequential and parallel actions are possible depending on the situation.

In this example, when another agent is detected, chase-agent is proposed. Once chase-agent has been proposed, prefer*chase-agent fires, creating a best preference so

```
elaborate*facing-agent
if an agent's direction is within +/-2 degrees,
then the robot is facing the agent

elaborate*not-facing-agent
if an agent's direction is not within +/-2 degrees,
then the robot is not facing the agent

propose*chase-agent
if the robot sees another agent,
then propose chase-agent

prefer*chase-agent
if chase-agent is proposed,
then create a best preference for chase-agent

apply*chase-agent*move
if chase-agent is selected and the robot is not moving,
then initiate move forward

apply*chase-agent*turn
if chase-agent is selected and the robot is not facing the agent,
then initiate turn to the direction of the agent
```

Figure 4.31
Rules for chasing another agent.

that chase-agent is preferred to other operators. Once chase-agent is selected, the two application rules fire (in parallel when appropriate). If the agent is already moving, then only the turn rule fires. As the robot chases the other agent, and the other agent turns, the apply*chase-agent*turn rule fires, dynamically adjusting the robot's heading so that the robot is pointed toward the other agent. Figure 4.32 shows how this could play out. After the robot has selected move-to-block, the other agent appears (1). Chase-agent is proposed and then selected (2). Since the agent is already moving, only apply*chase-agent*turn fires, and the robot turns toward the agent while moving forward. As the agent moves and turns, apply*chase-agent*turn continues to fire to correct the robot's heading until the robot is heading toward the agent (3). If the robot is fast enough, it will catch the other agent.

However, if the other agent goes into another room, and hides behind a wall, the robot no longer senses the agent and gives up on it, going back to trying to pick up a block. This arises because the robot didn't create any persistent structures describing the other agent in working memory. It based its behavior off of its perception so that

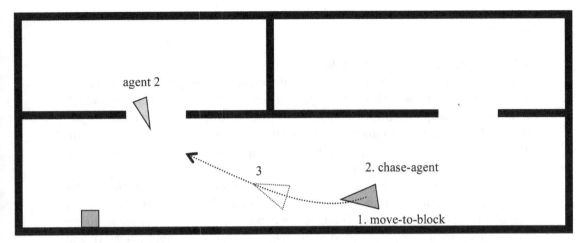

Figure 4.32
A robot chasing another agent.

when the other agent was "out of sight," it was "out of mind." A standard approach to remedy this problem involves the following steps. First, the sensory system is modified so that it maintains information about a perceived object for a second or two after it disappears, with an indication that it isn't visible. Second, an operator is added to record the last location of the object that disappeared. This creates a persistent structure in working memory that the robot can use. Third, an additional operator is added for moving to the last location. This could be further extended by using the speed and direction of the agent to predict where it will be in the future, and use that information to create a waypoint for the robot to move to. If the robot detects the agent while it is moving toward the saved location, chase-agent is proposed and takes control. An operator also needs to be added that removes the persistent structure if the robot gets to the last location without seeing the other agent. Finally, another application rule is added to chase-agent to also remove the persistent structure when the robot sees the other agent.

This example demonstrates how Soar can react immediately to its environment, and that it has the ability to explicitly remember transient structures.

4.5 Discussion

Although we have discussed many of the details of the individual components of Soar's processing cycle, some of its characteristics are best described and analyzed when the processing cycle is considered as a whole. In this section, we also discuss alternative designs that have been considered for Soar, including parallel operators and probabilistic representations, and why they are not included in the current Soar architecture.

4.5.1 Maintenance of Operator Selection

In Soar, once an operator is selected, it is maintained until the acceptable preference for the operator is retracted or another operator becomes the dominant choice through a change in other preferences. The first case is where the operator runs until completion or the external environment changes so that the operator is no longer relevant. The second case arises when an operator is interrupted by another operator that is a better choice for the current state.

Soar's approach to the first case (maintaining an operator until completion) is but one possible way to partition knowledge for the three different phases of operator execution: operator selection (deciding to select the operator), operator maintenance (once the operator is selected, deciding to maintain it as the current operator), and operator termination (once the operator is selected, deciding to terminate the operator). One can imagine alternative implementations where knowledge for each of the phases is encoded in different rules. This partitioning of knowledge is in addition to the knowledge involved in operator evaluation and operator application. Table 4.2 shows the four alternative formulations for operator maintenance that "make sense" using different partitions of the knowledge for proposing (P), maintaining (M), and terminating (T) an operator.

• Propose only (Soar's current approach). Once an operator has been selected on the basis of a proposal rule (P), it is maintained as long as the proposal rule matches (P), and it terminates when the proposal rule no longer matches (–P). With this scheme, care must be taken in defining the conditions for the proposal rule so that a temporally extended operator is maintained across multiple processing cycles as working-memory structures change and the operator applies. To achieve this, the conditions of the proposal must test working-memory structures that do not change until the operator terminates. For example, if an operator is proposed and selected to move a robot from one location to another, the operator proposal cannot test the

Table 4.2
Approaches to operator maintenance.

	Selection	Maintenance	Termination
1. Propose only (Soar)	P	P	–P
2. Propose and terminate (Soar 7)	P		T
3. Propose and maintain	P	M	–M and –P
4. Propose, maintain, and terminate	P	M	–M and (–P or T)

robot's original location or anything else that changes as the robot moves, such as the distance to the destination. It can test that it is not at the desired location, so that the operator proposal retracts when the robot achieves it final location. If dynamic information is important for the operator implementation, it can be maintained with operator-elaboration or state-elaboration rules. For example, the computation that the robot isn't at the location can be computed by a state elaboration that compares the current position to the desired position. Even though this rule matches different positions during movement, the working-memory structure that indicates it isn't in the desired position is maintained in working memory because a working-memory element doesn't go in and out of working memory if it is removed and re-added on the same cycle.

• Propose and terminate (Soar 7). This approach adds operator termination knowledge (T), which explicit indicates that current operator should be removed. Termination knowledge can be represented as one or more rules. Each termination rule has conditions that match termination situations, and when such a rule fires, its action causes the selected operator to be removed, so a new decision is made. In this scheme, once an operator is selected, it is maintained whether or not the proposal rule still matches, and when a termination rule fires, the operator terminates. If the operator is still proposed, it can be reselected, but this is a new application of the operator and through reselection, it allows apply rules to match and fire again in the new situation. The advantage of this approach is that the selection conditions do not need to be maintained throughout execution, and the termination conditions are not restricted to being the inverse of the proposal conditions (–P). A disadvantage is that additional knowledge must be learned (termination) and if it is learned incorrectly, an operator could be selected indefinitely. This approach was used in an earlier version of Soar (Soar 7).

• Propose and maintain. This approach adds operator maintenance knowledge (M), which can also be represented as one or more rules. In this scheme, once the operator is selected, it is maintained as long as at least one maintenance rule matches. The operator terminates when no maintenance rules match. One variant (illustrated in the figure) is that the proposal rule also serves as a maintenance rule. In contrast to the previous approach, knowledge in this approach describes the states in which the operator should not be terminated, whereas in the previous approach knowledge describes when the operator should be terminated.

• Propose, Maintain, and Terminate. This approach includes all three types of knowledge, so that once an operator is selected, it is maintained as long as maintenance or proposal rules match and termination rules do not.

The most obvious difference between these approaches is in the types of knowledge used to specify operator maintenance (P, M, and T). There is a tradeoff because the method that provides the most precision is specifying when an operator should be maintained and terminate (method 4) requires the most knowledge, which is a disadvantage for learning and knowledge acquisition. Our own experience with real systems is that –P is sufficient for specifying when an operator should terminate in almost all cases. In the cases where it is not, it is easy to add additional proposal rules or to add elaboration rules that compute abstract state properties that can be tested by the proposal rule. Moreover, if it desirable to specify other situations when the operator should terminate, this is possible to do through the addition of rules that create rejection preferences, which become a stand in for termination rules.

A deeper and more fundamental issue has to do with consistency of behavior. For all but the first approach, the agent's behavior can be inconsistent in that the behavior in a specific state differs depending on the history that led up to that state. Consider a situation A, in which an operator O1 is proposed and selected on the basis of conditions P. O1 remains selected in all approaches until a future situation B is encountered, in which P no longer holds. In situation B, assume that T doesn't hold in approaches 2 and 4, and that M holds in approaches 3 and 4. Thus, for approach 1, the operator O1 terminates and possibly a new operator is selected, whereas for approaches 2, 3, and 4 O1 remains selected. Now consider a situation where situation B isn't preceded by situation A or any other situation in which operator O1 has been proposed and selected. In situation B, approach 1 is consistent—O1 is not selected. However, all the other approaches are inconsistent. Whereas O1 is selected when B is preceded by A, O1 is not selected if B is not preceded by A.

In our own experience, developers often incorrectly assume situation B will never be reached without situation A preceding it and do not include the knowledge for when situation B arises on its own. That situation may be rare, but because of dynamics in the environment, it can happen. This leads to unexpected and often incorrect behavior.

4.5.2   Procedural vs. Declarative Representations of Operators

The native representation of the main components of operators in Soar is procedural—the knowledge to propose, evaluate, and apply operators is encoded in rules. That knowledge is accessible to the Soar architecture, but it isn't directly accessible to other knowledge encoded in Soar. Thus, it isn't possible for other knowledge to examine an operator's conditions or actions encoded as rules. The justification for this approach is that by restricting access, Soar can efficiently match rules to working memory to carry out the different aspects of operator selection and application. If the structure of rules was available to be matched by other rules, it would significantly expand working memory to include all rules, greatly increasing the computational effort required to match and fire rules. Moreover, it would force the representation of knowledge about operators to be the syntax used in Soar.

Although much of the structure of operators is represented as rules, when an operator is proposed, the structure created in working memory can include a declarative description of the operator's structure, including its preconditions and its actions. This allows other knowledge to examine the operator for evaluation and application, to the point where conventions can be defined so that general evaluation and application rules can interpret the declarative descriptions of operator preconditions and actions created in working memory. In that case, operator-specific evaluation and application rules are not necessary.

In systems like Soar, the important distinction between procedural and declarative knowledge structures is whether the structures can be accessed only by the architecture or whether they can also be accessed by other knowledge. Soar supports both types of access, but with a tradeoff: procedural knowledge is much more efficient to execute because it is interpreted directly by the architecture; declarative knowledge is more flexible (because it can be accessed by additional knowledge) but less efficient (because it is executed indirectly through other knowledge).

4.5.3 Parallel Operators

In Soar, only one operator can be selected at a time, forcing a sequential bottleneck. This design decision dates back to the original tasks implemented in Soar where an operator made a step in a problem space and generated a single new state. In that formulation, parallel operators would have generated multiple new states, pushing selection knowledge to the selection of the next state. After modifying Soar to enable it to interact with external environments, we maintained the restriction against parallel operators on the grounds that parallel operators could have conflicting actions that would be difficult for an agent to detect and recover from. Even with that restriction, there are multiple ways to generate parallel action in Soar.

Operator switching: As long as Soar is fast enough relative to the environment (which is the case in our experience), Soar can switch back and forth between operators which initiate independent external actions, giving the appearance of parallelism in the environment, even though only one operator is selected at a time. This requires operators that can be interrupted and resumed, which is straightforward using Soar's approach to operator maintenance.

Overlapping output actions: For temporally extended actions that do not require constant cognitive attention, multiple actions can be initiated either through sequential operator application or through mega-operators (below). For example, one operator can initiate the chew-gum action, while a second operator can initiate the walk action soon after chew-gum is initiated.

Mega-operators: In Soar, multiple rules can fire in parallel during the application of an operator, which can initiate multiple, independent output actions, as well as other changes in working memory. Thus, although there are no parallel operators, a single operator can initiate parallel actions. As we shall see in chapter 6, it is possible to learn these complex operators in Soar from more primitive operators that have only single action.

The first two alternatives apply when performing external actions; the final alternative applies to both external and internal actions.

4.5.4 Probabilistic Operators and State Structures

The only architectural support for probability and non-determinism in Soar as it has been described so far is in the selection of operators via numeric preferences. With the introduction of hierarchical operators in chapter 5, the implementation of an abstract operator (one implemented via suboperators instead of directly with rules) can be probabilistic via the probabilistic selection of suboperators that decompose the abstract operator into simpler, primitive actions.

However, there is no support for probabilistic representations of state information in working memory, nor does Soar support probabilistic calculations in rule firings to derive the structures in working memory beyond operator selection.

If probabilistic representations are necessary, there are four obvious alternatives to incorporating them into a cognitive architecture. The first is to explicitly represent them in working memory as attributes of objects. Thus, they would not be associated with individual working-memory elements. Any reasoning using the probabilities would have to be performed using knowledge encoded as operators and rules, so that it would be part performing a task. Although this doesn't require any modifications to the architecture, it means that reasoning about probabilities can interfere with task performance, and some of the potential for the probabilities influencing the operation of the architecture are lost.

A second approach is to build a cognitive architecture from the ground up with probabilities inherent to the internal representation of the state of the agent. When an operator applied, instead of adding and deleting working-memory elements, it would modify the likelihoods of individual working-memory elements, and add new structures that previously had no probability of existence. The calculation of the changes in the likelihood could be based on the probabilities of working-memory elements matched by the application rule. Similar calculations would be possible for state elaborations. In this approach, the calculation and maintenance of probability is a fixed overhead; however, the state representation would invariably have to be much larger because it must include all state structures that have some probability of being true. To take advantage of these probabilities, changes would have to be made to how rules are matched, possibly computing matches to all items with non-zero probability, which would greatly increase the match cost. One advantage of Soar's approach is that when a rule matches, it matches a mutually consistent set of structures that the agent believes can and do co-exist. It is at operator selection when the agent decides what to do and what to believe.

A third option is to maintain working memory as is, but allow probabilistic calculations to be made in determining the contents of working memory, so that the cost of match remains the same, but the calculation of changes in working memory is based on probabilistic information encoded in procedural knowledge that is combined during knowledge search to determine working memory. Markov Logic Networks (Richardson and Domingos 2006) are one example of this approach. Rosenbloom (2011) is also exploring this approach, where he is positing an implementation of cognitive architecture using factor graphs. His approach attempts to unify the different types of processing and memories in Soar within a single framework; however, it is too early to tell whether it can achieve the functionality in Soar. Moreover, the computational efficiency of this approach isn't clear. On the one hand, the probabilistic aspects require additional computation; on the other hand, it might be the type of computation amenable to massive parallel implementation.

A fourth option is to have a separate module for probabilistic reasoning, analogous to the mental imagery module or an external software system (Newell and Steier 1993). In this approach, probabilistic representations are maintained in a distinct module outside of working memory. As with mental imagery, there is an interface with working memory that allows an agent to create probabilistic structures in the module, initiate commands for performing probabilistic inferences, and create queries concerning structures in the module that result in symbolic structures being created in working memory. In this approach, Soar's main internal reasoning stays symbolic; however, it has access to a component that provides it with probabilistic reasoning. An advantage to this approach is that Soar's processing can continue independent of the module, maintaining reactivity and pursuing other approaches to problem solving without being limited by a potentially computationally expensive process. One disadvantage with this approach is that Soar doesn't have access to the internal processing of the external module and thus it cannot use its learning mechanisms to help improve it, nor can it provide additional task-dependent knowledge acquired from other sources to help constrain the processing.

To date, we have resisted including probabilities in Soar because of the expected computational cost, and because we have been successful at building agents that can work in non-deterministic and uncertain environments without them.

4.5.5 Reactivity

One of the requirements from chapter 2 is that a system be capable of deliberate, sequential behavior (including planning as we shall see in chapter 6), but without sacrificing reactivity. There are four aspects to reactivity. One is that the knowledge in the agent is available to respond to changes in the environment, the second is that the agent's internal representation of the situation is consistent with its perception, the third is that there is a bound on the processing required by the agent to react, and the fourth is that bounded processing is fast enough to respond to relevant changes in the environment. We consider each one in turn below.

Knowledge used to react to the current situation

In Soar, the knowledge to respond to changes in the agent's perception of the environment is used during selection and application of an operator. As the environment changes, the agent responds by selecting and applying an appropriate operator. Thus, the basic unit of reactivity is a single path through the processing cycle. In Rooms World, the agent responds to movement of another agent by changing its heading during a single processing cycle. One could imagine attempting to increase reactivity by allowing output to occur anytime during the processing cycle; however, it is only after operator selection that all proposal knowledge has been accessed, and it is only after quiescence in operator application that consistency is guaranteed.

Internal representation that is consistent with perception

To be reactive in complex, dynamic situations, an agent must respond to the situation as provided by the agent's sensors, but it must also maintain and respond to internal state to avoid erratic control when perception isn't stable. This is the classic tradeoff between reactivity and stability in control systems. To support reactivity, Soar automatically retracts the results of non-operator application rules when they no longer match so it is always selecting operators that are consistent with the current situation. This eliminates out-of-date information and the need to include additional knowledge to remove the results. When persistent structures are needed, either because of variations in perception or because historical information is important, operators can create structures that persist indefinitely (and must be explicitly removed). Another side to this issue is that it is important for the architecture not to maintain its internal data structures beyond the basis for their creation. This is exactly the issue concerning operator persistence described in subsection 4.4.1, where Soar maintains the currently selected operator only as long as it is supported by operator-proposal and operator-selection knowledge.

Bounded processing

The third aspect of reactivity is having a bound on the processing cycle. The dominant cost in the processing cycle is in matching and firing rules. In Soar, there is no guaranteed bound on matching and firing rules. The underlying implementation is efficient, and scales well to very large numbers of rules (Doorenbos 1994; Jones, Furtwangler, and van Lent 2011), but there are boundary cases where a single rule can perform combinatorial calculations and thus take a long time to match (Tambe, Newell, and Rosenbloom 1990). The boundary cases can be avoided by eliminating the ability to have multiple augmentations of an object with the same attribute. However, we have not eliminated this feature in Soar because it would make many types of knowledge more difficult to encode, and in practice the unbounded computations are easily avoided. Soar also can potentially have an unbounded number of knowledge accesses in a single processing cycle because each Elaboration subphase runs until quiescence, firing multiple waves of rules. To limit this problem, Soar has a bound on the number of Elaboration phases (100). When that threshold is met, Soar immediately proceeds to the next phase of the processing cycle. The only time this approach causes a problem is if a very long chain of elaborations is necessary to respond to changes in the environment. None of the systems developed in Soar have had this problem, as chains of elaborations rarely exceed a length of 5, so that exceeding this bound is an indication of a mistake in the agent's knowledge.

Soar does more than match and fire rules during a processing cycle. It runs the decision procedure, manages input and output. Although it isn't evident from the aspects of Soar we have described so far, additional processing is required to manage substates and run Soar's learning mechanisms. The important question is whether the processing time required for those activities is bounded and whether that time increases with increases in Soar's knowledge, the length of a run, and so on. It will not be possible to explore these issues until all Soar's components have been described, but in general, Soar's execution time is dominated by retrieving knowledge from its memories.

Fast enough processing

The final issue in reactivity is the raw speed of the processing cycle. To ensure appropriate reactivity, the frequency of processing cycle must be at least twice the rate at which task-relevant changes occur in the environment (the Nyquist rate; Black 1953). Anything less than twice that rate risks a loss of reactivity. This rate leads to a practical implementation constraint on the rate of the processing cycle. Psychological results and our experience in the real world suggest that a processing cycle of between 50 and 100 msec is required for real-time reactivity. Fortunately, current computers (and the underlying Soar implementation) are fast enough so that even though there is no bound on the processing, performance is not an issue for real-world applications. In chapter 5, we present results of running Soar in Rooms World where the processing is orders of magnitude faster than what is needed to maintain real-time reactivity. For the simple Blocks World agent described in this chapter, the processing cycle executes in under 0.03 msec, at least 1,000 times as fast as is required for real-time responsiveness. More complex agents have more changes in working memory on each processing cycle and are proportionally slower, but even in the worst case, our most complex robotic agents execute their processing cycles faster than real time. Evaluations of Soar on real-world applications, including TacAir-Soar, demonstrate that Soar's basic cycle time, even for agents with large procedural memories, is orders of magnitude faster than what is required for real-time behavior (Jones et al. 2011).

In developing an architecture that scales to large knowledge bases and achieves high performance, one of the most important lessons we have learned is that across all types of symbolic processing, the architecture should processes only changes in data it encounters as opposed to processing all of its available data from scratch. By processing only changes, the processing cost is proportional to the number of changes as opposed to the total available data. This lesson applies throughout the design of Soar. For example, in processing input, only changes in input are made to the input-link. This reduces data traffic between the input system and Soar and minimizes changes in working memory. Reducing the changes in working memory is important because Soar's method for matching rules also only processes changes in working memory so that the cost of matching rules is Soar is directly related to the number of changes in working memory, not the total number of items in working memory. A third example is in the design of the episodic memory system (chapter 9) where instead of taking a snapshot of working memory every cycle and saving it away, the episodic memory system only tracks the changes in working memory and creates data structures that store when an element enters working memory and then when it leaves working memory. Thus, whenever we design a new component in Soar, we consider how to minimize the computational overhead by processing only changes in data.

4.6 Analysis of Requirements

The components of Soar described in this chapter respond to many of the architectural requirements laid out in chapter 2. Below we evaluate how the components of Soar described in this chapter meet those requirements.

R0: Fixed structure. Soar makes a sharp distinction between the fixed underlying architecture and the knowledge encoded in the architecture. There are no task-dependent parameters to adjust, and the underlying Soar architecture remains constant across tasks.

R1: Symbol system. Production systems in general, and Soar in specific, fully support symbolic representations and reasoning.

R2: Modality-specific knowledge. As described so far, Soar doesn't provide support for modality-specific knowledge.

R3: Large bodies of knowledge. Production systems provide the means for representing knowledge bodies of procedural knowledge. As other knowledge types are added in future chapters, this requirement must be revisited.

R4:   Diverse generality of knowledge. By using production rules, Soar has the ability to represent a spectrum of generality for knowledge.

R5:   Diverse levels of knowledge. There must be rules that encode proposal and application knowledge for every operator. Additional knowledge can be added to control operator selection.

R6:   Distinct internal representation. Operators may create and maintain arbitrary internal representations in the state.

R7:   Rich action representation. Operators and production rules supports parallel, conditional actions; however, only with the introduction of substates in chapter 5 does Soar achieve rich action representation.

R8:   Goals at multiple time scales. At this point, there is no direct support for goals beyond representing them in working memory and reasoning about them using operators.

R9:   Incorporate innate utilities. No utilities, innate or otherwise are included in the architecture at this point.

R10:   Meta-cognitive knowledge. There is no direct support for meta-cognitive knowledge and reasoning.

R11:   Levels of deliberation. Production rules and operators provide two levels of deliberation, with rules providing uncontrolled retrieval of procedural knowledge and operators providing controlled deliberation. The overall processing cycle supports reactive behavior, and though there are no formal guarantees on bounded processing, in practice, processing is fast enough for real-world domains. The processing presented in this chapter doesn't directly support more complex and deliberate reasoning such as planning.

R12:   Comprehensive learning. No learning mechanisms have been presented so far.

R13:   Incremental, online learning. Although there are no learning mechanisms in the architecture as presented so far, production systems provide an appropriate representation for supporting incremental knowledge acquisition.

In summary, requirements R0, R1, R4, and R6 are achieved; requirements R3, R5, R7, and R11 are partially achieved; and requirements R2, R8, R9, R10, R12, and R13 are not yet achieved with the mechanisms in Soar that have been described to this point.

5 Impasses and Substates: The Basis for Complex Reasoning

In Soar as presented so far, the agents have sufficient knowledge to uniquely select and completely apply operators. This is a common assumption in reactive and expert systems built by hand, where knowledge search is sufficient for decision making and action execution and neither planning nor other types of complex internal reasoning are needed. However, general human-level agents often encounter novel situations where the knowledge that they can directly recall is incomplete, uncertain, or inconsistent. In this chapter, we expand on section 3.4 and describe how Soar responds to *impasses:* situations in which it is unable to make progress. When an impasse arises, Soar generates a *substate*, and then recursively employs problem-space search, using the same processing structure described in chapter 4. Impasses and substates provide an architectural mechanism for generating and pursuing immediate goals (R9) and meta-cognitive reasoning (R10) and one of the predictions from Soar is that complex reasoning, such as hierarchical actions, planning, mental imagery, and access to semantic and episodic memory, arises when procedural knowledge is insufficient to make progress.

Impasses arise in Soar when a new operator cannot be selected. The following sections describe the details of impasses (section 5.1); the structure of substates (section 5.2), the problem solving in substates and how it resolves impasses (section 5.3), how results are determined and returned from substates (section 5.4), and the processing that guarantees that substate processing is consistent with processing in higher-level states (section 5.5).

Section 5.6 includes demonstrations of many of the forms of complex reasoning that substates make possible, including hierarchical task decomposition, planning, perspective taking, and anticipation. Although many other architectures support similar types of reasoning, Soar is unique in that these types of reasoning arise in reaction to impasses and there are no separate modules or architectural structures to support them. Instead, they arise in service of operator proposal, selection, and application through the combination of impasses, substates, and problem spaces. The rationale for this approach is straightforward—when knowledge is sufficient to make a decision, complex reasoning isn't necessary. Complex reasoning is necessary when knowledge is incomplete, conflicting, or uncertain. Different types of complex reasoning arise naturally from the different types of available knowledge. Substates also provide a context within which an agent can reason about the state of its own processing, and the processing of others, thereby providing some aspects of metacognition.

5.1 Impasses

Soar makes decisions by processing preferences in the decision procedure as described in subsection 4.3.2. If the preferences are insufficient to determine a new dominant operator, then an impasse arises. An impasse doesn't indicate that there is an error, such as that the wrong operator was selected, but it indicates the inability of the agent to make progress with the information that is currently available. In Soar, the decision procedure detects four classes of impasses, and the impasses are mutually exclusive so that only one impasse can arise at a time.

An impasse is resolved when there is a sufficient change in the available preferences so that a new operator can be selected (or a different impasse arises). The change in preferences can be direct, through the creation of new preferences. It can also be indirect, through the creation or removal of working-memory elements that cause rules to retract existing preferences. The change can even be independent of the substate, such as if the perception of the environment changes working memory. When an impasse is resolved, the substate and all working-memory elements local to the substate are no longer relevant, so they are removed from working memory. Below is a short analysis of each type of impasse and the usual way in which it is resolved.

State no-change

A state no-change impasse arises when either there are no acceptable preferences or every candidate operator also has a reject preference. This impasse is usually a result of incomplete state-elaboration or operator-proposal knowledge. For example, if there are no operator-proposal rules, a state no-change impasse arises, indicating that operators must be proposed to make progress. This impasse can be resolved by the creation of acceptable preferences or by the creation of state elaborations that lead existing operator-proposal rules to fire.

Operator tie

An operator tie impasse arises when multiple operators are proposed, but the available preferences are insufficient to distinguish among them. This impasse usually indicates that the operator-evaluation knowledge is incomplete. For example, if there are only acceptable preferences, additional preferences are necessary to select between the proposed operators.

Operator conflict

This impasse arises when multiple operators are proposed and there are conflicting better/worse preferences. For example, if there are two operators proposed, A and B, and there are preferences A > B, and B > A, an operator conflict impasse arises. This impasse can be resolved by rejecting one of the conflicting operators or generating a new operator that is better than both A and B.

Operator no-change

An operator no-change impasse arises when a selected operator remains selected in the following decision. This impasse can arise because the knowledge to apply the operator isn't directly encoded in operator application rules. This impasse can also arise when an operator involves interaction with an external environment and multiple decision cycles are necessary for the operator's effects to become evident in the agent's perception.

5.2 Substates

Soar's response to an impasse is to create a new state, a *substate*, in working memory, which explicitly represents that an impasse has occurred and the reason for the impasse. An impasse can also arise in the substate, leading to a stack of states. In referring to substates, we use terminology where the stack grows downward, so that superstates as *higher* in the stack, whereas more recent states as *lower* in the stack, and we refer to the original state that has no superstate as the *top* state.

A substate is similar to the top state in that it provides the context for the selection and the application of operators. However, the purpose of the substate is to resolve the impasse as opposed to solve a task problem. The substate plays both the role of a state and a subgoal, as it contains representations of the progress in resolving the impasse as well as a description of the impasse that must be resolved, thus making meta-data about the decision process explicit. (In earlier descriptions of Soar, substates were called *subgoals*.)

As an example, figure 5.1 shows the most important working-memory elements that are created for a tie impasse among operators O31, O32, and O33 in state S20 (other working-memory elements, such as the substructure of state S20 are not shown). Soar generates the substate identifier (S23) and all of the associated working-memory elements. All substates share similar structures, including a "superstate" augmentation.

The substate also has an augmentation with the type of impasse (no-change, conflict, or tie). Tie and conflict impasses arise only for the operator, but a no-change can arise when the same operator is selected for multiple decisions (operator no-change) or when there is no operator selected and no viable operator is proposed (state no-change). The "attribute" augmentation contains either "state" or "operator" to

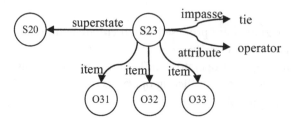

Figure 5.1
Substate structures.

distinguish which type of no-change impasse has arisen. Finally, for operator tie and conflict impasses, the operators that tied or conflicted are included as "item" augmentations. The structures that define the substate are maintained by the architecture and cannot be created or deleted by rules.

The "superstate" link between the substate and the superstate makes it possible for rules that match in the substate to access all working-memory structures in the superstate. Moreover, all the working-memory elements created in the substate are *local* to the substate, in that they exist independent of the superstate. They provide a mechanism for operators in the substate to create structures (sets of working-memory elements) that are not accessible by task operators in the top state. For example, structures can be created in the substate that represent hypothetical situations, or small variants of the superstate, so that the agent can evaluate the effect of selecting and apply alternative operators. As another example, the agent can create structures in a substate that it believes reflect the current knowledge of another agent and then use its own knowledge to discover what it would do if it were the other agent. Because the substate is inaccessible from the top state, the structures and the reasoning in the substate do not interfere with the reasoning in the superstate.

There are two important differences between the substate (S23) and the top state (S20). First, the top state doesn't have any augmentations relating to an impasse, nor does it have a superstate. Instead, the top state has "^superstate nil." The second difference is that only the top state has "io," "input-link," and "output-link" augmentations that connect to the perception and action systems. There are no independent "input-link" and "output-link" structures in substates, although it is possible to copy pointers to the top state structures in the substates.

5.3 Problem Solving in Substates

The processing in a substate uses the same PSCM processing cycle that is used in the top state: rules matching and firing to perform state elaboration and proposal, evaluation, selection, elaboration, and application of operators. The creation of the substate leads to the matching and firing of rules that test for the working-memory structures associated with the substate, which in turn leads to the selection and the application of operators in the substate. Even when there a substate, there is still only a single processing cycle, and during a phase rules fire for multiple states. In general, the rules that fire are those that respond to changes in the most recent substate; however, whenever there are changes in the top state from input or changes from results created in the substate, rules in the top state can fire, so that the agent stays reactive to its environment.

By using problem search in the substate, Soar has a much more powerful engine for accessing, generating, and combining knowledge than is possible with knowledge search alone. Remember from chapter 3 that knowledge search is restricted to retrieving knowledge the agent has encoded in long-term procedural memory, whereas problem search in a substate can use techniques that generate intermediate data structures that allow access to additional knowledge stored in long-term memory. Moreover, in the substate, the agent can use a different problem space than in the top state. For example, if there is a tie between task operators in the top state, a problem space can be used in the substate whose operators explicitly evaluate or compare tied operators. If there is an operator no-change impasse, the problem space in the substate can use operators that decompose the selected task operator into simpler actions.

For each of the different types of impasses, there are different types of problem spaces that are typically used. Below are some examples of the types processing that might arise to resolve each type of impasse.

State no-change

A state no-change impasse usually indicates that no operators have been proposed. This could arise when operators must be deliberately constructed. For example, there could be an operator construction problem space for the Blocks World, which has an operator that picks out a block to move, possibly by examining each block and determining whether it is clear. There could also be an operator that picks out a location to move the block to, making sure that location is not the block it is considering moving. Finally, there could be an operator that creates a Blocks World operator from the structures created by those earlier operators and the associated acceptable preference.

Operator tie

An operator tie impasse indicates that operators are proposed but there are not sufficient preferences to distinguish between them. If this arose in the Blocks World, problem solving in a substate could deliberately evaluate each of the proposed operators. The first step might be to create a copy of the top state, and then perform a one-step look-ahead search to determine whether or not applying the operator leads toward the current goal. The results of that search can be used to create preferences. This approach is demonstrated in subsection 5.6.1.

Operator conflict

An operator conflict impasse indicates conflicting knowledge, and the standard approach is similar to an operator tie: deliberately evaluate each operator and determine which should be selected.

Operator no-change

An operator no-change impasse indicates that the operator application knowledge is insufficient for immediately applying the operator. In the substate, there are four general classes of responses to this impasse, depending on the underlying cause.

• If the impassed operator is *abstract* and/or is difficult to directly encode as rules, operators from a different problem space can be used in the substate to apply the impassed operator by making incremental changes in the superstate. This is an example of dynamic task decomposition. In the Blocks World, moving a block in the real world might require using more primitive operators, such as moving a gripper to the block, grasping the block by closing the gripper, moving the gripper and block to the destination, and then opening the gripper to release the block. Examples of this type of operator no-change impasse are given in section 5.6.

• If the operator is proposed on the basis of its ability to achieve a goal, instead of on the basis of whether it can apply in the current state, an operator can be selected that cannot apply to the current state. This situation arises when mean-ends analysis is used, and is demonstrated for the Blocks World in subsection 5.6.3. In this case, the preconditions of the selected operator become the goal for operators selected in the substate. The operators in the substate change the superstate (which is technically part of the substate because of the superstate attribute) and eventually, the superstate is modified so that the selected operator applies.

• If the operator is incorrectly selected in a state where it cannot apply, preferences can be created that lead to selection of another operator. In the Blocks World, if an operator-proposal rule is overgeneral, an operator could be selected to move a block onto itself. Once the operator is selected, the application rules do not apply and a substate is created. In the substate, further operators can be selected to analyze why the block could not be moved, ultimately leading to the selection of an operator in the substate that creates a reject preference for the selected Blocks World operator.

• When an operator involves action in an external environment, it may be many processing cycles before perceptual feedback provides the changes to the state to indicate that the operator should terminate. In such cases, an operator no-change impasse arises when the operator is selected, and the processing in the substate can be as simple as repeatedly selecting an operator that waits. When the appropriate changes in input finally arrive, the task operator retracts, and another task operator can be selected, resolving the impasse. Examples are given in subsections 5.6.1 and 5.6.2.

5.4 Substate Results

In most programming languages, the standard approach for returning results from a function, procedure, or subroutine is to explicitly return a result upon termination, and the structure of the result must be known when the program is written. In contrast, results in Soar are determined on the basis of the connectivity of the working-memory elements created in a substate. Moreover, the processing in a substate may produce results incrementally, not just at termination. In fact, there is no signal from the processing in the substate that it should terminate. Instead, a substate terminates when the impasse is resolved. A result can contribute to resolving the impasse directly (if the result is a preference that changes which operator is dominate) or indirectly (if the result enables rules to match in the superstate that in turn leads to the creation of an appropriate preference).

5.4.1 Determination of Results

To provide maximum flexibility, Soar uses connectivity to the states in working memory to determine whether a working-memory element is a result. If a working-memory element is created by a rule that tests structures local to a substate, but it is connected to the superstate, meaning its identifier is linked directly or indirectly to the superstate, then it is a result. Figure 5.2 shows a simple example where S20 is the

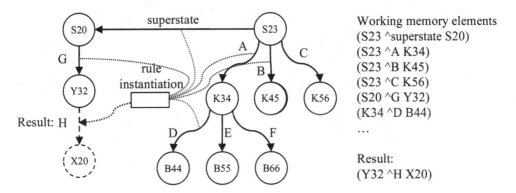

Figure 5.2
Example result.

superstate and S23 is the substate and has substructures shown as solid lines in the drawing. Some of the relevant working-memory elements are listed on the right side of the figure.

In this example, a rule matches a subset of those structures, shown with finely dotted lines, and creates an augmentation of a substructure of the top state, S20, with value X20. This new structure (Y32 ^H X20), shown with coarse dashed lines, is a result because it was created by matching structures in the substate and is in the closure of the superstate.

Not only can the firing of a rule create a new result, but the addition of one working-memory element can lead to other working-memory elements that were originally local to a substate becoming results. Figure 5.3 shows the structures in working memory before (on the left) and after the creation of a new working-memory element that links the superstate, S20, to a structure created in the substate with identifier K34. Once this element is created (S20 ^H K34), all the working-memory elements with K34 as their identifier are also accessible in S20, and thus they become results. The working-memory element (S23 ^A K34) isn't a result because it is still not accessible from S20.

5.4.2 Result Persistence

When a result is created, it has to also have an associated persistence. One possibility is to base the persistence of a result on the rule that created it, just as it is for working-memory elements created local to a state. Unfortunately, it cannot be this simple because the functional role for a working-memory element can differ between the substate and the superstate for which it is a result. For example, an operator application rule can create a working-memory element by testing the operator selected in

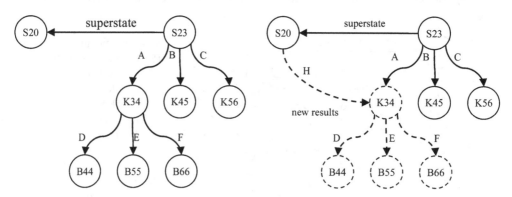

Figure 5.3
Multiple results created simultaneously.

the substate and modifying the superstate. However, from the perspective of the superstate, that working-memory element could be an elaboration of the superstate. A secondary problem is determining the conditions under which an i-supported result should retract. If it is retracted when the rule that created it no longer matches, that rule retracts when the substate terminates, making it impossible to return i-supported results that exist beyond the termination of a substate.

To explain how Soar determines the support of a result, we present an example in figure 5.4. In the figure, the working-memory elements above the horizontal dashed line are part of the top state and either existed before the substate was created, or were created by processing in the substate. All working-memory elements below the dashed line are local to the substate and are not accessible to the superstate.

In frame a, the substate has just been created. The identifiers and values are numbered in the order in which they are created. The top state has identifier 1; the substate has identifier 7. In this graphical depiction of working memory, the arcs are unlabeled to simplify the diagram, and we refer to the working-memory elements by their identifiers and values. For example [7, 1] refers to the working-memory element

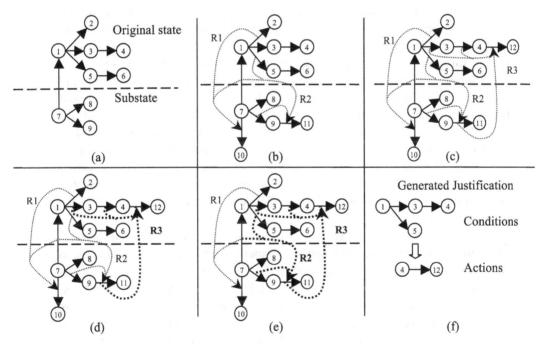

Figure 5.4
Determining a justification for a result produced in a substate.

that connects the substate to the top state with attribute ^superstate, which isn't displayed. At this point, working-memory elements [7, 1], [7, 8], [7, 9] are created by the architecture in response to the impasse.

In frame b, two rules fire: R1 and R2 (indicated by finely dotted lines). R1 tests [7, 1] and [1, 2] and creates [7, 10]. R2 tests [7, 1], [7, 9] and [1, 5] and creates [9, 11]. In frame c, rule R3 fires and creates [4, 12] while testing [9, 11], [1, 3], and [3, 4]. [4, 12] is a result because it is accessible in the top state and was generated by matching a structure in the substate.

Once a result has been created, a *justification* is created to determine the persistence of the result. The justification is a rule-like structure, where the conditions and actions are actual working-memory elements. The action of the justification is the result. The conditions of the justification are the working-memory elements in the top state that were tested along the path to generating the results. In order to determine those conditions, Soar maintains a memory of all rule firings in a substate, and then *backtraces* through the rule firing. In our example, this is shown first in frame d, where rule R3 is backtraced. At this point, working-memory elements [1, 3] and [3, 4] are used as the basis for conditions in the justification because they were tested in the rule and are accessible to the top state. Even though working-memory element [9, 11] was tested by rule R3, it isn't accessible in the top state, so it isn't included. However, Soar determines the reason for its existence by backtracing through its creation as shown in frame e, which adds [1, 5] to the set of conditions for the justification. Working-memory element [7, 9] was also tested in R2, but since it was created by the architecture in response to the impasse, no further backtracing is necessary. (If [7, 9] was an "^item" structure that referenced a tied or conflicted operator, it would be backtraced to the acceptable preference in the top state because that preference is the reason the "^item" structure was created in the substate.) Even though rule R1 fired in the substate and tested the working-memory element [1, 2] in the top state, that working-memory element isn't included as a condition because it wasn't in the backtrace and thus wasn't required to create the result.

Frame f shows an abstract version of the justification that is created. It tests for the existence of three working-memory elements and creates the result. The rule is analyzed to determine if it applies an operator, which would be the case if either [1, 3] or [1, 5] is part of a selected operator. If that is the case, the result receives o-support and since the justification is no longer needed, it is removed. If it isn't an operator application rule, the result gets i-support and the justification is maintained until it no longer matches, at which point the result is removed from working memory (and the justification is also removed). As we shall see in chapter 6, the creation of justifications is closely related to Soar's chunking mechanism for learning new rules.

5.5   Maintaining Consistency

When there are substates, rules can match and fire in all substates, although typically rule firing activity is localized to the most recently created substate and possibly the top state (because of changes from input). However, it is possible for inconsistencies to arise when persistent (o-supported) structures are created in substates and there are changes in the working-memory elements in superstates. To avoid problems, Soar's processing cycle maintains additional information and does some additional processing that guarantees that the processing in the substates is consistent with higher-level states.

The first potential consistency issue arises because the processing in the substates is dependent on and in service of the processing of superstates. When an impasse in a superstate is resolved, the processing in lower states is no longer relevant. If the processing in all states occurs in parallel, there is a risk that irrelevant and even conflicting processing can occur in substates. Consider a situation in which an operator is selected and leads to an operator no-change impasse. Also, assume that in the ensuing substate, operators are selected and applied. It is possible for information to become available in the superstate, such as from changes in perception, that leads to rules firing in the superstate that initiates actions in the world as part of an operator application. However, if a rule in the substate fires in parallel, it can initiate a conflicting action before the implications of the changes in perception eliminate the substate. The solution is straightforward (Wray and Laird 2003). Soar first processes the rules that make only local changes in the top state or a substate. This guarantees that there is no conflict between the actions of the rules across states. Processing then progresses from the top state, state by state. Rules are fired for a state, and if the changes resolve an impasse, it is removed along with all substates. If the impasse isn't resolved, Soar progresses to the next lower state, allowing non-local rules to fire, and so on. This guarantees that the information in the substates is consistent with the information in the superstates and that no inconsistent or irrelevant action is initiated in a substate.

The second issue can arise when rules in substates create local persistent structures through operator application. Those structures can become inconsistent with processing at higher states. Unlike i-supported structures (state elaborations and operator preferences) that automatically retract when the situation changes, the o-supported working-memory elements persistent until they are deliberately removed (or they become disconnected). For example, an operator in a substate can record the value of a sensor. When that sensor changes, the recorded value for that sensor in the substate remains unchanged, and becomes inconsistent with the current value of the sensor. That may have been the desired result if the agent wants to maintain a history of that sensor. However, an interesting thing has happened. Imagine that the substate was created *after* the sensor changed value. Then the processing would be different from the previous case because there would be different states, one with the saved sensor value and one with the new sensor value, even though the current situation as defined by the top state is exactly the same. It is this type of situation that can lead to inconsistent behavior, decreasing the agent's reactivity to the current situation. This is not a problem unique to Soar, and arises in any system that provides the ability to maintain persistent data structures as part of a task or goal hierarchy.

The technically correct solution requires that the architecture maintain a list of all working-memory elements in a superstate that had to exist (or not exist in the case of negated conditions) for each o-supported substate structure to be created. This includes superstate elements that contributed to the creation of other substate structures that ultimately led to the creation of the o-supported substate element. Then, whenever a superstate working-memory element is removed, all substate elements that were derived from it are removed. Unfortunately, this approach is logically complex and computationally expensive to implement, and the computational expense grows with the number of structures created in the substate. In a pilot implementation of this approach, the overhead for recordkeeping slowed Soar by as much as a factor of 10.

To avoid the slowdown encountered in the pilot implementation, Soar doesn't try to determine the consistency of individual working-memory elements. Instead, it determines the consistency of the complete substate (Wray and Laird 2003). If any of the processing in a substate becomes inconsistent, Soar removes the substate, and if the impasse remains, generates a new state. Once the new state is created, the knowledge in the state is guaranteed to be consistent with the current situation and the processing progresses from there. In operating systems terms, this guarantees that substates are reentrant—if the processing in a substate is disrupted, upon reentry, it returns to where it was (modulo non-deterministic decisions). This forces the system to be more reactive because it is never dependent on out-of-date memory structures. In practice, this approach adds no measurable computational overhead and rarely leads to the termination of a substate. Its most significant effect has been to change how Soar programs are written and how persistent structures are managed in substates.

5.6 Demonstrations of Impasses and Substates

In this section, we present examples of problem solving in substates in Soar, illustrating how substates support a variety of cognitive capabilities often encoded in other systems as separate modules. We demonstrate Soar systems that use substates for dynamic hierarchical task decomposition, operator subgoaling, look-ahead planning, and opponent anticipation. Soar systems have also used substates to generate new operators (Huffman and Laird 1995; Pearson and Laird 2005), correct errors in knowledge (Pearson and Laird 2005; Laird 1988), use analogy (Xu and Laird 2010), and access episodic and semantic memory (see chapters 8 and 9).

5.6.1 Hierarchical Task Decomposition: Blocks World

Hierarchical task decomposition is an important cognitive capability that was introduced in Planning GPS (Newell and Simon 1972) and ABStrips (Fikes, Hart, and Nilsson 1972) and has since been used extensively in Hierarchical Task Networks (HTNs; Ero, Hendler, and Nau 1994). Hierarchical task decomposition has been possible in Soar almost since its inception (Laird 1983; Rosenbloom et al. 1985). Task decomposition in Soar arises when an abstract task operator is selected and an operator no-change impasse arises because the knowledge encoded in rules is insufficient to apply the operator. In the substate, the agent can use operators from a different problem space that incrementally apply the original operator. The substate operators can be recursively decomposed into simpler operators until primitive operators are used. The more abstract operators can also be thought of immediate goals that the agent is pursuing, so that this is one way in which a hierarchy of goals (represented as operators) can arise.

One advantage of Soar's approach is that the same underlying computational approach is used to choose abstract operators (and thus goals) as well as primitive operators. This is because the PSCM is used in all states, albeit for different problem spaces and operators. Thus, the full power of the preference scheme and the decision procedure is available for all levels of a task hierarchy. In section 13.2, we describe in detail how TacAir-Soar makes extensive use of operator hierarchies. To illustrate this type of problem solving in a simple example, we use a reimplementation of Robo-Soar (Laird et al. 1991), an early Soar system in which a Puma robot arm and camera were used to stack real blocks. The reimplementation, which we call Hierarchical Blocks World (HBW), is an extension of the Blocks World example used in earlier chapters, but it uses a simulator as its external environment instead of a real robot.

In HBW, there are three levels of problem spaces as illustrated in figure 5.5. The primitive actions for controlling the gripper are applied using operators at the bottom level of the figure. The state of that problem space consists of the position and state of the gripper and the blocks in the environment. For this task, the gripper can be in either the movement plane, where it can move freely above blocks or above an empty space on the table (move-above), or the placement plane, where it can pick up or put down a block atop another block or the table using the open-gripper and close-gripper commands. The gripper can be moved up (move-up) into the movement plane, or moved down (move-down) in the placement plane. Once in the placement plane, the move-above operator cannot be used. The gripper can be opened (open-gripper), and if it is holding a block, the block is released. The gripper can be closed (close-gripper),

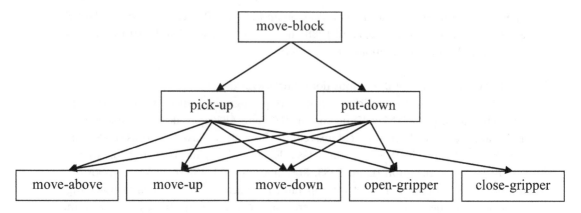

Figure 5.5
Three-level hierarchy of operators for hierarchical Blocks World.

and if the gripper is above a block in the placement plane, closing the gripper causes the gripper to hold that block.

The primitive operators are the operator-application problem space for the pick-up and put-down operators. Pick-up grabs any clear block with the gripper; put-down places a block that the gripper holds on top of another block or the table. The top problem space consists of the move-block operator described in earlier examples of the Blocks World and it moves a clear block on top of another clear block or the table. Move-block operators are applied via a pick-up operator followed by a put-down operator.

In this example, operator-evaluation knowledge is included that determines when each operator is selected. For example, if the gripper is open, in the placement plane, and above a block that is to be picked up, then the close-gripper operator is preferred. Later we will demonstrate how agents that do not have pre-programmed operator-evaluation knowledge can use either planning (subsection 5.6.3) or hierarchical reinforcement learning (chapter 7) to select operators across all levels of the hierarchy.

Figure 5.6 is a trace of the processing cycles involved in applying the operator that moves block A on top of block B. In this figure, time moves from top to bottom and to simplify the trace we use simple expressions, such as "(gripper open)," instead of displaying the actual working-memory elements. The numbering on the lines is for reference in the text and doesn't correspond to processing cycles. The descriptions of states are prefaced by "S:" and the selected operators by "O:". Whenever the state changes, the complete state is displayed, with the changes in the state underlined. Indentation indicates an operator no-change impasse, and subsequence substate. An arrow (as on line 6) indicates that a rule has fired to initiate a primitive action in the environment.

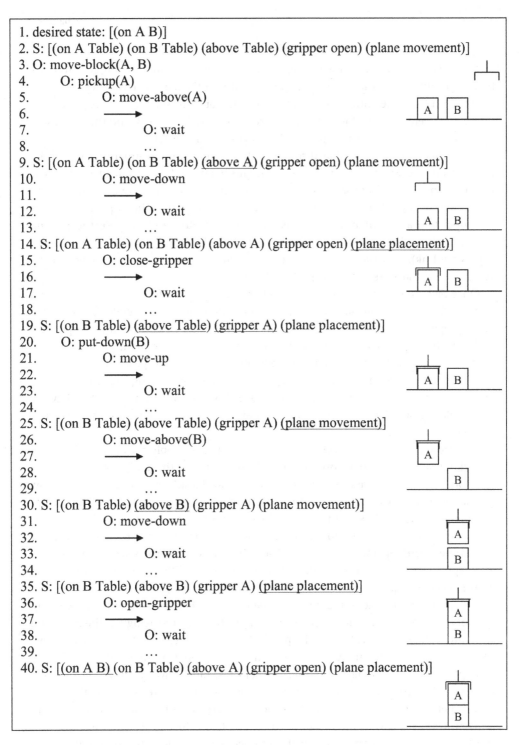

1. desired state: [(on A B)]
2. S: [(on A Table) (on B Table) (above Table) (gripper open) (plane movement)]
3. O: move-block(A, B)
4.　　　O: pickup(A)
5.　　　　　O: move-above(A)
6.　　　　　⟶
7.　　　　　　　O: wait
8.　　　　　　　...
9. S: [(on A Table) (on B Table) <u>(above A)</u> (gripper open) (plane movement)]
10.　　　　　O: move-down
11.　　　　　⟶
12.　　　　　　　O: wait
13.　　　　　　　...
14. S: [(on A Table) (on B Table) (above A) (gripper open) <u>(plane placement)</u>]
15.　　　　　O: close-gripper
16.　　　　　⟶
17.　　　　　　　O: wait
18.　　　　　　　...
19. S: [(on B Table) <u>(above Table)</u> <u>(gripper A)</u> (plane placement)]
20.　　　O: put-down(B)
21.　　　　　O: move-up
22.　　　　　⟶
23.　　　　　　　O: wait
24.　　　　　　　...
25. S: [(on B Table) (above Table) (gripper A) <u>(plane movement)</u>]
26.　　　　　O: move-above(B)
27.　　　　　⟶
28.　　　　　　　O: wait
29.　　　　　　　...
30. S: [(on B Table) <u>(above B)</u> (gripper A) (plane movement)]
31.　　　　　O: move-down
32.　　　　　⟶
33.　　　　　　　O: wait
34.　　　　　　　...
35. S: [(on B Table) (above B) (gripper A) <u>(plane placement)</u>]
36.　　　　　O: open-gripper
37.　　　　　⟶
38.　　　　　　　O: wait
39.　　　　　　　...
40. S: [<u>(on A B)</u> (on B Table) <u>(above A)</u> <u>(gripper open)</u> (plane placement)]

Figure 5.6
Trace of move-block applied in substates.

Line 1 is a description of the desired state, which in this simple example is to place block A on block B. Line 2 is a description of the initial state where blocks A and B are both on the table and the gripper is above the table, in the movement plane, and open. The operator move-block(A, B) is correctly selected on line 3, and the remainder of the trace shows how it is applied using operators in substates.

Since there are no rules that directly apply the operator, an impasse arises and a new substate is created. This substate is distinguished from the top state by the impasse information and the fact that it is a substate of a state where the move-block operator is selected. In the substate (not shown), a rule can match that the gripper is open in the superstate and that move-block is the superoperator, and propose the pick-up operator. Thus, the processing in the substate has direct access to top state (via the superstate link), and the selection and the application of operators is based on the structures in that state (which is part of the substate).

Once pick-up is selected on line 4, another impasse arises, followed by the creation of a substate. In that substate, rules can match and propose an operator to apply the pick-up operator. In this case, a rule matches that pick-up is selected in the superstate and that the gripper is open, above the table, and in the movement plane, and proposes move-above(A). Other operators (not shown) are also proposed, but an evaluation rule that prefers moving the gripper above the block being moved when the gripper is empty leads to the selection of move-above(A). Similar proposal and evaluation rules exist for the other operators that are selected below, but they are not discussed.

Once move-above(A) is selected at line 5, a rule fires to apply the operator, creating a working-memory element on the output-link to move the gripper to the correct location. However, the associated motor command doesn't execute instantaneously, so that move-above(A) stays selected across multiple processing cycles, and an operator no-change impasse arises, but there is no need for the agent to take additional action in the environment. It needs to wait for the motor action to complete. Thus, the agent selects the "wait" operator on line 6. When the wait operator is selected, it immediately applies and is repeatedly selected (indicated by an ellipsis on line 8) until the motor action completes.

When the motor action completes, perception changes elements in working memory, indicating that the gripper is now above block A. In the figure, the new state structure is shown on line 9, with the part of the state that changed underlined (above A). Although the state changed, the conditions for proposing move-block(A, B) and pickup(A) have not changed—neither of them test (above A), so they stay selected. However, the proposal for move-above tests (above A), so it retracts and the move-down operator is selected on line 10 to move the gripper into position so it can grab A. That again initiates a motor action that also takes time to execute, leading to a substate with wait operators. Once the gripper is in position, the proposal for the move-down operator is retracted and close-gripper is selected on line 15 and applied on line 16.

This completes the pick-up operator, so its operator proposal is retracted and put-down is proposed and selected. Problem solving continues with selections of the move-up operator on line 21 and others (lines 26–39) to apply put-down. When block A is finally on block B on line 40, the move-block proposal retracts and the substates are removed.

In this example, there are primitive operators to manipulate the gripper. Within a Soar agent, any number of lower levels can be accommodated by having additional lower (or higher) problem spaces and operators. This usually bottoms out when the appropriate representation for the next lower level of actions is non-symbolic (such as differential equations) or when a fixed control scheme exists to direct behavior in the motor system.

In applying an operator in a substate, different problem spaces can be used in different situations. As an extreme example, if the gripper breaks down, the agent could switch to a problem space that has operators that allow the robot to communicate with another agent to move the blocks. Operator no-change impasses also allow for a combination of rules and operators. If there are rules for partially applying an operator, those fire and problem solving in a substate fills in the gaps. For some operators, there may be simple situations in which rules apply the operator, whereas in other situations, problem solving in a substate is necessary. In addition, Soar's chunking learning mechanism (see chapter 6) converts problem solving in substates into rules, so that an operator that is initially applied by operators in a substate, is applied directly by rules.

5.6.2 Hierarchical Task Decomposition: Rooms World

A hierarchical decomposition can also be used for an agent in Rooms World (originally described in chapter 3). In this case, the agent "cleans" the rooms by moving all the blocks into a storage room. The actual robot can perform other tasks, such as patrolling rooms, chasing other agents, or randomly exploring the world; however, for simplicity we focus on room cleaning. Figure 5.7 shows the organization of the operators that are used to carry out that task. Indentation indicates operators that apply in substates. Underlined operators are primitive operators that initiate action in the environment. Italicized operators are shared across multiple problem spaces, including the operators used in substates to apply those operators. For example, go-to-adjacent-room is used in go-to-storage-room, go-to-unvisited-room, go-to-recorded-block, and go-to-unsearched-room.

This organization was deliberately designed and implemented by creating approximately 120 rules for state elaboration, operator proposal, operator evaluation, and operator application. The top problem space has many operators, some of which

Operator Name	Description of operator functionality
init-robot	[initialize robot data and parameters]
finish-cleaning	[detect that all rooms have been visited and cleaned, then halt]
record-block	[record the location of a sensed block]
record-room	[record all information about current room]
deposit-block	[if holding a block, move to storage room and drop it off]
detect-no-storage-room	[detect if no unvisited rooms and none are the storage room]
go-to-storage-room	[if location of storage room is known, go to it]
go-to-adjacent-room	[go to room that is connected to the current room]
go-to-location	[go to a specific location: doorway to next room]
set-waypoint	[set a location as a waypoint]
turn-to-waypoint	[turn to face the set waypoint]
turn-through-door	[turn so can go straight through door]
move-forward	[move forward]
stop	[stop]
avoid-object	[turn so as to avoid hitting obstacle]
go-to-unvisited-room	[if storage room is unknown, go to an unvisited room]
go-to-adjacent-room	[go to room that is connected to the current room]
drop-block-in-room	[move to lower left corner of room and drop the block]
go-to-location	[go to a specific location: lower left corner of room]
stop	[stop: before dropping block]
drop-block	[execute action to drop the held block]
get-block	[if do not have a block, find a block and pick it up]
find-block-in-room	[search room to find a block – if fail, mark room is clean]
record-direction	[remember initial heading]
record-turning	[record that agent is turning once the spinning starts]
spin	[start turning to search room]
stop-spin	[if spinning and achieved recorded direction, stop spinning and mark that the room is clean]
go-to-recorded-block	[go to a block in another room that was previously recorded]
go-to-adjacent-room	[go to room that is connected to the current room]
go-to-unsearched-room	[go to a room that has been visited but is not searched]
go-to-adjacent-room	[go to room that is connected to the current room]
go-to-unvisited-room	[go to an unvisited room]
pickup-block	[if block is visible, go pick it up]
go-to-location	[go to a location just in front of the block]
grasp-block	[if in front of the block, pick up the block]

Figure 5.7
Operator hierarchy for Room World agent that cleans rooms.

require substates, such as deposit-block and get-block. Some of the operators (such as those beginning with "record-") are operators that create persistent records in working memory for information that the agent senses. These operators build up a map in working memory of the rooms and doorways.

Operator-evaluation knowledge leads to the selection of get-block if the agent doesn't have a block. If a block is sensed directly, the agent goes to pick it up (pickup-block). Otherwise, the agent searches the room by spinning around (find-block-in-room). If that fails, the agent prefers going to a room where it has previously sensed a block (go-to-recorded-block). If there is no record of such a block, it then prefers going to a room it has visited, but didn't completely search for a block (go-to-unsearched-room). If there are no such rooms, it prefers going to a room it has not visited (go-to-unvisited-room). Many of these operators involve going to another room, which is achieved through a sequence of go-to-adjacent-room operators.

As part of the application of the go-to-location operator, the agent sets a waypoint for the location or object that it is attempting to go to. Once a waypoint is set, the agent receives detailed information for the waypoint, including its relative distance and bearing, which the agent uses to control its movement. By restricting detailed information to the current waypoint, the amount of data arriving from perception is greatly reduced.

Once the agent has a block, it attempts to deposit it in the storage area (deposit-block). If it has not found the storage area, it searches for it, using go-to-unvisited-room operators. Otherwise, it goes to the storage room (go-to-storage-room). Once it is in the storage room, it drops off the block, which leads it to a search for another block (get-block). In the agent described here, there is insufficient information to do anything but a random search—however, in subsection 5.6.4 we describe how the agent can use internal planning to find a path (a sequence of go-to-adjacent-room operators) to its destinations that is much more efficient. Figure 5.8 shows a trace of the agent's movement through Rooms World beginning in room 12, as it explores the map, and finds and then moves blocks from rooms 0, 2, 12, 18, and 19, to the storage room (room 16).

The overall behavior of the agent is as expected from the operator hierarchy in figure 5.7; however, there are a few points worth mentioning. First, there are elaboration rules that continually convert continuous data from perception into symbolic structures, such as converting angles to the closet cardinal directions, detecting when the agent is lined up with the waypoint it is attempting to move to, or detecting that a block is within range of its gripper. These symbolic structures are tested in operator-proposal and operator-evaluation rules.

The second point is that the computational resources required to run Soar in this domain are minimal. Most of the time, the agent is moving forward in a straight line toward some location and the agent isn't firing many rules. However, there are bursts

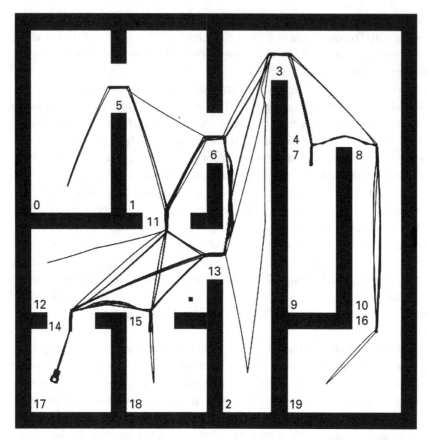

Figure 5.8
Trace of agent's movement through the room environment while moving five blocks (from rooms 0, 2, 12, 18, and 19) to the storage room.

of activity when the agent enters a new room and when it is deciding where to go next, either to explore unvisited rooms, pick up a previously seen block, or deposit a block in the storage room.

Figure 5.9 shows the maximum times recorded for processing cycles during the run illustrated in figure 5.8, which took just under 40 minutes. The data are collected in 10-second intervals, so that each data point represents the maximum time required to execute a processing cycle during that 10-second interval. Over the complete run, the agent averages under 0.01 msec per processing cycle. As the data show, some processing cycles take significantly longer, but the maximum time per cycle never exceeds 2 msec. Thus, the performance is at least an order of magnitude less than our target for real-time performance of 50–100 msec.

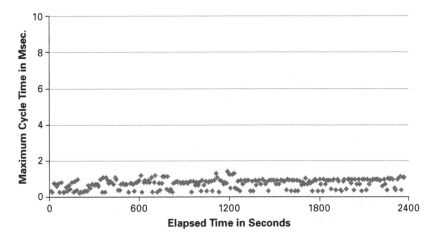

Figure 5.9
Maximum processing time per processing cycle during a representative run.

The reason for the disparity between average and maximum time is that the agent has bursts of processing. On average, the agent is firing only a few productions per cycle as it moves forward and passively monitors its sensors, and on average only about 20 working-memory elements change per cycle. However, as figures 5.10 and 5.11 show, there are cases when the maximum number of rule firings and the maximum number of changes in working memory are much higher than those averages. This occurs when an agent moves into a room and data about the previous room is removed and data about the new room is added. In these figures, the maximum number of rule firings and changes in working memory per processing cycle are once again aggregated in 10-second intervals. At the maximum, there are close to 50 rule firings and 400 changes in working memory and in a single decision; however, Soar processes those changes and rule firings in under 2 msec. (See figure 5.9.)

There are distinct patterns in the data and the maximum time for a processing cycle is correlated with the maximum number of production firings, and the maximum changes in working memory during that period. For example, if the agent stays in a room during a 10-second period, there are few changes in working memory, few production firings, and the maximum time is low. If the agent moves to a new room, there are many changes in working memory from perception and many production firings because the agent is creating data structures to represent the map. After approximately 1,300 seconds, all rooms have been visited and there are no more spikes in production firings (but there are still many changes in working memory because of changes in the agent's perception).

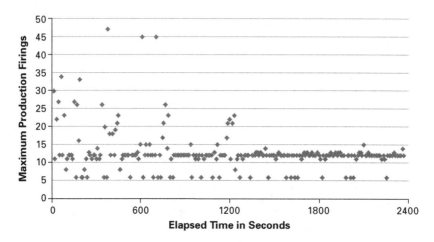

Figure 5.10
Rule firings per processing cycle during a representative run.

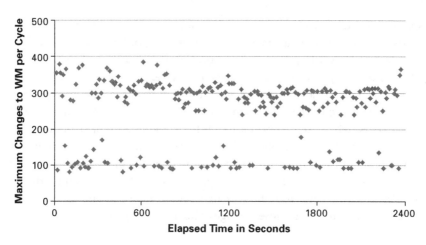

Figure 5.11
Changes in working changes per processing cycle during a representative run.

This example points out a problem that can arise when an agent senses its environment directly. If all aspects of the environment are added to working memory without any filtering, large changes in perception can sometimes result in large numbers of rule firings. In this example, there are spikes in processing; however, these are not sufficient to have a negative effect on reactivity. However, in RWA-Soar, where Soar was used to control a simulated helicopter, there were situations where changes in sensory data overwhelmed the agent when it flew over a hill and suddenly sensed a large number of new entities (Hill 1999). The solution was to add an attention mechanism that grouped objects and maintained a limit on the amount of data delivered from perception to working memory.

5.6.3 Operator Subgoaling (Backward Chaining): Blocks World

In the examples presented above, an operator is proposed and selected only when it can immediately apply to the current state. Problem solving might be required in a substate to apply the operator, but the operator-proposal rules test that all the operator pre-conditions are satisfied. Although that is one way for knowledge to be used to select operators, there are others. For example, many early AI "planning" systems, such as GPS and STRIPS, propose operators when their actions can potentially make progress toward the goal, using a technique called *means-ends analysis*. Attempting to work backward from the goal like this is often called *backward chaining*; however, the operators are not actually applied backward in the environment (which is usually impossible). Instead, if an operator is selected that cannot apply to the current situation, the unsatisfied preconditions act as intermediate goals for other operators to achieve.

Using operators as goals in this way is called *operator subgoaling*. This type of reasoning can arise in Soar when an operator-proposal rule doesn't test all the preconditions for applying the operator, but instead tests whether the operator can make progress toward the goal. Although the operator proposals do not test the operator pre-conditions, the operator application rules must still include those tests so that the operator is correctly applied. Thus, if an operator is proposed, it is possible that the application rules cannot fire. In this case, an operator no-change impasse arises, and in the substate, operators can be selected and applied that modify the original state (possibly through external actions) until the originally selected operator's application rules can fire.

Consider a Blocks World problem where the initial state has (on A Table) (on B C) (on C A) as shown in the first line in figure 5.12 and the desired state (DS:) is to have the blocks stacked in a tower with (on A B) (on B C) and (on C Table). To simplify this example, we assume move-block is a primitive operator and we ignore time delays for applying operators in the external environment, which were included in figure 5.5. We also do not show the clear property, which exists for blocks that do not have

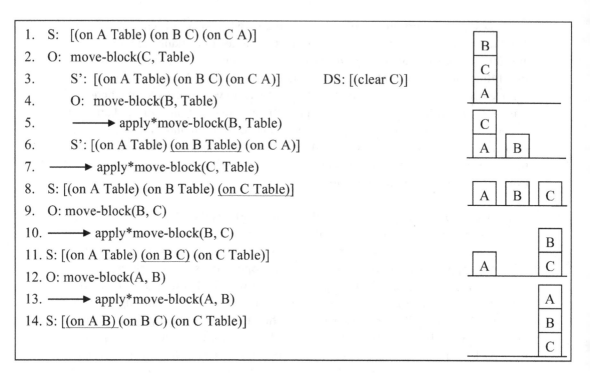

1. S: [(on A Table) (on B C) (on C A)]

2. O: move-block(C, Table)

3.   S': [(on A Table) (on B C) (on C A)]   DS: [(clear C)]

4.   O: move-block(B, Table)

5.   ⟶ apply*move-block(B, Table)

6.   S': [(on A Table) (on B Table) (on C A)]

7. ⟶ apply*move-block(C, Table)

8. S: [(on A Table) (on B Table) (on C Table)]

9. O: move-block(B, C)

10. ⟶ apply*move-block(B, C)

11. S: [(on A Table) (on B C) (on C Table)]

12. O: move-block(A, B)

13. ⟶ apply*move-block(A, B)

14. S: [(on A B) (on B C) (on C Table)]

Figure 5.12
Example trace of operator subgoaling in Blocks World.

other blocks on top of them. In this example, an operator is proposed if it moves a block into its "on" position in the desired state. In our example, B is in its desired "on" position on C. However, A is not on B, so an operator is proposed for moving A onto B. In addition, C is not on the table, so an operator is proposed for moving C onto the table. For this example, we assume that there are indifferent preferences so that a random choice is made between these options, and in this case, we assume move-block(C, Table) is selected on line 2.

When move-block(C, Table) is selected, the rule to apply this operator cannot apply because C is not clear (block B is on it), so an impasse arises. The ensuing substate (S') shares the structures in the top state, so that when these structures are modified in the substate, the top state is also modified. In the substate, elaboration rules create the desired state in S' to achieve a state in which C is clear, as shown on line 3 of figure 5.12.

Operator move-block(B, Table) is selected on line 4 so that C can be clear. The operator applies on line 5 and modifies the state so that B is on the Table and C is clear in the state structure on line 6. Because the state structures are shared, the application of the operator changes the substate (S') and the top state (S). In the modified state, the rule for applying move-block(C, Table) fires immediately on line 7, without the selection of another operator. In this example, the problem is solved through the selection and the application of operators without further impasses on lines 8–14.

One difference between operator subgoaling as it arises naturally in Soar and as it is usually applied in other means-ends planners is that in Soar, the reason that an operator fails to apply isn't always explicitly available. In other means-ends planners, the unsatisfied pre-conditions of the stalled operator become subgoals. However, in Soar, the non-matching conditions of the rules that apply the operator are not automatically made available in working memory. Instead, the only information available to the agent is that the operator didn't apply. Thus, additional rules must be included that test each precondition and record in working memory whether or not the precondition is satisfied. This was done in the example above in order to compute that the desired state on line 3 should consist of (clear C). With this additional information, the problem solving in the substates can be directed to achieving that precondition. Otherwise, it would have to blindly search for a state in which the operator application rules apply. The rationale for the approach in Soar is that there are situations where the agent doesn't know why an operator doesn't apply and the architecture should support all levels of knowledge (R5).

Operator subgoaling can coexist with hierarchical task decompositions. When used in combination, a single substate can have operators from the top problem space selected (through operator subgoaling) and applied to move the state so that the operator's preconditions are met. It can also have operators that apply a selected operator. For example, in figure 5.12, once move-block(B, Table) is selected on line 4, it can be applied in a substate using the operators pick-up and put-down (and the lower level if required), replacing the rule firing on line 5.

5.6.4   Deliberate Reasoning about Control: Blocks World

In the previous demonstrations, the operator application knowledge encoded in rules was insufficient to apply the operators, but there was always sufficient operator-evaluation knowledge to select the appropriate operator for a state. In this section, we consider situations where the operator-evaluation knowledge encoded as rules is insufficient to select the next operator so that a tie impasse arises, and deliberate reasoning about operator selection is necessary. Once again, the key distinction here is that the processing within a single processing cycle is limited to accumulating knowledge from the firing of rules (knowledge search), and that the processing in a substate is open to any type of deliberate reasoning (problem search) as long as there are appropriate problem spaces and associated knowledge. Thus, one important hypothesis in Soar is that complex search strategies arise because a lack of directly encoded operator-evaluation knowledge, where the agent must resort to problem search to make a decision during a task.

The Soar architecture doesn't dictate any specific response to a tie impasse. However, we have developed a problem space, encoded in rules, that provides a general approach for deliberately reasoning about which operator should be selected. This problem space is called the *selection* problem space because it is used to select between competing operators. Within the problem space, there are operators for evaluating tied task operators, comparing evaluations of task operators, generating preferences, and so on. The key to the generality of the selection problem space is that it provides task-independent operators for deliberately evaluating task operators, but the implementation of the task-independent operators involves substates in which task-specific knowledge is used.

To illustrate the selection space, we use an example from the Blocks World, where there is no operator-evaluation knowledge encoded in individual rules. Instead, we assume that the agent has knowledge (encoded in state-elaboration rules) that allows it to evaluate a state by counting the number of blocks in place. In this example, a block is in place only if the block it is on top of is also in place. Thus, when the agent attempts to build a tower with blocks A, B, and C, block B is only in place if it is on top of block C, and block C is on the table. The more blocks that are in place, the better the state is.

Below we show how substates and problem spaces provide a control structure so that an agent can use state evaluation knowledge for operator selection. The agent requires some additional knowledge about the task, including knowledge about the structure of the task states and operators, knowledge about how to simulate the effects of an operator on an internal copy of the state (an *action model*), and knowledge about how to evaluate the desirability a state (described above). An underlying hypothesis is that these forms of knowledge are often more directly available to an agent than knowledge to directly evaluate an operator, which is an assumption also shared by planning systems.

In the example, the selection problem space combined with the state evaluation knowledge leads to a one-step look-ahead hill climbing search. We use two figures to show two different perspectives on how behavior plays out for this search. Figure 5.13 shows a textual trace of the processing, showing operator selections, impasses, and states. Each line is numbered for reference. The line numbers do not correspond directly to processing cycles, as many lines list the current state to show progress in the problem solving. Figure 5.14 show a graphical depiction of states, operators, and substates where time moves left to right and substates arise below impasses in superstate. The numbers in small squares in figure 5.14 match the line numbers in figure 5.13.

Line 1 shows the initial state. Three operators are proposed, but because there are only acceptable preferences, a tie impasse arises on line 2. In the ensuing substate,

---

1. S: [(on A Table) (on B Table) (on C A)]
2. Tie Impasse: move-block(B, C), move-block(C, Table), move-block(C, B)
3.   O: evaluate(move-block(B, C))
4.   S: [(on A Table) (on B Table) (on C A)]   *copy of original state*
5.   O: move-block(B, C)
6.   S: [(on A Table) (on B C) (on C A)]   *evaluation = 0*
7.   O: evaluate(move-block(C, Table))
8.   S: [(on A Table) (on B Table) (on C A)]   *copy of original state*
9.   O: move-block(C, Table)
10.   S: [(on A Table) (on B Table) (on C Table)]   *evaluation = 1*
11.   O: evaluate(move-block(C, B))
12.   S: [(on A Table) (on B Table) (on C A)]   *copy of original state*
13   O: move-block(C, B)
14.   S: [(on A Table) (on B Table) (on C B)]   *evaluation = 0*
15. O: move-block(C, Table)

Figure 5.13
Trace of problem solving in Blocks World with tie-impasses, the selection problem space, the evaluate operator, and no-change impasses.

selection-space rules fire and propose instances of the *evaluate* operator, one for each of the tied task operators. As part of proposing the evaluate operators, indifferent preferences are created because the order of evaluation does matter. In the figure, evaluate(move-block(B, C)) is then selected at random on line 3.

There are no operator application rules for the evaluate operator, so operator no-change impasse arises and a substate is created, on line 4, with the goal of the substate being to apply the evaluate(move-block(B, C)) operator.

The look-ahead is performed within the context of evaluating the task operator. This is done by creating a copy of the original task state in which the tie impasse originated. This is the state for which a task operator needs to be selected. The copy of the task state is made by state-elaboration rules that create copies of the working-memory elements that have the task state identifier. It is at this point that additional task knowledge is needed, so that the copy rules "know" which of the aspects of the task state to copy. This knowledge is encoded as an elaboration of the state, and it consists of working-memory elements that list the attributes of the task state (and task operator) that should be copied. The state is copied in a single decision, and at the same time a preference is created to select the task operator being evaluated, which in this case in move-block(B, C). That operator is selected on line 5.

Applying the operator in this situation requires that the agent have an internal model of the effects of the operator actions. The operator actions can be encoded as

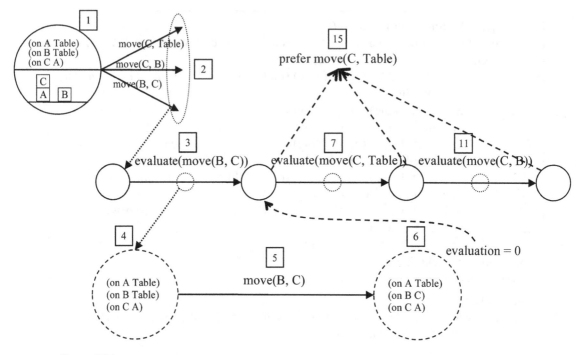

Figure 5.14
Graphical depiction of processing illustrated in figure 5.13.

an operator-application rule and in this example, we assume the necessary rule exists to apply the operator, which is rule P10 from figure 4.18 in chapter 4. After rule P10 fires and applies the operator (line 6), the resulting state is evaluated. In this case, the state-elaboration rules mentioned earlier compare the state to the desired state and determine that none of the blocks are in place, so an evaluation of 0 is created. The evaluation rules add it to the superstate, and it completes the application of evaluate(move-block(B, C)), so that evaluate(move-block(B, C)) terminates, and the next evaluate operator is selected, on line 7.

In the remainder of the trace (lines 7–15), the two other tied task operators are evaluated, producing an evaluation of "1" for move-block(C, Table) (because it places C in place) and an evaluation of 0 for move-block(C, B) (because no blocks are in place). State-elaboration rules in the selection space compare the evaluations and generate preferences for the task operators, with move-block(C, Table) being better than the other two operators, which are made indifferent to each other. At this point, there are sufficient preferences to resolve the tie and select move-block(C, Table) on line 15. This would be followed by another tie impasse, with evaluations of the tied operators, leading to the selection of move-block(B, C), which would be followed by a search leading to the selection of move-block(A, B), which achieves the goal.

When using a standard programming language, the knowledge to control a search method is encoded as a sequential algorithm, and reprogramming is required to change the method. However, because of Soar's impasse and substate structure, the critical steps of a search are the selection and the application of an operator (the evaluation operator), which can easily be influenced by additional knowledge, so that the overall pattern of the search is determined dynamically by what knowledge is available, not by a pre-specified procedure or algorithm. For example, if there is sufficient knowledge to select a single task operator, no impasse results, and there is no search. If ever there is insufficient knowledge to evaluate the result in the bottom substate, then after one step in the sub-substate, the agent is once again faced with a decision for selecting another task operator. For that state, there may be sufficient task knowledge to make a selection, and search proceeds; however, whenever knowledge is insufficient, another tie impasse arises. If another tie impasse arises, the approach recurs, leading to a heuristically guided depth-first search. With additional task-independent knowledge, the agent can keep track of the depth of the search across impasses, and maintain evaluations for different depths, terminating a search whenever a new depth is reached, leading to an iterative deepening search (or even mini-max or alpha-beta if the indecision arises in the course of a two-player game).

Figure 5.15 shows the results, as measured by mean numbers of processing cycles, for different search methods, and with levels of control knowledge based on the operator-evaluation rules, P6 and P7, described earlier in chapter 4. Adding rules P6 and P7 limits the number of operators tied in many states and thereby decreases the search required to determine which operator to apply. At the far left are the runs discussed in chapter 4, in which indifferent preferences lead to random decisions in the external environment without any internal search. Second from the left is a one-step look-ahead hill climb, where the evaluation function of the state described earlier is used. Third from the left is a depth-first search that arises when the only evaluation is success or failure. Failure is detected when a state is reached in which no operators are available, which arises when the blocks are stacked into a tower that isn't the final state. Knowledge is included so that the agent rejects moving the same block twice in a row to avoid pursuing useless paths. Without this knowledge, the searches can be quite deep as the system can get into loops. On the right is the performance achieved when iterative deepening is used, where the agent first searches to depth 1 for all tied operators, then depth 2, and so on until a solution is found.

None of the internal search methods creates or saves an overall plan for achieving the goal. Instead, at each impasse, they perform a search to determine the next external operator to select, and after taking that step, they perform another search to

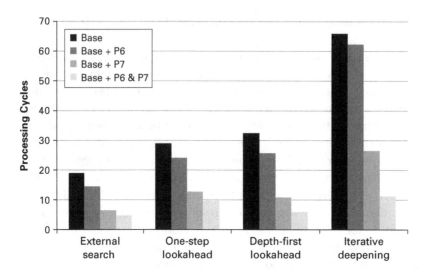

Figure 5.15

Processing cycles to solve Blocks World problems with varying methods that use additional selection-space knowledge.

determine the next operator. As a result, there is redundant processing for the depth-first look-ahead and iterative deepening searches. What is missing at this point is any memory of the results of their processing that can be used to guide future behavior beyond the current decision. In chapter 7, Soar's chunking mechanism is introduced, which automatically learns rules that eliminate the redundant processing, and significantly decreases the number of cycles required to find a solution.

The external search, where task operators are selected at random, requires the fewest total processing cycles. However, all of its operators are task operators performed in the external environment. In the other approaches, the vast majority of the processing cycles involve applying internal operators, including the evaluation operators or internal versions of the task operators. The value of these internal searches is that they minimize external actions, where the time to perform an action, such as picking up a block, can be orders of magnitude longer than performing an internal action. Figure 5.16 shows the total external actions taken by these methods, and demonstrates that the total external actions taken by the other methods are significantly less than the purely external search. Moreover, iterative deepening requires the largest number of total cycles because of its exhaustive approach, but it always finds the optimal solution in terms of external actions. In this example, one-step look-ahead also finds the optimal solution, but that is a reflection of the simplicity of the problem and the quality of its evaluation function.

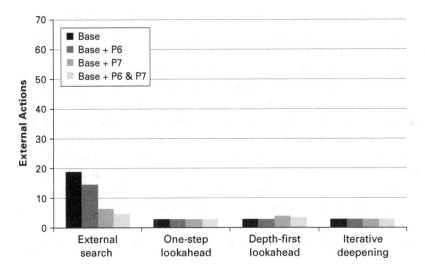

Figure 5.16
Average numbers of external actions required by different methods.

These results are what is to be expected from an architecture that uses these methods; however, the point of the demonstration is that Soar naturally uses the knowledge that is available to switch between approaches. These changes didn't require modifications to the Soar architecture or the top problem space, except for the removal of the indifferent preferences that lead to the random selection of the external operators. This reiterates the point that in Soar, there are not a series of pre-programmed methods to choose from. Instead, as was noted in section 1.1, Soar supports a *universal weak method* (Laird and Newell 1983) that is available for every task.

A critical feature of this approach to planning is that the method knowledge is encoded as operators (and rules) in problem spaces for substates, and not in an external module written in some other language. As a result, the planning process is temporally distributed over many decisions in Soar, so that even when the agent is planning, the primitive unit of decision making remains the selection and the application of a single operator. When planning, the operators involve evaluating task operators and apply-ing internal models of task operators. One advantage of this approach is that planning is immediately interrupted if changes in perception lead to changes in preference knowledge. For example, there can be proposal and evaluation rules that test for a dangerous situation and create preferences that force the selection of an operator to respond to that situation.

The type of planning demonstrated here is *state-space planning*, where the planning occurs by searching through the states of the original task problem space using internal models of the original task operators, attempting to achieve the desired state. An alternative approach is *plan-space* planning, where the search is through states that are partial plans of task states and operators (Sacerdoti 1977; Tate 1977). The operators in plan-space planning are not the original task operators, but instead manipulate the partial plan by adding task operators, task states, or reordering the components of the partial plan. Such an approach is possible in Soar, but it doesn't arise naturally, and it requires adding the plan-space operators, as well as explicit knowledge about the pre-conditions and post-conditions of task operators. Moreover, once a plan is created, it must be returned as a result and maintained in working memory. Executing the plan requires additional operators that keep track of where the agent is in the plan, and then some form of processing (encoded as rules) that examines the plan and creates preferences to select the current operator in the plan.

5.6.5 Combined Hierarchical Task Decomposition and Deliberate Control: Rooms World and Blocks World

As discussed in the previous section, whenever there is insufficient operator-evaluation knowledge, substates arise from tie impasses to deliberately reason about control. Similarly, when there is insufficient operator application knowledge, substates arise from operator no-change impasses leading to hierarchical operator application. These naturally combine when both types of knowledge are not directly available, so that deliberate reasoning about control is used across multiple levels of an operator application hierarchy. In cases where the agent has abstract models of operator application, internal planning doesn't have to descend to the level of primitive actions.

Rooms World

As an example of these combinations of methods, consider the Rooms World agent whose task knowledge is described in figure 5.7. If we eliminate the indifferent preferences that lead to random wandering in the environment, the agent encounters tie impasses when it is choosing which room to move to next (go-to-adjacent-room). In response to those impasses, it can perform an internal search to find the shortest path to the room its goal. In some cases, the agent is trying to find a path to a specific room (go-to-storage-room). In other cases, it is trying to find the closest room that has a block (go-to-recorded-block), the closest room that has not been completely searched (go-to-unsearched-room), or the closest room that has not been visited (go-to-unvisited-room). Although the go-to-adjacent-room operator isn't a primitive operator and must be decomposed into simpler operators when executing in the environment, the agent can internally simulate its abstract effects during the look-ahead search. This is achieved by including an operator application rule that models the agent moving directly to the next room without executing the lower level operators. This rule has conditions so that it applies only when the agent is attempting to move between rooms when it is evaluating tied operators, and it doesn't apply when the agent is attempting to move between rooms in the external environment.

To constrain the search, we include knowledge so that the agent computes the Euclidian distance from one room to the next, providing a lower-bound on the distance the agent has to travel to get to other room. Using this knowledge, as well as additional task-independent knowledge for computing and comparing partial paths, the Rooms World agent performs a modified best-first search where it maintains and updates estimates of the total cost of reaching the desired location and biases the search toward the estimated shortest path. This is essentially a variant of IDA* (Korf 1985).

Using the look-ahead planning, our Rooms World agent no longer wanders aimlessly through the world when it searches for a room. Instead, it uses a combination of its model of the environment, which consists of the map it has built up, together with a simple model of its movement between rooms, to internally search for its destinations. It still must search in the environment to find the storage area and all the blocks, but that search is directed without the redundancy of a random search.

The left side of figure 5.17 shows a trace of the agent's behavior when planning was used. On the right side is a trace of the agent's behavior when there was no

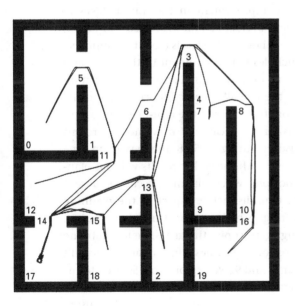
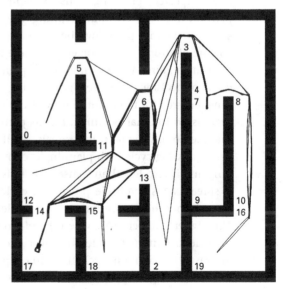

Figure 5.17
Traces of agent behavior with planning (left) and without (right).

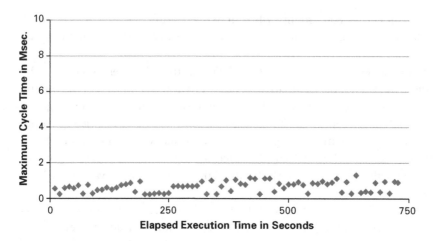

Figure 5.18
Maximum processing time per processing cycle with planning.

planning (see figure 5.8). As is evident from the figure, planning eliminates useless wandering and the agent moves directly to the rooms it needs to go to, such as when it is delivering a block to the storage room, or searching for a block in a room it has not yet visited.

As expected, planning leads to significant improvement in the time it takes to perform this task. Without planning, the agent averages about 2,400 seconds (about 40 minutes); with planning, the agent averages about 780 seconds (about 13 minutes). For the planning agent, the elapsed time includes both movement in the world and the time required to perform internal planning. Even though planning involves hundreds of decisions, it is negligible owing to the overall speed of processing and the time required for the robot to move from room to room. For the non-planning agent, there is no internal planning, but its path is longer, because of movement to rooms that are not on the path to its goals. As illustrated in figure 5.18, the maximum time per processing cycle with planning is consistent with the earlier results without planning and is also less than 2 msec. There is no spike when planning occurs because it is spread across multiple processing cycles. One distinctive aspect of the planning agent is that the maximum number of rule firings is higher (approximately 60 vs. 35). The higher numbers arise when the planning agent copies the task state to a substate to create an internal model; however, the cost of these rules is minimal and doesn't increase the maximum cycle time. In chapters 8 and 9, we explore how Soar performs on a much larger map (100 rooms), and examine the effect on performance of maintaining map information in working memory and semantic memory, as well as using episodic memory to keep track of object locations.

```
1.  S: [(on A Table) (on B Table) (gripper open)]
2.  Tie Impasse: move-block(A, B), move-block(B, A)
3.      O: evaluate(move-block(A, B))
4.          S: [(on A Table) (on B Table) (gripper open)]
5.          O: move-block(A, B)
6.              S: [(on A Table) (on B Table) (gripper open)]
7.              Tie Impasse: pick-up(A), pick-up(B)
9.                  O: evaluate(pick-up(A))
10.                     S: [(on A Table) (on B Table) (gripper open)]
11.                     O: pick-up(A)
12.                         S: [(on A none) (on B Table) (gripper A)]
13.                         Tie Impasse: put-down(B), put-down(Table)
14.                             O: evaluate(put-down(B))
15.                                 S: [(on A none) (on B Table) (gripper A)]
16.                                 O: put-down(B)
17.                                     S: [(on A B) (on B Table) (gripper open)]        achieves (on A B)
18.                     O: pick-up(A)
19.                     S: [(on A none) (on B Table) (gripper A)]
20.                     Tie Impasse: put-down(B), put-down(Table)
21.                         O: evaluate(put-down(B))
22.                             S: [(on A none) (on B Table) (gripper A)]
23.                             O: put-down(B)
24.                                 S: [(on A B) (on B Table) (gripper open)]            achieves (on A B)
25.                     O: put-down(B)
26.                     S: [(on A B) (on B Table) (gripper open)]                        achieves (on A B)
27. O: move-block(A, B)
```

Figure 5.19
Trace of hierarchical task decomposition and look-ahead planning.

Hierarchical Blocks World

As a second example, we can use the Blocks World agent when it has neither operator-evaluation knowledge nor an internal operator action model for move-block, but it does have an internal action model for put-down and pick-up. Consider an agent attempting to stack block A on B using the hierarchical Blocks World described in subsection 5.6.1. As illustrated in figure 5.19, the agent first encounters an operator tie-impasse for selecting move-block operators at line 2. This is followed by the selection space, where it attempts to evaluate one of the move-block operators and selects it on line 5 in a substate of the evaluate operator. However, the move-block operator cannot be directly applied (since the agent doesn't have an action model for it), so an operator no-change impasse arises on line 6, and it then attempts to apply move-block via pick-up and put-down operators. In this case the gripper is open, so only pick-up operators are proposed and a tie arises between pick-up(A) and pick-up(B). Pick-up(A) is evaluated first and applied on an internal copy of the state, followed by another tie impasse, but this time between put-down operators. In this case, put-down(B) is tried and found to be successful in carrying out move-block on line 17. This success leads to pick-up being selected as the appropriate operator as the first step in move-block(A, B). Additional impasses (lines 20–24) are required to determine that put-down should be applied because there is no memory that it was the second step after pick-up (chunking provides this memory as is described in chapter 6). Finally, on line 27, move-block(A, B) is selected.

When move-block is selected, it is decomposed into the appropriate pick-up and put-down operators, which are in turn decomposed into primitive operators for opening the gripper, closing the gripper, and moving the gripper (not shown). Eventually, the agent solves the problem. For the problem where the initial state has (on C A), (on A Table), (on B Table), where the desired state is (on A B), (on B C), and (on C Table), it takes an average of 850 decisions. The minimum number of steps required if there are no tie impasses is 42, which includes execution of primitive operators, such as open gripper, and the selection of the abstract operators move-block, pick-up, and put-down.

The behavior that arises from an agent responding to impasses appears to be complex; however, it doesn't involve a complex underlying method or program that must be created by a human to generate it. Instead, the complex behavior arises naturally from the interaction of the available (and unavailable) knowledge and Soar's decision procedure, impasses, and substates.

5.6.6 Meta-Cognitive Processing

The previous demonstrations emphasize how Soar agents use complex cognitive reasoning in substates. One additional important property of substates is that they provide a context for meta-cognitive reasoning and representing situations that are not directly related to the agent's current beliefs about its current situation. Moreover, even though an agent cannot directly examine its own procedural knowledge (encoded as rules), it can get access to it indirectly by creating hypothetical situations for itself, and then "observing" which actions it takes in those situations. Those actions can be simulated physical actions, and we have seen examples of this when Soar agents perform look-ahead searches, but it can be used more generally for an agent to essentially learn more about its own behavior.

An agent can also use a similar approach to model the behavior of other agents, under the assumption that another agent's reasoning and knowledge is essentially the same as its own reasoning and knowledge. The agent does this reasoning in a substate by creating a representation of what it believes the other agent's knowledge of the situation is—that is, the other agent's current state. Without any additional architectural mechanisms, the agent can discover what it would do in the other agent's situation by allowing its own knowledge to select and apply operators to its internal model of the other agent's state. An agent can also employ additional knowledge about the biases and preferences of the other agent to modify the selection of operators and predict behavior different from its own. We used this approach in an agent that played a two-person version of the game Quake II (Laird 2001b). When the bot was in a situation where it could sense the enemy, but was unable to attack because the enemy was too far away, the bot would attempt to predict the enemy's actions. It would do this by creating an internal representation of the enemy's situation and goals in a substate, and then allow its own knowledge to select operators, thereby predicting where the enemy would go. Using its predictions of the enemy's actions, the bot would set up an ambush in a room that it expected the enemy bot to go to, but that it could get to first. We further extended the agent so that it would observe the enemy's preferences and use those preferences in predicting the enemy's actions.

This approach also can be used in the simulation approach to theory of mind (Goldman 1989) and suggests that it is possible to model theory of mind behavior without any special architectural mechanisms. In addition, it suggests that declarative representations of the agent's (or other agents') knowledge and behavior isn't always necessary for reasoning about simple situations. All that is needed is the ability to create a sufficiently rich internal description of a situation, which then enables existing procedural knowledge to generate the predictive behavior of other agents.

5.7   Discussion

One of the hypotheses in Soar is that impasse-driven problem solving is the source of complex cognitive behavior, including different types of hierarchical task decomposition, internal search, planning, and perspective taking. The two key architectural mechanisms required to support this behavior are detecting the impasse, and creating a new state structure that represents the reason for the impasse. The substate provides the context for problem solving to resolve the impasse without disrupting the processing in the original state. These mechanisms place Soar toward the lean end of the spectrum in terms of architectural support for complex reasoning. Many architectures directly support specific methods or forms of complex reasoning. For example, Icarus (Shapiro and Langley 1999) directly supports means-ends analysis, whereas planning architectures such as STRIPS (Fikes and Nilsson 1971) and PRODIGY (Veloso et al. 1995) directly support specific representations of planning knowledge. Although these approaches innately provide more powerful problem solving for every problem represented in them, they are not as flexible as Soar in terms of the variety of types of knowledge and approaches that can be encoded in them for complex reasoning.

Although Soar's substates provide a natural way to represent goals that arise automatically from impasses, there are some types of goals that might be more appropriately implemented in other ways in Soar. For example, one disadvantage of using abstract operators to represent task goals in Soar is that only the operators currently selected are represented explicitly. There is no declarative representation of potential future behavior that the agent can deliberately manipulate or communicate to other agents. An agent can do hypothetical reasoning to discover its own future plans, but in many cases, it could be much more convenient to have a declarative representation of current and future goals. Such representations can be implemented in Soar by creating plan or goal structures in the state and using operators to manipulate those structures, and this approach is used in TacAir-Soar (see chapter 13) to maintain and manage the agent's mission information. Deliberately created goal structures can support subgoal suspension, parallel subgoals, and provide finer-grain control of the persistence of goals. However, they require additional knowledge and processing to manage them, and they do not easily provide the local independent state structures that can be useful for hypothetical reasoning and perspective taking (as well as additional benefits associated with chunking (chapter 6) and hierarchical reinforcement learning (chapter 7)).

At the other extreme, for goals that are always being pursued, such as survival goals or goals that arise to achieve states with high utility (R8), the need to pursue those goals can be implicit in proposal and evaluation rules for operators that attempt to achieve those goals. Thus, the agent just "knows" when it should pursue those goals/ operators without explicitly testing for a declarative representation of a goal. For example, satisfying thirst can be pursued by having operators proposed for drinking whenever the agent is low on water. These responses can be programmed from the start or possibly learned through experience with reinforcement learning (see chapter 7), as long as the appropriate reward is generated at the appropriate times. The advantage of implicit goals is that the agent is always prepared to pursue them and that the decision procedure in Soar can be used to select between them if ever they compete. The disadvantage is that it is difficult for the agent to deliberately reason about them and their relation to other goals except when they are proposed.

5.8 Analysis of Requirements

In terms of the architectural requirements laid out in chapter 2, impasses and substates significantly expand the capabilities of Soar. Below is a list of the affected requirements.

R5: Diverse levels of knowledge. Substates support using problem search to generate and retrieve knowledge when directly available knowledge is incomplete. Thus, a spectrum of knowledge can be encoded and used.

R6: Distinct internal representations. Substates provide a mechanism to support distinct representations so that processing in a substate doesn't disrupt the processing in the top task state. Substates provide the necessary structure to represent hypothetical situations that are critical for planning and perspective taking as well as other forms of complex reasoning.

R7: Goals at multiple time scales. Substates, especially those generated in response to operator no-change impasses, provide a mechanism for representing and reasoning about immediate goals that the agents is currently pursuing. Longer term goals, and goals that required knowledge-based management must be represented as state structures in working memory that are manipulated by operators.

R9: Rich hierarchical control knowledge. Impasses and substates make it natural to represent hierarchical operators that support extended, conditional execution of external actions.

R10: Meta-cognitive knowledge. Substates provide the representation of meta-information and allow the use of meta-cognitive knowledge in reasoning (Rosenbloom, Laird, and Newell 1986). Whether this meta-information is sufficient for all meta-cognitive activity is an open question.

R11: Levels of deliberation. Substates provide a straightforward way to achieve more complex and deliberate reasoning such as planning, internal search, and perspective taking. Soar integrates this with reactive deliberation that is applied via operator selection/application and supports dynamic transitions between these levels. These mechanisms do not interfere with Soar's ability react quickly to environmental changes.

In combination with the requirements discussed at the end of chapter 4, with substates, Soar achieves or at least partially achieves requirements R0, R1, R3, R4, R5, R6, R7, R9, R10. Requirements R2 (multi-modality representations), R8 (innate utilities), R12 (comprehensive learning), and R13 (incremental, online learning) have yet to be addressed, and they motivate the architectural mechanisms presented in chapters 6–11.

6 Chunking

In chapters 4 and 5, we presented the basic capabilities of Soar that support decision making, problem solving, and planning. With these capabilities, Soar meets many of the architectural requirements from chapter 2, but up to this point it ignores the requirements that relate to learning (R12 and R13). This chapter introduces Soar's first learning mechanism: chunking, an automatic mechanism for learning production rules. The original work on chunking was inspired by work on the power law of practice by Newell and Rosenbloom (1982), which was followed by Paul Rosenbloom's thesis work on procedural chunking. Rosenbloom demonstrated that it is possible to achieve the power law of practice in a computational architecture that includes both performance and learning (Laird, Rosenbloom, and Newell 1986a). These ideas were the basis for chunking in Soar (Laird, Rosenbloom, and Newell 1986b). From the PSCM perspective, chunking is an automatic means of converting problem-space search in a substate into knowledge (encoded as rules) that can be directly accessed via knowledge search. More generally, chunking converts deliberation into reaction, thereby eliminating repetitive internal reasoning, and speeding behavior.

Many of the ideas in chunking overlap with early work on explanation-based generalization (Mitchell, Keller, and Kedar-Cabelli 1986) and explanation-based learning (DeJong and Mooney 1986). All three approaches use the trace of a solution to a problem to determine which features of the task are important for directing behavior toward goal achievement. Possibly the most important distinction between Soar and explanation-based learning systems is that in EBL systems the analysis is of a behavior trace to the solution of a task problem. In these systems, learning influences the decisions made along the path to the solution. In Soar, the trace is based on behavior that generated a result in a substate, which doesn't necessarily correspond to success or failure—it is some structure that was created by processing in the substate and linked to the superstate. Moreover, the trace is compiled into a single rule, so that in the future, all of the decisions captured in the trace are not modified, but are completely bypassed. Chunking also shares many features with the production composition learning mechanism in ACT-R (Anderson 1993), which creates new rules by combining rules that fire in sequence. Lewis (1987) was the first to explore the idea of production composition, predating the work in Soar and ACT-R. The name "chunking" derives from the fact that it combines multiple knowledge elements into "chunks" of knowledge, in this case rules. For a more extensive review and analysis of chunking, see Rosenbloom 2006.

This chapter presents the mechanisms for learning rules in Soar via chunking and discusses the implications of including chunking in Soar, followed by demonstrations of chunking in Blocks World, Rooms World, and multi-column arithmetic. It also discusses the assumptions chunking makes about the problem solving that it learns over and to what extent these assumptions are met by the current implementation in Soar. Finally, it summarizes the contributions chunking makes to meeting the requirements for cognitive architecture from chapter 2.

6.1 Chunking in Soar

The basic idea behind chunking is relatively simple. When a result is produced during problem solving in a substate, Soar determines which working-memory elements that existed in the original state were instrumental in creating that result. It then builds a rule whose conditions test those working-memory elements and whose actions create that result. Once the rule is built, it fires in similar situations in the future, allowing processing to proceed without an impasse. Thus, impasses are replaced with rules, and the agent's performance speeds up as internal deliberation is eliminated in situations where the agent has experience.

Chunking creates new rules by generalizing justifications. (See subsection 5.4.2.) Recall that justifications are created in a substate whenever a result is created, and they make it possible for Soar to automatically determine the persistence of a result. The difference between a justification and a rule is that a justification includes tests for specific working-memory elements, including the specific identifiers (such as S03) that existed in working memory when the result was created. In a rule learned by chunking, the conditions that test working-memory elements are generalized by replacing identifiers (such as S03) with variables (such as <s6>). The identifiers in the actions are similarly replaced with variables. All instances of the same identifier in a rule are replaced with the same variable, and all distinct variables are forced to match distinct identifiers. Because a justification includes the original identifiers, a justification is useful only when it is created. In future situations the identifiers are different and the justification has no chance of matching. With the replacement of identifiers with variables, a rule can match new objects with different identifiers, testing for the same structure as defined by the connectivity of the variables together with the tests for the attributes and the values.

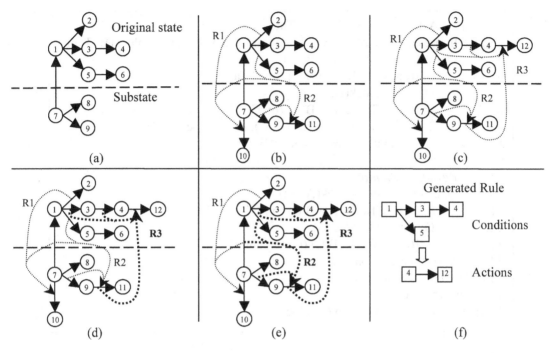

Figure 6.1
Determining a rule for a result produced in a substate.

Figure 5.4 showed the derivation of justifications. Figure 6.1 duplicates that figure except for labeling the final structure in panel f, replacing "justification" with "rule" and replacing the circles (representing identifiers) with squares (representing variables). Panel c shows the structures built up through the firing of rules R1, R2, and R3. R3 creates the structure [4, 12], which is a result. When the result is created, backtracing through R3 and R2 (but not R1, because it didn't create any structure that was necessary for the creation of [4, 12]) determines the conditions: [1, 3], [1, 5], and [3, 4]. In the future, when those conditions match new structures in working memory, the rule fires and executes the action to create a new working memory [4, 12].

The generality of the resulting rule is dependent on the generality of the processing in the substate. All working-memory elements tested in the substate in service of generating the result are included in the learned rule. If many irrelevant elements are tested, the learned rule is overly specific and applies in only limited situations in the future. If the processing in the substate is general and tests only those elements necessary to produce the result, then the learned rule is general.

1.   S: [(on A Table) (on B C) (on C Table)]
2.   Tie Impasse: move-block(B, A), move-block(A, B), move-block(B, Table)
3.   O: evaluate(move-block(B, A))
4.   S: [(on A Table) (on B C) (on C Table)]
5.   O: move-block(B, A)
6.   S: [(on A Table) (on B A) (on C Table)]
7.   Tie Impasse: move-block(B, C), move-block(B, Table), …
8.   O: evaluate(move-block(B, C))
9.   …
9.a   *Result: evaluation = 3*
10.   O: evaluate(move-block(A, B))
11.   S: [(on A Table) (on B C) (on C Table)]
12.   O: move-block(A, B)
13.   S: [(on A B) (on B C) (on C Table)]
13.a *Result: evaluation = 1*
13.b *Result: move-block(A,B) > move-block(B,A)*
14. O: move-block(A, B)
15. S: [(on A B) (on B C) (on C Table)]

Figure 6.2
Trace of Blocks World using selection space with chunking.

Figure 6.2 shows the trace of depth-first problem solving for the Blocks World, originally shown in figure 5.13. Rules are learned for all results that are created including the preferences created in the substates that arise from the tie impasses (line 13b), and the evaluations computed in substates that implement the evaluation operator (lines 9a and 13a). The evaluation is computed on the basis of the distance to the goal, so a smaller evaluation is better. For this example, we focus only on the results created at line 13 and not those created between lines 9 and 10.

Once the state at line 13 is generated by applying the operator, a task-specific rule notices that the desired state is achieved and generates an evaluation of 1. The evaluation indicates that the goal can be achieved in one step using the operator being evaluated. The evaluation is a result and in response to the result, Soar generates a new rule. An English version of the rule is shown in figure 6.3. All the relations tested in chunking were necessary for determining that the desired state had been achieved.

Another rule is learned when the preference move-block(A, B) > move-block(B, A) is created on the basis of the fact that an evaluation of 1 is better than an evaluation of 3. This rule depends on the processing in the substate that led to the creation

```
If the selected operator is evaluate and
    it is evaluating the superoperator move-block(A, B) and
    the there is no evaluation for that superoperator and
    the superstate is (on A table) (on B C) (on C table) and
    the desired state is (on A B) (on B C) (on C table)
then
    create an evaluation structure with value 1 for the superoperator
```

Figure 6.3
Rule learned from generating evaluation "1" in substate.

```
If operator move-block(A, B) is proposed and
    operator move-block(B, A) is proposed and
    the problem space is the blocks-world and
    the state is (on A table), (on B C), (on C table) and
    the desired state is (on A B), (on B C), (on C table)
then
    create a preference move-block(A, B) > move-block(B, A)
```

Figure 6.4
Rule learned from generating preference preferring move-block(A,B) over move-block(b, A).

of the evaluation of 3 for move-block(B, A) and 1 for move-block(A, B), so that rule also tests all of the relations in the state and desired state as shown in figure 6.4.

In both of the learned rules in figures 6.3 and 6.4, there are explicit tests for the names of the blocks: A, B, and C. Thus, these rules do not apply in problems with blocks with different names, or even in isomorphic problems where the labels on the blocks are rearranged. This is a reflection of the state and rule representations, where rules must test for the equality of block labels (which are constants) to determine if a block is in place. Chunking doesn't generalize over constants, so these tests are not replaced with variables. It is possible to analyze the rules from which the justification was derived to determine if the identity of the constants were tested or whether variables were used (Kim and Rosenbloom 2000); however, the current version of chunking analyzes only the trace of behavior and not the original rules. The additional level of generality can be achieved with the existing version of chunking by modifying the representation of the original problem so that the representation of the desired state shares the object structures for the blocks and table as in the current state. Then the rules that test whether an object is in the correct position in the state can do so by testing whether the identifier of the objects are the same instead of whether the labels are the same.

There are cases where a result is produced where a rule isn't created. Specifically, when the generation of the result is dependent about the existence of an ensuing no-change impasse, which indicates there are no other options available. For example, if an operator is being evaluated in the selection problem space, it is possible that it can lead to a state in which no other operators can apply. During a depth-first search in our Blocks World domain, if moving block C onto block B is being evaluated, when block B is already on block A, the only legal operator for the ensuing state is to move block C back on the table. However, if that operator is rejected during a look-ahead because it cannot possibly lead to an optimal solution, a state no-change impasse arises. For this task, that indicates a failure, and an evaluation of failure can be returned for moving C onto B. However, no rule is created, because the result is based only on the existence of the second impasse, and that reason cannot be captured in a rule, so no rule is created (nor are any rules created for future results depending on that result). This is a case we call *failure from exhaustion*. Soar can learn rules from other types of failure when it detects an illegal state or even a duplicate state. It is only when it bases a decision on a lack of knowledge, which in Soar means testing for the existence of an impasse, that it is unable to learn from failure.

6.2 Implications of Chunking in Soar

The most significant effect of chunking is that it eliminates processing in substates for situations similar to ones experienced in the past, eliminating repetitive impasses and thus speeding up future processing. The effect of such a speed up can be dramatic and have a qualitative effect on an agent's behavior by providing an exponential collapse in the reasoning required to solve a problem. This is especially true in dynamic environments, where compiling deliberate behavior into a skill can be the difference between knowing in principle how to perform a task, and being able to perform it under the time constraints of the environment.

The functional role of chunking within the context of the PSCM is to convert problem-space search to knowledge search. Although chunking is a simple learning mechanism, it is can learn knowledge for all PSCM functions: state elaboration, operator proposal, operator evaluation, and operator application, which is an important step toward comprehensive learning (R12). The creation of individual rules during problem solving is consistent with the need for incremental, online learning (R13).

Not only does chunking apply to all types of impasses in Soar, within an impasse, chunking is agnostic as to the type of processing used in a substate to generate results. Any method can be used, such as analogy, look-ahead search, task decomposition, or planning, as long as it is encoded in Soar. One way to think of chunking is that it transforms knowledge from more deliberate, general forms into a more efficient, compiled form. Chapters 8 and 9 include examples where chunking converts deliberate retrievals from semantic or episodic memory into automatic retrieval of knowledge from rule-based procedural knowledge. Thus, the power of chunking comes from using a simple learning mechanism in concert with powerful, knowledge-based problem solving.

This generality has made chunking useful in a wide variety of tasks where many different problem-solving strategies are used (Rosenbloom et al. 1985; Steier et al. 1987; Rosenbloom, Laird, and Newell 1993). For many years, chunking was the only learning mechanism in Soar. During that time, we investigated the hypothesis that chunking is sufficient for all learning (and the related hypothesis that rules are sufficient to encode all types of knowledge). On face value, chunking appears to be solely a mechanism for speeding up learning, and thus is often dismissed because the agent isn't acquiring *new* knowledge, just compiling the existing knowledge that is implicit in its rules, into new rules. However, if the problem solving in a substate is generative—meaning it creates new structures—it is possible to use chunking to learn declarative knowledge, using a process called *data chunking* (Rosenbloom 2006). This type of learning has been demonstrated in a variety of applications, including language understanding (Lehman, Lewis, and Newell 1991), concept acquisition, and instruction taking. SCA (Miller and Laird 1996) used chunking to inductively learn new categories. Instructo-Soar used instructions to create new operators, hierarchies of new operators, and control knowledge for selecting operators from natural-language instruction (Huffman and Laird 1995). Improv (Pearson 1996; Pearson and Laird 2005) learned planning knowledge, and it also learned to correct that knowledge with experience. These latter two systems were combined to support a combination of learning by instruction and autonomous learning by experience (Laird, Huffman, and Pearson 1997).

Although chunking can be used to learn declarative knowledge, it is cumbersome, often requiring the agent to deliberately reason about what should be learned. That reasoning can interfere with the agent's pursuit of its current tasks. Moreover, the methods for learning declarative structures require domain-specific knowledge about the potential structure of the knowledge that is to be learned, making it cumbersome to use on a new task. As a result, data chunking is rarely used in Soar systems except for research on declarative learning, such as in the systems described above. In addition, over the years, psychological and neurological evidence has accumulated that indicates that there are multiple, independent learning memory systems in humans. Together, the combination of functional needs and inspiration from humans led us to investigate additional learning mechanisms, which are described in chapters 7–9.

6.3 Demonstrations of Chunking

In our demonstrations of complex reasoning in section 5.4, we showed how impasses and substates arise in Soar, and how in those substates, different internal search methods can be used. In this section, we demonstrate the effect of chunking in agents that use different types of substates.

6.3.1 Speed-up Learning in Blocks World

Figure 6.5 shows a simple demonstration of speed-up learning when an agent uses look-ahead search in the Blocks World. The figure shows the number of processing cycles for runs of depth-first look-ahead searches without chunking, with chunking, and then a subsequent run on the same problem after rules have been learned. These data are the means, averaged over all twelve of the Blocks World problems presented in chapter 4. Processing cycles are shown instead of execution time because the execution time is so short, which makes reliable measurement difficult owing to the resolution of available timers. Subsection 6.3.2 presents execution-time results for a graph search problem in which the total execution time is sufficient for reliable measurement.

Figure 6.5 demonstrates that chunking improves performance not only on ensuing runs but also within a single trial. In such *within-trial transfer*, rules learned during the look-ahead search (the "with chunking" condition) apply within the same problem, eliminating some of the impasses and reducing search. On later runs (the "after chunking" condition), there is *across-trial transfer*, in which rules learned in earlier runs eliminate impasses, and thus decrease, and in some cases, eliminate internal search. These data also demonstrate that providing additional knowledge to constrain the search (in the form of operator evaluation rules P6 and P7, presented in chapter 4) is

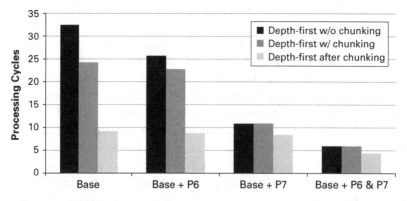

Figure 6.5
Chunking for depth-first look-ahead search in Blocks World.

additive with chunking. Both improve performance, and together they improve performance more than either one individually.

One reason for within-trial transfer in the look-ahead search is that when the look-ahead search without chunking finds a path from the initial state to the goal, the agent doesn't retain any memory of that path. The only memory that is retained from the impasse and substate is the preference for making the current decision. Thus, each time an external action is selected, a new search to the goal must be taken. However, with chunking, when a path to the solution is found during the look-ahead search, and evaluations are passed back as results, preferences are created to prefer the operators at each decision. Chunking creates rules that create those preferences in similar states in the future.

Although chunking converts processing in substates into rules, in some cases it isn't possible for chunking to create a rule that summarizes the processing in a substate (see section 6.1). And because of the original design of the selection space, the runs after chunking don't always eliminate all internal search. (See figure 6.5.) In the version illustrated in figure 6.5, a preference for a tied operator is created as soon as its evaluation is created. Thus, when an operator is found to lead to failure, a worse preference is created for it. However, no rules are created for these preferences because they were originally based on failure from exhaustion. If all but one of the tied operators leads to failure, and if the failed ones are evaluated before the operator that leads to success, the correct operator is selected (because all others have worse preferences), but because the decision is based on failure from exhaustion, no rules are learned. With additional experience, the agent eventually explores the correct choice, and learns a rule to prefer that choice.

Instead of relying on additional experience, we can make a small modification to the evaluation knowledge to defer the creation of evaluations until after all operators are evaluated. This ensures that an operator on the path to success is evaluated, which ensures that a preference is generated for it, and a corresponding rule is learned. This leads to additional processing during initial problem solving but has the potential to improve post-chunking performance.

Figure 6.6 shows how this modification effects problem solving in the Blocks World. For each different knowledge level, we show three additional results using the deferred evaluation method without chunking, with chunking, and after chunking. Because of the deferred conversion of evaluations to preferences, the internal searches take longer before and during chunking. However, after chunking, search is eliminated. This leads to a tradeoff between the cost of the initial search and the final performance after learning, analogous to the tradeoff of exploration and exploitation in reinforcement learning (Singh et al. 2000).

Another observation is that P7 reduces internal search relative to P6 and the base case, but in a few cases it leads to a non-optimal solution even when using the deferred

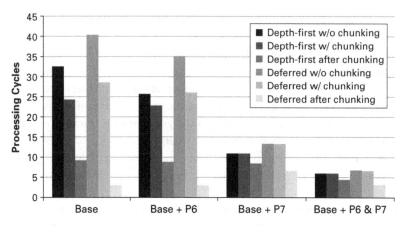

Figure 6.6
Chunking comparisons with deferred evaluations.

approach. This occurs because we are using a heuristically guided depth-first search that exploits a solution as soon as it finds it and has no guarantees of optimality. With, P7 non-optimal solutions are found and chunking captures those for the future. If a method was used that finds optimal solutions, such as iterative deepening or A*, chunking would capture the optimal solution.

The next demonstration of chunking in the Blocks World confirms that rules learned in one problem can transfer to different problems that have the same desired state. This is to be expected as many of the problems have solutions that are subsets of other problems. Figure 6.7 shows results for the twelve initial states that were introduced in subsection 4.4.1. For each problem, we display the average transfer ratio between the problems, which gives the ratio of improvement for a problem if it is first trained on another problem. Transfer ratio is computed by taking the solution length for a problem when it is solved in isolation minus the solution length after solving another problem, divided by the solution length for the problem solved in isolation. Higher numbers indicate more transfer, so that a value is 1 the maximum possible when there is complete transfer. A value of 0 indicates no transfer. Each data point is the average transfer gained for a problem by taking the rules learned by chunking for each of the other problems individually and then using them for the problem. Thus, the transfer for problem 1 (0.52) is the average transfer achieved for this initial state (on C A), (on A B) after using the rules learned from each of the other problems individually (there is no pooling of rules from multiple problems).

Chunking can also be used in the hierarchical version of the Blocks World that was presented in section 5.6.5 where look-ahead searches are used for all levels of the

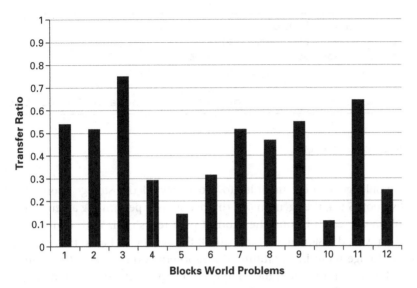

Figure 6.7
Transfer across problems for deferred evaluations.

hierarchy. The operator application substates do not provide an opportunity for significant speed up through chunking as the rules learned for such substates do not eliminate significant internal reasoning, but just convert operators into rules. However, chunking does eliminate the impasses that arise when the agent is performing internal look-ahead searches. For the problem where the initial state has (on C A) (on A Table) (on B Table), with the desired state is (on A B) (on B C) (on C Table), it takes an average of 850 decisions without chunking. During chunking, while rules are being learned, the average is 558 decisions (averaged over 30 trials). After chunking, 42–44 decisions are required, depending on which solution path was found during the look-ahead searches.

6.3.2 Rooms World

The next demonstration is with the Rooms World agent described in chapter 5. The Rooms World agent interacts with a continuous real-time environment, using significantly more knowledge than the Blocks World agent. As in the Blocks World example above, we consider only the cases where chunking learns rules from resolving tie impasses, as learning over the other impasses has little effect on performance in these tasks.

Tie impasses arise in the Rooms World agent whenever the agent must decide which room to go to next in order to move to some desired location. For example, the agent picks up a block in a room that is far away from the storage room, it must decide

```
If the agent is in room 1 and
   the desired location is room 9 and
   an operator is proposed to go to room 2 and
   a second operator is proposed to go to room 0
then
   create a preference the first operator > the second operator.
```

Figure 6.8
Example rule learned in Rooms World.

which room it should go to next in order to move toward the storage room. As described in subsection 5.6.4, the agent makes this decision by performing a heuristic-constrained, look-ahead search to find the shortest path to its goal. With chunking, rules are learned for each decision along that path. If the agent ever has to move from that room to the storage room in the future, the appropriate rules fire, without any internal search. Moreover, if the agent has to move from any of the rooms along that path, the learned rules cover all of those decisions and no search is required.

Figure 6.8 shows the English version of a rule learned via chunking by an agent in Rooms World when it is in room 1 and it is trying to determine which room it should move to in order to pick up a block it had seen in room 9. The rule tests the agent's current location and its desired location and the existence of two operators, which are proposed to move to different rooms that are adjoining the current room. The operator that moves the agent closer to the room is preferred. The rule is specific to the rooms, the operators, and the locations of those rooms (not shown in figure 6.8 but included in the actual rule). The tests for the locations of the rooms are necessary because the reasoning in the substates is dependent upon distances between rooms (and intermediate rooms), so specific locations are important. Although those details are captured by the rule, no additional aspects of the problem or state are tested. This rule fires whenever that agent is trying to achieve room 9 and is in room 1, no matter what the reason for going to room 9 is.

The overall effect of adding learning to this problem is minimal because the amount of time spent planning is a small percent of overall execution time. The only visible difference is that without learning the agent pauses for a second to plan, whereas after learning there is no pause. To provide a more compelling demonstration, we can take the same search algorithm and apply it to a graph search problem where the only actions are to move between nodes in a graph. Here, we are using exactly the same selection space and rules that control the application of the evaluate operators that were used in Rooms World above, but using them within the context of a problem space where the states consists only of a graph structure with nodes and links, and where an operator corresponds to moving along a link connecting one node to

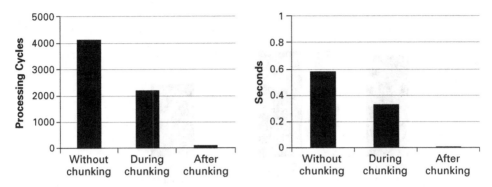

Figure 6.9
Performance on a graph search problem: without, during, and after chunking.

another. The nodes still have spatial locations so that the search can take into account the distances between nodes; however, the time to move between nodes isn't dependent on traversing physical distances, but involves teleporting from one location to another. For this problem, the search to find a path from one node to another completely dominates the time it takes to solve the problem, so that the effect of chunking is more pronounced.

Figure 6.9 shows two measures of performance for a sequence of searches through a graph of twenty-one nodes. Each figure shows performance without chunking; during chunking, where rules learned early in the searches aid later decision making; and then after chunking, where the problem is solved a second time using rules learned earlier. In all cases, the optimal solutions are found and in the after-chunking condition, the solutions are found in the minimal number of processing cycles. Whereas the during-chunking condition shows within-trial transfer, the after-chunking condition shows across-trial transfer. The right panel shows that the time required to solve each problem tracks the changes in processing cycles.

Figure 6.10 shows the time per processing cycle for each condition, demonstrating that in this case chunking doesn't have a negative effect on reactivity. Although there is overhead involved in creating the rules and adding them to procedural memory in the during-chunking condition relative to the before-chunking condition, in this case, the additional processing is minimal. In the after-chunking condition, there is a decrease because chunking eliminates the architectural processing required to create substates, justifications, new rules, and remove substates. The average time per processing cycle is more than that from the Rooms World example in subsection 5.6.2 because every decision in this problem involves the selection and the application of task operators as well as the overhead associated with the substates generated during the search. In Rooms World, in contrast, very few rules fire in the vast majority of processing cycles.

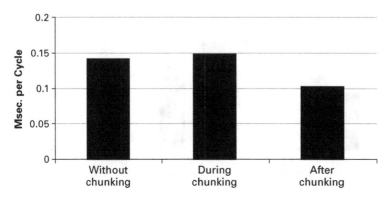

Figure 6.10
The effect of chunking on processing time on a graph search problem.

6.3.3 Multi-Column Arithmetic

One of the important characteristics of chunking is that it applies not just to one type of impasses, nor does it learn just one type of knowledge. Chunking learns rules for all PSCM functions, in all impasses and substates, except when there is failure from exhaustion. The previous tasks we described use chunking to learn operator-evaluation knowledge by means of look-ahead searches. To illustrate chunking over a hierarchy of operators with distinct problem spaces, where operator application rules are learned, we use multi-column arithmetic. The task is to solve simple multi-column arithmetic problems (subtraction and addition) by using simple procedures (such as counting to derive addition/subtraction facts). Although this isn't an efficient way for a computer to do arithmetic (and Soar can directly perform arithmetic calculations in the actions of rules), this approach illustrates the use of chunking within the context of a complex mental procedure. The procedure uses only symbolic manipulation and makes no use of built-in knowledge of addition or subtraction, nor basic arithmetic facts such as $2 + 3 = 5$. Instead it uses knowledge about the order of digits (0, 1, 2, 3, . . .) and simple counting procedures. It also knows that 0–9 are single-digit numbers, whereas 10–19 are two-digit numbers.

We use an addition procedure that processes the problem column by column, beginning from the right. If the sum for a column is greater than ten, the ten's digit is carried over to next column to the left. Subtraction problems follow the same procedure with minor modifications for borrowing instead of carrying.

Figure 6.11 shows the internal representation of a problem in Soar's working memory. Not all structures in working memory are shown, just those directly related to the representation of the arithmetic problem. Each arithmetic problem has a structure for the arithmetic operation (addition) and a structure that points to the right-

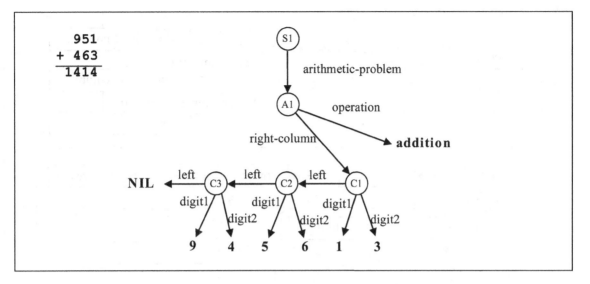

Figure 6.11
Representation of the problem 951 + 463.

most column (C1). That column then has pointers to the column to its left (C2) and the two digits in the column (1 and 3). ^digit1 always refers to digits in the top number (951) and ^digit2 refers digits in the other number (463). This representation of the internal state is consistent with representations used in similar models of addition and subtraction (Rosenbloom et al. 1991; Brown and VanLehn 1980).

Figure 6.12 shows the problem-space decomposition for the arithmetic task in Soar for addition. Subtraction reuses this structure with minor additional operators for borrowing in place of carrying. Dashed arrows represent the execution flow of between Soar operators and solid arrows represent the creation of substates when impasses are encountered in applying an operator. Rectangles with rounded edges represent the substate. In the top state, the agent is in a loop of applying the operators process-column, and go to next-column, until the last column is finished. If there is a carry after computing the last (left-most) column, a new column is created to hold the carry.

When executing process-column, the agent needs to access and add the two digits, which requires multiple operators and thus involves a substate. If there is no carry from the previous column, digit1 is retrieved with a direct execution of the get-digit1 operator. If there is a carry from the previous column because the sum wasn't a single digit, then the get-digit1 operator requires a substate in which it computes the result of adding 1 to the current digit1 using the compute-result operator. Compute-result

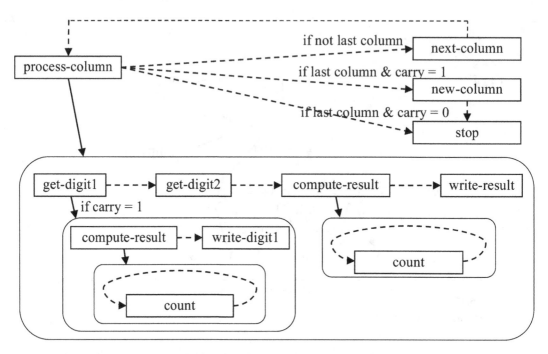

Figure 6.12
Problem-space decomposition of an addition problem.

is a general operator that can add any two digits and it does this in a substate
by counting up on the first digit (the accumulator) as it counts up on a temporary
structure until that structure has the value of the second digit. In this example, 1 + 3
is converted to the problem of adding 3 more numbers beginning from 1. Therefore,
one counter (the accumulator) starts at 1 to record the total count, and one counter
starts at 0 to keep track of the number being added. When the second counter reaches
the number being added (3), the first counter stops at the answer (4). Counting up is
done by moving through a linked list that encodes the ordering relationships between
the digits. If the counting goes above 9, then a carry is recorded and the accumulator
is set to 0.

With chunking, Soar learns rules that apply the operators that are implemented in
substates. Below are the types of rules learned for addition problems, beginning from
the deepest substates (compute-result), up through the top (process-column). Similar
rules are learned for subtraction:

Compute-result.   By counting in the substates, the agent determines the sum of two
digits. For example, it learns that if it is adding 5 + 6, the result is 1 and a carry. 100
rules are learned to cover all pairs of digits 0–9.

Get-digit1.   If there is a carry from a previous column, get-digit1 relies on a substate to add 1 to the current digit and rewrite the value of digit1. 10 rules are learned for adding 1 to 0–9 and rewriting digit1.

Process-column.   Adds together the first digit, any carry, and the second digit, to create the result for that column. 200 rules are learned, which cover all pairs of digits 0–9, with and without a carry.

Once all the process-column rules are learned, the agent selects the process-column operator, once for each column, and then a single rule fires, computing the appropriate result. This is followed by the selection and the application of next-column until the last column is reached. In adding 358 to 741, there is a "hanging" carry, so a new column is created and that carry is written as a 1. Thus, chunking converts the time it takes to solve a problem from being dependent on the sum of all of the digits in the two numbers to being dependent on only the number of columns. For example, adding 358 + 741 originally requires on the order of 7 + 4 + 1 = 12 steps to perform all the count operators. By adding knowledge for picking the base to be the larger number, this can take 3 + 4 + 1 = 8 steps. No matter what strategy is taken originally, after chunking only one step per column is necessary, plus one more step if there is a final carry; thus, in this example, four steps are required.

6.4   Assumptions Inherent to Chunking

The success of chunking in Soar is predicated on assumptions about the processing in a substate and general properties of the architecture. In some situations, the architecture guarantees that those assumptions are met; in others there is empirical evidence that they are met; in still others, the fact that Soar is a learning system means that the assumptions are violated in some cases.

6.4.1   Consistency Assumption

A major assumption of chunking is that the structures in a substate are consistent with the structures in all superstates. In early versions of Soar, structures could be created in a substate that persisted beyond what was justified by the structures in superstates, especially in dynamic environments. As was discussed in section 5.5, problems can arise when a persistent substate structure is created by testing structures in a superstate, and those superstate structures change. If such a situation is allowed, tracing back through rules to determine the conditions for a learned rule can lead to working-memory elements that no longer exist in working memory. The resulting rule could test collections of structures that never existed at the same time in working memory, a problem we called *non-contemporaneous rules*. The solution to this problem is to force problem solving in a substate to be always consistent with superstates and this is implemented as was described in section 5.5. The problem of non-contemporaneous rules was identified long before the underlying problem of maintaining consistency between state and substate, although both problems are now solved by the same mechanism.

6.4.2 Efficiency Assumption

A second assumption of chunking is that it creates representations of knowledge that can be matched and retrieved in time that is much less than required to create the results in the original substate. The strongest version of this assumption is that rules can be added to production memory with little or no effect on the overall time it takes to match and retrieve the knowledge in rules. When this assumption isn't met, there is the *utility problem* where the addition of knowledge doesn't always lead to improvement in behavior (Minton 1995). Empirically, the efficiency assumption holds for the vast majority of problems implemented in Soar and it held in our example in subsection 6.3.2. The scalability of the rule matching algorithms underlying Soar's procedural memory was established by extensive research in high-performance production match (Doorenbos 1994).

However, there are cases where Soar can learn rules that are computationally expense to match, called *expensive chunks* (Kim and Rosenbloom 2000; Tambe, Newell, and Rosenbloom 1990). Expensive chunks can arise when chunking overgeneralizes beyond the problem-solving paths from which they were learned, which in some cases can convert finding a single solution to a problem into a rule that computes all solutions to the problem. The underlying root of this problem is that Soar allows working-memory structures with multiple values for each attribute, called *multi-valued attributes*. Rules become expensive to match when they include multiple conditions that test values of a multi-valued attribute. For these conditions, the matcher maintains all possible matches between these conditions. Consider a hypothetical example for representing information about students, with each student represented as an attribute on the state, with a separate identifier for each student, and with additional data about each student as shown in figure 6.13.

```
(S1 ^student x1 ^student X2 ^student X3        ...)
(X1 ^name billy ^age 8.5 ^eye-color green ^height 4.2)
(X2 ^name sam   ^age 8.2 ^eye-color blue  ^height 4.5)
(X3 ^name sue   ^age 8.1 ^eye-color green ^height 4.6)
...
```

Figure 6.13
Example multi-valued attribute structure in working memory.

With these structures, a rule can be written that finds children with common features, such as the same eye color. That rule would first need a set of conditions that matches any student and his or her associated eye color. It would then have another set of conditions that matched another student and tested that his or her eye color was the same. In matching this rule, every student's eye color would have to be compared against every other student's eye color, and this requires at least N^2 comparisons. For two or three students, the number of comparisons isn't large; for large numbers of students, however, the computational cost can be substantial. Soar tries to avoid this problem by automatically ordering the conditions of rules to minimize intermediate matches, but in some cases such as this, it cannot be avoided. This problem could be solved by restricting Soar's working-memory representations to a single value for each attribute (Tambe, Newell, and Rosenbloom 1990); however, for ease of representing data structures with multiple elements, we allow multiple values for an attribute, which puts some onus on a programmer to avoid writing rules that are expensive to match as well as to avoid processing in substates that leads to expensive rules.

6.4.3 Closed-World Assumption

Fundamental to chunking is the assumption that it is possible to capture the reasons for generating the actions of the learned rule in its conditions. Looking at this from the perspective of consistency, Soar assumes that the rules that it builds create the same structures in working memory that would be created by the processing that would arise in the substate if the rule didn't exist. Clearly, this is true in the exact situation in which the rule was created. However, in building rules, Soar makes a "closed-world assumption" that whatever it doesn't know to be true at the time it builds the rule is assumed to be false, or at least to be irrelevant to producing the result on which the rule is based. Another way to say this is that Soar assumes that its knowledge of the world is sufficiently complete so that the addition of more knowledge will not change a decision in the future. This is a problem for chunking because it impossible for the agent to know everything beforehand and as knowledge increases, new possibilities can be discovered that lead to a different decision in the future.

The clearest example of this problem is from the Blocks World example in subsection 6.3.1. In that example, a failure evaluation is created when there are no operators available in a state. If a new operator is learned in the future, the rule learned from the failure will be incorrect. Another example is when a rule tests for the absence of a working-memory element in the substate. The absence of working-memory elements that exist in a superstate isn't problematic, because those tests are included by chunking. However, it is computationally intractable for chunking to correctly capture all of the reasons that a negated test for a structure *local* to the substate succeeded. Soar would have to analyze all the rules that could produce that structure and determine why they *didn't* fire. Soar could ignore such conditions in creating rules (and it did for many years), but that can lead to over general rules—ones that apply in situations for which they are inappropriate because they do not test all the conditions they should. To avoid this problem, Soar doesn't create rules that test for local negation (although a user can override this if desired). This problem can be avoided (with some effort) by replacing local negated tests with negated tests of structures of the superstate.

It is also possible to violate the closed-world assumption in Soar's preference scheme for selecting operators. Consider a case in which chunking learns a rule on the basis of the processing in a substate where in one state a single operator is proposed, selected and applied. Assume that there is another operator that would have been proposed in that state with a best preference if additional structures were in the state. In a future situation where those structures are in the state, the second operator would be selected, leading to a different result. Thus, implicit in the selection of an operator is that other operators will not be proposed that dominate it via the preferences. Attempting to capture all of the reasons why another operator wasn't proposed or evaluated to be better than a selected operator requires an analysis similar to that required for testing for the absence of structures on the substate. To avoid learning the overgeneral rules that would be built in such situations, Soar provides a mechanism to disable chunking in specific states.

6.4.4 Summary of Assumption Discussion

Meeting all the assumptions inherent to chunking is challenging. In response, we take a multi-pronged approach. When possible, Soar is designed to either satisfy the assumption, such as in the case of the consistency assumption; not learn rules when the assumption is violated, such as with exhaustion through failure or local negations; or use heuristics to avoid violation, such as when learning over probabilistic decisions or retrievals from semantic and episodic memory. If incorrect or over general rules are learned from violations of the closed-world assumptions, all is not lost. Soar has the capability to use problem solving in substates and chunking to recover from incorrect knowledge through deliberate correction of decisions (Laird 1988; Pearson and Laird 2005).

In attempting to meet the efficiency assumptions, we have decided that for now it is worth maintaining the representational expressiveness that Soar affords, while depending on agent developers to create agents that do not violate those assumptions and allowing them to disable chunking when avoiding those violations is too difficult. As we move to agents that learn most of their knowledge, one challenge will be to see if our learning mechanisms and the initial knowledge from which they work can avoid these problems or whether it will be necessary to restrict the expressiveness of Soar.

6.5 Analysis of Requirements

Chunking is the first step in achieving the two requirements from chapter 2 related to learning: R12 and R13.

R12: Support diverse, comprehensive learning. Chunking provides an important learning mechanism for the procedural knowledge used in Soar. It can learn all of the different forms of PSCM knowledge and it can learn from all types of processing in substates. We have demonstrations of using chunking to learn operator selection and application knowledge, and these arise naturally from the use of the selection-space and operator-implementation substates. However, there are not many examples of chunking being used to learn operator-proposal knowledge, in part because we have not developed general problem spaces for creating new operators. Thus, one important challenge for the future is to develop a comprehensive theory for the origin of operators (see chapter 14 for more discussion of this issue). For other forms of knowledge, our experience with using chunking to learn declarative knowledge suggests that additional mechanisms need to be investigated to achieve comprehensive learning. Furthermore, there is no easy way to use chunking to capture statistical regularities related to experience and utility. These final issues are addressed in chapters 7–9.

R13: Incremental, online learning. Chunking is incremental and online. It learns rules as results are produced in substates, and those rules are immediately available to influence behavior. Although there is some computational overhead required to support chunking, in practice it is minimal and doesn't affect reactivity.

7 Tuning Procedural Knowledge: Reinforcement Learning

In the previous chapter, we introduced chunking, which learns new rules that are based on problem solving in substates. However, chunking doesn't take advantage of innate likes and dislikes of the agent (R8) unless they are explicitly reasoned about in a substate, nor does it easily capture statistical regularities of an agent's experiences. Moreover, it only adds new rules; it doesn't modify or tune existing rules. In this chapter, we extend Soar to include *reinforcement learning* (RL), which uses experience in an environment to tune the values of numeric preferences in operator-evaluation rules.

Reinforcement learning is the study of learning mechanisms that use *reward* as a source of knowledge about performance (Sutton and Barto 1998). A reward can be external (either positive or negative, such as pleasure or pain received directly from the environment) or internal (e.g., a predisposition to prefer novel situations) (Singh, Barto, and Chentanez 2004). Using experience, reinforcement learning algorithms adjust the agent's expectations of future rewards for its actions in different situations. These stored expectations are then used to select actions that maximize expected future reward. In general, RL approaches depend on a gradual accumulation of experience rather than on learning from a single experience, and thus are robust over noise and non-determinism in the agent's interaction with the environment.

A simple model of reinforcement learning for an agent interacting with an environment is illustrated in figure 7.1. The agent tries to take actions that maximize its expected future reward. The reward is a signal, which in this agent comes from the external environment. The agent's internal state is determined by its perception of the environment. The agent maintains a value function, called the Q *function*, which provides a mapping from the state to expected rewards from the environment for each possible action that can be applied to the state.

In its simplest formulation, the value function is a table that lists the expected value (called the Q *value*) of every state-action pair, although many different representations of value functions are possible. The action-selection module applies the value function to the internal state to find the Q value for each possible action. The action-selection

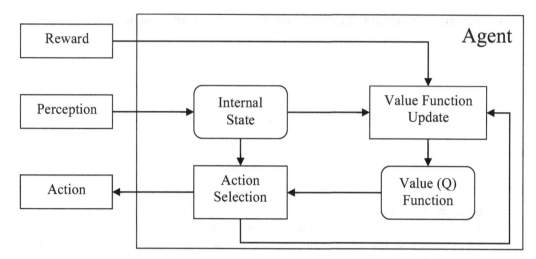

Figure 7.1
Structure of a reinforcement learning agent.

module then uses the Q values to make a probabilistic selection, and the selected action is executed in the environment. Learning occurs by updating the Q function for a state-action pair on the basis of the reward received after executing the action and the discounted expected future reward, which is derived from the actions available in the next state.

After numeric preferences were added to Soar (Wray and Laird 2003), it became clear that reinforcement learning can be mapped onto Soar (Nason and Laird 2005). The internal state of the simple RL agent in figure 7.1 maps onto a state in Soar, and action selection maps onto operator selection. The value function of the RL agent is analogous to operator-evaluation rules, specifically rules that create numeric preferences. What must be added to Soar is the concept of reward and a mechanism for updating the value function, which in Soar involves modifying the values of numeric preferences in the actions of operator-evaluation rules.

From the PSCM/Soar perspective, the functional role of reinforcement learning is to tune operator-evaluation knowledge, adjusting procedural knowledge so that an agent improves its ability to receive future rewards. From the perspective of reinforcement learning, Soar provides a broad and rich architecture in which RL is a surprisingly natural fit. The preponderance of research in RL studies specific variants of RL applied to specific problems and doesn't address the issue of how RL can be used across a wide variety of problems when there are multiple types of knowledge for controlling both internal and external actions. Integrating RL with Soar also opens the opportunity to study the integration and interactions of RL with additional mechanisms that acquire other types of knowledge via chunking, episodic memory, and semantic memory. Finally, Soar supports extensions to basic reinforcement learning, including relational state representations, hierarchical RL, and operator-specific value functions.

Section 7.1 describes the details of reinforcement learning in Soar. Beyond the integration of RL with a general cognitive architecture, what makes RL in Soar unusual, if not unique, is the use of rules to represent the value function. Section 7.2 explores how that representation supports learning over large state spaces. Section 7.3 presents demonstrations of RL in Soar across a variety of domains. This is followed by a discussion of the role RL plays in meeting the requirements presented in chapter 2.

7.1   Reinforcement Learning in Soar

This section presents the details of how reinforcement learning in implemented in Soar, including the representation and setting of reward, the representation of value functions, the selection of operators, the updating of RL rules, the use of RL in substates, and a discussion of model-free vs. model-based RL in Soar.

7.1.1   Reward

To provide support for both externally and internally generated rewards, Soar maintains a reward structure on each state. For maximum flexibility, the reward value is set by knowledge (rules) in the agent. The agent can base an external reward on input from the environment, in the simplest case by copying a value from a specific reward sensor. The agent can use its own determination of an internal reward to create the appropriate value on the reward structure.

To illustrate the basic concepts of RL, we use the Blocks World and assume that the agent repeatedly attempts to solve the same problem of stacking blocks A, B, and C. The simplest way to add the calculation of reward is to modify rule P12 so that when the agent detects that the desired state has been achieved it also creates a reward (figure 7.2). For an agent that exists for extended periods, rewards are created throughout its existence, not just at termination.

7.1.2   Representing the Value Function

The value function in Soar is represented by operator-evaluation rules that create numeric preferences. For convenience, we call these *RL rules*. RL rules match state structures and a proposed operator, and create numeric preferences for that operator. The values of the numeric preferences for an operator are combined to give a single

```
P12*halt*all-blocks-in-desired-position
If block A is in its desired position and
   block B is in its desired position and
   block C is in its desired position
then
   create a reward of 1 and
   halt
```

Figure 7.2
Goal detection rule for Blocks World with three blocks.

```
P13*evaluate*move-block*RL*stack-A-B-C*A-Table*B-Table*C-Table*moveA-B
If the state has problem space move-single-unit-block and
   the desired is (on A B) (on B C) (on C Table) and
   the state is (on A Table) (on B Table) (on C Table) and
   an operator is proposed to move A on B
then
   create a numeric preference for the operator with value 0.0
```

Figure 7.3
Example RL rule for Blocks World.

value, which is used in the selection of the operator. This combined value is the expected value of the operator for the current state. In the terminology of RL, it is called the Q *value*.

In reinforcement learning, the simplest form of a value function is a tabular representation. A table has a separate Q value for each distinct state-operator pair. The table is indexed by the current state and a proposed operator, and the associated Q values are used to select the next operator. To achieve the same functionality in Soar, RL rules are created for state-operator pairs. For each desired state in the Blocks World, this requires 29 rules. Since there are 13 distinct desired states, this requires $13 \times 29 = 277$ rules to cover all Blocks World problems. Figure 7.3 shows an example of a rule where the desired state is (on A B) (on B C) (on C Table), the current state is all the blocks on the table, and the operator is to move A onto B.

Although it is straightforward to capture a tabular representation using a set of non-overlapping rules (as described above), rules provide a flexible representation for defining a mapping from states and operators to Q values. As will be presented in section 7.2, rules can test a subset of a Soar state, and multiple rules can match a single Soar state, so that their values combine to compute the current Q value (see subsection 7.1.3). Moreover, an agent can represent and learn different value functions for different problems by including problem-specific RL rules that test aspects of the desired state as well as aspects of the current Soar state.

Another advantage of using rules in Soar to represent the value function is that rules in Soar support relational representations and not pure propositional representations (as is common in most RL systems). In propositional representations, the state isn't a graph structure; instead it is a list of independent features. A relational representation is more expressive, so more complex structures can be expressed; however, the additional expressiveness usually means that the set of possible states is much larger (sometimes infinite), which can make encoding the value function challenging. Soar has a variety of mechanisms to support learning over large state spaces.

7.1.3   Operator Selection

As was noted in chapter 4, all numeric preferences created for an operator are added together. In reinforcement learning, this forms the Q value for that specific operator. Although the Q values contain useful information, the symbolic preferences are given precedence because they provide definitive information about the desirability of the operators. Thus, the decision procedure first filters the proposed operators using symbolic preferences, then uses the Q values to select from among any remaining operators. If the symbolic preferences are sufficient to determine a single choice, the numeric preferences are unnecessary and are ignored in decision making (although their values are still updated by the procedure described below).

Where a decision depends on a probabilistic selection based on numeric preferences, Soar supports both epsilon-greedy exploration and Boltzmann exploration. When using epsilon-greedy exploration, with probability ε, the agent selects an action at random (with uniform probability). Otherwise, the agent takes the action with the highest expected value. When using Boltzmann exploration, if the agent has proposed operators $O_1, \ldots, O_n$ with expected values $Q(s, O_1), \ldots, Q(s, O_n)$, the probability of operator O_i being selected is

$$\frac{e^{Q(s,O_i)/\tau}}{\sum_{j=1}^{n} e^{Q(s,O_j)/\tau}}$$

where τ is the temperature. Lower temperatures lead to a strong bias in the selection to the operator with the highest Q value, such that when $\tau = 0$ the best item is always selected. Higher temperatures lead to a more random selection, such that when $\tau = \infty$ the selection is completely random. If $\tau = 1$, the operator is selected from a uniform distribution on the basis of the Q values. For example, if there are three operators, with Q values of 0.15, 0.1, and 0.25, the probability of selecting each of those operators will be, respectively, 30 percent, 20 percent, and 50 percent. By biasing the selection toward the operators with the highest Q values, these schemes attempt to exploit learning and speed convergence. However, except when τ and ε are 0, both schemes

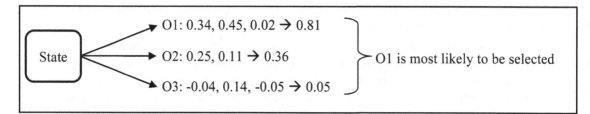

Figure 7.4
Example operator selection using values created by RL rules.

maintain some probability of selecting other operators to ensure that other options are explored and not ignored just because one operator led to success early on. Soar supports reducing both τ and ε using either an exponential or a linear decay so that the amount of exploration decreases.

Figure 7.4 shows three operators that have been proposed for the state: O1, O2, and O3. The values of the numeric preferences for an operator are added together to give the Q value (O1: 0.81, O2: 0.36, O3: 0.05). These values are processed by the chosen selection scheme (epsilon-greedy or Boltzmann), and an operator is selected. In this case, O1 is the operator most likely to be selected, because it has the highest value, although either of the other operators could be selected.

7.1.4 Updating RL Rules

The learning part of reinforcement learning involves updating the value function, which in Soar means modifying the values of the indifferent preferences in RL rules. Soar supports both Q-learning (Watkins 1989) and SARSA algorithms for Temporal Difference (TD) learning (Rummery and Niranjan 1994). In both procedures, the value function is updated on the basis of the reward received for taking an action and a discount of the expected future reward.

The TD update uses the current value and a modification that is the difference between the discounted expected future reward and the current reward. Specifically, the TD update function is

$$Q(s, O) \leftarrow Q(s, O) + \alpha[r + \gamma Q(s', O') - Q(s, O)],$$

where s is the current state, s' is the next state, O is the current operator, and O' is the operator applied to s'. The current value, $Q(s, O)$, is modified by adding

$$\alpha[r + \gamma Q(s', O') - Q(s, O)].$$

The reward received is r, and the discounted expected future reward is $\gamma Q(s', O')$. The discount of the future reward is a parameter, γ; it is included because there is uncertainty as to whether the future reward will be received. A learning-rate parameter, α,

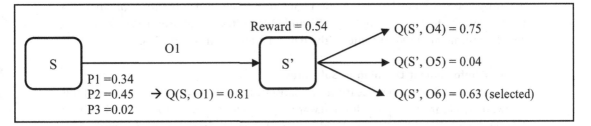

Figure 7.5
Updating the evaluation rules using RL.

moderates the effect of change in the expected reward. The discount and the learning rate take values between 0 and 1.

Figure 7.5 shows an example of a situation in which the agent begins in state S and selects operator O1 on the basis of rules, P1, P2, and P3, whose combined values give a Q value of 0.81. After the operator has been applied, a reward of 0.54 is received, and three operators, O4, O5, and O6 are proposed. If operator O6 is selected, the update proceeds as follows.

In SARSA, the expected future reward is taken to be the Q value of the next selected operator, which in this case is O6 with a value of 0.63. For our example, we can fill in the values in the update:

$\alpha[0.54 + \gamma*0.63 - 0.81]$.

If we use $\gamma = 0.9$ and $\alpha = 0.1$, our update becomes

$0.1*[0.54 + 0.9*0.63 - 0.81] = 0.1*[0.54 + 0.567 - 0.81] = 0.1*[0.297] = 0.0297$.

In Q-learning, the expected future reward is the maximum value of the proposed operators, which in this case 0.75 for O4. Thus, when Q-learning is used, we can fill in the values for an overall update of

$0.1*[0.54 + 0.9*0.75 - 0.81] = 0.1*[0.54 + 0.675 - 0.81] = 0.1*[0.405] = 0.0405$.

For both methods, the update is divided among the rules that contributed to the Q value of the applied operator. In this example, there are three rules. When SARSA is used, each is adjusted by adding 0.01 (0.0297/3 rounded); the new values for the rules then are P1 = 0.35, P2 = 0.46, and P3 = 0.03.

If it is impossible to compute the expected future reward because there are no numeric preferences for the next selected operator (under SARSA) or proposed operators (under Q-learning), the reward is recorded, and the update is computed when it is possible to compute an expected future (with a cumulative discount based on the number of intervening operator selections). This process fills the "gaps" that can arise when operators do not have numeric preferences. Soar also supports *eligibility traces* (Sutton and Barto 1998) for both SARSA and Q-learning. (Eligibility traces, which can speed learning, are used in some of the demonstrations in section 7.3.)

7.1.5 Reinforcement Learning in Substates

Soar supports reinforcement learning in substates. In each substate, Soar maintains a reward structure that provides a reward specific to the operator selected in that substate, and RL rules are updated using the procedure described above. This overall structure of RL across substates in Soar is analogous to MAXQ, a hierarchical version of RL (Dieterich 1998, 2000). One important difference is that RL in Soar applies to all types of impasses and substates, whereas MAXQ supports only hierarchical task decomposition. Thus, the structure of Soar allows for RL to be applied not only to subproblems involving task decomposition and operator application (operator no-change impasses), but also to subproblems involving operator creation (state no-change impasses) and operator evaluation (tie and conflict impasses). In Soar, each state's reward structure is maintained independently, and rewards in one state can be based on rewards in other states. For example, an external reward can be copied down from the top state to a substate, or can be combined with a local reward.

One complication in hierarchical RL is that during an operator no-change impasse the impassed operator stays selected across multiple processing cycles during which there could be multiple rewards. When the operator terminates and a new operator is selected, the RL rules for the impassed operator are updated using the total reward that was experienced during its selection.

7.1.6 Model-Free vs. Model-Based Learning

In the RL community, a distinction is made between using RL when the actions being learned over are executed in an external environment and using RL when the actions are simulated using an internal model of the environment. The first is called *model-free* learning, because it doesn't require an internal model of the effects of actions in the environment; the second is called *model-based* learning, because the model is used to support the learning. One advantage of model-based learning is that the internal search can often be performed much more rapidly than the external search, in which the dynamics of the external environment can take additional time.

Soar's implementation of RL is agnostic as to whether learning is model-free or model-based. If the problem space being learned over involves interaction with an external environment, Soar learns from the reward received from the environment as in executes actions in the environment. If the problem space being learned over has operators that are executed internally on a model of the environment using rules to simulate the effects of those operators, Soar learns from the reward generated internally. All the demonstrations of Soar using RL in section 7.3 are model-free, involving direct interaction with an environment. Although not reported here, model-based learning has been used in other tasks in Soar (Xu and Laird 2010).

7.2 Learning over Large State Spaces

One of the challenges of using RL for real-world problems with large state spaces is that the agent may rarely encounter the same state more than once, so that improvement in behavior is slow if learning is specific to state-operator pairs,. For example, if a state includes the exact x, y, z position of every block in the Blocks World and the position of each block in different instances of the problem vary, learning a value function on the basis of those positions will rarely aid problem solving on new instances of the problem.

7.2.1 General RL Rules

One approach to dealing with large state spaces in Soar is to use RL rules that can match multiple state-operator pairs. Rules can ignore certain state structures by not testing them in conditions. In addition, instead of matching specific values of working-memory structures, rules in Soar can test for equality, inequality, as well as relative values and ranges of numeric quantities. Thus, each rule associates a Q value with the subset of the states and operators that match the conditions of the rule. The expected value of a general RL rule is then the average of all state-operator pairs that the rule matches, weighted by how often each pair is experienced. Furthermore, when general rules overlap, their values are combined to determine the Q value of a proposed operator. This provides a mechanism for *coarse coding* and *tile coding* (Sutton and Barto 1998).

It is also possible, by using rules that test only a subset of the problem's description, to encode general knowledge that applies across multiple problems. At the extreme, for knowledge that is independent of a specific problem, such as "Don't jump off a cliff," RL rules can ignore the problem description completely and test only a few features of the state and operator. This generality also extends to testing operator descriptions, where rules can test general features of an operator (it puts a block on the table) without testing all of the details (it puts block B on the table).

One implication of learning with rules that vary in generality is that learning proceeds from general to specific. The general rules get more training instances, because they cover more states; the specific rules get training instances with lower variance, so they provide a more accurate prediction of future reward. By including both general and specific rules, the system learns the general, less accurate knowledge quickly, then refines it through learning the values for the specific rules (Wang and Laird 2007, 2010).

7.2.2 Enriched State Representations

A related approach is to enrich the state representation by including state-elaboration rules that compute abstract features, such as converting the specific locations of blocks to "on" relations. RL rules can test the abstract features and ignore the specific locations of the blocks. A similar example is where state-elaboration rules test for ranges of numeric feature values, discretizing continuous features into symbolic features and thus reducing the dimensionality of the state space that is learned by RL.

7.2.3 Operator-Specific Value Functions

Another approach to covering large state spaces is to use RL rules that test different subsets of state features in the RL rules for different operators. The correct selection of one operator may depend on only a small number of features; other operators may depend on a different set of features. The ability to represent operator-specific value functions decreases the total number of RL rules, and can speed learning because experiences accumulate more quickly for each rule.

7.2.4 Combining Symbolic and Numeric Operator-Evaluation Rules

Soar also provides the flexibility of combining rules that create numeric preferences (tuned by RL) and rules that create symbolic preferences. Symbolic preferences have precedence, but if they are insufficient to determine a dominant choice, numeric preferences are used. Since RL is applied to only a subset of the space, the learning required is greatly reduced, similar to the approach used in heuristically accelerated learning (Bianchi, Ribeiro, and Costa 2008). Section 7.3 includes a demonstration of how a few rules using symbolic preferences (P6 and P7 from chapter 4) can greatly reduce the search space and speed learning via RL.

7.2.5 Incomplete Value Functions

With Soar, it isn't necessary to have operator-evaluation rules that cover all state-operator pairs. This is especially important in domains where not all state features are known beforehand. When there are state-operator pairs that are not covered by either symbolic or numeric preferences, tie impasses arise between the competing operators and in the ensuing substate, the agent can use other methods to choose an operator. As was noted in chapter 5, impasses and substates provide a general mechanism for dealing with uncertainty—especially for novel situations, where general reasoning approaches can analyze the alternatives, and deliberately evaluate them. Chunking (as described in chapter 6) provides the mechanism for capturing the process in the substates and creating new operator-evaluation rules that create either symbolic or numeric preferences. If the new rule creates a numeric preference, it is automatically tuned in the future by RL, so that the value function is dynamically extended through a combination of processing in a substate and chunking (Laird, Derbinsky, and Tinkerhess 2011).

7.3 Demonstrations of Reinforcement Learning

This section presents three demonstrations of RL in Soar. The first demonstration takes place in the standard Blocks World we introduced in chapter 4 and shows how symbolic operator-evaluation knowledge works synergistically with RL. The second demonstration takes place in the hierarchical version of the Blocks World introduced in chapter 5 and shows how RL can be applied to the selection of operators across a hierarchy of substates. The third demonstration takes place in the Infinite Mario domain created for the Reinforcement Learning Competition. In contrast to the other demonstrations, in the Infinite Mario domain the agent doesn't have complete perception of the environment, and the environment changes independent of the agent. We delay a demonstration of RL in the Rooms World environment until chapter 11, where a variant of Rooms World is used to demonstrate the use of a theory of emotion to generate internal reward for RL. For all demonstrations, we use the default parameter settings in Soar: SARSA, epsilon-greedy, with $\alpha = 0.3$, $\varepsilon = 0.1$, and $\gamma = 0.9$. (For additional demonstrations of agents using RL in conjunction with episodic memory and mental imagery, see chapter 12.)

7.3.1 Blocks World

As a simple demonstration of using RL in Soar, we can add RL rules to the Blocks World problems introduced in chapter 4. Initially, we include one RL rule for every state-operator pair in the problem space, which ends up being a total of 29 rules. For example, in the state with (on A B) (on B Table) (on C Table), there is one RL rule for each possible operator: moving A onto the table, moving C onto A, and moving A onto C. All RL rules are all initialized with 0.0 for their Q values. The agent is run multiple times on the problem. In the RL community, each attempt at solving a problem is called an *episode*; however, owing to the use of episodic memory in Soar, using that term is confusing, so in this book, we refer to each attempt as a *trial*. On successive trials, the agent can use knowledge learned in earlier trials.

Figure 7.6 shows the average number of cycles required, across multiple trials, to solve the 12 problems that have a desired state (on A B) (on B C) (on C Table), averaged over 30 runs, where a run is an instance of an agent running through all trials. Reward was received when the desired state was reached. The x axis represents the number of trials; the y axis represents the number of processing cycles required to solve the problem. Averaged over all 12 problems, the optimal number of cycles to solve the problem is 3.

Figure 7.6 shows the performance in the Blocks World using different levels of knowledge. RL alone has no additional knowledge with which to control operator selections; the other levels of learning include combinations of rules R6 and R7. In chapter 4, we demonstrated how adding rules P6 and P7 significantly decreases the number of cycles that are needed to search for the solution in the Blocks World

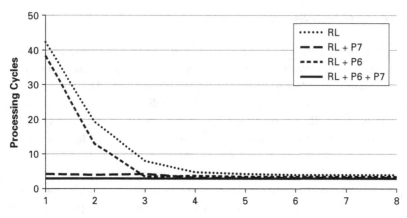

Figure 7.6
Performance using RL with different levels of initial control knowledge.

problems, and together they eliminate any need for search. As the figure demonstrates, RL quickly tunes the RL rules, and the addition of P6 and P7 speeds performance and learning.

7.3.2 Hierarchical Blocks World
In chapter 5, we introduced a hierarchical version of the Blocks World, with the problem-space structure illustrated in figure 7.7. In that version, we had two conditions: one in which operator-evaluation rules were hand-coded for the operators in all three problem spaces so that the correct operator was always selected for each state, and a second where look-ahead planning was used to find the correct sequence of operators. With RL, the system can learn when to select the operators on the basis of experience without planning, so it need not have an internal model of its actions. RL still requires operator-proposal rules, RL rules for each operator, and a means for computing reward. Each of these types of rules is described below.

Operator-proposal rules
The operator-proposal rules are the same rules used in chapter 5. They propose each operator whenever it can legally apply in the appropriate substate. For example, when move-block is selected in the superstate, an instance of pick-up is proposed for every clear block when the gripper isn't holding anything. Open-gripper is proposed when either pick-up or put-down is selected in the superstate and the gripper is closed.

RL rules
RL rules (operator-evaluation rules that generate numeric preferences) are included for each state-operator pair for all three levels of the problem-space hierarchy in

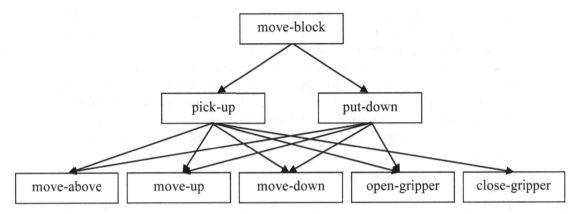

Figure 7.7
Three-level hierarchy of operators for move-block.

figure 7.7. It is necessary to determine which state features should be tested in these rules, and the answer is different for each level of the operator hierarchy. Our approach is to include all features that are potentially relevant to achieving the goal of that level, and to ignore all other features.

In the top problem space, the features are exactly the same as those used in problem described in subsection 7.3.1, in which move-block is the only operator. Thus, we use the 29 operator-evaluation rules described there and ignore details concerning the position of the gripper.

For the middle problem space, where pick-up and put-down are the operators, the agent needs to learn when to pick up an object and where to place an object using put-down. For pick-up, the important state features include the object that is being moved by move-block, and the object that should be picked up. In fact, these are the same (the agent should pick up the object being moved), but this is what the agent must learn. Therefore, we generate RL rules for each possible pair of objects being moved (blocks A, B, and C) and objects that can be picked up (blocks A, B, and C). This generates nine RL rules for pick-up. For put-down, the agent must learn to prefer operators that put down the object that is held at the destination of the move-block operator, and learn to avoid put-down operator for all other situations. For put-down, there are three possible objects that can be held, and three possible destinations (the blocks that are not held and the table), so nine operator-evaluation rules are needed.

For the operators in the bottom problem space that directly manipulate the gripper, the agent needs to learn when to perform each of those actions dependent upon the state of the gripper (open/closed, up/down, above a block/table) and the superoperator being applied (either pick-up or put-down). If pick-up is the superoperator, then it must also test the block being picked up; if put-down is the superoperator, the destination of put-down is tested. For example, for close-gripper, the RL rule tests which block is being moved (A, B, C), the position of the gripper (up, down), and which object it is above (A, B, C, Table). This requires 24 rules, and the agent must learn to prefer closing the gripper when it is down and above the same object as the object being moved (close gripper is never used in putdown). All the other operators at this level require two sets of RL rules because the states they are preferred in depend on whether pick-up or put-down is the superoperator. Across all levels, more than 200 RL rules are required.

Reward

The reward for completing the total task is not sufficient to get timely learning in this task. To improve the rate of learning, we provide reward for each level of the hierarchy for successfully implementing the selected superoperator. Negative reward is also supplied when a state is reached that is inconsistent with applying the superoperator. At the top level, a reward of 1 is given for successfully solving the problem. This leads to learning which move-block operator should be selected at each state in that problem space.

In the problem space with pick-up and put-down, a reward of 1 is given for successfully applying the selected move-block superoperator, which occurs when the block being moved by move-block is placed on the destination of move-block. A reward of –1 is given if a block is placed on the block being moved. With RL, these rewards lead to learning which instances of pick-up and put-down should be selected at each state in the middle problem space.

In the bottom problem space, where the gripper is directly manipulated, a reward of 1 is given for successfully applying the superoperator, be it pick-up or put-down. For pick-up, the reward is given if the block being picked up is picked up (held in the gripper), and a reward of 1 is given if the block being put down is put down on the correct destination. A reward of –1 is given if when attempting to apply pick-up for a block, another block is picked up. A reward of –1 is also given if when attempting to apply put-down, the block being held is put on an incorrect destination. These rewards lead to learning when the gripper manipulation operators should be selected to apply pick-up and put-down.

Discussion

Together, the knowledge described above is sufficient for learning to solve these problems in relatively few trials. In creating the RL rules, the developer isn't specifying in which state which operators should be selected, as was done in chapter 5, but is only specifying which state features are relevant to making those decisions. In RL terms, this knowledge determines the value function and selecting the correct features for these rules has a direct effect on the speed and convergence of learning. If we include additional features that take on different values during problem solving, learning is slower; if critical features are not included, the learning is not likely to converge. One of the distinguishing features of our implementation is that by representing the value function as rules, it makes it easy to have different value functions for each operator in a problem space, which decreases the total size of the value-function space and speeds learning. Although more than 200 operator-evaluation rules are needed to cover all situations, Soar has facilities to make it trivial to generate the variants required for each operator.

Results

To illustrate learning across all levels of the hierarchy, we present results from four different conditions. In all conditions, the results are the median of 100 independent runs, using the Soar default RL settings. The x axis represents the number of training trials, all on the same problem; the y axis represents the number of processing cycles on a log scale. In three conditions, operator-evaluation knowledge is included so that RL is used in only one problem-space level. In level 1, learning occurs only in problem space of the move-block operator, whereas in level 2 learning is only in the problem space of pick-up and put-down. Similarly, in level 3 learning is only in the bottom problem space for directly manipulating gripper. All these conditions quickly converge to optimal behavior, which shows that each individual level is relatively easy to learn. (See figure 7.8.)

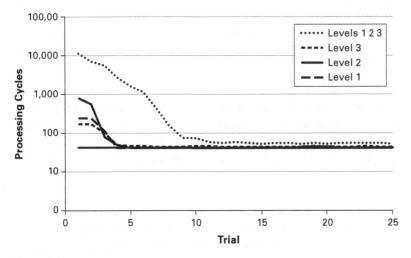

Figure 7.8
Learning curve averaged over all problems using RL.

When learning for all levels (level 1, 2, 3), finding a solution initially takes many more cycles (the y axis is a log scale), and more trials are required for convergence, although it achieves very good performance within 10 trials. This condition's median performance doesn't converge to the optimal (the straight line in the figure) within 25 trials, in part because this experiment was done with using epsilon-greedy search, where $\varepsilon = 0.1$, so that 10 percent of all decisions are made at random. In this condition, there are over 40 decisions that have to be learned; in the other conditions, decisions for only one level (about 10–15) decisions are open to learning and random decisions.

There are additional factors that influence the time it takes to converge in hierarchical RL systems that are in play here:

• Initially, none of the levels has sufficient operator-evaluation knowledge to select correct operators, so there is search across all levels.
• Lack of knowledge at the top levels has a multiplicative effect on increasing total search, because selecting the wrong move-block operator leads to useless searches in substates.
• Learning occurs at the lower levels independent of the success of the problem solving (or learning) at the higher levels. For example, even when the agent has a selected the wrong move-block operator, there is learning in the substates.
• The feedback for a high-level operator can be incorrect when its implementation is not yet learned. For example, the correct pick-up operator can be selected at the appropriate time, but until that operator is correctly learned the implementation can pick up and move the wrong block, so that the selection of move-block will not be correctly updated. Moreover, the opposite can happen: the wrong pick-up operator is selected, but the underlying implementation performs the actions of the correct pick-up operator, so the wrong pick-up operator gets a positive reward.

Because the search required to find a solution would be orders of magnitude longer, a baseline comparison of learning using only the lowest-level operators without the hierarchy isn't included. That approach would entail solving the problem with the level-3 operators, with a solution depth of 23 and a branching factor that averages 3 (it varies from 2 to 4), which gives a search space of 3^{23} (which is approximately 10^{11}).

Transfer
One of the main advantages of hierarchical decomposition is that it splits a larger problem into smaller problems, each of which can have an exponentially smaller search space, so that the sum of those searches is much less than the original. A second advantage is that each smaller problem can occur multiple times in the solving

of the overall problem, providing within-trial transfer, so that learning to apply one operator aids in its execution later in the problem. Moreover, these smaller problems can occur as subproblems in related problems. Thus, in hierarchical systems, a significant form of transfer can arise because different problems are decomposed into similar subproblems. In the hierarchical Blocks World, when the agent attempts a problem, not only does it learn how to solve that problem; it also learns how to solve the subproblems of how to implement move-block, pick-up, and put-down. For Blocks World problems, there is perfect transfer of these learned implementations to new problems. Thus, although the first problem requires an extended search, subsequent problems are significantly faster as they only need to solve the problem at the move-blocks level, and not the lower levels. The identity of subproblems is also the major source of transfer in chunking; it was identified by Thorndike (1932) as critical to transfer.

7.3.3 Infinite Mario

Infinite Mario was developed for the Third Annual Reinforcement Learning Competition at the 2009 International Conference on Machine Learning. It was inspired by Nintendo's Super Mario World, a side-scrolling video game featuring destructible blocks, enemies, fireballs, coins, chasms, and platforms. It requires the player to move to the right to reach the finish line, earning points and powers along the way by collecting coins, mushrooms, and fire flowers and killing monsters. We created an agent in Soar to play Infinite Mario to discover what problems arise in applying RL to a dynamic, complex, continuous task (Mohan and Laird 2011). The domain comes with a sample agent, which we used for comparison.

The position of an object in the world is represented by a pair of real numbers, but the domain is divided into a two-dimensional (16 × 22) matrix of tiles, where each tile can have one of the 13 values that determine if the corresponding tile in the scene is a brick, or contains a coin etc. These 13 values include all possible combinations of objects that can occur in a tile at once. An agent perceives the contents of the tile. If the tile contains a monster, the agent also perceives the monster's type, its current location, and its speed in both the horizontal and vertical directions. An agent controls Mario, the character shown in the middle of the screen near the bottom of figure 7.9. The actions available to the agent are same as those available to a human player through the game pad in a game of Mario. An agent can move right or left or can stay still. It can jump while moving or standing. It can move at two different speeds. Acceleration is finite, so changing velocity takes time.

An agent's actions have immediate effect only on the locations near Mario, so we simplified the state to include only the 5 × 5 tile space around Mario (as opposed to the 16 × 22 total scene). We created an initial RL agent that had the above actions.

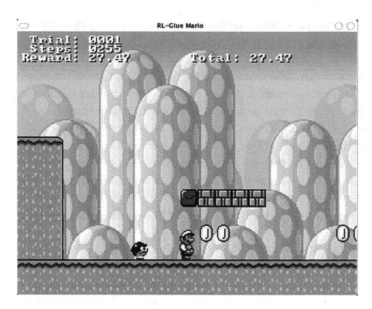

Figure 7.9
Screen shot from Infinite Mario.

It dynamically generated more than a million RL rules to cover each of the states it encountered. This agent failed to show any significant learning after training on 2,000 trials.

To facilitate generalization and learning, we introduced modifications to both the state structure and the operator structure. In the state, we used state elaborations to create an object-based representation relative to the agent. A typical Mario trial contains many objects, including monsters, coins, pits, question blocks, pipes (which may or may not contain a monster), raised platforms and the finish line. Thus, the state representation changes from the form "the tile at position (x, y) is type t," to "there exists a pit at a distance of three tiles." Because a tile can include multiple objects, this new representation explicitly decomposes a conjunction (the type) into its component objects and then makes them relative to the agent. Representing position relative to the agent is more likely to generalize to future situations because of the locality of agent actions.

We also modified the operator structure by adding hierarchical operators, similar to approaches described in the Blocks World. The hierarchy is based on a GOMS analysis (Card, Moran, and Newell 1983) of Mario performed by John, Vera, and Newell (1990) that predicted behavior of a human expert playing Mario. That analysis was implemented in an early version of Soar and demonstrated that using some very simple hand-coded heuristics, the model could predict the behavior of the human expert. Their analysis makes a distinction between keystroke-level and functional-level operators. Keystroke-level operators (KLOs), the primitive actions available to the human user, can be performed using a keyboard or a joystick. For Infinite Mario, these include moving right or left, jumping, and changing speed. Functional-level operators (FLOs) are a collection of keystroke-level operators that, when performed in succession, perform a specific task—for example, moving toward goal or grabbing a coin.

The game of Mario contains a limited number of functional-level operators, as do most computer games. For completing most trials successfully, a few FLOs are sufficient, such as move-toward-goal, tackle-monster, grab-coin, search-question-block and avoid-pit. In the GOMS analysis, a human expert selects between these FLOs on the basis of local conditions. If nothing is in the way, the human moves to right toward the goal; if a monster is nearby, tackling the monster gains preference. For this agent, we enriched the state by creating state-elaboration rules that used the distance of the objects from the agent to compute attributes such as "is-threat" for monsters and "is-reachable" for coins and question blocks. These attributes convert specific values of distance into qualitative ranges, which decreases the effective state space.

Figure 7.10 shows the operator hierarchy used in our agent. At the top level (level 1), five operators are proposed. All of these except for "Move to Goal" can be

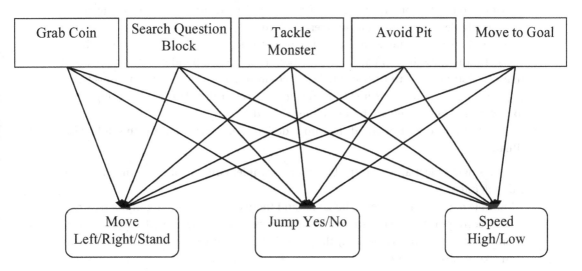

Figure 7.10
Problem-space hierarchy for a Soar agent.

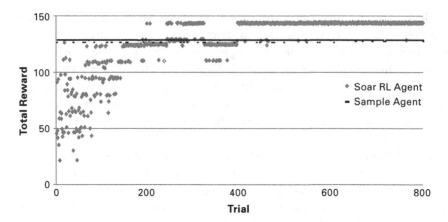

Figure 7.11
Performance of an RL agent learning both KLOs and FLOs in comparison to a hand-coded sample agent (level type 0, difficulty 0, seed 121).

instantiated with multiple objects; for example, the agent has two operators proposed for "Grab Coin" if it perceives two coins. These operators are implemented via the primitive KLOs move left/right, jump yes/no, and speed high/low. This structure is programmed into Soar via operator-proposal rules. The RL rules for the FLOs test for a proposed operator and the object relevant to that operator. For example, the RL rule for Grab-Coin tests for the existence of a coin and its relative position to the agent. This greatly decreases the total number of RL rules.

Figure 7.11 shows the agent's performance as it learns RL knowledge for both the FLOs and the KLOs in comparison to the performance of a hand-coded sample agent that was distributed with the Infinite Mario environment. Note that the agent is learning at two levels at once. As it is learning when to select the FLOs, it is learning when to select the KLOs necessary to apply the selected FLOs.

The current object-oriented learning design performs well in the following situations:

• Only single object affects agent behavior. Example: Only a coin or a monster is in close vicinity.

• Multiple objects can influence behavior and there exists an ordering in the selection of the corresponding FLOs so that both objects can be dealt with appropriately. Example: If two coins are present, the coin that is closer can be collected before the coin that is farther away.

• Multiple objects can influence behavior but there is a clear preference between the execution of the FLOs related to the objects. Example: If a coin and a monster are nearby, tackling the monster is always preferred over collecting the coin.

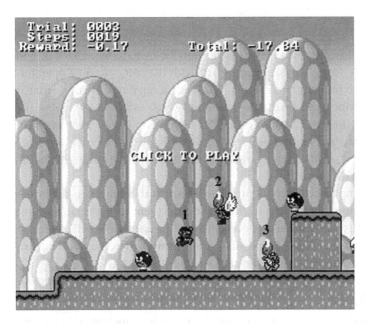

Figure 7.12
Example of a situation in which the independence assumption of the RL object-oriented approach
fails.

In some situations where there are multiple objects, the independence assumption
that is implicit in the design of the RL rules can break down so that the agent fails to
learn the best policy. The current design forces the agent to select a single object at a
time to respond to. Consider the example scenario in figure 7.12, where there is a
flying koopa (labeled 2) and a walking koopa (labeled 3). In the current design, the
agent selects between two instantiations of the "Tackle Monster" operator—one for
the flying koopa and one for the walking koopa. If it selects "Tackle Monster" for the
flying koopa (2), the converged policy dictates that the agent take a step toward
the right, because in doing so it can avoid the flying koopa and move a step closer to
the goal. However, this results in the agent's colliding with the walking koopa (3),
which is moving to the left, and the game ends with a high negative reward. If the
agent selects "Tackle Monster" for the walking koopa, the agent should execute a
right-jump step that eliminates the walking koopa. However, in the current situation
the agent collides with the flying koopa in the air and earns a huge negative reward.
Moving left is the correct move, but it is a sub-optimal move in both the policies. The
object-oriented design greatly decreases the number of rules needed for each operator,
and in general it speeds learning. However, performance suffers in cases where the
independence assumption fails.

7.4   Analysis of Requirements

Adding reinforcement learning furthers the achievement of requirements R12 and R13. In the case of R12 (comprehensive learning), RL adds the ability to tune operator-evaluation rules that use numeric preferences. This adds a capability beyond what is possible in chunking, which can learn new rules but which is not able to tune the preference values of existing rules. More generally, there is no direct mechanism in chunking to capture statistical regularities. In the case of R13 (incremental learning), RL is incremental, with a small constant overhead for updating the values of the RL rules involved in recent decisions.

Reinforcement learning is related to R8 (innate likes and dislikes) in that it provides a mechanism for learning from them by incorporating them as internal rewards. However, RL doesn't determine the likes and dislikes of an agent. (We will return to R8 in chapter 11, where we explore the possible relationship between appraisal theories of emotion and a subset of possible innate likes and dislikes.)

Although the addition of RL is an important piece of providing comprehensive learning, there are still open research questions to be pursued relating to RL in Soar:

• Although rules are an expressive representation for the value function, there are no capabilities in Soar to refine the conditions of rules once they have been created. Chunking does provide a means to learn RL rules by creating rules when the reasoning in the selection space returns numeric preferences.

• Currently there are many parameters for RL in Soar, such as whether eligibility traces are used, whether SARSA or Q-learning is used (for evidence that Q-learning is what is used by humans, see Walsh and Anderson 2010), and then within each of those schemes there are specific values or control policies for learning rate and temperature/epsilon decay. We need to converge on a single implementation that is used for all tasks. One approach would be to determine a single set of specific parameter values; however, in view of the inherent variation in tasks and rewards, that seems unlikely to be possible. A more promising approach would be to develop algorithms that automatically adjust these parameters on the basis of an agent's performance and experience. For example, the ALeRT algorithm uses trends in reward sequences to automatically adjust both the learning rate and the exploration rate (Cutumisu et al. 2008).

8 Semantic Memory

with Yongjia Wang and Nate Derbinsky

This chapter describes Soar's semantic memory, a repository for long-term declarative knowledge that supplements what is contained in short-term working memory (and production memory). Episodic memory, which contains memories of the agent's experiences, is described in chapter 9. The knowledge encoded in episodic memory is organized temporally. Specific information is embedded within the context of when it was experienced (such as a memory of attending a football game in Michigan Stadium), whereas knowledge in semantic memory is independent of any specific context, and represents more general facts about the world (such as that Michigan Stadium is where the University of Michigan football team plays its home games).

For many years, Soar didn't have separate long-term declarative memories; all knowledge had to either be maintained in working memory or encoded in production memory. Although long-term declarative knowledge can be maintained in working memory, such an approach is problematic. To access information in working memory, rules must have conditions that test the appropriate working-memory elements, starting from the state, in order to match the desired structure. Therefore, all long-term data must be linked to the top state, either directly or through other structures. In order to provide uniform access to long-term facts stored in working memory, there must be a common representational structure for all facts, such as representing all long-term entities as substructures of the state via the common attribute, such as ^entity. Unfortunately, even though the performance of Soar scales well with the number of rules, the rule-matching algorithm doesn't scale well when there are large numbers of structures sharing a common attribute in working memory. For an agent that pursues a variety of tasks and exists for days and months, the long-term data that accumulate in working memory would overwhelm the rule-matching algorithm.

An alternative approach to storing such information in working memory is to store it in production rules. In this approach, rules are created with conditions that test for a query, such as "Ann Arbor & state," and the action creates the result, such as "Michigan." Data chunking (described in chapter 6) uses chunking to create such rules, and it would also be possible to have another architectural mechanism create such rules. The issue with using rules to store semantic information in Soar is that a separate rule is required for each way the data can be accessed. In the example above, one rule is required to retrieve Michigan as the state of Ann Arbor and another rule is required to retrieve Ann Arbor as a city in Michigan. In general, if the goal is to allow access to data using any subset of its structure, a combinatorial number of rules are required to support access via all possible subsets of attributes of the declarative knowledge. For example, if an object has five attributes, 31 rules are required. Such an explosion in rules for objects with many attributes would require large amounts of memory and could ultimately slow performance.

The major problem with both working memory and production memory is that they are not designed to efficiently store and retrieve large bodies of declarative knowledge. To avoid their shortcomings, Soar has a separate long-term declarative memory, called *semantic memory*, where the agent can store structures that originate in working memory but may be relevant to some future situation or task. Semantic memory can also store knowledge preloaded from some other existing knowledge bases, such as Cyc (Lenat and Guha 1990; Lenat 1995) or WordNet (Miller 1995). In both cases, procedural knowledge must exist to retrieve knowledge from the semantic memory at appropriate times.

Under this approach, working memory maintains structures that are directly relevant to the current task, including an agent's perception, its current goals, entailments of its perception and goals (computed via state elaborations), the results of deliberate inferences (computed by operator applications), and any history of events that are relevant to its current decision making (maintained by operator applications or retrieved from episodic memory). In contrast, semantic memory holds facts, goals, and other structures that may be useful in the future, such as "Ann Arbor is in Michigan," "birds are a kind of animal," or "room 37 is connected via a doorway to the east to room 45." The agent can access semantic memory, but that access requires a deliberate retrieval.

Consistent with our earlier distinction between knowledge search and problem search (see chapter 3), retrieval of knowledge from semantic memory is knowledge search. It doesn't involve a combination of knowledge search and problem search, as is found in systems like Cyc. Instead, any problem search, such as deductive or inductive reasoning over retrieved facts, including initiating multiple cascading retrievals from semantic memory, is controlled by the deliberate selection and application of operators (which is itself controlled by procedural knowledge). Consider, as an example, an agent's attempt to determine (for the first time) the time of day in Ann Arbor when the morning sun first hits the Eiffel Tower. The approach described here involves a combination of retrievals from long-term memory, such as determining what city the Eiffel Tower is in (Paris), what country it is in (France), what time zone it is in, what is the time difference with Ann Arbor, and so on. Procedural knowledge initiates the appropriate retrievals, then uses and combines the results to create follow-on retrievals until enough data have been retrieved to allow computation of the answer.

In order to be both general and flexible, there are no built-in relations (such as "isa" or "part-of") with specialized inference. Such relations and the associated procedural knowledge for interpreting them can be encoded in Soar, but they are not built in. Thus, Soar's module for semantic memory is relatively simple, sharing many properties of a relational database, although there are important subtleties in how it interacts with the rest of the architecture. This approach is consistent with the implementations of long-term declarative memories in other cognitive architectures, such as ACT-R (Anderson 2007) and CLARION (Sun 2006), but is a departure from knowledge-representation systems, such as Cyc, in which extended inference during knowledge retrieval is possible.

The combination of working memory and semantic memory is analogous to memory hierarchies in computer systems, where there are multiple types of memories with different performance characteristics. There are small, fast memories (such as registers and caches), and there is main memory (which is significantly larger, but slower to access). These memories contain the information relevant to active processes. However, these memories are volatile, and they are small relative to the amount of information required for all tasks, so computers also have secondary memories, implemented in a non-volatile but slower technology (such as magnetic disk or flash memory). In Soar, working memory holds the information that directly affects current decision making by influencing which rules match, whereas structures in semantic memory must first be deliberately retrieved into working memory before they can affect decision making.

Semantic memory has long been an active area of research in psychology. ACT (Anderson 1983) was the first cognitive architecture to have a long-term declarative memory module. In ACT-R, the long-term declarative memory holds all the structures that occur in the system's buffers. The specific properties of ACT-R's declarative memory are based on a rational analysis of how to retrieve the best item from long-term memory, thus providing important functionality (Anderson and Schooler 1991). In addition, the details of the declarative memory allow ACT-R to model a rich set of psychological phenomena and human data, such as the Fan effect (Anderson and Reder 1999), category learning (Anderson 1988), and theory of list memory (Anderson, Bothell, Lebiere, and Matessa 1998). Our implementation of semantic memory doesn't yet include all the functionality of the declarative memory found in humans or in

ACT-R. Instead, we have initially focused on basic functionality and efficiency (Derbinsky and Laird 2010), because the native long-term declarative memory in ACT-R doesn't scale well to large knowledge bases (Douglass, Ball, and Rodgers 2009). An active goal of our research is to expand the functionality of Soar to match that of human memory while maintaining an efficient implementation.

There has also been significant research in incorporating semantic memories in other cognitive architectures, including Icarus (Langley and Choi 2006), Companions (Forbus and Hinrichs 2006), and LIDA (Franklin and Patterson 2006). There have also been attempts to incorporate large knowledge bases in cognitive architectures. The Companions architecture uses a subset of the Cyc knowledge base, and there have been efforts to integrate WordNet with ACT-R (Douglass, Ball, and Rodgers 2009; Emond 2006), Cyc with ACT-R (Ball, Rodgers, and Gluck 2004), and WordNet with Soar (Londsdale and Rytting 2001), but these approaches haven't achieved the performance required for a real-time agent.

Knowledge is retrieved from semantic memory using operator application; however, it can indirectly support any PSCM function when it is used in a substate. The general approach is that the information retrieved from semantic memory is one step in the reasoning required to generate the results of a substate, and it can end up elaborating the superstate, creating a preference for the superoperator or modifying the superstate as part of applying the superoperator. As a side effect, chunking compiles the processing in the substate into a rule, so that in the future repeated retrievals from semantic memory for the same situation are not necessary.

From the broader perspective of the PSCM, semantic memory extends the representation of state beyond working memory. Instead of representing everything that the agent knows about the world in the state in working memory, the agent only represents what is important for performing PSCM functions. The agent can access information in semantic memory, but that requires a deliberate decision with additional knowledge search, creating a tradeoff between minimizing the directly available state and introducing processing to manage the contents of the state. Thus, semantic memory helps maintain bounded access to procedural memory by eliminating the need to match a large number of working-memory elements to production memory. From a problem-space perspective, we are expanding problem-space search by adding operators to access semantic memory in order to maintain bounds on knowledge search in procedural memory.

Section 8.1 presents an overview of semantic memory in Soar. Section 8.2 provides the details of how structures are encoded and stored in the long-term semantic store. Section 8.3 describes how semantic structures are retrieved. Section 8.4 includes demonstrations of using semantic memory in Soar. Section 8.5 presents an analysis of its role in meeting the requirements of chapter 2, and lays out our plans for future work on semantic memory.

8.1   Semantic Memory in Soar

Figure 8.1 shows the basic structure of working memory and semantic memory in Soar, independent of procedural memory, the decision procedure, the input and output components, and other components. The structures in semantic memory can be preloaded or can be incrementally built up by an agent by storing structures from working memory. The representation of knowledge in semantic memory is the same as in working memory—both include graph structures that are composed of elements consisting of an identifier (circles), an attribute (arrows), and a value (circles or constants). As was noted in chapter 4, the values can be either identifiers (non-terminal nodes in the graph) or constants (terminal nodes). For simplicity, the attribute labels are not shown in figure 8.1, and the numbers 1, 2, and 3 are used as representative constants. As illustrated in the figure, the elements in working

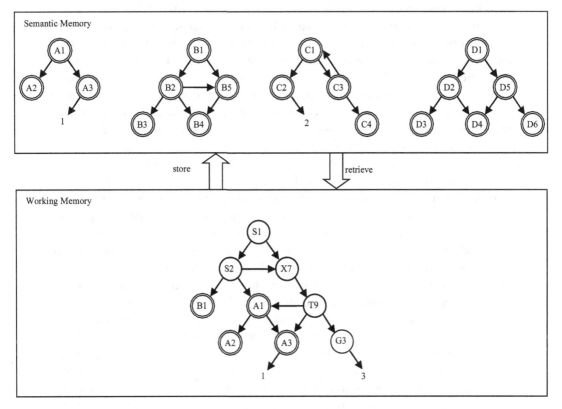

Figure 8.1
Example of interaction between working memory and semantic memory.

memory form a single connected graph structure, whereas the elements in semantic memory form multiple disconnected graphs because they are based on stored subsets of working memory.

The interaction between the two memories occurs through storage from working memory to semantic memory or retrieval from semantic memory to working memory. Retrieval is based on a *cue*—a partial description of an object in semantic memory, where an object is defined as the set of working-memory elements that share a common identifier. A cue can contain specific attributes and values, and/or attributes with unspecified (variable) values. The retrieval process searches for the object in semantic memory that best matches those structures. In order to retrieve the most recent information, retrieval is biased toward the most recently created and accessed structures. If a match is found in semantic memory, and the object doesn't already exist in working memory, the object is created in working memory and linked to the *retrieved* structure on the state (not shown in figure 8.1). If the matched object already exists in working memory, a link is created to it from the retrieved structure.

There isn't necessarily a direct correlation between all structures in working memory and semantic memory. There may be transient structures in working memory that are never stored into semantic memory (for example, the position of blocks relative to each other in the Blocks World, or the exact sensory values in the current state). Moreover, there are usually many structures in semantic memory that are not in working memory. For example, the names of cities in the state of Michigan may be stored in semantic memory and do not need to be retrieved into working memory when an agent is attempting to solve a math problem.

Figure 8.1 also shows an important change that was necessary to support the connection between semantic memory and working memory. In the original design of Soar, all working-memory elements and their constituent parts were transient. Identifiers were created dynamically as needed in working-memory elements; their purpose was to provide a means of connecting structures in working memory together. With the introduction of semantic memory, some structures continue to exist in semantic memory even after they are removed from working memory. In order to maintain the identity of structures in semantic memory, the identifiers of structures stored in semantic memory maintain their identities throughout the existence of the agent. Examples of such *long-term identifiers* are shown in figure 8.1 as double circles. All identifiers in semantic memory are long-term identifiers and those long-term identifiers are used when a structure from semantic memory is retrieved to working memory; identifiers that exist only in working memory are short-term identifiers. In general, a long-term identifier represents a concept or an object that the agent could encounter or make reference to in the future. If semantic memory is preloaded with a knowledge base, long-term identifiers are allocated for the identifiers of the concepts and objects in the knowledge base.

In figure 8.1, identifiers A1, A2, A3, and B1 are long-term identifiers that have been retrieved into working memory. The long-term identifiers also allow working memory to contain a subset of a larger long-term graph structure, such as the element with B1 as the value. In this case, B1 is in working memory, but the structures for which it is an identifier are only in semantic memory (the elements that include B2, B3, B4, and B5). If B1 alone is sufficient for the agent's reasoning, the remainder of the B structure need not be retrieved. However, if additional detail is required, the agent can retrieve the remainder of the B graph structure at any time by retrieving the substructure of the B1 long-term identifier directly from semantic memory.

Long-term identifiers are one means of creating new global symbolic constants. Besides existing in semantic and working memory, such identifiers are stored in productions learned via chunking, and in structures in episodic memory. (See chapter 9.)

8.2 Encoding and Storage

Encoding is the step of determining which working-memory elements should be stored in long-term memory; storage includes how the elements are represented and stored in the memory. In theory, initiation of encoding can be either deliberate or automatic. Soar currently uses deliberate initiation, in which the agent's procedural knowledge designates which working-memory structures are to be stored in semantic memory.

We have adopted the deliberate approach because the obvious method of storing all structures that occur in working memory in long-term semantic memory has some unresolved problems, and we have yet to develop an alternative automatic mechanism. One problem is that many structures in working memory are transitory and indicate only that something is true in a certain situation. Thus, the fact that block A was on block C at some point during problem solving is not a general fact about the world worth storing in semantic memory. Moreover, an agent can create hypothetical situations in working memory, which contain "facts" that might never be true. For example, a Soar agent can imagine being driven off a cliff and destroyed. If those structures are automatically stored in semantic memory without some annotation that they were imagined, the agent could become confused. One property of Soar that underlies these issues is that working-memory elements do not have associated truth values. The truthfulness (and usefulness) of elements in Soar is determined by how they relate to other structures, such as whether they are created in a substate in which hypothetical reasoning is being pursued. For these reasons, Soar currently supports only deliberate encoding; however, whether it is possible to develop an automatic encoding scheme that avoids the issues listed above is a topic of active research.

Encoding for semantic memory is initiated by a rule (usually as part of an operator application) that creates a working-memory element that links the object to be stored to a special structure on the state (the smem link), similar to the way output is initiated. As will be illustrated in figures below, the smem structure exists on all states, and all semantic-memory operations can be performed locally on every state. All of the working-memory elements of the object being stored (all of those that share the same identifier) are added to or updated in semantic memory. As part of storing the working-memory elements, all short-term identifiers in those working-memory elements are converted into long-term identifiers. The letter-number combination that labels an identifier (such as A2 or S1) becomes permanent, and subsequent retrievals of semantic-memory elements with that identifier produce the same associated letter and number. Long-term identifiers are maintained in rules learned by chunking and in structures learned by episodic memory, thus providing a means for binding long-term structures together. Future storage commands for this identifier overwrite previously stored attributes and values of that identifier, thus providing a mechanism for updating long-term semantic-memory structures.

Figures 8.2 and 8.3 show how new semantic knowledge is encoded for a simple example from the arithmetic domain using the processing structure described in chapter 6. The difference here is that the information about the relationships between digits (^next and ^previous) represented at the top of each of these figures are in semantic memory, whereas in chapter 5 this information was completely and solely represented in working memory. In this example, the agent is poised to add two numbers (1 and 3) in the rightmost column of a problem.

The lower left panel of 8.2 shows a subset of the contents of working memory before any calculations have taken place; the lower right panel shows the contents of working memory after the calculation. The structure is the same as that used in figure 6.9, except that in this case we use an expanded representation of each number in which there is a long-term symbol for every digit from 0 through 9. This expansion allows there to be multiple properties and relations for a number. In working memory, N2 and N4 are long-term identifiers and have been retrieved from semantic memory. This shows how the same structure is represented in both working memory and semantic memory at the same time. Using identifiers N2 and N4, the agent can access the primitive features of a number, such as the digit representing the number ("1") and the English word used to refer to the number ("one"), and relations to other numbers (via next and previous attributes), which are used when counting. The figure also shows the existence of the ^smem link (which is where commands for initiating store to and retrieval from semantic memory are created, and where results from a retrieval are deposited).

The lower right panel of figure 8.2 shows the contents of working memory after the operator compute-result creates a new structure, with the newly created attribute

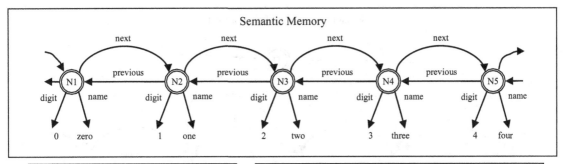

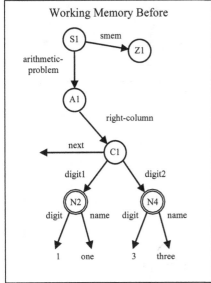

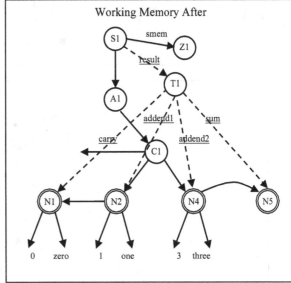

Figure 8.2
Subset of semantic and working memory during addition problem before and after a result is created in working memory.

names underlined and the new links shown as dashed arrows. This structure has identifier T1, and includes not only the sum of the addition, but also links to the symbols that stand for the two numbers added together (^addend1 and ^addend2). In computing the sum, all that is necessary is to create the ^sum link from T1 to N5; thus, at this point the substructure of N5 isn't retrieved into working memory. In addition to computing the sum, the carry is computed; it is "0." Computing the carry requires knowing that "0" is the value, so the value is retrieved along with the long-term identifier, N1. Additional structures, such as the relation between N4 and N5 and the relation between N2 and N1, were retrieved from semantic memory when

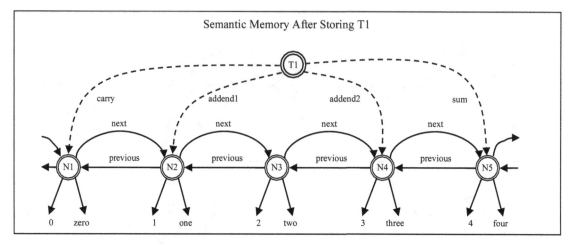

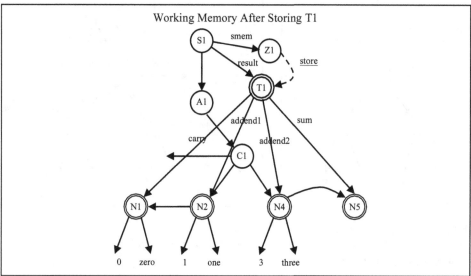

Figure 8.3
Semantic and working memory before and after result is stored.

N4 and N2 were first retrieved; for simplicity, those are not shown in the left panel of figure 8.2.

Once the result structure (T1) is created, the agent can store it in semantic memory for future use. Figure 8.3 shows how this is done: the agent creates a working-memory element using the attribute store, which links the ^smem command structure to identifier T1. After this element is created, Soar converts T1 to a long-term identifier and copies all the working-memory elements that have T1 as their identifier into semantic memory. If T1 already exists in semantic memory, all of the structures with T1 as their identifier are replaced with the structures in working memory. Structures that were in semantic memory but not in working memory are removed. Note that working-memory elements with T1 as their values (such as Z1 ^store T1) are not added to semantic memory; only those with T1 as their identifier are stored into semantic memory. In this case, all the values of the working-memory elements are already long-term identifiers; however, if they were not, they would be converted to long-term identifiers as part of the storage process. The storage is only "one level," so any deeper substructures not already in semantic memory would have to be explicitly stored.

8.3   Retrieval

Retrieval is initiated by the creation of a cue on the semantic-memory command structure. The cue is a set of working-memory elements that share the same identifier. If the value of a working-memory element in the cue is a long-term identifier (or a constant), then that value must exactly match a structure in semantic memory. If the value in the cue is a short-term identifier, it acts like a variable and the object must have that attribute, but there is no constraint on the value.

The left panel of figure 8.4 shows an example of a simple cue for the digit "1" (solid lines). After the cue is created, semantic memory is searched. If a successful match is found, the structure from semantic memory is recreated in working memory, including all attributes and values of the matched identifier. If multiple semantic memory structures are found that correctly match the cue, the structure that was most recently stored or retrieved is retrieved. If no exact match is found, a working-memory element signifying failure is created on the ^smem structure. In this case, the search is for a structure that has the attribute "digit" and the value "1." N2 is found, and, as shown, all of elements that have it as their identifier are added to working memory. The retrieved structures have dashed lines.

The right panel of figure 8.4 shows the result of a more complex cue. In this case, the agent created a cue to recall a previously learned addition fact so that it could be used for a subtraction problem. In this case, the agent created a cue to solve the equation "5 + ? = 8." As the figure shows, the retrieval was performed using long-term

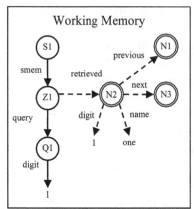
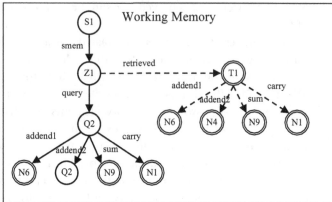

Figure 8.4
Example retrievals from semantic memory in working memory.

identifiers for "5," "8," and "0" (for the carry). The result is the structure with the value of addend2 filled in with long-term identifier for "3," which in this case is N4. N4 on its own can be used for some internal reasoning, and only when the structure underlying the long-term identifier is needed does an additional retrieval have to be performed on that identifier. In this case, a retrieval of N4 would recover its entire substructure, including that it represents the digit "3."

Semantic memory doesn't directly support retrieval using a multi-level cue in which there are working-memory elements that constrain the substructure of the values in the top-level working-memory elements of the cue. The effect of a multi-level retrieval can be approximated by first retrieving long-term identifiers that have the desired substructure, then using those long-term identifiers as the values in a single-level retrieval.

To speed the retrieval process, semantic memory implements two optimizations (Derbinsky and Laird 2010). First, the cue elements are internally ordered using metadata from semantic memory, such that rarely used attributes and attribute-value pairs are considered before those that are more common. Because retrievals are conjunctive, this minimizes retrieval candidates and detects failure early, thereby eliminating searching and reducing the overall retrieval time. The second optimization is to maintain an inverted index on the graph of semantic-memory elements. With this structure, it is efficient to retrieve a list of long-term identifiers augmented by just an attribute or an attribute-value pair. As we show in subsection 8.4.3, the retrieval process, which in the theoretical worst case scales linearly with the number of long-term identifiers in semantic memory, shows little or no degradation in retrieval time over a large set of cues in very large knowledge bases.

8.4   Demonstrations of Semantic Memory

In section 8.4.1, we use multi-column arithmetic to demonstrate the use of semantic memory to store and retrieve structures that are accessed in multiple ways. In section 8.4.2, we use Rooms World to demonstrate the use of semantic memory to encode static knowledge about an environment—in this case, the layout of rooms that the agent encounters. The large knowledge base task provides us with an environment in which we can evaluate the performance of semantic memory.

8.4.1   Multi-Column Arithmetic

Semantic memory provides a means of transferring knowledge from one situation to another. In the arithmetic example, facts about sums of number pairs are recorded in semantic memory when they are computed by the counting procedure. These transfer to future situations when the same numbers are added or subtracted. The general counting procedure requires multiple operator applications and rule firings in Soar (linear with the magnitude of the second number being added or subtracted); the memory retrieval requires a single access to semantic memory. More specifically, semantic memory associates a question and its answer by recording the structure representing a fact as shown in figure 8.4, such as "5 + 3 = 8" being encoded as (T1 ^addend1 5 ^addend2 3 ^sum 8 ^carry 0). In a later situation, if "5" and "3" are again presented as the value for ^addend1 and ^addend2 respectively, this structure is retrieved and eliminates the need to perform the counting again.

   If the problem is structured so that the calculations are performed in substates, chunking learns rules that directly produce the answer for specific problems. Moreover, if a problem is decomposed so that each arithmetic calculation is computed in a separate substate, chunking will learn rules for each calculation. The benefit of learning declarative structures is that the arithmetic facts learned from addition can be reused for subtraction and vice versa, whereas chunking learns rules for the specific calculation that was performed. For example, when "5 + 3 = 8" is learned, if it is stored and retrieved appropriately in semantic memory, it eliminates computation not only for "5 + 3 = 8" and "3 + 5 = 8" but also for "8 – 3 = 5" and "8 – 5 = 3," because the addition problem and the subtraction problem depend on the same arithmetic fact. In general, this is the transfer learning effect that arises from a flexible declarative representation compared to using production rules.

   Orthogonal to transfer issues, chunking can chunk over semantic retrieval and compile the entire procedure into a single rule to speed execution in the future. Although Soar can transition directly from the counting procedure to chunks, it would then be unable to take advantage of the transfer provided by the semantic memory between addition and subtraction problems. Semantic-memory retrieval is more expensive than firing a single rule because it requires multiple operators to create a

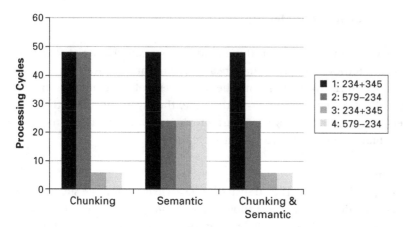

Figure 8.5
Interaction between semantic learning and chunking in multi-column arithmetic.

cue and access the retrieved structure, as well as incurring the cost of searching semantic memory. Therefore, chunking over a semantic retrieval can provide further increases
in speed. Intuitively, chunking speeds execution via practice, whereas semantic learning acquires flexible knowledge structures that can transfer to different procedures
without having practiced in exactly the same situation. Figure 8.5 shows the improvement obtained from the two different types of learning.

The addition problem in this test is "234 + 345 = 579." The subtraction problem is
"579 – 345 = 234." Each is the reverse of the other, and both depend on the same set
of arithmetic facts. In this experiment, the agent alternates between addition and
subtraction, first doing addition (labeled 1 in the legend of figure 8.5), then subtraction (2), then repeating addition (3), and then repeating subtraction (4). Without any
learning, the task takes 47 cycles for both the addition problem and the subtraction
problem. Chunking provides no benefit for the subtraction problem, because the
chunks are learned for solving addition. However, chunks are learned for all levels of
the hierarchy, including how to process a column completely. Thus, only six cycles
are required to solve a problem that agent has experienced before: three for processing
the columns, two for advancing to the next columns, and one for terminating the
problem). With semantic learning, the facts do not transfer within a problem, but the
facts learned in the addition problem transfer to the subtract problem (and to future
addition problems). The facts replace only the counting in the compute-result sub-
problem, because no facts are stored for the results of a completed column. Column
facts are more specific because they include the positions of numbers in the problem
and whether there are carries. Column facts could be stored, but that would involve
deliberately storing facts that would rarely be used. When chunking and semantic

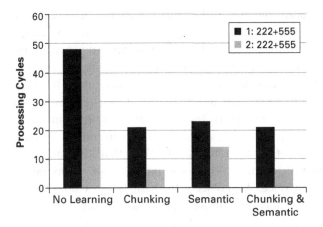

Figure 8.6
Within-trial and across-trials transfer using semantic learning and chunking in multi-column arithmetic.

memory are combined, the first subtraction problem gets the benefit from semantic memory, and the repeated problems get the gains from chunking.

Both chunking and semantic memory will see within-trial improvement if the numbers in two columns are repeated. For example, if the problem is 222 + 555 = 777, there is significant improvement the first time the problem is attempted when either learning mechanism is used (figure 8.6). Here the no-learning case takes 48 cycles. Chunking learns from the first column, and the learned rule immediately transfers to the remaining columns. Semantic memory is able to transfer the addition fact for 2 + 5 = 7 learned in the first column. Chunking and semantic memory both see improvements on a second trial, because the first column can then be solved from memory. When both mechanisms are used, chunking eliminates the need for all retrievals from semantic memory.

In this formulation, there is no direct role for reinforcement learning, as no underlying search is needed to determine which operator to select at each stage of the problem. The agent already knows the procedure for performing multi-column addition and subtraction and is learning the facts associated with its execution so it can perform it more efficiently. If the agent did not have knowledge of the procedures, reinforcement learning could learn the ordering of operators, such as when to do a carry, using feedback received from correct and incorrect answers.

8.4.2 Rooms World

In Rooms World, there are no immutable facts, such as the arithmetic facts from the multi-column arithmetic domain; however, there are stable aspects of the environment, including the location of walls and doors in a room. There are two problems with maintaining these structures in working memory. First, for very large environments, working memory grows to be very large, which can make it costly to match rules. Second, if the agent ever moves to a novel environment and doesn't maintain the structures from the first environment, it loses all memory of the first environment and will be unable to access that information if it ever returns to the original environment. Thus, one role for semantic memory is as a long-term memory of an agent's knowledge of the relatively stable aspects of its environment. Toward this end, we implemented a variant of our agent for Rooms World that stores all room and object information in semantic memory. The information about rooms never changes, so it has to be stored only once. With objects, the basic features of an object don't change, so they too are stored only once; however, an object's location changes when it is moved, and the agent updates this information in semantic memory whenever it changes.

Storing information about the rooms and their connections in semantic memory requires some changes in how the agent accesses that information. To motivate these changes, we take a step back and describe how room information is used and stored in the original agent. First, the agent uses room information to determine which rooms it can move to next and to estimate distances to other rooms. The data structure for each room includes information about location of the room, its walls, doorways, and the neighboring rooms each doorway connects to. Other important room information includes whether a room has been visited and whether it has been cleaned. Initially, an agent has only information about the room in which it starts and information about the existence of neighboring rooms. When the agent moves into a room, it senses the locations of all walls and doors and the existence of neighboring rooms (but not their identity). When an agent is searching for blocks, it attempts to visit rooms that it knows exist, but which it has not visited or which are not completely emptied of blocks.

In the original agent, everything it knows about a room is in working memory. That isn't true when the data have been stored in semantic memory. Thus, it is easy in the original agent to have a rule that matches all rooms that have not yet been visited and proposes an operator for visiting each of those rooms. In the semantic-memory agent, there is no guarantee that the information about such rooms is in working memory, so instead the agent must query semantic memory to find a room that has not been visited (or cleaned). This changes the search for such information from a search over working memory by rules to a search over semantic memory. This change introduces a bias because semantic memory retrieves the unvisited (or uncleaned) room that the agent most recently visited or discovered. A similar change must be made to retrieve information about objects that haven't been moved to the storage room.

Although these are significant changes in how information about rooms and objects is retrieved, the effect on the agent's design is localized to the proposal of a few operators. For the most part, the agent is unchanged, because the majority of its reasoning is about information related to the room it is currently in, and in both the original and the semantic-memory agent the information about the current room is maintained in working memory.

The semantic-memory agent does include some additional changes. Specifically, it includes operators that deliberately store information about objects, rooms, walls, doorways, and the connections between rooms into semantic memory when it first visits a room. The semantic-memory agent also attempts to minimize the number of elements in working memory by deliberately removing room structures that are distant from the agent's current position. When the agent revisits a room, the relevant structures are retrieved from semantic memory.

The external behavior of the semantic-memory agent is unchanged from the original agent. Although operators are added to store and retrieve data from semantic memory, selecting and applying these operators has no observable effect on the time it takes the agent to perform its tasks.

The semantic-memory agent does have an advantage in that it doesn't require that the contents of working memory be maintained throughout the execution of the task. If working memory is cleared because the agent is taken to another environment, the semantic-memory agent dynamically retrieves from semantic memory the information it needs to perform its task. In the original agent, there is no way to recover information about the map once it has been removed from working memory.

One remaining question concerns how storing and retrieving structures from semantic memory affects the reactivity of the agent. The empirical question is whether the cost of matching large numbers of structures in working memory with rules is higher or lower than the cost of deliberately storing and retrieving those structures from semantic memory, and whether either of those costs is excessive. To explore this question, we created a simulation of the third floor of the University of Michigan's Beyster Building. Our simulation, which was based on the building's architectural plans, is shown here in figure 8.7. (For a more detailed evaluation of the use of declarative memories in the Rooms World agent, see Laird, Derbinsky, and Voigt 2011.) The third floor has about 200 rooms and doorways. As before, the agent's task is to find specific types of objects (square blocks) and move them to a specified room. In this case, there are four square blocks it must find and move to a nearby room. It takes the agent about an hour to explore the floor, find the four objects, and move them.

When the entire map is maintained in working memory, the total size of working memory grows to be approximately 8,500 elements. When semantic memory is used, there are, on average, approximately 800 elements in working memory. However,

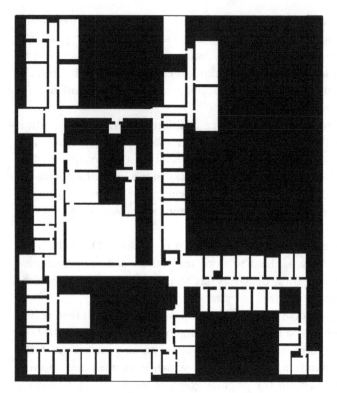

Figure 8.7
Floor plan of building used in experiments.

when the agent is planning a path to another room, it must retrieve room information from semantic memory into working memory for each room it considers during the search. This leads to an increase in the size of working memory. In long internal searches, working memory can grow to 2,000 elements.

Figure 8.8 shows the maximum time required for a processing cycle for the case in which the map and the object data are stored in working memory and the case in which they are stored in semantic memory. Both approaches are sufficiently efficient to support real-time behavior—their maximum cycle times are at least five times as fast as is required. Moreover, their average cycle times (not shown) stay below 0.02 millisecond. There is an upward trend when using working memory, which we attribute to the increasingly large amounts of data in working memory slowing the matcher. With semantic memory, there is little or no upward trend, and the maximum cycle time is usually significantly less than it is when only working memory is used. There are a few outliers for when semantic memory is used; these arise during look-ahead planning when the agent retrieves room information from semantic memory.

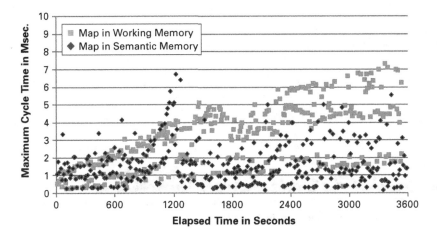

Figure 8.8
Maximum cycle time for a Rooms World agent that stores map information in either working memory or semantic memory.

These results suggest that each of the approaches is sufficient from a computational standpoint for problems of this size (and larger). In fact, we are surprised at how well the working-memory agent performs when there are 200 rooms and doorways in working memory, which is a testament to Soar's Rete matcher (Doorenbos 1994). Although not evident in this example, the performance of the working-memory agent is more susceptible to performance problems, because it is easy to write rules that partially match large combinations of rooms. To illustrate this point, we added a single rule that tests for combinations of rooms that are neighbors of the current room. This rule generates large numbers of partial matches—numbers that grow as more rooms are explored and added to its internal map, even though the rule never matches completely. Figure 8.9 shows the maximum cycle times for the agents from figure 8.8 with this additional rule, with the y axis extended from 10 to 60 milliseconds.

The cost of using working memory to store the map is obvious and increases as the map grows, ultimately exceeding our threshold of 50 msec. The agent using semantic memory sees some degradation in performance; however, it ability to maintain only a small subset of rooms in working memory minimizes the effect. In general, semantic memory spreads potentially expensive knowledge searches over multiple processing cycles so that the reactivity of a single processing cycle is never in jeopardy.

8.4.3 Large-Declarative-Memory Task

For a semantic memory that accumulates large bodies of knowledge, efficient access poses a significant computational challenge. As an example, Douglass, Ball, and

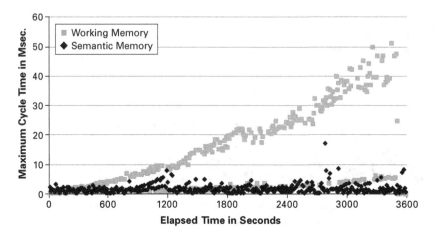

Figure 8.9
Maximum cycle time for Rooms World agents with expensive rule added.

Rodgers (2009) developed a cognitive model that made use of a large subset of the WordNet lexicon (Miller 1995) to aid communication with Air Force officers. They found that the native ACT-R declarative memory module was unable to load their full knowledge base (232,500 ACT-R declarative structures), and they found a statistically significant and intractable relationship between the number of declarative chunks and the retrieval time (peaking at about 190 msec for a four-element cue on 77,510 ACT-R declarative structures).

To incorporate their large store of declarative knowledge, Douglass et al. developed a custom module to outsource declarative retrieval matching to the PostgreSQL relational database management system. They reported retrieval times of about 40 msec with cues of 1–4 constraints on a derived subset, totaling 232,500 structures, of the WN-LEXICAL (Emond 2006) conversion of the WordNet 3 lexicon.

To evaluate the ability of Soar's semantic-memory implementation to encode large knowledge bases and to support efficient retrievals, we extended this empirical evaluation to the entire WN-LEXICAL data set (Derbinsky and Laird 2010). The full knowledge base has more than 820,000 structures, and once added to Soar's semantic memory (including all indexing structures) it requires about 400 megabytes of memory. We measured retrieval times for cues comparable to those issued by Douglass et al., randomly choosing ten nouns and forming a cue of seven elements from their full WordNet sense descriptions. Retrieval times were approximately constant, averaging 0.3 msec over ten runs each (SD = 0.01). Thus, our implementation demonstrates 100× faster retrievals on a comparable set of cues, scaling to a 3× larger store of declarative knowledge.

8.5   Analysis of Requirements

Adding semantic memory furthers the achievement of requirements R3, R4, R5, R12, and R13 without compromising other requirements, specifically those related to maintaining reactivity (R11).

R3:   Use large bodies of knowledge. Semantic memory directly supports efficient encoding and retrieval of long-term knowledge in very large declarative memories. The retrieval mechanism provides a rich language for cue-based retrieval, and the semantic memory supports storing all types of knowledge that is represented in working memory.

R4:   Use knowledge at different levels of generality. Semantic memory provides the mechanisms for long-term storage of symbolic information, including hierarchical representations that can be accessed via cue-based retrieval. The cues can be specific, including many features, even unique identifiers, or they can be general, with only a few features.

R5:   Represent diverse amounts of knowledge. Semantic memory provides a mechanism for the incremental accumulation of declarative knowledge, and agents can have varying levels of knowledge for different tasks.

R12:   Comprehensive learning. Semantic memory adds the ability to maintain long-term declarative structures, offloading working memory so that only information relevant to the current situation needs to be maintained there.

R13:   Incremental learning. Semantic memory is incremental and both storage and retrieval are implemented efficiently within Soar.

Semantic memory is a relatively recent addition to Soar, and there are still many open research questions. Three major research issues related to semantic memory are the following:

• Currently, Soar supports only deliberate storage to semantic memory. This requires the agent to attend to storing relevant structures, which can disrupt its task performance. We chose deliberate storage because the simple approach of storing all working memory structures in semantic memory was untenable. An automatic mechanism must detect when a structure isn't transitory or merely hypothetical, or at least must include sufficient context to determine its status. Our current hypothesis is that we can use meta-data maintained by episodic memory to determine which structures in working memory should be stored in semantic memory; however, this is speculative and requires more research.

• An additional problem that is related to the first is that Soar's semantic memory maintains only a single representation of a concept, whereas often it is useful to have different "views" of an object based on some limited context. Such a context is different from the specific temporal context when a concept is acquired, which is the basis for episodic memory. Fahlman's Scone system (Chen and Fahlman 2009) provides an example of a knowledge base with multiple contexts that could provide direction for this research.

• Currently, the matching of a cue for a retrieval is all-or-nothing and is biased only by the history of memory accesses (Derbinsky and Laird 2011). The memory retrievals are not influenced by the current context of the retrieval (for example, the contents of working memory or the activation of working-memory elements), or by other structures in semantic memory. For example, if an agent wants to retrieve the meaning of the word "bank," it can initiate a retrieval of the meaning for that word, and the history of retrievals will affect the current memory selection. However, in our current system there are only limited opportunities for agent knowledge to bias the retrieval with additional information, such as that it is related to a "body of water" or, alternatively, to a "financial institution." ACT-R supports soft constraints and additional mechanisms for biasing memory retrievals, but at a computational cost that makes it infeasible for knowledge bases with more than a few hundred elements (Douglass and Myers 2010). We need to explore alternative data structures, algorithms, and possibly different formulations of the problem of efficiently and effectively accessing semantic memory with more flexible matching than is currently supported.

9 Episodic Memory

with Andrew M. Nuxoll and Nate Derbinsky

Episodic memory, first described in detail by Tulving (1983), is a record of a stream of experience. It is what you "remember," and it includes contextualized information about specific events, such as a vacation or a dinner. In contrast, semantic memory is what you "know." It consists of isolated facts that are free of the specific context in which they are learned—they are not embedded in specific experiences, and they are useful in reasoning about general properties of the world. Episodic memories make it possible to extract information and regularities that may not have been noticed during the original experience and to combine them with current knowledge. Episodic memory also has a temporal structure that make it possible to retrieve a sequence of episodes that can be used to predict behavior and environmental dynamics in similar situations.

Episodic memory is a capability that we humans take for granted, except when an accident or disease disables it. When that happens, the resulting amnesia is devastating (Corkin 2002). Our goal in adding episodic memory to Soar is to capture the most important functional aspects of episodic memory without necessarily modeling all the details of human episodic memory, many of which are still unknown and may depend on the specifics of the underlying implementation technology of the brain.

At an abstract level, episodic memory provides a memory of previous events and supports additional cognitive capabilities that enhance the reasoning and learning capabilities of an integrated intelligent agent. For example, although episodic memory allows an agent to answer questions about the past, it also can improve an intelligent agent's reasoning about the current situation by allowing the agent to envision the state of the world outside of immediate perception, and to use experience to predict the outcomes of possible courses of action. Episodic knowledge also enables an agent to deliberately reflect on past events, using its knowledge of the results of its actions in the past to influence future behavior. Deliberate reflection can also lead to improvements in other types of learning, by making it possible to replay an experience more carefully when time for reflection becomes available.

There are limited examples of computational implementations of episodic memory for integrated agents. Cognitive architectures such as ACT-R and EPIC do not have task-independent architectural episodic-memory systems with the properties discussed in this chapter. The "basic agent" created by Vere and Bickmore (1990) had a primitive episodic-memory capability (a linked list of previous states), which was used only in a limited capacity (such as to answer questions). Ho, Dautenhahn, and Nehaniv (2003) describe an agent that uses a task-specific implementation of episodic memory to locate previously encountered resources. LIDA (Franklin and Patterson 2006) and CLARION (Sun 2006) have episodic memory, but few details of their operation or examples of their use have been made available. Icarus (Stracuzzi et al. 2009) recently added the ability to associate temporal ranges with concepts, but their approach doesn't directly support the retrieval of complete episodes; rather, it focuses on retrieving individual concepts, which makes it more similar to semantic memory with time stamps. In addition, according to Stracuzzi et al., "the cost of matching (inferring) concepts grows with the number of temporally distinct beliefs added to the memory," bringing into question whether this approach is practical for a long-lived agent.

Case-based reasoning (Kolodner 1993) is related to episodic memory, but in most CBR systems a case describes the solution to a previously encountered problem that the system retrieves and adapts to new problems. Furthermore, the structure of a case (the specific fields in the problem and the solution) is typically designed by a human for a specific task or set of tasks, which limits its generality. For example, continuous case-based reasoning (Ram and Santamaría 1997) relies on cases that consist of the agent's sensory experiences, but doesn't include internally generated abstractions. In addition, outside of continuous case-based reasoning, CBR systems rarely capture moment-to-moment experiences.

The role of episodic memory in the problem-space computational model is similar to the role of semantic memory. Episodic memory provides an additional long-term memory that can be accessed to enrich the state. The standard approach is to have episodic memory be accessed as part of operator application, although it can be used in a substate to support any PSCM function in a superstate, including state elaboration, operator proposal, operator evaluation, and operator application. One important feature is that chunking can then capture the retrieval that occurred in the substate so that in similar situations in the future an episodic-memory retrieval isn't necessary, as its processing has been compiled into a rule. More generally, episodic memory provides a record of the agent's experiences, so that behavior can depend not only on the current situation and general facts retrieved from semantic memory, but also on situations the agent experienced in its past.

Section 9.1 gives an overview of how episodic memory is implemented in Soar. Sections 9.2–9.4 describe the stages of operation of Soar's episodic memory (encoding information from the current situation, storing it into episodic memory, and retrieving episodes) in more detail. Section 9.5 provides demonstrations of tasks that use episodic memory to improve their behavior. Section 9.6 compares episodic memory to semantic memory, focusing on their relative strengths and weaknesses. Section 9.7 evaluates episodic memory in relation to the requirements set forth in chapter 2 and proposes future research.

9.1 Episodic Memory in Soar

Our design for episodic memory in Soar is driven by a desire to capture the functionality of what we commonly consider to be episodic memory in humans: an automatic, architectural symbolic memory that supports cue-based retrieval and autobiographical representation of the agent's moment-to-moment experiences (Nuxoll and Laird 2004, 2007). As with semantic memory, our ultimate goal is that episodic-memory retrieval is sufficiently efficient to support real-time reactivity over long agent lifetimes.

Figure 9.1 includes all the components of Soar that have been presented so far. Like semantic memory, episodic memory is a separate long-term memory that interacts directly with working memory. In contrast with semantic memory, episodes are stored

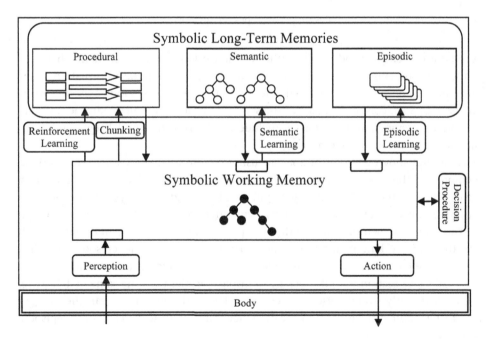

Figure 9.1
A block diagram of Soar.

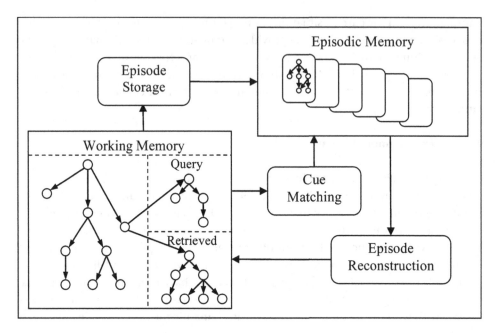

Figure 9.2
Processing and memories modules supporting episodic memory.

automatically. Each episode is a snapshot of the working-memory elements that exist at the time the episode is stored. Episodes also include temporal information; thus, once an episode has been retrieved, the next episode or a previous episode can be accessed. In Soar, episodes consist of the symbolic structures available in the top state of working memory, and do not yet include images or other modal representations, such as are available in mental imagery.

Figure 9.2 shows a subset of Soar, focusing on the interactions between working memory and the components of episodic memory. The structures in working memory are captured by the episodic-storage module and encoded in the episodic memory. To retrieve an episode, an agent constructs a cue on a state in working memory. In contrast to semantic memory, the queries for episodic memory can be multi-level graph structures of working-memory elements. During retrieval, the episode that best matches the cue is found and is reconstructed on the state off a link where the cue was made. (See section 9.3.) If there are multiple episodes with the same match score, the most recently stored episode is retrieved. The retrieved episode can then trigger rule firings, and can be used to create a new cue for further searches of episodic memory.

As in semantic memory, the information retrieved from episodic memory doesn't directly perform the PSCM functions for proposing, evaluating, or applying an operator. Instead, the knowledge embedded in an episode must be interpreted by rules in order to contribute to a PSCM function. Consider a somewhat contrived example: a robot has proposed operators for moving into two rooms, but because there are no additional preferences an impasse arises. In the ensuing substate, the agent constructs queries to retrieve a memory of each room. If one of the rooms leads to recalling an episode in which danger or pain was encountered but the other one doesn't, the agent could create preferences for avoiding the first room. Thus, the memories are state elaborations that are precursors to inferences that lead to the performance of other PSCM functions, which in this example is the evaluation of proposed operators. Episodic memory provides access to past experiences, including the properties of states that have been visited, operators that have been applied, and possibly results that have been produced. It is up to other knowledge to determine how the information about the past will be used for decision making and action within the current task.

9.2   Encoding and Storage

Encoding involves capturing a memory so it can be stored in long-term memory. For many learning mechanisms, this stage can involve significant analysis to determine the contents of the memory, such as generalizing over multiple data elements. However, episodic memory is the simplest of learning mechanisms: it just records the current situation. Moreover, in our implementation, encoding records only changes in working memory. (See subsection 9.5.3 for more details.)

Inherent to episodic memory is that it is an ongoing record of the agent's experience, so episodes are stored automatically. There is some flexibility as to what marks the transition from one episode to another, and Soar supports two different approaches. In the first approach, each episode corresponds to a single processing cycle, so changes are recorded at the end of each processing cycle. This ensures a fine-grain record of the agent's experience. However, often the agent is doing little processing across many cycles as it waits for the environment to change, such as when the robot is moving through a room. Thus, Soar also supports recording only when the agent executes an external action. This captures an agent's interactions with its environment, but doesn't record changes that occur in between agent actions.

The second design decision is concerned with which working-memory elements are stored in an episode. Soar stores working-memory elements that are linked to the top state, as well as some limited meta-data related to the time of storage. Substates aren't stored, because the top state captures all of the perception and situational awareness of the agent, which is the basis for most uses of episodic memory. Moreover, in many cases the structure of a substate can be reconstructed from the top state.

Storing substates greatly increases the amount of data stored and complicates the storage and retrieval processes. Soar also doesn't store retrievals from episodic memory, as storing them could lead to extremely large episodes. Not storing substates and episodic retrievals eliminates some memories, so we may have to revisit this decision if the current implementation excludes an important capability.

The third design decision related to storage is whether there are any changes in an episode once it has been stored, such as merging or generalization of episodes. To date, we have not explored such possibilities, mostly because we have concentrated on the basic aspects of episodic memory, and the computational requirements of adding mechanisms that analyze episodes aren't clear. Thus, in the current implementation, episodes do not change. There is no automatic generalization process that analyzes episodes and looks for regularities, nor is there any forgetting mechanism (Nuxoll et al. 2010).

9.3   Retrieval

Retrieval can be initiated in any state, and can be initiated in one of two different ways. The most common type of retrieval is via the creation of a cue made of working-memory elements, which is then matched against the stored episodes. This is similar to how retrievals are initiated for semantic memory, although with episodic memory the cues aren't restricted to a single level of working-memory elements. The second type of retrieval can follow the first. When a cue successfully retrieves a stored episode, the retrieved episode is recreated as a structure on the state, as illustrated in figure 9.2. Once an episode has been retrieved, a command exists to retrieve the *next* (or *previous*) episode. This type of retrieval allows the agent to move forward (or backward), re-experiencing episodes in the order in which they occurred or in reverse order.

For example, in Rooms World, if the agent decides to use memory to determine where another agent is taking blocks, the agent can create a cue to retrieve when it saw the other agent with a block. It can then use repeated "next" retrievals to "fast-forward" to an episode in which the other agent is moving into another room. Of course, this assumes that the agent actually saw the other agent pick up a block and move it, but it allows the agent to recall this information even if the agent didn't originally reason about it.

Both methods for retrieval in Soar are deliberate—the agent decides to attempt a retrieval by selecting an operator that creates a cue or uses a next (or previous) command. An alternative (not implemented in Soar) is for retrieval to be automatic, so that the complete top state is used to continually attempt a retrieval from episodic memory. One advantage of deliberate over automatic retrieval is that deliberate retrieval allows the agent to specify a subset of the situation as a cue, or even a hypothetical situation for the cue, and is not limited to retrieval based on the current situation. A second advantage is that the cost of retrieval can be high, especially when the cue is the complete state, and deliberate queries initiate a retrieval only when the agent needs information to perform PSCM functions.

Similar to semantic memory, a cue for episodic memory is a conjunction of working-memory elements, although cues for episodic retrievals can contain multiple levels of working-memory elements. In the limit, the complete state can be used as a cue to recall a situation similar to the current state. To further enhance the expressiveness of retrieval, it is possible to specify negative features—working-memory elements that should not be in the retrieved episode. For example, an agent in the Rooms World can use negative features to recall when it saw a block that was *not* also seen in the storage room. Without these negative features, blocks that have already been placed in the storage room would be recalled.

Soar retrieves the episode that best matches the cue. If at least one episode exactly matches the structure in the cue, the most recent episode that exactly matches the cue is returned. If there is no exact match, the most recent episode that matches the most features in the cue is returned.

A cue can also specify that particular episodes, or episodes with particular features, are not be retrieved, so that the agent can filter out previously examined episodes. This is helpful in our first example, in which the agent is recalling another agent moving blocks to the other room. It is possible that the agent retrieves an episode in which the other agent just dropped the block in the room, and did not move it to the other room. By inhibiting those episodes, the agent can recall other situations in which the other agent picks up and moves other blocks.

Soar uses a combination of optimizations to speed up the search of episodic memory for the best match (Derbinsky and Laird 2009). Once the best-matching episode has been found, it is reconstructed in working memory. Additional meta-data as to whether the match is exact or whether it is a partial match are provided, and the number of elements that match is reported. If no episode matches any features, a failed retrieval is reported. It is up to the agent to decide whether an exact match is necessary, or whether the results of a partial match are useful. In the cases reported in section 9.4, the agents require exact matches; however, we have used partial match results in other agents (Nuxoll 2007).

Although the expressiveness of the queries could be extended beyond the positive and negative features currently allowed, there is a tradeoff between expressiveness and computational expense for the retrieval, and we are biased toward simple queries and efficient retrievals. For example, adding arbitrary disjunction to the queries could be useful in some situations, but would cause a significant increase in the computation required for finding the best match. If a complex cue is required that cannot be expressed in our existing cue language, the agent can make repeated retrievals, explicitly filtering out retrievals that don't meet its criteria.

9.4 Use of Episodic Memory

Just as in the use of semantic memory, the use of episodic memory depends on procedural knowledge encoded as rules. To initiate retrieval, an operator is selected that creates the appropriate cue and then processes the results returned to working memory. How the results are used is not constrained; however, episodic memory supports a set of *cognitive capabilities* that are useful for a general intelligent agent. A cognitive capability is implemented as a general problem space and associated knowledge (sometimes individual operators or sets of operators) that an agent can use in a variety of problems. Informally, it appears that some type of episodic memory is necessary (and sufficient) to achieve these capabilities: most if not all of the capabilities require the recording and retrieval of the agent's experiences, and many rely on the temporal structure of episodic memory. Attempting to achieve these capabilities with only working memory and semantic memory would be extremely challenging and probably would require indirect implementations of much of the functionality inherent to episodic memory.

Our list of cognitive capabilities supported by episodic memory is organized according how they aid perception, reasoning, and learning. We demonstrate virtual sensing and action modeling in section 9.5. Retroactive learning and remembering success and failure were demonstrated in Nuxoll 2007.

9.4.1 Perception

Episodic memory can aid perceptual processing and situational awareness by providing a point of comparison of current perception to previously perceived data in a similar situation. We have identified three perception-related cognitive capabilities that episodic memory can aid.

Noticing familiar or novel situations
It can be valuable for an agent to detect when it is in a familiar situation or one that is novel. Episodic memory can provide a basis for determining novelty by using the current situation as a cue for retrieval. If the retrieval fails, the agent probably is in a novel situation. If the retrieval succeeds, the agent can compare the retrieved memory against the current situation to detect similarities and differences that could be relevant to the task at hand.

Detecting repetition
In many problems, an agent attempts to explore an environment or to generate distinctive states. If a familiar situation is detected, the agent can attempt to determine whether the current situation is so similar to an earlier situation that the agent may have returned to the same place by mistake, which can in turn be used to adjust its

control knowledge so to avoid such repetition in the future. The agent can also use the *next* command to move forward through episodes to determine which action(s) it took in similar situations, so as to avoid repeating them in the present situation.

Virtual sensing

An agent's perception of its environment is limited both spatially and temporally—that is, to the here and now. Episodic memory allows that agent to use its memory to expand its perception to include what it has sensed in other locations and at other times, giving it effectively a much broader awareness of its situation outside of immediate perception. Using episodic memory in this way can answer queries such as "Where did I park my car?" or "Where is the nearest drinking fountain?" Semantic knowledge, described in the previous chapter, can provide answers to similar questions when the agent has deliberately considered the question before, but episodic knowledge allows the agent to think back and to extract knowledge that was available in the original experience but might not have been originally considered worth noting.

9.4.2 Reasoning

Episodic memory stores the agent's history, which can be used to improve reasoning by providing an additional source of knowledge for predicting the effects of future actions and changes in the world, and for explaining past actions.

Action modeling and environmental dynamics

In many situations, it is useful for an agent to know the potential effects of its actions in the environment, so as to select actions that help achieve its goals. This is the basis for means-ends analysis where operators are selected on the basis of how well their actions contribute to achieving the current goals. More generally, modeling the actions of operators allows an agent to plan by creating an internal model of a situation and then trying out alternative operators. Episodic memory provides a crude but effective way for an agent to predict immediate changes in its environment that result from an action by retrieving similar situations in its past wherein it took that action (Xu and Laird 2010). The agent can then retrieve the immediately following state to recall the result of that action and either use that result to evaluate the proposed operator or continue to perform a further look-ahead search that might lead to a more informative result.

Remembering previous successes and failures

A more specific type of learning about the environment is remembering successes and failures. This can augment action modeling so that the agent can retrieve not only the result of an action in terms of predictions to changes in the state but also how those changes are related to the agent's goals.

Explaining behavior

The ability to remember what you did in the past allows you to relate your actions to others, possibly explaining why you did what you did. Explanations are useful in teaching others, but also for learning from your own successes and mistakes, such as during a debriefing session or in self-explanation (Chi and Vanlehn 1991). An agent can use its episodic memory to recall the solution of a problem, step by step, as well as the context for each decision, which can be used as the basis for explaining why a decision was made.

Prospective memory

When an agent plans future activities, episodic memory can act as a repository for future goals. For example, if you decide to stop at the store on the way home, the memory of the decision could be recalled on the way home and lead to an attempt to achieve that goal. This capability, which involves recalling an action or an intention, has been called *prospective memory* (McDaniel and Einstein 2007).

9.4.3 Learning

Although episodic memory is itself a learning mechanism, albeit a simple one, it can aid other types of learning by providing a memory of previous experiences that can serve as training instances for other learning mechanisms. The episodes can be recalled and reprocessed when more time or additional information is available.

Retroactive learning

Often an agent is unable to process the implications of a situation completely in real time because the agent lacks the specific information or resources that it needs in order to learn. For example, an agent in a real-time environment may not have time to apply an iterative learning algorithm while performing a task. However, when time becomes available, the agent can internally replay the events and learn from them then. Episodic memory allows experiences to be more fully analyzed once the resources are available. Thus, episodic memory can "boost" other learning mechanisms.

9.5 Demonstrations of Episodic Memory

9.5.1 Virtual Sensing

Episodic memory expands an agent's knowledge of its environment beyond its current perception by allowing the agent to access information from the recent past. This is effective if the environment changes slowly relative to the activities of the agent. We illustrate these capabilities in Rooms World.

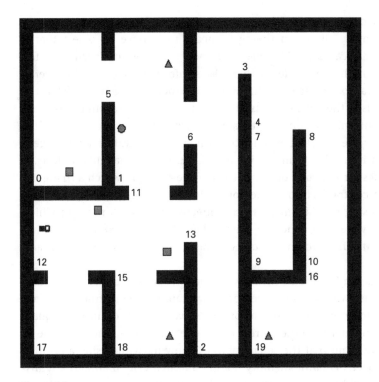

Figure 9.3
Example of a Rooms World environment for virtual sensing demonstrations.

Figure 9.3 shows a configuration of Rooms World in which the agent has already visited all of the rooms and perceived the objects. At this point, the agent is in room 12 and can perceive two square objects in that room. In this example, we expand the capabilities of the agent (through additional problem spaces and operators) so that a human can give it simple instructions, such as to fetch an object in another room. Without any long-term memory, the agent must use working memory to maintain a record of all objects it has ever perceived. As discussed in chapter 8, this is problematic for a long-lived agent that experiences large numbers of objects.

An alternative is for the agent to deliberately record the location of every object it perceives in semantic memory. This is the approach taken in chapter 8. It works for simple cases, such as if the human instructs the agent to "fetch the square object." In response to that instruction, the agent queries semantic memory for a square object. When a square object is retrieved from semantic memory, one of the features associated with the object is the room in which it was perceived, and the agent can use that information to fetch it (if the object hasn't moved). Semantic memory works well when the agent needs to access information about an object that it explicitly stored. Semantic memory fails when the agent needs to retrieve an object that it didn't explicitly store because at the time it seemed unimportant (such as a fire extinguisher), or when the agent needs to retrieve information using the overall context in which it was experienced. If the human instructs the agent to "fetch the triangular object that is in the same room as the circular object," the agent can directly retrieve the correct information only if it has explicitly stored a relationship (e.g. "in-same-room-as") for the objects it experiences, which is unlikely. Instead, the agent must use repeated retrievals. For example, it can first retrieve all triangular objects. It can then create queries for a circular object in each of the rooms in which a triangular object was found. In contrast, episodic memory automatically captures the relevant data, and the agent using episodic memory can directly query for a room in which objects of both types were seen. Once an episode has been retrieved, the agent has the information about which room the objects was in (in this case room 1), and correctly fetches it.

As was noted in chapter 8, episodic memory enables an agent to create queries that would be difficult to use with semantic memory. For example, the instructor can ask the agent to go to a room where there was once a square object, even if no square object is there now. To determine the correct room, the agent uses a negative cue to inhibit retrieval of the room that the square object is now in, while using a positive cue for the square object. Semantic memory doesn't automatically maintain any historical information; thus, in order to support this type of retrieval, an explicit history of previous rooms would have to be maintained for each object.

9.5.2 Action Modeling

Action modeling involves using episodic memory to learn a model of the actions performed by an external operator—an operator that changes the agent's environment. Once the agent has acquired a model of its actions, it can internally simulate its operators on an internal model of the environment state for planning. We have already seen Soar agents use action models during look-ahead planning in subsection 5.6.4, where a Blocks World agent used rules that internally simulated the move-block operator. In subsection 5.6.5, agents in Blocks World and Rooms World used action models for planning in multiple problem spaces. Now we will see how an agent can learn an action model for Blocks World using episodic memory.

As a starting point for this demonstration, we use the agent that performed a one-step look-ahead hill-climbing search in subsection 5.6.4. It used a simple evaluation function to compare internally generated states. An example of that agent's behavior was illustrated in figure 5.13. Here we use the same agent, except that in this case the agent doesn't know how to internally simulate a move-block operator—it is missing rule P10. That critical piece of knowledge can't be derived from the other procedural knowledge that the agent has. Instead, the agent must use its experience to learn knowledge that is equivalent to that rule.

In this example, we assume that the agent previously worked on similar problems and has episodic memories of some of the situations in which it applied operators. We also assume that it has an additional problem space that includes operators that support action modeling using episodic memory: an operator for creating queries to retrieve previous episodes (query), an operator for dealing with failed retrievals (failed-EM-retrieval), an operator for advancing to the next episode (next-episode), and an operator for using the results of a query as the result of a superstate operator application (update-superstate). This problem space is appropriate for operators with deterministic external actions.

The trace reproduced in figure 9.4 shows the beginning of problem solving. The lines do not correspond to a processing cycle in Soar, as the trace includes descriptions of impasses and important states. The trace is identical to the original trace in figure 5.13 through line 5, where move-block(B, C) is selected to apply to a copy of the original state. The purpose of applying the operator is for the agent to imagine what would happen if that operator applied, then evaluate the resulting state.

---

1.   S: [(on A Table) (on B Table) (on C A)]
2.   Tie Impasse: move-block(B, C), move-block(C, Table), move-block(C, B)
3.   O: evaluate(move-block(B, C))
4.   S: [(on A Table) (on B Table) (on C A)]   *copy of original state*
5.   O: move-block(B, C)
6.   O: query[(on A Table) (on B Table) (on C A); move-block(B, C)]
7.   O: failed-EM-retrieval   *evaluation = retrieval-failure*
8.   O: evaluate(move-block(C, Table))
9.   S: [(on A Table) (on B Table) (on C A)]   *copy of original state*
10.   O: move-block(C, Table)
11.   O: query[(on A Table) (on B Table) (on C A); move-block(C, Table)]
12.   O: next-episode
13.   O: update-superstate
14.   S: [(on A Table) (on B Table) (on C Table)]   *evaluation = 1*
15.   O: evaluate(move-block(C, B))
...

Figure 9.4
A trace of problem solving in Blocks World in which episodic memory is used for action modeling.

In the trace reproduced in figure 9.4, the agent doesn't have a model of its own actions, so there is no rule to fire. For that reason, an impasse arises after line 5, which results in the creation of a substate (not shown). On line 6, the query operator is selected to recall a similar situation in which the move-block operator was applied. This operator creates a cue, which consists of the important structures in the state and the relevant task operator. In this case, we assume that the agent had not previously experienced this exact state and operator, so the query fails to find an exact match. Because of this failure, the agent is unable to model the effects of this operator to this state. At this point, the failed-EM-retrieval operator detects the failure and is selected. It creates an evaluation of "retrieval-failure" for the evaluate operator in the superstate, which will be used for creating preferences for the move-block(B, C) operator once evaluations are created for the other tied operators.

On line 8, move-block(C, Table) is evaluated. In the ensuing substate, the agent attempts to apply that operator to the internal copy of the state. As before, there is no rule to apply the operator, so an operator no-change impasse arises, and the agent attempts to retrieve an earlier state in which it applied this operator to this state on line 11. In the case, we assume the agent has experienced this combination of a state and an operator before, and the retrieval succeeds. In response to the success, the agent selects the next-episode operator, which retrieves the next episode from episodic memory. The agent then selects the update-superstate operator on line 13, which compares the retrieved episode to the superstate, and modifies the superstate (by adding and removing working-memory elements) so that the superstate corresponds to the retrieved episode. This completes the application of the move-block operator, which then leads to an evaluation of the new state by elaboration rules on line 14. In this case, the evaluation is "1" because block C is in place and no other blocks are in place.

The evaluation of move-block(C, B) begins on line 15. If the agent has previously experienced this step, this operator is evaluated using episodic memory, which leads to an evaluation of "0" because none of the blocks are in their correct positions. At this point, there are three evaluations: "retrieval-failure," "1," and "0." Elaborations within the selection space compare the numeric values and create a better preference, preferring the selection of move-block(C, Table) to move-block(C, B). "Retrieval-failure" must also be translated into some type of preference. It might be tempting to create a preference to avoid operators that led to a retrieval failure; however, the agent has no way of knowing whether such an operator is useful or not; it knows only that the operator has not yet been tried. In this case, it is better to try the operator in the real world and discover what state it leads to, which has the side effect of creating a memory that can be used in the future for performing a look-ahead. Thus, in this case, a best preference is created, and move-block(B, C) is selected.

Selecting and applying move-block(B, C) in the environment leads to a state in which the blocks are stacked (on B C), (on C A), and (on A Table). In this state, only move-block(B, Table) is available, and it is selected and applied, taking the agent back to the state in line 1. Although the external state is the same as in line 1, episodic memory now has a memory in which the agent moved B on C for that state. The agent does its one-step look-ahead, determines that move-block(C, Table) is better than either of the two alternatives, selects move-block(C, Table), and applies it in the environment. The search continues from this point, and the agent eventually solves the problem.

Figures 9.5 and 9.6 show the results of using episodic memory for this problem in comparison to the following agents.

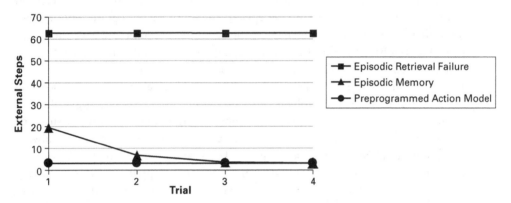

Figure 9.5
External steps required to solve a Blocks World problem.

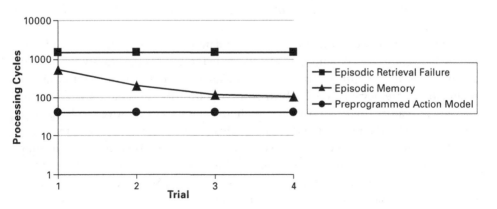

Figure 9.6
Processing cycles required to solve a Blocks World problem.

Episodic retrieval failure: Episodic memory is disabled, so all retrievals fail and the agent makes random decisions.

Episodic memory: The agent uses episodic memory for its action model. Episodes are learned incrementally on the basis of experiences with the world.

Pre-programmed action model: The agent includes rule P10 for the action model and uses the same one-step look-ahead as the episodic-memory agent.

Figure 9.5 shows the total number external steps required by each agent, where the agents perform the same task on repeated trials. The agent that has the pre-programmed action model produces optimal behavior in terms of actions in the external environment. The episodic-memory agent is in the middle. Initially, it must take actions in the environment that are not on the path to the solution, so it is not optimal, but even on the first trial it is better than the agent that always fails on retrieval. Over the next two trials, the episodic-memory agent acquires enough episodes so that it can match the behavior of the agent pre-programmed with the action model. One trial isn't enough, because the agent sometimes takes random actions in the environment that are not on the optimal path to the solution.

Figure 9.6 shows the same agents, but displays the total number of processing cycles required to solve the problem. In this figure, the y axis is a log scale. The behavior of the agent without episodic memory or an action model never succeeds with an episodic retrieval. This is the worst case for processing cycles as it always attempts a retrieval, always fails, and then makes a random decision. The agent with the pre-programmed action model takes many internal steps for each external step (approximately 12 internal steps for each external action), but it still takes fewer internal steps than any other agent. The agent that uses episodic memory for its action model must take more internal steps for each external action, because it must perform the episodic retrieval. It averages between 16 and 20 internal steps for each external action; however; it shows significant improvement as it learns the correct external actions to take.

The trace reproduced in figure 9.4 and the data plotted in figures 9.5 and 9.6 do not include chunking. When chunking is enabled, the first opportunity for learning a new rule is at line 7 in the trace, where the failed-EM-retrieval operator creates an evaluation of "retrieval-failure," which is the result of the substate for applying the evaluate operator. There is no direct result for applying the move-block operator, because the episodic retrieval failed. This evaluation could potentially lead to a new chunk; however, that rule would be overly general because it is based on the assumption that no additional episodes will ever be available in the future (the closed-world assumption). Thus, to avoid learning an overgeneral rule, Soar automatically disables chunking when the result is dependent on a failed retrieval. Note that Soar can learn from dead ends or from encountering illegal states in a search space. It is only that when Soar fails on the retrieval from a memory that chunking is disabled.

The next opportunity for chunking to be used is line 14, where a result it produced for applying move-block(C, B). In this case, a rule is learned. Chunking is unable generalize the rule, because the processing was dependent on the specifics of the cue and the result retrieved from episodic memory. Thus, although Soar learns action models for the operator in this problem space, it learns them one by one, for each state-operator pair. Xu and Laird (2010) describe how it is possible to generalize the action models so that learning from one situation can apply to a similar situation. Their technique uses a combination of reinforcement learning (to learn more general cues) and analogy (to map a similar episode onto a new situation). These techniques use existing mechanisms in Soar, but they involve additional problem spaces and additions to the problem space for retrieving episode memories to use in action modeling.

At line 15, a rule is learned for the evaluation operator. As problem solving continues, additional rules are learned for applying move-block operators as well as evaluate operators. In addition, rules are learned that create preferences for comparing operators, such as that move-block(C, Table) is better than move-block(C, B). Learning these rules speeds problem solving the first time a problem is attempted by eliminating redundant processing; it also speeds processing when the same problem is tried a second time.

Figure 9.7 shows the effects of chunking for the agent that has the pre-programmed action model and for the agent that uses episodic memory. In both cases, the number of internal steps decreases, and for the action model agent it decreases to the optimal number after the first trial because it has learned to select the correct external operators in every state. The episodic-memory agent also improves, but it takes longer. As

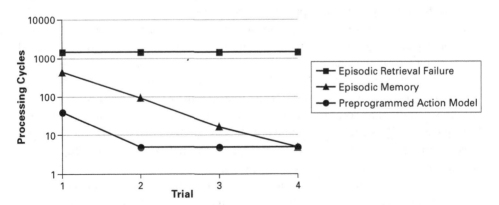

Figure 9.7
Processing cycles required to solve a Blocks World problem while using episodic memory and chunking.

it gathers more episodes, it is able to perform more internal simulations and then learn from them. It also reaches optimal performance by the fourth trial. The number of external steps doesn't change with chunking. In this case, episodic memory is responsible for improvements in external behavior whereas chunking is responsible for eliminating unnecessary internal steps. Together, episodic memory and chunking allow an agent that initially doesn't have any internal action-model knowledge to achieve optimal performance in both external and internal processing.

9.5.3   Evaluating Performance in Rooms World

Maintaining bounded episodic processing as an agent contends with multiple, complex tasks over a long lifetime presents a significant computational challenge. Here we focus on the Rooms World agent, using the expanded map of the University of Michigan's Computer Science and Engineering building map presented in chapter 8 to evaluate the performance of Soar's episodic-memory mechanism. The design of that mechanism was motivated by the need to minimize the growth in processing time for storage, cue matching, and reconstruction as the number of episodes increases. If working memory is unconstrained, reconstruction can become costly. However, over long agent lifetimes, cue matching during retrieval has the greatest growth potential. The overall design is meant to minimize the time required for that operation without significantly affecting the amount of memory or time required for other operations.

The intuition behind the performance optimizations in Soar's episodic memory (Derbinsky and Laird 2009) lies in the observation that one episode usually differs from the previous one (and the next one) in a relatively small number of features. Thus, processing throughout the mechanism considers only changes in working memory between episodes, as opposed to the entirety of any episode. For example, when encoding an episode, the mechanism only stores information about the working-memory elements that were removed and those that were added, so that instead of recording a complete snapshot, Soar maintains the temporal intervals when working-memory elements existed in working memory. Consequently, when a Rooms World agent maintains a large map in its working memory, episodic storage stores only the changes that occur in the map, minimizing encoding cost and total storage. During cue matching, the components of the cue are matched against the temporal intervals for each working-memory element, interval matches are combined, and the best episode is reconstructed in working memory.

To evaluate Soar's episodic memory, we ran the Rooms World agent on the task described in subsection 8.4.2, which involves a map of the third floor of the University of Michigan's Computer Science and Engineering Building. In addition to the results illustrated in figure 8.8, we ran the Rooms World agent with episodic memory, with episodic memory used to determine the location of blocks that need to be picked up.

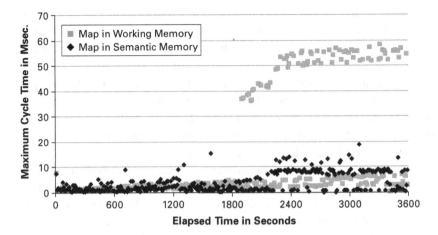

Figure 9.8
Performance of Rooms World agents using episodic memory.

In these runs, data for episodic memory are recorded whenever the agent takes an external action. These are the situations in which the changes in agent's situation are relevant to the agent's behavior. In addition, only changes in internally generated working-memory structures are recorded; changes in low-level perception are not. In this agent, and in most others, internal elements are the ones that are relevant to decision making.

Figure 9.8 compares an agent that stores the map in working memory against an agent that stores the map in semantic memory. The higher cost of storing the map in working memory is attributable to the fact that each episode contains the entire map, so that a copy of the entire map is added to working memory when an episode is retrieved. The first retrieval is performed after 1,800 seconds. From that point on, reconstruction of the map as part of a retrieval accounts for the sharp rise in cycle times. In contrast, when the map is stored in semantic memory only a small subset of the map is maintained in working memory, and thus the amount of data stored in an episode is much smaller and the reconstruction costs are much less. Even though there is clearly a cost to using episodic memory when using semantic memory to store the map, it is small enough so that the agent easily retains its reactivity.

9.6 Comparison of Episodic Memory and Semantic Memory

Thanks to our experience with both episodic and semantic memory, we can give some indications of the different strengths and weaknesses of each. In our current implementation, semantic memory is most useful when the agent has pre-existing procedural knowledge as to when it should store and update isolated facts, such as the location and structure of a room or an arithmetic fact. Especially for immutable facts, semantic memory provides efficient and effective long-term memory for storage and retrieval. In contrast, because episodic memory automatically captures the agent's experience, it is most useful for accessing information that co-occurred as it was experiencing the world, independent of whether the agent deliberately attended to it at the time. In addition, episodic memory has a temporal structure that we can exploit to recall and then predict the dynamics of the environment, including the effect of an agent's action in a similar situation that it experienced in the past.

Are both of these memories necessary? Could one of them perform both functions? Although an agent can use semantic memory to maintain the structures stored in episodic memory by deliberately storing all working-memory structures in semantic memory, doing so would disrupt the agent's ongoing reasoning. Episodic memory does this automatically, independent of the agent's reasoning. Probably more important, episodic memory is efficient (both in time and in space) in storing episodes. Semantic memory would be unable to take advantage of the temporal structure of experience that episodic memory takes advantage of when storing episodes. This would lead to a huge increase in data in semantic memory. Moreover, semantic memory is designed for efficient retrieval of a single level of data (an individual object), whereas episodic memory can be cued using a hierarchical structure that includes relations among many objects for retrieval, and it retrieves a complete context.

The alternative is to use episodic memory for all long-term declarative structures. From our experience, the advantage of having a separate semantic memory is that it provides a locus for maintaining stable information. With semantic memory, all information about a fact and about its permanent relations with other facts is maintained, is easily and efficiently accessible, and can be deliberately updated by the agent, so that as the agent's knowledge of the world changes the changes are reflected in its long-term memory. With episodic memory, information about the same object can be spread across multiple episodes, and the agent must access episodic memory repeatedly to build up a complete description of an object and its relations. Moreover, when an episode is retrieved there is no guarantee that it reflects the agent's most recent set of beliefs about the world. Finally, owing to the current state of our implementations, episodic memory is computationally more expensive to access, especially as episodes accumulate with experience.

Our conclusion is that both memories are necessary, and that each provides unique functionality. Attempting to use a single memory might be possible, but that would be awkward and probably computationally expensive. There are real and significant computational advantages to designing the underlying storage and retrieval mechanisms to take advantage of the unique structures of semantic and episodic memory.

9.7 Analysis of Requirements

Like semantic memory, episodic memory furthers the achievement of requirements R3, R4, R5, R12, and R13.

R3: Use large bodies of knowledge. Episodic memory provides a mechanism for accumulating and using information about the agent's experiences. We have demonstrated that it supports the efficient encoding and retrieval of experiential information, although there are still open issues for learning over long time periods.

R4: Use knowledge at different levels of generality. Episodic memory includes whatever information was represented in working memory, be it specific or general. Retrieval from episodic memory allows the agent to recall specific situations it experienced, as well as any generalizations it derived at the time.

R5: Represent diverse amounts of knowledge. Episodic memory provides a mechanism for the accumulation of experiential knowledge.

R12: Comprehensive learning. Episodic memory adds the ability to maintain a history of the agent's experiences, which supports a variety of cognitive capabilities that are difficult if not impossible to achieve with other learning mechanisms in Soar.

R13: Incremental learning. Episodic memory is incremental in that episodes are added one by one throughout the lifetime of the agent.

Owing to the continual growth of episodes acquired via experience, it isn't possible to guarantee bounded retrieval time, which is a necessary constraint if requirement R11 is to be achieved. There are four possible responses to this problem:

• Develop new algorithms that meet these requirements. In view of the inherent need for more and more memory to store episodes, this is not likely to be achieved with von Neumann architectures for arbitrary numbers of episodes.

• Modify the dynamics of episodic memory so that the number of episodes is bounded. One possible approach is to introduce a forgetting mechanism that automatically removes episodes that have a low probability of being useful.

• Determine the bound on the number of episodes that can be efficiently processed and restrict our use of episodic memory to problems that meet that limit.

• Develop heuristic approaches that do not guarantee finding the best match, but have performance guarantees so that they are bounded.

Initially, we have adopted the third approach while continuing to try to improve the efficiency of the underlying processes (the first approach). We use and experiment with episodic memory in agents we develop, but we are limited to the length of our system's experiences by the computational demands of episodic memory (which corresponds to roughly 40 hours of human experience). The other approaches deserve future research.

There are still many challenges ahead in our use of episodic memory. Our plans for future research on episodic memory include the following:

• Evaluate the usefulness of episodic memory for additional cognitive capabilities. An important part of these evaluations is developing general procedural knowledge so that a capability can be used across many tasks without starting from scratch. The implementations of the current capabilities approach this, but their generality will have to be tested in a range of tasks.

• Explore activation-based retrieval. At present, retrieval is based on a cue deliberately created by the agent, and the retrieval is biased using recency. In the past we did some work in which activation of the elements in the cue, and elements in the memories, was used to bias retrieval toward the "more important" memories. That work was a proof of concept and didn't include extensive exploration of the space of possibilities, their computational overhead, and their effect on behavior. Incorporating activation in the retrieval process, and perhaps incorporating quantities related to appraisals (see chapter 11), could improve the robustness of the retrieval process so that the retrieved episode would be more likely to be the one most relevant to the agent's current processing and goals. Incorporating these influences may also force us to reconsider some of the data structures and algorithms we are using for retrieval.

• Expand episodic memory so it contains not only symbolic structures but also imagery. With the recent addition of mental imagery to Soar (chapter 10), there is the possibility of including spatial representations and images in episodic memory. Supporting mental imagery in episodic memory will enrich the agent's ability to recall structures, and will allow it to more fully utilize mental imagery (which, as we have shown, is critical to robust behavior in spatial environments) (see Wintermute 2010).

10 Visuospatial Processing with Mental Imagery

with Scott Lathrop and Samuel Wintermute

The previously discussed aspects of Soar rely on symbolic working memory to represent an agent's understanding of the current situation. The generality and compositional power of symbolic structures make them central to knowledge representation and processing in cognitive architectures. However, perception-based representations can provide important functional advantages for specific types of reasoning. Our work on visuospatial cognition was inspired by research on mental imagery (Kosslyn, Thompson, and Ganis 2006) and by the possibility that perception-based representations are ubiquitous in human reasoning (Barsalou 2008).

As part of our expansion of Soar's capabilities, we have added memory and processing structures to directly support perception-based representations. Accordingly, this addition to Soar focuses on two forms of perceptual representations, spatial and visual, and brings together two related lines of research previously presented separately (Lathrop and Laird 2009; Wintermute and Laird 2009). The research includes multiple implementations. The first, called *Spatial-Visual Imagery* or SVI (Lathrop 2007), focused on modeling many of the characteristics of human mental imagery. The second, named *Spatial/Visual System* or SVS (Wintermute 2009b), built upon the foundations specified in SVI, but with increased emphasis and expansion on the functionality afforded by the combination of concrete spatial representations and abstract symbolic representations. This chapter presents a synthesis of the two systems under the SVS name. Although SVI and SVS were fully functional, they didn't have the robustness required of releasable software. The current implementation of a visual system in Soar is a reimplementation of SVS and is consistent with the descriptions in this chapter, although in some cases it doesn't support the full functionality of SVI and SVS. In the conclusion, we will summarize the differences between these systems.

Although behavioral and biological evidence influence the design of SVS, functionality is the primary driver of theoretical commitments and design decisions, specifically in tasks rich with spatial or visual properties. As computational benefits of perception-based representations have been well studied in isolation (Larkin and

Simon 1987; Lathrop and Laird 2007), our focus is on the capabilities gained by integrating low-level spatial and visual information with higher-level symbolic abstractions. Here, we call the processes involving interaction between abstract symbolic and concrete perceptual representations *mental imagery* processes, with *spatial imagery* being a special case where the concrete representation is spatial. For example, imagine that you are facing south and we ask you to simulate the following movements: step forward, turn right, step forward, turn right, and step forward. If we then ask you what your final location and orientation is, most people respond that they are to the west of where they began, facing north. This type of reasoning requires that you infer a global spatial relationship (your final location and orientation) from a set of local spatial relationships provided in the task instructions. Spatial imagery is especially useful for reasoning when the precise metric details of space matter, making abstraction into symbolic information difficult—for example, when steering a car through a field of obstacles.

Visual imagery is useful for the detection of spatial or visual properties when the specific shape or visual texture of the object(s) is necessary for the inference. For example, consider the reasoning involved when the following questions are given verbally rather than in writing: Does the letter 'A' have an enclosed space? The letter 'E'? When asked, most people respond that they create a visual image of the letter and then "look at" the image to answer the question. This type of reasoning requires a visual depiction, as the inference involves detecting a visual topological feature (e.g., enclosed space) to formulate an answer. Of course, the system could encode this information symbolically, but making these types of properties explicit for all shapes and objects requires either significant *a priori* knowledge engineering or significant processing during perception that is rarely useful. Both approaches are unlikely to be scalable across the range of spatial and visual properties that might be useful to a human-level agent.

Specialized spatial and visual cognition has been well studied, both from a functional point of view (e.g., Funt 1976; Gelernter 1959; Glasgow and Papadias 1992; Larkin and Simon 1987) and from a human-modeling point of view (e.g., Gilhooly, Logie, and Wynn 1999; Levine, Jankovic, and Palij 1982; Zwaan and Radvansky 1998). These approaches are valuable, but they are not constrained by what is known about other aspects of cognition (short-term and long-term memories, reasoning, decision making, and so on). Previous unified computational theories of spatial and visual cognition have focused almost exclusively on reasoning with abstract symbolic representations (Baylor 1971; Carpenter, Just, and Shell 1990; Lyon, Gunzelmann, and Gluck 2008; Moran 1973). Such theories and corresponding computational models normally assume that perception is a transducer whose primary purpose is to transform raw sensory data into abstract symbolic representations that concisely capture the relevant properties of salient objects. This basic scheme is shared by many AI designs, from early planning systems (Fikes and Nilsson 1971) to modern probabilistic inference systems (e.g., Richardson and Domingos 2006), that rely solely on abstract symbolic representations while disregarding perceptual-level data.

Other architectures integrate symbolic reasoning with perceptual-level visual and spatial cognition, but focus on fidelity rather than functionality (Gunzelmann and Lyon 2007; Harrison and Schunn 2002); still others take a knowledge-intensive (rather than architectural) approach and apply it to a particular problem domain, such as geographic reasoning and diagrammatic reasoning (Barkowsky 2007; Kurup and Chandrasekaran 2006; Tabachneck-Schijf, Leonardo, and Simon 1997). Other comprehensive theories for this integration have also been put forth (Barsalou 2008; Grush 2004), but not as implemented architectures. Kosslyn developed a complete theory of mental imagery (Kosslyn, Thompson, and Ganis 2006), which inspired the development of SVS. However, Kosslyn has implemented only a subset of this theory (see, e.g., Kosslyn et al. 1992).

Within the context of the problem-space computational model (PSCM), spatial and mental imagery provide Soar with innate problem spaces for representing and manipulating spatial and visual information. Symbolic working memory maintains its centrality as the interface between all of Soar modules. Spatial and visual structures have both symbolic and non-symbolic aspects; the non-symbolic aspects are stored outside of working memory. Every object represented as a spatial and visual structure also has a working-memory representation of its identity. For example, there are working-memory elements representing that there is block named blockA. Other symbolic properties of spatial and visual structures are accessible only indirectly, via commands, in a way similar to how semantic and episodic memories are retrieved. For example, the agent can query for whether or not blockA is next to blockB. Specialized processing over the separate non-symbolic representation of the blocks then calculates the property and adds a symbolic representation of the result to working memory, where it can be accessed by the other parts of Soar. A significant achievement has been the development of the appropriate interfaces so that spatial and visual imagery can be used within the context of the PSCM. Thus, the addition of imagery doesn't change the processing cycle or the way decisions are made. It does include additional long-term memories for perception-based information that can be recalled and used for spatial and visual reasoning.

10.1 Visual and Spatial Representations

Our hypothesis is that there are three distinct representations that support spatial and visual cognition: amodal symbolic, quantitative spatial, and visual depictive, all of which are shown in figure 10.1. To support cognitive processing, these representations and their associated processes are used together.

Representation / Aliases	Information	Processing	Uses	Example

Symbolic
 	
Sentential
 	
Propositional
 	
Descriptions
	▪ Perceptual information
	  o Object identities
	  o Spatial properties (optional)
	  o Visual properties (optional)
	▪ Non-perceptual information
		Symbolic manipulation
		
		Logic
		
		Entailment
			General reasoning
			
			Explicit visual feature recognition
			
			Qualitative spatial reasoning
				object (tree)
				feature(tree, curve)
				color (tree, green)
				
				object (house)
				feature(house, corner)
				color(house, blue)
				
				left-of(tree, house)

Quantitative spatial
 	
Sentential
 	
Metric diagram
 	
Spatial image
 	
Perceptual symbols
	▪ Object labels
	▪ 3D Spatial Properties (explicit)
	  o General shape
	  o Location
	  o Orientation
	▪ 3D Spatial Properties (implicit)
	  o Size
	  o Topology
	  o Direction
	  o Distance
		Mathematical manipulation (including motion simulation)	Spatial perception
			
			Spatial imagery
			
			Spatial reasoning *(General shapes)*
				tree:
				  location <-2,4,0>
				  orientation 0
				  shape coordinates
				  <1,3,1>;<2,8,1>;<1,3,0>..
				
				house:
				  location <9,4,0>
				  orientation 0
				  shape coordinates
				  <8,3,1>;<2,3,1>;<4,3,0>..

Visual depictive
 	
Iconic
 	
Analog
 	
Visual image
 	
Perceptual symbols
	▪ Object labels
	▪ 2D Visual Properties (explicit)
	  o Shape
	  o Texture
	  o Empty space
	▪ 2D Spatial Properties (implicit)
	  o Location
	  o Size
	  o Topology
	  o Direction
		Mathematical manipulation
		
		Depictive manipulation
			Visual perception
			
			Visual imagery
			
			Spatial reasoning *(Specific shapes)*	

Figure 10.1
Multiple representations supported by Soar.

The amodal symbolic representation is a stable medium that is useful for general reasoning (Newell 1990). From a spatial and a visual perspective, symbols may denote an object, visual properties of an object, and spatial relationships between objects. In general, these symbols are qualitative properties rather than quantities. They are sentential, in that their meaning depends on context and interpretation rather than on their spatial arrangement in memory. For example, the right-hand column in the first row of figure 10.1 represents two objects, a tree and a house, with symbols denoting visual (e.g., color(tree, green)) and spatial (e.g., left-of(tree, house)) properties. In addition to spatial and visual properties, symbols can represent non-spatial or non-visual content, which is necessary for associating an object with other modalities and concepts such as love, justice, and peace.

The quantitative spatial representation is also amodal, but it is perception-based. The location, orientation, and rough shape of objects in space are determined by the agent's interpretation of visual, auditory, proprioception, and kinesthesis senses. Computationally, the representation uses three-dimensional Euclidean space with symbols to label objects. Spatial processing is accomplished with sentential, mathematical manipulations. Motion may be simulated by linear transformations (i.e., translating, rotating, and scaling) or by non-linear dynamical systems. The second example in figure 10.1 represents the metric location, orientation, and rough shape of the tree and the house. Direction, distances between objects, size, and rough topology can be inferred from this information.

In contrast to the symbolic and spatial representations, both of which are sentential structures, space (including empty space) is inherent to the visual depictive representation. The depiction is from a privileged viewpoint, and the structure of the patterns resembles the objects in a perceived or imagined scene. Computationally, the depiction is a bitmap with associated processing that uses either mathematical manipulations (e.g., filters or affine transformations) or specialized processing that takes advantage of the topological structure through what we call depictive manipulations (discussed later). This imagery processing can be used to extract cognitively useful visual features (e.g., lines, curves, enclosed spaces) or to reason about the details of specific shapes. Similar to spatial imagery, visual imagery can manipulate the depiction to simulate physical processes.

Each representation has functional and computational tradeoffs that depend on the details of a task. For example, given appropriate inference rules and the symbolic representation in figure 10.1, one can infer that the green object (the tree) is to the left of the blue object (the house). However, one cannot infer the distance between the tree and the house, or that the top of the house is a triangle. One can infer these properties from a symbolic representation only when the relevant property is encoded explicitly or when task knowledge supports the inference (e.g., if three lines intersect, then there exists a triangle). Even if equivalent information is present in each representation, processing efficiency may vary across them.

These tradeoffs can be characterized on a scale between discretion and assimilability (Norman 2000) or on a scale between scope and processing cost (Newell 1990). The symbolic representation is high in discretion and scope. It is high in discretion because it conveys just enough information required for general reasoning. For example, the predicate description, on (apple, ground), is sufficient for general inferences, such as "if the apple is on the ground then grasp it." Symbols have greater scope than spatial and depictive representations in that they can represent incomplete knowledge, such as negation and uncertainty, as in "if the apple is not in the tree but is on the ground or on the table then grasp it." Reasoning in this context doesn't have to be concerned about the exact location or shape of the objects.

At the other extreme, the spatial and depictive representations are low in discretion and scope. They provide many details, but these details are limited to spatial and visual information. However, for spatial and visual properties, they have a lower processing cost and are easier to assimilate. For example, information from the visual image listed in figure 10.1, such as that the roof of the house is a triangle and overhangs the frame of the house, is directly accessible. What is lost in scope is gained in efficiency.

10.2   Visuospatial Domains

To motivate the architectural discussion, examples from the Pegged Blocks World domain and the Scout domain will be used. Pegged Blocks World problems are very simple, but require both precise spatial reasoning and broad generalization for success. The domain has been designed to be minimal in order to clearly demonstrate the benefits of multiple representations and imagery. In contrast, the Scout domain is relatively complex, including comprehensive agents that demonstrate the broad capabilities of the architecture. In addition, it requires the use of visual information (not just spatial information), so it covers more parts of the architecture.

An agent in the Pegged Blocks World domain (figure 10.2) perceives blocks and can act to move them from place to place. In contrast with similar domains, however, the blocks cannot be placed freely on a table. Instead, there are two fixed pegs, and each block must be aligned to one of the pegs—essentially, there can only be two towers, and their positions are fixed. The agent is presented with a simple goal, such as to stack A on top of B on top of C on top of D, all on peg2. Blocks can be moved from the top of one tower to the other; however, the blocks vary in size, and the pegs are close enough that blocks may collide, depending on the exact sizes of the other blocks in the towers. Blocks can also be moved out of the way to a storage bin that has unlimited space to hold blocks. Each move has a certain cost, manifested as a negative reward. The agent's goal is to solve the problem with minimal cost. A reward of –1 is

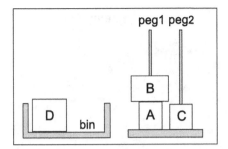

Figure 10.2
A state in Pegged Blocks World. Source: Wintermute and Laird 2009.

received for moving a block from one peg to another without collision, a reward of −20 for moving a block to or from the bin, and a reward of −1,000 for causing a collision. It is in the agent's best interest to solve a problem by moving blocks between the towers, using the bin only if necessary and never causing collisions.

The agent must solve a series of problems, all of which have the same goal. Performance is judged cumulatively across multiple episodes, where block sizes vary across instances (so the agent cannot perform well simply by following a fixed action sequence). The agent perceives the spatial state of the world, which is represented to the agent as labeled polyhedrons in 3D space. There are an infinite number of such states, though, so the state space must be abstracted in some way if the agent is to avoid planning from scratch in each new instance. However, in this domain there is no obvious way to abstract the spatial state. A standard Blocks World abstraction (e.g., predicates such as on(A,B)) is insufficient, since collisions cannot be predicted in terms of it. However, we will show that this problem can be overcome by using a spatial representation and imagery.

The Scout domain (Lathrop and Laird 2009) is motivated by research in developing autonomous scouts to provide situational awareness for an Army unit. In addition to autonomously maneuvering to a position, the Army wants scouts to coordinate and improve their positions autonomously. The scout team must cooperate to gain and maintain observation with an approaching adversary's three-vehicle reconnaissance element. The team's goal is to keep their higher commander informed of the opposing force's movements by periodically sending observation reports (through the lead scout) of their best assessment of the enemy's location.

The problem of creating an agent performing the task of the lead scout is considered here. Figure 10.3 shows a typical situation the lead scout might face. Here, the agent perceives a certain view of the world (a), and its teammate perceives another view (b), both reflecting some actual situation (c). The agent must combine the information it can directly perceive, information communicated from its teammate, and background

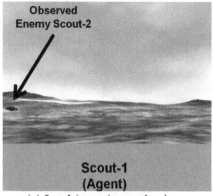

(a) Lead (agent) scout's view

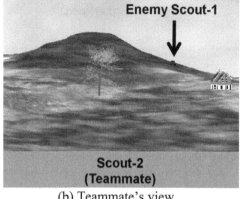

(b) Teammate's view

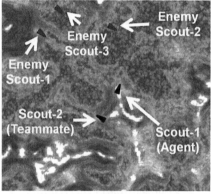

(c) Actual situation

Figure 10.3
Various views from the Scout domain.

knowledge (such as formations typically used by the enemy) to form hypotheses about the number and location of the enemies. It has a terrain map of the area to help with this. On the basis of these hypotheses, the agent can adjust its orientation or that of its teammate to better track the enemy units. As will be shown, spatial and visual representations are necessary to solve this problem.

10.3   SVS

The overall design of SVS, our instantiation of the theory in section 10.1, is illustrated in figure 10.4. Combined with the rest of Soar, this results in a comprehensive cognitive architecture for spatial and visual processing. The non-SVS aspects of Soar are shown at the top of figure 10.4. Boxes are short-term memories; circles are processes.

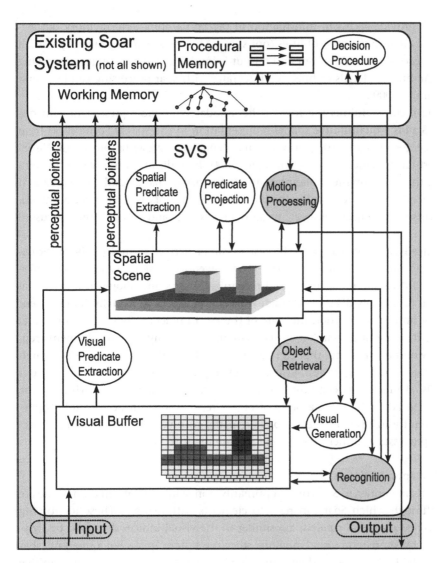

Figure 10.4
Soar/SVS Architecture.

Gray circles provide access to information in perceptual long-term memory (knowledge). There are implicit control lines (not shown) between working memory and all of the processes shown. SVS input and output is implemented as changes in working memory. Additional details of how SVS integrates with Soar processing can be found in Wintermute 2009b.

Working memory fulfills the role of the amodal symbolic representation in our theory. SVS adds a quantitative spatial representation in the Spatial Scene short-term memory (center of figure 10.4) and a visual depictive representation in the Visual Buffer short-term memory (bottom of figure 10.4). In addition to the two short-term memories, there is a long-term memory in SVS for visual, spatial, and motion data; it is called *Perceptual LTM*. To simplify the diagram, this memory is not explicitly shown, but is accessed by object retrieval, motion processing, and recognition (discussed below).

Theoretically, all information in the system can be derived from depictive information added to the visual buffer by a low-level perception system. Conceptually, processes in Soar/SVS should segment and recognize objects and should use 2D visual information to estimate 3D spatial structure. However, complete domain-independent computer vision is well beyond the state of the art. In practice, SVS is used in virtual environments without a complete visual system; many simulated environments represent the world in structures that can be directly fed into the spatial scene. Although it isn't used for bottom-up vision, visual processing still plays a prominent role in our system. Visual imagery is cognitively useful and can be implemented without true perception. In addition, some aspects of object recognition can be fruitfully implemented, even though the broader problem remains unsolved. In the following subsections, the processes and memories inside SVS are discussed briefly.

10.3.1   Perceptual Pointers

Although the memories in SVS contain primarily non-symbolic information, there are symbols through which Soar can refer to elements within them. These identifying symbols, called *perceptual pointers*, are similar to the visual indices described by Pylyshyn (2001) for short-term visual memory, since the system "picks out a small number of individuals, keeps track of them, and provides a means by which the cognitive system can further examine them in order to encode their properties . . . or to carry out a motor command in relation to them." However, that theory limits the number of objects to four or five, a limitation we do not model.

Perceptual pointers are similar in concept to identifiers. Every item in Perceptual LTM has a corresponding symbol in Soar, implemented as a perceptual pointer that is the equivalent of a long-term identifier. Every item in a short-term memory, whether it is the Spatial Scene or the Visual Buffer, has a perceptual pointer that is the equivalent of a short-term identifier, in addition to an associated long-term identifier if the item is known to be an instance of something in Perceptual LTM. The convention in SVS is to name the attribute associated with long-term identifier *class-id* and to name the attribute associated with a short-term identifier *id*. The values of these identifiers are simply string symbols that refer to an object in Perceptual LTM, in the Spatial Scene, or in the Visual Buffer. Strings for class-id perceptual pointers are consistent across agents and can be incorporated into rules, whereas id strings are not consistent and are intended to be matched with variables.

Figure 10.5 shows Pegged Blocks World information represented in Soar/SVS. Dotted arrows are perceptual pointers. Only those created by SVS have arrows in the figure, but instances of the same strings elsewhere (e.g., blockB:i1 and blockC:i1 in the

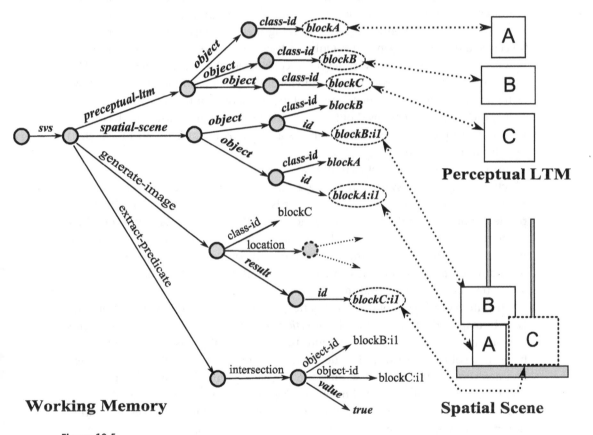

Figure 10.5
Pegged Blocks World information in Working Memory, Perceptual LTM, and Spatial Scene. Working-memory elements labeled in bold italics are created by SVS.

intersection structure) are also pointers to the same objects. The processes of image generation and predicate extraction represented in the figure will be explained in detail shortly.

The visual and spatial details of the objects in SVS (e.g., their coordinates in space or their pixel values) are *not* represented in Soar's working memory. Working memory instead holds the perceptual pointers and qualitative information. The qualitative information includes data retrieved from one of the long-term memories, or data extracted from the spatial scene using the processes outlined below.

10.3.2 Memory Encodings

Internally, the spatial scene (center of figure 10.4) is a set of three-dimensional objects grounded in continuous coordinates. The symbolic perceptual pointers to the objects in the scene are represented in Soar's working memory organized as a hierarchy of objects and their constituent parts. Only the leaves of this tree correspond to primitive polyhedrons, but nodes at every level are considered objects; this enables symbolic reasoning to refer to the whole or to individual parts. For example, the house shown in figure 10.1 might be encoded as two polyhedrons, one for the roof and one for the frame, each a part of a "house" object. The agent can reason at either level, considering the roof independently or the house as a whole. For simplicity, this hierarchy is not shown in figure 10.4.

Since the scene grounds objects at locations in 3D space how the coordinate frame affects the rest of the system might be a matter of concern. Is the scene from the perspective of the agent (i.e., egocentric), or is the coordinate system specified independently of the agent's frame of reference (i.e., allocentric)? In fact, the coordinate frame of the scene is arbitrary; it doesn't affect most spatial processing. Intuitively, this is because the properties that the higher-level parts of the system care about are qualitative properties of objects relative to one another—properties that are preserved across translation, scaling, and rotation.

The internal encoding of the visual buffer (bottom of figure 10.4) is a set of bitmaps. Each bitmap in the buffer is called a *depiction* and has a perceptual pointer presented to working memory (not shown in figure 10.4). Individual pixels in the depiction can be set to a color, or to a special value indicating emptiness. Typically, there is at least one depiction in the set representing the perceived scene from an egocentric viewpoint, but others may be created through image processing. Having a set of depictions allows multiple objects to exist at the same visual location; it also serves as an attention mechanism, as processing can focus on specific regions.

The Scout agent uses depictions in the visual buffer to encode its perceived map, along with other visual structures it creates during problem solving. Figure 10.6 shows an overlaid set of these depictions. The background image is a perceived map. The triangle-like region is a depiction of an area visible from a specific perspective,

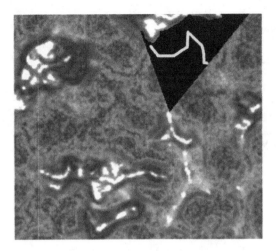

Figure 10.6
Visual depictions used in a Scout agent.

and the squiggly line in its center is another depiction overlaid on the previous two that enables the agent to recognize a potential enemy path. The agent uses these depictions to determine whether the enemy's paths would be visible from its location or from the location of its teammate. How these images are created will be explained below.

The internal representation of perceptual LTM is more heterogeneous than the other parts of SVS. It stores spatial objects and the quantitative relationships between them, visual textures, and motion models (e.g., the motion model of a particular vehicle). Long-term perceptual pointers are available to Soar agents for all of these constructs. In the current implementations, the knowledge engineer encodes these items in perceptual LTM on the basis of the domain. For example, spatial objects can be designed in using an external 3D modeling tool, then imported into perceptual LTM. A useful research direction would be to attempt to learn such information and then gradually add and modify the information in the agent's Perceptual LTM. Our hypothesis is that such learning would work in conjunction with the learning mechanisms in Soar's other long-term memories (i.e., episodic and semantic).

10.3.3 Predicate Extraction
Predicate extraction provides symbolic processing in Soar with qualitative properties of the contents of the spatial scene and visual buffer. These processes are architectural; there is a fixed set of properties that can be extracted, and those properties are not learnable by the agent. In contrast to perceptual pointers, qualitative predicates are created in working memory only when requested by Soar. There is a great deal of

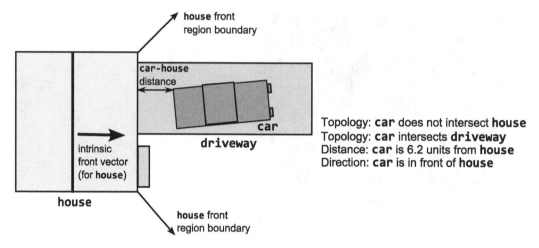

Figure 10.7
Information derivable through spatial predicate extraction.

qualitative information implicit in the memories of SVS, each piece of which can take substantial calculation to derive, so this top-down control is needed to make the system computationally tractable.

For the spatial system, there are three important kinds of relationships between objects that can be queried: topology, distance, and direction. (See figure 10.7.) Topological relationships describe how the surfaces of objects relate to one another. In the current implementation of SVS, the only relationship that is detected is whether or not two objects are intersecting.

Distance queries are similarly simple. Currently the system can query for the distance between any two objects in the scene along the closest line connecting them. This information is non-qualitative, although it is certainly "less quantitative" than the contents of the spatial scene, as it reduces three-dimensional information to a scalar quantity. However, it is extremely useful in practice. The closest obstacle to the agent might be detected by extracting the distance from the agent to all of the obstacles and comparing to determine the closest.

Direction queries are implemented as in the approach of Hernández (1994). For each object, a set of surrounding acceptance regions are defined, which correspond roughly to concepts such as left and right. An object is in a particular direction if it lies within the acceptance region. Every object has an associated "front" vector, defining an intrinsic frame of reference, upon which the regions are based; however, this could easily be extended to allow queries using frames of reference of other objects, or using a global coordinate frame.

Figure 10.5 shows a simple example of predicate extraction in Pegged Blocks World. The agent has created an image of block C on peg2 and has used predicate extraction to detect that this imagined block intersects block B. To do this, Soar rules created a query structure in working memory, which SVS processing detected and responded to. The working-memory representation has been simplified in the figure, but the essentials are the same.

The visual system also supports predicate extraction. For example, there is a predicate that reports whether or not a depiction has any non-empty pixels. Typically, visual generation and top-down visual recognition processes (discussed below) result in a depiction that will have some pixels filled in if some property is true (e.g., an object exists) and no pixels filled in if the property is not true, so predicate extraction there is simple. One way visual predicate extraction is used in the Scout domain is to determine whether the path in figure 10.6 overlaps with the perceivable region (the partial triangle). Similar to spatial predicate extraction, a symbolic query structure is created in working memory to focus SVS processing. Visual processing searches the pair of depictions for the overlapping path and view pixels. SVS augments working memory with the resulting distance of the overlapping path, which can then be used for subsequent reasoning.

For both spatial and visual predicate extraction, our theory allows a wider variety of predicates than those that are present in the current system. In particular, previous implementations have allowed for spatial predicates encoding size, orientation, and a larger variety of topological relations, and for visual predicates encoding topological relationships, size, and distance. The architectural commitment is that predicate extraction is a distinct, fixed process in the system, not that the implemented set of predicates is complete.

10.3.4 Image Creation

Often the information provided to Soar through perceptual pointers and predicate extraction about objects that the agent can perceive is not sufficient to allow general-purpose problem solving: predicate extraction alone doesn't provide enough information about the outside world. Instead, imagery processes must be employed. Though imagery has often been proposed for problem solving, the exact means by which images are created in a problem-independent manner have rarely been specified.

10.3.5 Predicate Projection

Creating a new spatial image often involves translating a qualitative description to a quantitative representation in the scene. To allow this, SVS incorporates a process of predicate projection (Wintermute and Laird 2007). Predicates supported by SVS include geometric concepts such as "hull" and "intersection." A hull image is the convex hull of two or more objects in the scene; an intersection image is the region of intersection of two or more objects. In addition, SVS supports predicates (such as "on") that specify qualitative spatial relationships between objects, but not about the shape of the image.

Like predicate extraction, predicate projection is a fixed process, but there is no strong commitment that the current library of available operations (described more fully in Wintermute 2009b) is complete. Further research is needed to determine what kinds of predicate projection are necessary for human-level functionality.

In Pegged Blocks World, predicate projection can be used to create images of blocks in new positions. Such an image is shown in figure 10.5, but with the predicate projection portion (the location structure) of its symbolic specification omitted. To arrive at the image, the location structure should encode that the block is on the surface of the table, centered with respect to peg2.

10.3.6 Memory Retrieval

In contrast to predicate projection, which describes the qualitative properties of the spatial or visual image, memory retrievals extract specific quantitative information from perceptual LTM (e.g., objects, quantitative spatial relationships, motion models, visual textures, etc.) via perceptual pointers. SVS uses this information to construct or augment the spatial scene. For example, an agent can imagine a car without qualitatively describing its shape or the relationship of the wheels to the body. Images can be created by a combination of both processes, for example, by imagining a specific object in long-term memory at a qualitatively described location. The image of block C in figure 10.5 is an example of this, as the shape of the block is retrieved from LTM. This retrieval is implicit in the specification: a class-id attribute is present, whose value is a perceptual pointer to an LTM item. SVS then instantiates the object with the class-id in the spatial scene, adding the resulting object id, or perceptual pointer to Soar's working memory.

10.3.7 Motion Simulation and Motor Imagery

Although the previous approaches to image creation are powerful, they are insufficient to solve problems involving non-trivial motion. For example, consider predicting whether a turning car will hit an obstacle (figure 10.8). The agent must determine whether or not the car can drive to the goal, via the waypoint, without colliding with an obstacle. The path of the car when steering toward the waypoint, then toward the goal, is shown. An agent able to derive this path can check whether the car intersects obstacles, solving the problem. For a general agent that is capable of the same range of behavior as humans, there are many types of motion that the system may need to predict, including the outcome of its own actions, the motions of others, and the motions of objects not under the control of any agent (e.g., the path of a bouncing ball).

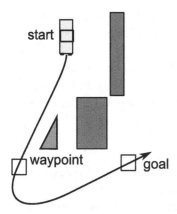

Figure 10.8
An example of a motion problem.

In SVS, information of this type is encoded in *motion models* (Wintermute and Laird 2008). By transforming one continuous spatial state to another, motion models provide the fine-grained quantitative resolution that representing motion accurately requires. Motion models are in perceptual LTM, and can be applied to any object in the spatial scene, resulting in a motion simulation. This simulation is a sequence of steps, controlled by Soar. The agent can use predicate extraction between each time step, gaining information from the simulation, such as whether or not the car intersects an obstacle in figure 10.8.

Motion models can be used to simulate many kinds of motion, including the motion of the agent's own effectors. In a system incorporating real effectors, motion models should be intimately tied to their control (Wintermute 2009a 2010). For this reason, the motion-processing module in figure 10.4 is connected to the output of the system.

Motion models are encoded as task knowledge and are not architectural, as an agent may encounter any number of distinct motion patterns in its life. Hypothetically, an agent encountering a car for the first time would learn the model at that time. This learning process is an area for future research. In the current implementation, motion models are written as C++ functions by the knowledge engineer.

10.3.8 Visual Generation
If SVS were a more comprehensive model of human processing, perception would directly create structures in the visual buffer, and internal processing would derive the spatial scene from those structures. In imagery contexts, the visual buffer would be modified in top-down fashion on the basis of information in the spatial scene and in symbolic working memory. This process, called *visual generation* (Lathrop and Laird

2008), is supported by SVS. To support generation, the agent specifies the point of view and which object(s) in the spatial scene to render. The result of this process is a new depiction instantiated in the visual buffer.

This process entails a conversion from a 3D to a 2D representation, so it can be used directly to solve problems of the form "can object A be seen from the perspective of object B?" It also is useful to generate visual depictions to support further processing, such as predicate extraction or visual recognition.

10.3.9   Visual Recognition

The visual system in SVS enables recognition processes to make use of properties of the depictive representation. Supporting visual recognition in general is a major challenge, but allowing simple recognition processes in certain domains can be useful. SVS realizes visual recognition either through mathematical manipulations (e.g., edge detectors) or through "depictive manipulations" that encode pixel transformations to create new depictions (Furnas 2000; Lathrop and Laird 2009). A pixel-rewrite rule, specified in Soar and then passed to SVS for processing, includes a left-hand-side condition and a right-hand-side action. Rather than being symbolic, however, the pixel-rewrite rule conditions and actions test and modify bitmaps. When a rule matches a region, the right-hand-side action rewrites the appropriate pixel(s). As a simple example, the left panel of figure 10.9 illustrates two depictive rules. The upper rule states "if there is a black pixel adjacent to a gray pixel then change the gray pixel to white." The lower rule says "if there is a black pixel diagonal to a gray pixel then change the gray pixel to white." The asterisk values represent wild-card values, and a pixel rewrite rule may specify rotations (90°, 180°, 270°) for which a match fires the

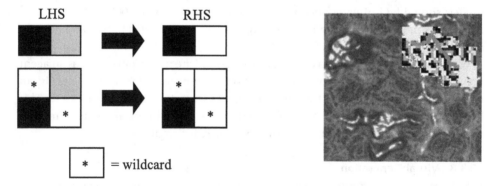

Figure 10.9
Depictive manipulations. Left: An example of two depictive rules for manipulating a bitmap. Right: The output of depictive rules used in the Scout domain to detect a likely path through terrain.

rule. With appropriate rules, the result of this process can be meaningful depictions, such as an outline of the enclosed space in an object.

A Scout agent can use depictive manipulations to recognize sophisticated properties of the world. The agent must identify paths that an enemy might follow through terrain, and rules can create such a path. This process is shown in the right panel of figure 10.9. Because these processes derive meaningful visual information from undifferentiated pixels, we consider them recognition processes. To support visual recognition, the depictive manipulation rules are encoded in Soar's working memory as the results of operator application and sent to SVS for processing. The symbolic results of that processing then augment working memory.

10.4   Demonstrations of Spatial and Visual Imagery

Agents for the two imagery domains covered here will now be discussed in more detail. We have used these spatially and visually rich environments to demonstrate the capabilities of Soar with, and in some cases without, its imagery component. Additional experimental results are reported in Lathrop 2008, Lathrop and Laird 2007, Wintermute and Laird 2009, Wintermute 2009, and Wintermute 2010.

10.4.1   Simulated Army Scout

In this domain, the agent makes decisions by analyzing the situation and choosing a course of action. Analyzing the situation involves reasoning about known and hypothesized friendly and enemy positions, terrain, and obstacles. If the scout doesn't know the locations of all expected enemies, it can use knowledge of how the enemies typically maneuver to imagine their location. The agent can also use imagery to analyze an action's outcome before executing it. For example, the lead scout can imagine hypothetical enemy destinations, possible enemy paths, the teammate's view, and its own view. Using this information, it can make a decision about whether or not to re-orient itself, its teammate, or both.

In our experiments, we have found that an agent using imagery provides more information about the enemies than a comparable agent without mental imagery (Lathrop and Laird 2009). Figure 10.11 illustrates that the agent using mental imagery provides more information sooner and for a longer period of time than the agent without mental imagery. The x axis represents the simulation time. The y axis represents the amount of information provided by the agent per unit time, 1.0 meaning perfect information and −1.0 meaning no information, averaged over the three enemy entities. It is calculated as follows:

$$I_t = -1 \text{ if no observation}$$

$$= 1 - d \text{ otherwise},$$

where

$$\delta = \frac{\sqrt{(\mathrm{obs}_x - \mathrm{act}_x)^2 + (\mathrm{obs}_y - \mathrm{act}_y)^2}}{d_{\mathrm{acceptable}}}.$$

Here $(\mathrm{obs}_x, \mathrm{obs}_y)$ is the reported location of an entity at time t, $(\mathrm{act}_x, \mathrm{act}_y)$ is the actual location of an entity at time t, and $d_{\mathrm{acceptable}}$ represents the square "box" within which an error δ is calculated. If the distance between the observed and actual location of the entity falls outside this "box," then the information is -1.0 for that entity during that time. Results were averaged over 30 trials.

For comparison, a hand-calculated baseline is shown, representing the information an idealized scout team provides if each scout had the ability to observe one enemy from the beginning to the end of the simulation, which ends up being $(1 + 1 - 1)/3 = 0.33$. In the simulation, the terrain makes this approach impossible. At its best, the team can cover the enemy vehicles only partially. The agent using imagery provides more information sooner and for a longer period of time than the agent not using imagery. The imagery agent in this domain uses the comprehensive capabilities of Soar/SVS, especially the capabilities of the visual system, to manipulate the depictive representations, recognize topology (e.g., what portion of a path is covered by the agent's view), and measure distance (what is the length of the observed portion of the path). The agent with mental imagery provides more information, as its spatial and visual reasoning is more accurate than reasoning with abstract symbols, taking advantage of the explicit representation of space in the visual buffer and

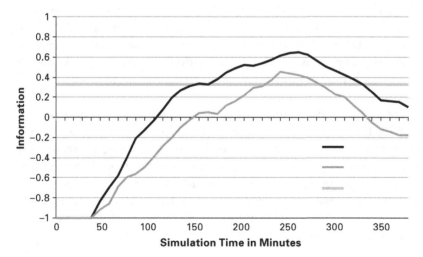

Figure 10.10
Results from simulation of agents in the Scout domain.

corresponding specialized processing within the architecture. The computational advantage frees resources to perform other cognitive functions (e.g., observe, send and receive reports), and using Soar for control allows the agent to maintain reactivity by interrupting mental imagery processing when new information arrives from either the teammate or perception.

10.4.2 Pegged Blocks World

In the Pegged Blocks World domain, it is difficult to create an abstract state representation that captures all relevant problem states so that optimal behavior can be encoded. However, it is easy to make spatial predictions with imagery. The resulting states of these predictions can be abstracted, and decisions can be made in terms of the predicted abstract states.

Figure 10.11 shows an example using SVS's spatial system. Starting at the left, two different possible states of the world are shown: instance A and instance B. When these are abstracted into symbolic representations using predicate extraction operations (thick arrows), they produce equivalent descriptions. If decision making is based only on this state, it would be impossible for the agent to always choose the right answer. Imagery allows the agent to disambiguate instances where states have the same abstraction, but different action effects. The transition from state 2 to the two possible state 3's is produced by the agent imagining the effect of an action (move D onto C) via predicate projection in the spatial level. After imagery, instances A and B lead to different states, one in which there is not a collision (A) and one in which there is (B). These collisions can be detected through predicate extraction, providing symbolic representations that distinguish the two states.

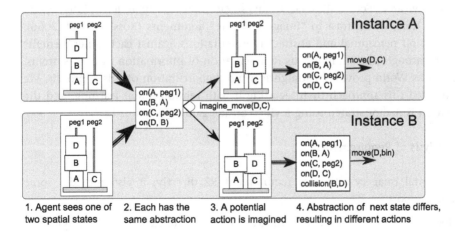

1. Agent sees one of two spatial states   2. Each has the same abstraction   3. A potential action is imagined   4. Abstraction of next state differs, resulting in different actions

Figure 10.11
Example of imagery-based decision making in Pegged Blocks World.

An alternative approach might be to determine a better means of abstracting spatial information, so as to improve the agent's predicate extraction system. However, there doesn't seem to be a method of abstracting spatial information that can work well in arbitrary domains (Forbus, Nielsen, and Faltings 1991), so an agent in a task-independent architecture probably will have to deal with imperfect abstractions of spatial state (Wintermute and Laird 2009). One theme in work with SVS has been investigating how imagery can be useful to compensate for imperfect abstractions.

An agent has been built to perform in this domain to demonstrate this basic process, which we call *simulative imagery* because it is a specific use of imagery to simulate the effects of actions (Wintermute 2009c). The agent has knowledge in the form of an imagery-conditional plan that works in the manner of figure 10.11 to disambiguate states at decision points. The plan knowledge used by the agent is compact, encoding fewer than 15 different choices, but imagery allows the agent to be sensitive to minute differences in block shapes that could cause collisions. Thus, the agent benefits from representing state at multiple levels of abstraction: the spatial level allows for precise predictions, whereas the abstract symbolic level allows for compactly represented knowledge, which leads to generalization. Though the abstract representation is imperfect, imagery compensates when precision is needed and the agent can act intelligently. In this example, simulative imagery is used for one-step look-ahead, but the same mechanisms could be used for arbitrarily deep search. One-step look-ahead is used to make this agent more representative of agents in domains where aspects of the environment are difficult to model (e.g., the actions of others, or random events); this makes deep searches unreliable, though the local consequences of the agent's own actions may still be predictable.

Though this domain is simple, approaching it from a functional standpoint in a comprehensive architecture allows us to investigate a previously underexplored aspect of imagery. Here, in contrast to "imagery debate" arguments (Kosslyn et al. 2006), which often pit perceptual and abstract representations against each other, benefits are gained through the simultaneous representation of information in both systems. Pegged Blocks World provides a straightforward demonstration of this approach. We have extended this approach by integrating it with reinforcement learning, and the combination is demonstrated using a video arcade game in section 12.2.

10.5   Analysis of Requirements

Adding mental imagery addresses requirement R2 directly; it also provides some important support for R7.

R2: Modality-specific knowledge: With SVS, Soar isn't restricted to purely symbolic representations for its reasoning, but can take advantage of the efficiency and accuracy afforded by perceptual reasoning.

R7:   Rich action representation. SVS also includes motion models, which allow precise control of actions that would be difficult to achieve through purely symbolic control.

SVS is a significant step forward; however, it still has shortcomings that future research will have to address.

Beyond objects: Currently the system is restricted to object-based spatial representations. It doesn't have a means of perceiving empty space, such as a doorway, except to consider the space or location as some kind of pseudo-object that isn't directly sensed.

Connecting real perception: The current implementation has been used with simulated environments. The next step is to connect SVS to real sensors and algorithms for object detection and identification. One possibility is that imagery can facilitate these processes, although significant research is required as to how systems such as SVS can provide appropriate information to object detection and identification routines. Although SVS has not been connected to real sensors, other Soar robotic systems have, but they have relied on bottom-up conversions of sensor data to symbolic structures and have not used mental imagery.

11 Emotion

with Robert P. Marinier III

The fundamental components and the extensions of Soar we have discussed in previous chapters are standard memory and processing units that have obvious functional value for a cognitive architecture. In this chapter, we consider emotion and some possible computational models of how it interacts with cognition. Folk psychology often implies that emotions are a negative distraction, and that from a functional/logical perspective we would be better off without them (consider the Vulcans in *Star Trek*). However, extensive research by psychologists, neurologists, physiologists, and sociologists supports the theory that emotion and cognition are inexorably interlinked, and there is wide agreement that emotions are necessary to ensure effective behavior and learning (Damasio 1994). Although it is clear that emotion influences behavior in humans, the exact functional benefit of emotion is less clear.

The purpose of our investigations is to discover whether and how computational agents can utilize some of the functional capabilities of emotion—that is, to bring the functionality of emotions to cognitive architectures. This is in contrast to most existing computational models of emotion, which focus primarily on creating believable agents (Gratch and Marsella 2004; Hudlicka 2004), modeling human data (Gratch, Marsella, and Mao 2006; Marsella and Gratch 2009), or entertainment (Loyall et al. 2004).

In this chapter we describe how we integrated some aspects of emotion with cognition, both for cognitive architectures in general and more specifically for Soar. The work described here is in an early state, and thus is not yet included in the Soar release. In exploring this integration, we found that although the problem-space computational model as defined in chapter 3 provides an abstract characterization of the structure of behavior, it is agnostic as to the content of the state and the specific operators. Neither Soar nor the PSCM specifies a set of primitive operators or data structures for the state. Newell (1990) proposed that a set of abstract functional operations (collectively called PEACTIDM) are ubiquitous in immediate behavior, in which decisions are made quickly in response to the current situation without extensive deliberation or planning. Our hypothesis is that these operations provide a context for integration of one aspect of emotion, specifically that PEACTIDM can provide general content for immediate tasks within the structure of the PSCM.

Our work on emotion draws on appraisal theories (Gratch, Marsella, and Petta 2009; Roseman and Smith 2001). We hypothesize that appraisals provide the data required for PEACTIDM's abstract functional operations as well as for generating an internal reward signal for reinforcement learning. Further, we hypothesize that PEACTIDM's abstract functional operations provide a framework for computing and using appraisals, and we develop an extension to Soar for computing and using appraisals within the context of PEACTIDM. We demonstrate this integration and the effects of appraisals on decision making and reinforcement learning in a new agent for an early version of Rooms World. One interesting result of our investigations is that appraisals provide innate utilities and thus provide some of capabilities required for achieving R8.

This chapter draws on Marinier, Laird, and Lewis 2009 and on Marinier 2008. There are many consequences of our model; for example, it assumes a non-categorical model of emotion (every unique combination of appraisal values is a unique emotion), that intensity is generated the same way for all emotions, and that there is some ordering to appraisal generation. This is in contrast to many previous computational models (Neal Reilly 1996; Marsella and Gratch 2006) and some emotion theories that assume a categorical representation of emotion, but it meshes well with Scherer's (2001) appraisal theory, which has been the focus of our implementation.

11.1   Appraisal Theories of Emotion

Appraisal theories of emotion postulate that an agent is constantly evaluating its situation along a number of *appraisal dimensions*, many of which take the current goal into account. There are many different appraisal theories (for several examples see Scherer, Schorr, and Johnstone 2001), and the number of dimensions in a theory varies from five to more than fifteen, although most theories overlap extensively in their proposed dimensions. The values for these dimensions influence the current emotion, resulting in what we might call fear, anger, joy, and so on. The emotion may have multiple effects; for example, the agent may attempt to cope with the emotion in some way. In our work, we explored emotion-driven learning.

The particular appraisals that we have investigated are a subset of the appraisals described by Scherer (2001), and are listed in table 11.1. The appraisals we use are split into three main groups: appraisals that help the agent decide which stimulus to attend to (Suddenness, Unpredictability, Intrinsic Pleasantness, Relevance); appraisals that help the agent understand the implications of the situation (causal agent and motive, outcome probability, discrepancy from expectation, conduciveness); and

Table 11.1
Appraisals we have investigated.

Suddenness	Extent to which stimulus is characterized by abrupt onset or high intensity
Unpredictability	Extent to which the stimulus could not have been predicted
Intrinsic pleasantness	Extent to which stimulus is pleasant independent of goal
Relevance	Extent to which stimulus is important with respect to goal
Causal agent	Who caused the stimulus
Causal motive	Motivation of causal agent
Outcome probability	Probability of stimulus occurring
Discrepancy from Expectation	Extent to which stimulus did not match prediction
Conduciveness	Extent to which stimulus is good or bad for the goal
Control	Extent to which anyone can influence the stimulus
Power	Extent to which agent can influence the stimulus

appraisals that help the agent decide what do in response to an attended stimulus (control, power).

Consider our agent that has to clean the rooms in Rooms World. If the agent has the goal of cleaning a room and it sees a block, it may evaluate the situation as not particularly Unpredictable (because it has seen blocks before) but very Relevant (because it needs to clean up that block). The situation isn't really Conducive, since the agent realizes that it has more work to do. The value of Discrepancy from Expectation depends on what the agent predicted before this situation arose: if the agent expected the room to be clean already, then Discrepancy is high; if it expected to find a block, Discrepancy is low. These dimensions have continuous values. Causal Agency, on the other hand, has a categorical value: self, other, or nature. If the agent is alone in the environment, the agency will probably be attributed to nature (unless the agent knows that it placed the block here). On the other hand, if a cat is present, the agent may attribute agency to it.

Appraisal theories postulate a fixed mapping from appraisals to emotions, possibly modulated by other factors, such as physiology. For example, in the situation described above, Novelty is low, Relevance is high, and Conduciveness is low. Suppose the agent knew the block would be here because it had seen it before, resulting in a high Outcome Probability and low Discrepancy from Expectation. Further, suppose that agency is attributed to nature. This set of appraisals may map onto boredom because nothing special is happening.

On the other hand, if the agent was sure the room was clean, then the Outcome Probability associated with that prediction would be high and Discrepancy from Expectation would also be high, perhaps resulting in dismay. In general, the interaction between Outcome Probability and Discrepancy from Expectation influences

Table 11.2
Relationship among outcome probability, discrepancy from expectation, and intensity.

	Discrepancy low	Discrepancy high
Outcome probability low	High intensity (surprising)	Low intensity (not surprising)
Outcome probability high	Low intensity (not surprising)	High intensity (surprising)

the intensity of the experienced emotions, but not the valence (see table 11.2). Finally, if agency is the cat (other), the agent may experience anger, since it has something to blame.

11.2   Abstract Functional Cognitive Operations

Although there is significant empirical support for appraisal theories (Scherer et al. 2001), there are no comprehensive computational theories of how the data generated and processed by appraisals combines with cognition to produce purposeful behavior (but see Smith and Kirby 2001 for an attempt). Cognitive architectures are one attempt at producing the computational answers. Cognitive architectures such as Soar and ACT-R specify processing units, storage systems, data representations, and the timing of various mechanisms. However, they provide only the structure in which knowledge is encoded; they do not provide a theory of operators that support immediate behavior by interacting with and responding to an external environment. PEACTIDM provides a framework in which to bring appraisals and cognitive architecture together to address these deficits. Relative to the PSCM, PEACTIDM defines a higher-level set of functions that would be implemented, perhaps implicitly, via the PSCM; our specific implementation is discussed below.

Newell (1990) proposed that an agent performs certain abstract functional operations in the service of immediate behavior:

Perceive (getting raw perceptual information from the environment),
Encode (transforming that information into something cognition can process),
Attend (focusing cognition on one of potentially many stimuli),
Comprehend (generating structures that relate the stimulus to the task),
Tasking (performing goal maintenance),
Intend (choosing an action in response to the Attended stimulus),
Decode (transforming the action into a form that can be executed)
Motor (executing motor actions).

In our implementation, we extend PEACTIDM by including a prediction generated as to the outcome of the action it Intends. These operations are performed in a cycle as shown in figure 11.1.

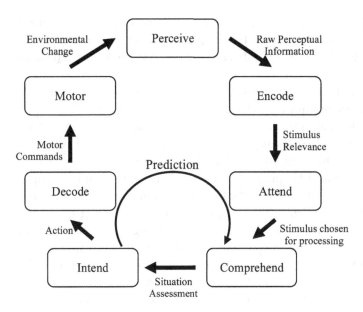

Figure 11.1
The basic PEACTIDM cycle. Tasking is not shown.

In general, there are data dependencies among these steps: an action cannot be executed by Decode and Motor until Intend chooses one, Intend cannot choose an action until the stimulus has been put in context by Comprehend, Comprehend cannot understand the stimulus until a stimulus has been focused on by Attend, and Attend cannot focus on a stimulus until at least one has been Perceived and Encoded. There are exceptions to some of these dependencies, as in pure stimulus-response reflexes, but if cognition is involved, we claim this holds.

Thus, there is a PEACTIDM cycle that repeats, enabling the agent to generate behavior in response to an ever-changing situation. Tasking, which includes creating goals and subgoals, marking goals as completed, and giving up on goals, is special in that the agent typically doesn't change tasks very rapidly relative to the length of the PEACTIDM cycle. That is, in some cycles the agent may engage in Tasking instead of executing an external action, but we hypothesize that this takes virtually the same form: instead of Attending to an external stimulus, the agent Attends to the internally represented possibility of Tasking. The potential Tasking operation, e.g. creating a subgoal, can be Comprehended in the context of the situation, e.g., determining if it is a good idea, and Intended, i.e., actually doing it and predicting the outcome. The goal selected by Tasking serves as input to the Encode and Comprehend steps.

In the cleaning task in Rooms World, all these functions are performed: the agent chooses to clean a room (Tasking), sees a block and a doorway (Perceive and Encode), focuses on the block (Attend), determines that the block is preventing goal achievement (Comprehend), decides to pick the block up and predicts that doing so will allow it to make progress in the task (Intend), and actually picks up the block (Decode and Motor).

The PEACTIDM functions are abstract since, in terms of any particular architecture, they may be mapped onto multiple primitive operations. Following Newell's lead, we mapped PEACTIDM onto Soar in the following way: Perceive and Encode are a combination of stimulus input on Soar's input-link and parallel elaboration rules that create additional structure, including the internal Tasking stimuli, and Attend is an operator that selects a stimulus for processing. Comprehend and Intend are implemented as complex operators that are initially implemented in substates via multiple primitive operators. With experience, chunking collapses the processing into single decisions. Decode and Motor map onto Soar's output processing. Thus, relative to the PSCM, in our model PEACTIDM is a hypothesis as to the structure of a generic top-level problem space. Indeed, even though the agent described in this chapter is a direct implementation of PEACTIDM (Newell 1990, p. 262), complex agents must implement these steps in one manner or another. Table 11.3 shows how the PEACTIDM steps

Table 11.3
Comparison of PEACTIDM implementation across two different agents.

Abstract functional operation	Emotion agent	Original agent
Perceive	Perception system	Perception system
Encode	Perception system State elaboration	Perception system State elaboration
Attend	Attend operator	Perception system
Comprehend	Comprehend operator	Compiled into operator proposals
Tasking	Intend (internal) operator	Abstract operators: deposit-block go-to-storage-room go-to-next-room go-to-location
Intend	Intend operator	External action operators: move-forward set-waypoint stop avoid-object turn-through-door turn-to-waypoint
Decode	Motor system State elaboration	Motor system State elaboration
Motor	Motor system	Motor system

manifest themselves in the agent described here and in the Rooms World agent described in chapter 5. Note that the original agent doesn't explicitly comprehend; the task is highly reactive, and thus the comprehension knowledge has been incorporated into the proposals for the various Tasking and Intend operators. Also note that Perception and Motor are external to these agents, although the Emotion agent does perform the Attend task explicitly.

The comparison above gives some hint as to how a general mapping between PEACTIDM and PSCM may be developed, as PEACTIDM stands; however, such a mapping would be imperfect. PEACTIDM was originally developed to explain immediate behavior only; support for long-term behavior would have to be added, as hinted at by the abstract operators under Tasking.

When Newell presented PEACTIDM, he described only the processes involved—namely, these abstract functional operations. Newell didn't describe the data generated or consumed by these various processes, much less the representations. We hypothesize that appraisal theories of emotion can help fill in these missing pieces.

11.3   Unifying Cognitive Control and Appraisal

Our primary hypothesis is that appraisal theories provide some of the data that are generated and consumed by parts of the PEACTIDM process. (For the specifics, see table 11.4.) For example, Perceive and Encode generate information that Attend can use to choose a stimulus to focus on. Appraisals such as Suddenness, Unpredictability, and Goal Relevance are examples of information that can be used to influence Attend.

Table 11.4
Integration of PEACTIDM and appraisal.

Appraisals	Generated by	Required by
Suddenness	Perceive	Attend
Unpredictability Intrinsic pleasantness Relevance	Encode	
Causal agent Causal motive Outcome probability Discrepancy from Expectation Conduciveness Control Power	Comprehend	Comprehend, Task, Intend

Indeed, Scherer (2001) includes these in what he calls the Relevance dimensions. In our original example, the agent had two stimuli it could Attend to: a doorway and a block. Since its goal is to clean the room, the block is considered highly Goal Relevant; the doorway is not. Thus, the agent Attends to the block.

Similarly, Comprehend generates information that Intend can use to choose an action. Again, there are a number of appraisal dimensions whose information are useful here, including Causal Agency (Who put the block here?), Discrepancy from Expectation (Did I expect a block to be here?), Conduciveness (Is it good or bad that there is a block here?), and so on; Scherer calls these the Implication and Coping Potential dimensions. In our example, the agent determines that the block isn't Conducive to its goal, that the Causal Agent was the cat, and that Discrepancy is high.

In terms of implementation, each continuously valued appraisal can take on a value in the [0, 1] range or in the [–1, 1] range. The range depends on whether the appraisal appears to be valenced (e.g., the endpoints seem equally "intense" but have opposite meaning) or not. For example, Conduciveness has values in the [–1, 1] range, since something can be very good or very bad, and these are both "intense" (i.e., non-zero) values. A zero value, then, means that something is neither good nor bad. Discrepancy, on the other hand, is in the [0, 1] range, since a complete match wouldn't seem to be intense and thus should correspond to a zero value.

This unification of PEACTIDM and appraisal theories demonstrates that appraisal generation is inherent to generating behavior. That is, to the extent that PEACTIDM accurately describes how behavior is generated, appraisals must be generated.

11.4   Emotion, Mood, and Feeling

Given this unification, we can turn to the question What is emotion? "Emotion" is a broad term that covers many phenomena. For our purposes, we find it useful to distinguish three concepts: emotion, mood, and feeling. Appraisal theories claim that appraisal values map to emotional responses; thus, we define emotion as the current set of appraisal values. Thus, we use a continuous representation for emotion; see Barrett 2006 for a discussion of why categorical models may be flawed. Mood, on the other hand, is a more temporally extended phenomenon; thus, we define mood as a decaying average over recent emotions. Thus, mood is represented as another set of appraisal values. This implementation of mood is a gross simplification; mood would theoretically include many other factors, among them physiological effects. In our theory, the agent doesn't experience emotion or mood directly. Instead, emotion is combined with mood to generate a feeling, which is what the agent actually perceives. The details of our simplified theory of how emotion and mood are combined into feeling are complex and beyond the scope of this chapter (see Marinier 2008). Again, however, feeling is simply represented as a set of appraisal values; thus, emotion, mood, and feeling share a common representation. In this theory, emotions are not inherently categorical, with labels such as "joy" or "fear." The agent can use socio-cultural knowledge to map regions of appraisal values onto such labels, but it is the appraisal values that affect behavior and learning. Our agents don't generate these labels, but for debugging purposes a function generates them using Scherer's (2001) appraisal theory.

In Soar, the feeling is calculated on the basis of the appraisals computed by an agent and deposited on a special "link" in working memory, which is much like the links for input, output, semantic memory, episodic memory, and SVS. When the agent puts appraisals on the link, feeling appraisals appear on a corresponding link. The mood is managed automatically by Soar, and is apparent only through its effect on feeling. Note that in the absence of emotion the agent may still experience a non-neutral feeling, since mood takes time to decay. Mood has parameters that control the decay rate and how much it is influenced by each new emotion. (Mood can also be disabled.)

11.5   Emotion and Reinforcement Learning

The unification of cognitive control and appraisals raises a question: Why are appraisals not simply part of the vast knowledge the agent uses to generate behavior? In terms of cognitive architecture, the question is whether there is some direct interaction between emotion, mood, and feeling and other architectural modules. Although it is likely that emotion interacts directly with many cognitive modules to influence the decision making as well as the physiology of an agent, we have limited our exploration to using feeling as an internal reward signal to drive reinforcement learning.

The general idea of using internal data for reward is called *intrinsically motivated reinforcement learning* (Singh, Barto, and Chentanez 2004). Various types of internal data structures have been suggested as the basis for intrinsic reward, including some that are related to appraisals such as discrepancy from expectation (Schmidhuber 1991). Hogewoning et al. (2007) treat reward history as an emotion representation, and use reward trajectories to automatically adjust the exploration rate. Salichs and Malfaz (2006) generate rewards based on happy and sad emotions. The emotions are triggered by stimuli that satisfy current drives (e.g., if the agent is hungry and there is food, it is happy; if there is no food, it is sad). Fear, generated when state values have a large variance, influences action selection to bias against "dangerous" actions. In short, it appears that our work is unusual in using the feeling computed from a wide variety of appraisals as a reward signal.

In our approach, intensity and valence values are derived from the agent's feeling. The idea of decomposing emotion into these two dimensions comes from another set of emotion theories called *circumplex models* (Yik, Russell, and Barrett 1999), and suggests a unification of appraisal theories and circumplex models. To combine these into a reward signal, we consider a few cases. For example, suppose intensity is very high but valence is close to neutral. In this case, reward should have some medium value, since it simultaneously appears to be important but unclear. On the other hand, if intensity is very high but valence is exactly neutral, reward must also be neutral (zero), since there is no way to classify the situation as good or bad. The simplest function that achieves these properties is for reward to be the product of intensity and valence.

The calculation of intensity is based on a number of criteria. First, expectations should be a dominant factor in determining intensity (Neal Reilly 2006). That is, if Outcome Probability is high and Discrepancy is low, intensity should be low, since nothing special is happening. On the other hand, if Outcome Probability and Discrepancy are both high, we would expect intensity to be high, since something the agent was sure about didn't happen. Similar arguments can be made for when Outcome Probability is low for each value of Discrepancy. To capture this aspect of intensity, we compute a "surprise" factor based on these two appraisals.

Another criterion is that no single appraisal value should dominate the result. This is a common shortcoming with simple computational models when there are only a few appraisals—typically, the appraisal values are multiplied together, which means that if any one of them is zero then the values of the rest don't matter. To capture lack of dominance, we multiply the surprise factor by the average of the absolute values of the rest of the numeric appraisals; categorical appraisals do not influence intensity in our system. The resulting intensity equation is

$$I = [(1 - OP)(1 - DE) + (OP \cdot DE)] \cdot \text{AVG}(|\text{other appraisals}|) .$$

Thus, intensity is a value in [0, 1].

Valence is the average of all valenced appraisals (those whose values are in [–1, 1]). As was stated earlier, reward is the product of intensity and valence, resulting in a reward in [–1, 1].

This integration is illustrated in figure 11.2. Appraisals are represented in working memory as objects with an attribute for each available appraisal dimension. The appraisal representation is processed by the emotion module, which passes it to the Mood and Feeling modules, which also maintain their data organized by appraisal dimensions. The intensity and the valence are computed by the Feeling module and feed into reinforcement learning; the feeling appears in working memory.

11.6   Demonstrations of Emotion Processing

Our primary goal in developing an application with the system was to test to see if this integration provides some additional functionality. Secondarily, we wanted to investigate which appraisals have the greatest effect on performance.

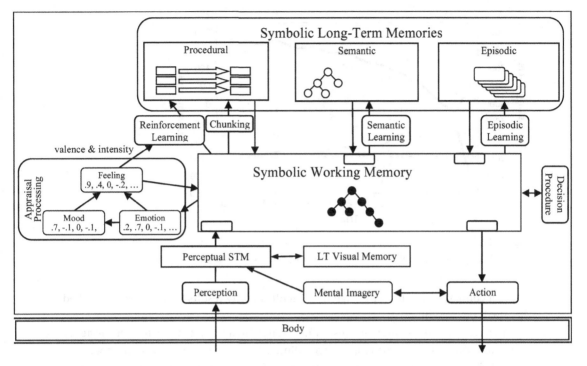

Figure 11.2
The integration of emotion, mood, feeling, and Soar.

We tested the system in multiple environments and tasks. Here we show results from the cleaning task in Rooms World (with no other agents). As table 11.3 shows, this agent differs from the agents described in previous chapters: it is organized on the basis of the principles of PEACTIDM and appraisal theories, the emphasis is on learning via reinforcement learning, and it doesn't plan.

The stimuli are the rooms, doorways, and blocks in the world, and tasking options such as creating a subgoal to clean a room or to go to another room. As a simplification, each stimulus has only a single action associated with it. (The actions are checking the room for blocks, moving through a doorway, picking up a block, and executing the Tasking operation.) Thus, the agent is learning what to Attend to, within the situations it ends up in as a result of its previous choices. The only learning mechanism we use in this experiment is reinforcement learning.

For the experiments described here, we disabled mood, so feeling was just emotion. We ran 50 repetitions of 15 trials each. A trial was a single run of the task. Learning was retained across trials. The results described here were achieved using an earlier prototype of the Rooms World environment. The difference in implementation makes

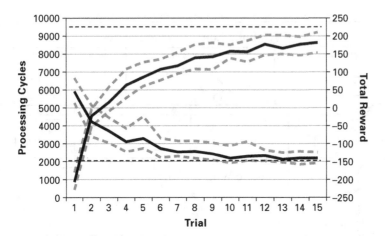

Figure 11.3
Processing cycles and total reward results for the Conduciveness experiment.

a direct comparison to the other agents difficult, so only results for the agent described here will be presented.

First, we tested the Conduciveness dimension, which is related to whether the agent is making progress toward its goal. This dimension alone is sufficient to generate a reward signal, since it is valenced. (In this case, intensity is just the absolute value of Conduciveness.) Conduciveness is measured by counting how many blocks have to be moved and how many rooms have to be checked. These quantities vary as the agent moves blocks, checks rooms, and discovers more blocks and more rooms.

Figure 11.3 shows the median number of processing cycles to complete the task (decreasing from left to right) and the median total reward accumulated in each trial (increasing from left to right). The medians are surrounded by the first and third quartiles, to give an idea of the variability in the data. The horizontal dashed lines show the approximate optimal values. In some cases the agent's performance of the task was poor. To avoid very long runs (which would make running the experiment impractical), we cut the agent off after 10,000 processing cycles. We counted a run in which we did so as a failure. Failure data are aggregated three ways: total failures (how many of the 15 × 50 = 750 runs failed), trial failures (how many trials had at least one failure run), and final-trial failures (how many trials had a failure in the final trial). Failure data are reported in table 11.5.

As illustrated in figure 11.3, the agent learned to complete the task in fewer processing cycles, and it learned to accumulate more reward; this indicates that its performance improved. The failure data in table 11.5 show a number of failures, but there were fewer failures in the final trial, which implies that the agent generally overcame

Table 11.5
Failure results for Conduciveness experiment.

Failures on final trial	Repetitions with any failures	Total failures
3 (6%)	12 (24%)	57 (7.6%)

whatever difficulty it had had in the intermediate trials. Finally, the agent learned quickly—a problem of this size would take a typical reinforcement learner hundreds or thousands of trials, but it took this emotion-driven agent only about ten. The primary reason for the faster learning is that, whereas a typical reinforcement learner receives a reward only when the task has been completed, this agent received frequent rewards based on how well it was performing the task, which resulted in much faster learning. Indeed, the agent that received a reward only at the end failed 100 percent of the time on all 15 trials.

This success may demonstrate that appraisals other than Conduciveness are unnecessary. To explore this question, we added two more appraisals: Outcome Probability and Discrepancy from Expectation. Note that we had to retain the Conduciveness dimension, as it is the only one with valence, which is required to generate reward. Adding these new dimensions requires generating a prediction about the outcome of an action, computing its associated probability, and comparing the resulting situation against the prediction. To support this, the agent creates a task model. As it executes actions in the world, it records sequences of Attended stimuli. Thus, the agent creates a network of the stimuli it experiences, with the links reflecting how recently and frequently that transition occurred. Given an Attended stimulus, the agent predicts that in the next cycle it will Attend to whatever stimulus is most strongly connected to the current stimulus. Note that this doesn't account for the action the agent chooses, since there is only one action per stimulus in this experiment. The Outcome Probability reflects how strong that link is relative to the other links. That is, it isn't strictly a probability, but it functions in much the same way. Discrepancy from Expectation is computed as a simple match or mismatch between the prediction and the next Attended stimulus.

Adding these appraisals does little to change the qualitative shape of the graph of the processing cycles or the total reward (not shown). However, they have a dramatic effect on the failure rates. (See table 11.6.)

Why does adding these appraisals reduce the failure rate? First, most failures occur because of infinite reward cycles. The agent finds a way to repeat a few actions that give it overall positive reward, and it learns to do those actions forever. Previously these cycles were broken by the cutoff. Now, however, they are broken because of the change in the way these appraisals interact with reward. When the agent repeats the

Table 11.6
Failure results for Conduciveness + Outcome probability + Discrepancy from expectation experiment.

Failures on final trial	Repetitions with any failures	Total failures
0	0	0

same actions many times, the links in the task model quickly shift to predicting those stimuli with high Outcome Probability. While the agent is actually doing these things, the Discrepancy from Expectation is low. This results in a low intensity, which results in a low reward. Thus, when the agent is stuck in cyclical behavior, the behavior ceases to be rewarding (that is, the agent gets bored). The only way to get more reward is to do something else, so the agent breaks out of the cycle.

We performed additional tests involving additional appraisals, inclusion of mood, changes to architectural integration, and other domains. For architectural integration, we automatically modulated reinforcement learning's exploration and learning rates on the basis of emotional state. In general, these explorations led to improvements in learning, although mood didn't have much effect in Rooms World. Interested readers are referred to Marinier 2008 for details.

11.7 Analysis of Requirements

The major achievement of this work is that we have developed a preliminary structure in which appraisal knowledge can be used, but we do not have a general method for computing all appraisals across a wide variety of tasks. Some appraisals appear to be straightforward to compute, as they relate directly to goal achievement; however, we do not yet have a general method to compute, for example, Discrepancy from Expectation. In the model described above, this was computed using a task-specific method, but what is needed is a task-independent approach that scales to complex problem spaces. There is a possibility that episodic memory can provide a general capability for generating expectations based on past experience, but that is an open research question. Thus, it is premature to claim that our current implementation of appraisal theory achieves any of the requirements set forth in chapter 2.

In this chapter, we demonstrated appraisal theories' potential to aid in achieving R12 and R13, but overall its contribution may be across many different components and across many requirements. Possibilities include the following:

• providing a theory for a subset of utilities related to decision making and goal achievement (R8)
• influencing episodic and semantic memory storage and retrieval, so that episodes and facts with high intensity are more likely to be stored and retrieved

- providing an indirect way to access meta-cognitive knowledge related to goal achievement, and expectation of success (R10)
- increasing the types of knowledge that are represented and used in an agent (R5).

As is obvious, there are still many open research questions, beyond solving the problem of computing appraisals. For example, a complete model of emotion must be embodied to take advantage of non-verbal communication (e.g., facial expression) and to allow exploration of things like action tendencies and basic drives (e.g., hunger and thirst), which should interact with cognition to generate goals and thus influence appraisal generation. Socio-cultural interaction is an area that also has potential interactions with appraisals. Many appraisal theories, including Scherer's, include dimensions and emotions specific to social or cultural situations; for example, Internal and External Standards Compatibility is the degree to which one is conforming to one's own or community standards, and is hypothesized to influence emotions such as guilt, shame, and pride. There have also been previous efforts to model the interplay between culture and cognition in Soar (Taylor et al. 2007). Model validation is also an issue. Previous work attempted to use humans to judge believability, although attempts to use human data have also been gaining traction (Marsella and Gratch 2009).

Finally, what forces the agent to generate values for these particular appraisals, or to follow PEACTIDM at all, remains a major architectural issue. Although we have argued that appraisals provide the information that PEACTIDM requires, nothing architectural actually forces the agent to follow the PEACTIDM steps or generate the appraisal symbols that the system recognizes. This suggests that some architectural structures may be missing.

12 Demonstrations of Multiple Architectural Capabilities

with Nate Derbinsky, Nicholas Gorski, Samuel Wintermute, and Joseph Xu

Chapters 6–11 introduced new memory and processing components to Soar and demonstrated how those components support various cognitive capabilities. This chapter presents Soar agents that employ the following novel synergistic combinations of those components:

• using reinforcement learning to acquire the knowledge that determines when and how retrievals from episodic memory are made, as well as learning to use what is retrieved to support future decision making
• using mental imagery to support look-ahead search in spatial tasks (playing classic arcade video games), then using the result of the look-ahead as part of the state for reinforcement learning
• using a wide variety of methods—including rules, task decomposition, episodic memory, semantic memory, and mental imagery—to support action modeling for look-ahead searches.

12.1 Learning to Use Episodic Memory with Reinforcement Learning

All our previous agents that used episodic memory included hand-coded procedural knowledge that determined how to retrieve memories from episodic memory as well as how to use the retrieved information. For example, in the Rooms World agent hand-coded rules propose the operator that attempts to retrieve a memory of seeing a block that is not in the storage room. These rules test whether the agent has decided to get a block but doesn't yet know which block to get. Episodic memory is used to recall a block the agent has seen and where it was located. There are also rules that extract the relevant information (the room the block is in) to direct behavior (select an operator to move to that room). Thus, the Rooms World agent is pre-programmed with the knowledge it needs to use episodic memory effectively in its environment.

In the project discussed in this section, we developed an agent that uses reinforcement learning to learn when to retrieve memories from episodic memory, and then to learn which operators should be selected once an episode is retrieved. Not only does this research extend earlier work on episodic memory in cognitive architecture; it also extends work on using reinforcement learning to learn control knowledge for accessing internal memories while learning to perform a task. (This section is based on Gorski and Laird 2010.)

In some earlier work, RL algorithms were used to learn to control internal memory mechanisms. Littman (1994) and Peshkin, Meulaeu, and Kaelbling (1999) developed RL agents that learned to toggle internal memory bits, Pearson et al. (2007) showed that an RL agent can learn to use a simple symbolic long-term memory, and Zilli and Hasselmo (2008) developed a system that learned to use both an internal short-term memory and an internal spatial episodic memory. Our work extends these previous studies in three ways. First, our episodic-memory system automatically captures all aspects of experience. Second, it learns when to access episodic memory, how to construct conjunctive cues, and when to use those cues. Third, it takes advantage of the temporal structure of episodic memory by learning to advance through episodic memory when that is useful (a property shared by the Zilli-Hasselmo system, in which it is used for simpler task representations and episodic-memory representations).

12.1.1   Environment Description

The agents we have developed exist in the Well World domain. Well World is simple enough to be tractable for learning, but rich enough so that episodic memory can improve performance. The goal for an agent in Well World is to satisfy two internal drives: thirst and safety. Figure 12.1 shows the Well World environment, in which there are three locations. At two of the locations, there are wells (which provide the water resource); at the third location, there is shelter (which provides the safety resource). The agent perceives information only about its current location—for example, it cannot see the shelter from Well 1.

Figure 12.1
Objects, resources, and adjacency in Well World.

The agent can move between locations and consume the resource at a location if that resource is available. The safety resource is always available, but the water resource is available only at one well at a time. If water is available at Well 1 and the agent consumes it, the well becomes empty and water then becomes available at Well 2; when the agent consumes water at Well 2, that well becomes empty and water is then available again at Well 1. Thus, the well that provides water alternates every time the agent consumes water.

Since the agent must remember where it last drank water in order to know which well currently has water, it needs some form of memory in order to perform optimally. That memory could be held in working memory or in semantic memory, but both of those would require task-specific knowledge to store the information for later retrieval. Episodic memory automatically creates memories of states, and the question is whether the agent can learn to exploit that memory. Furthermore, the agent has no background knowledge of the semantics of the environmental features it perceives. The agent doesn't know that if a well is "empty" then it can't consume "water" there, doesn't know that "thirst" is a drive that is quenched by "water," and it doesn't know about "safety" or "shelter." The meanings of these features must be learned, and the only signal from which the agent can learn is reward (the specifics of which are discussed below).

When the agent's thirst is quenched, its thirst drive is 0; thirst increases linearly by 0.1 on every time step. After passing the threshold of 1.0, the agent is considered thirsty until it quenches its thirst by consuming water, which resets the thirst drive to 0. The agent's drive for safety is constant and is satisfied by consuming the safety resource at the shelter. The agent's reward structure is as follows: To penalize unnecessary actions, agent incurs a reward of –1 each time it takes an external action (moving and consuming resources); internal actions (such as initiating a retrieval from episodic memory) incur a reward of –0.1. (In a real-world setting, internal actions would presumably take orders of magnitude less time to complete than external actions.) The agent receives a reward of –2 on every time step that it is thirsty, and a reward of +2 when it consumes the safety resource and it isn't thirsty. Satisfying thirst results in a reward of +8. Concurrent rewards (e.g., the agent is thirsty and takes an external action) are summed.

The agent's initial knowledge consists of the following operators, which are proposed in all states: consume resource, move to a neighboring location, create a cue to initiate a retrieval from episodic memory. There is also an operator to advance episodic memory forward in time to retrieve the next episode. That operator is proposed only when there has been a previous successful retrieval. The agent's state includes the agent's location (potential locations are shown in figure 12.1), the values of its drives (thirst and safety), and the results of any retrievals from episodic memory. The agent also has an RL rule for each possible state, and all these RL rules are initialized with numeric preferences of 0.0.

12.1.2 Experiments

Our experiments in Well World evaluate various strategies for using episodic memory. (Additional experiments are presented in Gorski and Laird 2010.) In the first experiment, we test an agent's ability to learn to select a cue for retrieval from episodic memory. The second experiment tests an agent's ability to learn to use the temporal aspects of episodic memory. This set of experiments investigates all the ways retrievals can access Soar's episodic memory. We present details of the first experiment and summarize the results of the second experiment. In all experiments, the agents learn using reinforcement learning to select the operators in each state to achieve maximum reward. Results are the average of 250 trials, smoothed, and rescaled so that an average reward of 0 per action is optimal in each experiment.

The first experiment tests the basic behavior of using RL to learn to use an internal episodic memory. The agent must learn that when it becomes thirsty it should perform a retrieval from episodic memory, using a cue of "resource: *water*," and then use the retrieved knowledge when learning which action to take.

Agents in Well World cannot perceive which well contains water while at the shelter, and thus must use memory to know which well it consumed from last when it becomes thirsty. The agent's optimal behavior, then, is to move to the shelter and consume the safety resource when it isn't thirsty. When it becomes thirsty, it must select the cue "resource: *water*" to retrieve the well that it last visited (and hence consumed water from) from episodic memory. It then moves to the other well and consumes water there.

The agent must learn which action to select in every situation it encounters. With RL, the agent learns to associate an expected reward with each situation-action pair, and eventually it learns which action for a situation will lead to the greatest reward. Note that it is not learning the general concept of moving to the opposite well here, as the agent performs no generalization: it must learn both that when it retrieves Well 1 it should move to Well 2 *and* that when it retrieves Well 2 it should move to Well 1 independently.

Figure 12.2 plots the performances of an agent under the following conditions: only the correct cue is available to be used for retrieval (labeled "No distractors"); the correct cue and five distractors are available ("5 distractors"); and a baseline condition in which episodic memory is lesioned and the agent cannot perform retrievals ("Lesioned ep. mem."), which demonstrates how an RL agent lacking internal memory would perform. The five distractor cues result in either failed retrievals or episodes in which the agent was at the shelter; retrievals made using those cues are not useful for solving the task.

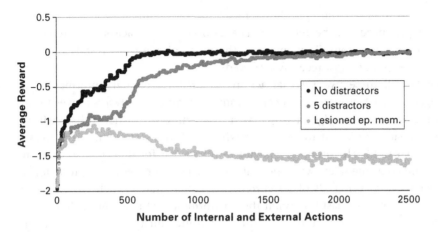

Figure 12.2
Performances of agents learning to retrieve episodic memories.

When only a single cue is available for retrieval ("No distractors"), the agent quickly learns both when to act in the environment and when to use its internal memory so as to receive the maximum amount of possible reward. The agent learns to select actions to satisfy its safety and thirst drives at appropriate times, eventually generating the optimal behavior. In the second condition, the presence of the distractors ("5 distractors") slows learning because the agent has to gain sufficient experience in using each cue to learn which cue leads to a retrieval that makes it possible to reliably go to the correct well, and thus to a higher reward. Finally, when an agent's episodic memory is lesioned, there is never enough information in the state to enable the agent to reliably determine which well contains water when it becomes thirsty, and thus its average reward is low. The results in figure 12.2 indicate that the agent can learn how to use its internal memory while learning how to interact with its environment.

In the first experiment, the agent retrieved episodic memories of the last time it perceived the water resource, which was sufficient knowledge to determine which well to move to in order to find water. In the second experiment, an alternative strategy is explored: the agent retrieves a past situation that closely resembles the agent's current situation, then advances to the next memory to retrieve what the agent did the last time it was in a similar situation. The agent thus uses episodic memory to store knowledge of which action it took the last time it was in a similar situation to inform its current behavior. In this experiment, the agent has available the normal actions in the environment (moving and consuming resources). It also has two internal actions available. The first of these actions is a cue-based episodic-memory retrieval that uses a cue consisting of all of its current perceptual knowledge. When an agent uses this cue to retrieve from episodic memory, the most similar situation that the agent has experienced will be retrieved. The second internal action is a temporal retrieval that advances episodic memory to the next episode (the episode that was stored after the episode most recently retrieved).

In Well World, these two internal actions can recover enough information so that the agent can act properly in the environment. If an agent always moves to the well that has water, knowledge of which well it last moved to when thirsty will be sufficient to enable the agent to determine which well has water when it is thirsty again (the other well). The optimal behavior in this task is for the agent to move to the shelter and consume safety when not thirsty. When it becomes thirsty, it performs a cue-based retrieval using all of its current perceptual state (which results in its remembering when it was last thirsty). It then performs a next retrieval (which results in its remembering where it moved to after last being thirsty at the shelter). The agent then moves to the other well (not the well it last moved to, as that well will now be empty).

An agent must learn when to perform the cue-based retrieval (when the cue is the complete state), when to advance its retrieval, and what action to take in the world given the knowledge retrieved from episodic memory. This provides a primitive envisioning or planning capability similar to the action modeling presented in chapter 9: the agent can use its history to predict potential future situations. Through RL, the system learns when and how to perform such primitive planning.

The performances of the agent under two conditions are plotted in figure 12.3. In the first condition, the agent learns when to make a cue-based retrieval and when

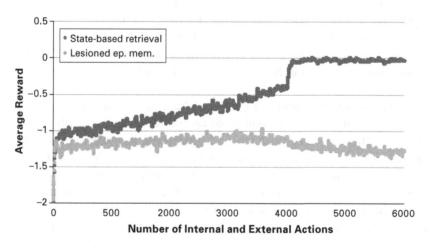

Figure 12.3
Performances of agent using temporal control of episodic memory after retrieval.

to advance the episodic memory, although the next action cannot be selected until a cue-based retrieval has taken place (this condition is labeled "State-based retrieval"). The second condition is a baseline comparison in which episodic memory is lesioned.

There is a dramatic improvement in performance after the agents have taken 4,000 actions. In this experiment, the exploration parameter decays linearly. On the 4,000th action, and every successive action after that, the agent ceases to select actions randomly and selects only the actions with the best-learned value estimates. The dramatic difference in performances between when the agent is selecting random actions very rarely (e.g., just before the 4,000th action) and never (e.g., immediately after the 4,000th action) indicates that a minute amount of random action selection in this task has a significant negative effect on behavior. In the previous task, random action selection didn't interfere with an agent's ability to recover and complete the task.

In this task, there is a precise sequence of actions that must be executed, which explains the agent's sensitivity to exploratory actions. If an agent becomes thirsty and randomly selects to consume the safety resource, then when the agent next becomes thirsty and attempts to retrieve a memory of when it was last thirsty and what it did next, that memory will not be informative as to which well contains water—which in turn leads the agent to bias its learned behavior against performing retrievals. Effectively, any random action selection is disruptive when episodic memory is used to remember a sequence of actions.

Taken together, these experiments show what the possible interactions between RL and episodic memory are, where RL learns when to make retrievals, what cues should be used for retrievals, and what actions to take after the retrievals. Even though the task is very simple, it takes hundreds if not thousands of trials for RL to learn the correct behavior. Thus, one conclusion to draw is that RL can be used but there must be severe restrictions over the space of what must be learned. In Soar, knowledge or external advice can greatly constrain when operators are proposed, and RL can be used to fill in where knowledge is missing and when there is uncertainty. Gorski and Laird (2010) describe additional experiments, some performed in a more complicated Well World configuration that involved constructing cues from multiple features, and others that compare learning to use episodic memory to an agent that learns to use a simple bit memory.

This research opens up the possibility of extending the range of tasks and behaviors modeled by cognitive architectures. To date, scant attention has been paid to the richness of episodic memory or to many of its more complex properties, such as its temporal structure or the fact that it doesn't capture only isolated structures and buffers but instead captures working memory as a whole. Similarly, although RL has made significant contributions to cognitive modeling, it has been predominantly used to learn to control external actions. This research demonstrates that cognitive architectures can use RL to learn more complex behaviors that are dependent not just on the current state of the environment, but also on the agent's experience—learning behaviors that are possible only when RL and episodic memory are combined.

12.2   Using Mental Imagery with Reinforcement Learning

In this section we discuss a unique integration of reinforcement learning, planning, and the imagery system. As in subsection 10.4.2, the imagery system is used to predict the state resulting from an action using simple models of physical processes in spatial domains, and this prediction is abstracted into qualitative information in working memory. In this demonstration, RL rules are included that test the abstracted prediction, and a policy is learned to control behavior. Thus, whereas conventional Q-learning learns the value of each action in each state, Reinforcement Learning using Abstraction and Imagery (ReLAI) learns the value of state-action pairs sharing common predictions. ReLAI is implemented as task-independent knowledge within Soar that relies on Soar's RL and imagery components. Using ReLAI, Soar agents learn to solve problems in Pegged Blocks World, and to play classic computer games (including Space Invaders and Frogger II) faster and with better asymptotic performance than a comparable system with RL alone. (This section is based on Wintermute 2010a and Wintermute 2010b, which contain additional details beyond those provided here, including a description of using ReLAI in Pegged Blocks World.)

Formally, ReLAI is a technique for aggregating state-action (s,a) pairs in the table of values learned by Q-learning. What aggregate (or *category*) an (s,a) pair belongs to is determined by the predicted next abstract state resulting from action a in concrete state s. If abstract states are related in the right way to the concrete state space, and predictions are accurate, Q-learning with ReLAI converges to the optimal policy, sometimes much faster than it would without aggregation. (For more details on ReLAI and the theory behind it, see Wintermute 2010a,b.)

Figure 12.4 is a gray-scale screen shot of the game Frogger II (the original game is in eight-bit color). The agent doesn't play the whole game; it has a simpler goal: navigating the frog to the top of the screen without colliding with any of the moving obstacles or leaving the area shown. Without considering the rest of the game, this problem is still very difficult. The position of the frog is discrete in the vertical direction (there are nine rows to move through), but many horizontal positions are possible. Most of the obstacles move continuously at uniform speed to the right or the left, although some move vertically or diagonally. Obstacles are constantly appearing and disappearing at the edges of the screen. A slow current in the water pushes the frog to the right at a constant rate, so inaction still results in motion. The frog has five possible actions: to move in one of four directions and to do nothing. The agent

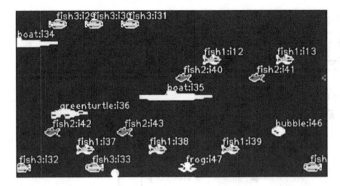

Figure 12.4
Gray-scale screenshot of Frogger II annotated with object classifications.

plays multiple instances of the game, and the initial state of the game differs across instances (initially the obstacles are in different positions).

The original game code for these games runs on an Atari 2600 emulator on the same computer Soar runs on, and the two-dimensional bitmap information from the screens is fed into the Soar agent. As illustrated in figure 12.5, a low-level perception system segments, tracks, and labels the objects perceived. (Its labels are shown in figure 12.5.) This information is passed to the spatial scene, which represents objects geometrically in Euclidean space. High-level perceptual processes act on this representation to extract qualitative properties of the objects and their relations to one another and deposit them into Soar's symbolic working memory, where they are accessible to Soar's decision process. Though the low-level perception system is custom-built for Atari games, the rest of the architecture, including high-level perception and imagery, is based on the task-independent components described in chapter 10.

In complex domains such as Frogger II, the qualitative properties that can be extracted from the perceptual scene by a task-independent architecture are rarely sufficient for learning, and an agent's designer must come up with a good abstraction and hope for the best. The hypothesis behind ReLAI is that imagery operations provide the ability to create more useful state information that leads to better decision making and better learning. This information is based on highly accurate short-term imagery-based predictions of the outcomes of actions and the dynamics of the environment. For example, in figure 12.5 the frog and two fish are identified by low-level perception and added to the spatial scene. High-level perception (SVS predicate extraction) extracts the relative positions of the frog and the fish and deposits them in working memory (shown on the left side of the working-memory structure in figure 12.5). Procedural knowledge creates a command for SVS to imagine the locations of the frog and other objects after the frog has moved up. In this case, SVS creates new

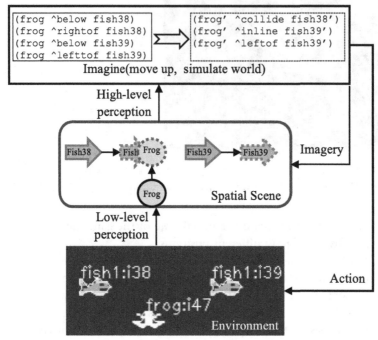

Figure 12.5
Change in working memory after imagined move up in Frogger II.

objects (dashed outlines) for the future positions of the objects in the scene. When high-level perception is applied to the modified (imagined) scene, it creates the working-memory elements on the right for the imagined objects (frog', fish38', fish39'), and the agent can detect that the frog will collide with a fish if it moves up. After making predictions for each action, the agent decides on one, which is sent to the environment directly.

The imagery-based predictions (such as that the frog will collide with a fish) elaborate the agent's state and provide useful information for decision making. For example, the ReLAI agent can base its action choice on a precise prediction of whether or not it will collide with an obstacle in the new state, whereas without the prediction an agent can only base its decisions on the current state, which includes information (obstacle adjacency) that only roughly predicts future collisions between moving objects. This enhanced information also becomes available to reinforcement learning, which makes it much easier to learn which actions to take because predictions of the outcomes of the actions are directly available.

In order to support reinforcement learning, a reward function similar to that of the game score has been implemented: there is a reward of 1,000 for winning (reaching the top row), and –1,000 for losing (colliding with an obstacle or leaving the area). There is a reward of 10 for moving up, and a reward of –10 for moving down to encourage the frog to move up to the top. At every time step, there is also a reward of –1, to encourage short solutions.

The abstract perceptions, which are similar to those illustrated in figure 12.5), encode the following information in working memory:

the vertical position of the frog (one of the nine rows)
a rough horizontal discretization of the frog's position into left, middle, and right regions
a determination as to whether or not the frog currently collides with an obstacle
a determination as to whether or not an obstacle (or screen edge) is adjacent to the frog in each of the four directions.

As a state representation, this abstraction loses potentially useful information, and it is not Markovian (since the agent could make better decisions by remembering where it has seen obstacles). However, it is compact. Just as important, it can be composed from the simple perceptual operations available in the architecture.

The same abstract state representation is used in a baseline agent using conventional Q-learning and in a ReLAI agent. Both agents choose an action every 15 game frames (four per second). The ReLAI algorithm as used in Soar is illustrated in figure 12.6. In this example, action categories are determined by using imagery to project

---

for each episode
  for each step in the episode
    perceive the concrete state s and any reward, store s in the spatial scene
    for each action a
      use imagery to simulate a in the spatial scene, along with any environmental changes
      apply high-level perception to the imagined scene, derive the next abstract state $A(s')$
      look up the learned value of a in s based on the category of (s, a), which is $A(s')$
    given the current action values and the reward, apply a Q-learning update to the
        category of the previous action (if any)
    choose an action using epsilon-greedy policy
  repeat until s is terminal
repeat for all episodes

Figure 12.6
ReLAI algorithm.

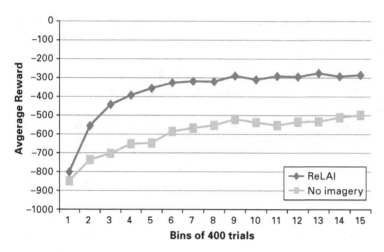

Figure 12.7
Results for Frogger II.

forward the motion of the obstacles near the frog and the effect of the action on the
frog, then applying the abstraction to that imagined state. In addition to abstract
perceptions, in this domain the ReLAI agent also encodes the proposed action as part
of the abstract state. This is because perceptions about the next state alone cannot
capture the immediate reward for the transition, since moving up or down a row
affects reward (not just being in a particular row).

Experiments were run using the original game running in emulation. Q-learning
with epsilon-greedy exploration was used with the Soar default RL parameters. Thirty
trials of 6,000 episodes each were run in each condition. Figure 12.7 shows the results,
with groups of 400 adjacent trials binned together, averaged across all trials in the bin
and across all trials. (Each point represents 12,000 games. A random agent's average
reward is –1,000.) The graphed results do not show the ability of the agents to play
the game well: epsilon-greedy exploration meant that the agent acted randomly 10
percent of the time (often with fatal results), and some of the randomly chosen start
states were unwinnable because every possible action led to a collision. These factors
contributed to high variability in the data, necessitating the averaging of many games
per data point.

To examine the final policy, 700 games were run in each condition using the final
policies, but without exploration and with unwinnable games filtered out. Of these,
the non-imagery baseline agent received an average reward of –66 and won 45 percent
of the games, whereas the ReLAI agent received an average reward of 439 and won 70
percent of the games.

The ReLAI agent clearly outperforms the baseline agent: it learns a better policy, and learns it faster. When the same perception system was used with and without simple local predictions based in imagery, much better performance was achieved with the simple local imagery-based predictions.

Because Atari graphics are simple, the perception system can be configured to work in many games. Agents for two other games (Space Invaders and Fast Eddie) have been implemented, with results similar to what was achieved in Frogger II. As task independence has been a priority of the design of Soar's imagery components, no architectural modification outside of the low-level emulator interface was necessary to create Soar agents for these games.

This work demonstrates the benefits of multiple representations and imagery for AI systems. Previous research had identified that imagery can ease the problem of abstraction in particular tasks, such as motion planning (Wintermute 2009a), and in versions of the Blocks World (Wintermute and Laird 2009). However, the results above demonstrate that this approach can apply much more widely. In that way, it is a step toward a better understanding of how perception, internal representation, decision making, and learning are related.

12.3   Diverse Forms of Action Modeling

In order to plan, an agent must have knowledge about how its actions affect the environment. This knowledge is called an *action model*. In chapter 5 we demonstrated that an action model can be encoded in rules as well as through successive operator decompositions, and that Soar can perform look-ahead searches by using these action models. In chapter 9 we demonstrated how episodic memory can also be used as the basis of an action model, and how action-model rules can be learned using chunking. In this section, we use a simple board game to show that, in addition to those other forms of knowledge, Soar can use semantic memory and mental imagery for action modeling, and that it can use all of these forms of action modeling on a single task. These mechanisms vary along many dimensions, including generality, reportability, learnability, computational expense, and the types of problems where they are appropriate, so it is to an agent's advantage to have a diverse set of mechanisms for action modeling. Forbus and Gentner (1997) posited a similar diversity of processing to support mental models, although they didn't focus on architectural mechanisms as we do here. (This section is based on Laird, Xu, and Wintermute 2010.)

12.3.1   A Simple Board-Game Task

To illustrate how these approaches work, both independently and in unison, we use a simple board game, illustrated in figure 12.8. In this game, the Soar agent must slide

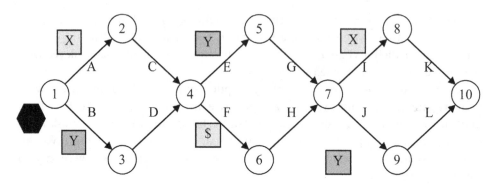

Figure 12.8
Board-game task.

the hexagonal marker on the left along the directional paths to numbered nodes until it gets to the end (node 10). As the marker slides along a path, it may touch one of three different objects, labeled X, Y, and $. If the marker hits an object, the agent gets points. In our examples, we assume that the agent has semantic knowledge that $ is worth 20 points, but doesn't initially know the values of the other objects (X is worth 10 points; Y is worth 5). The goal is to get to the end with the highest possible score, which is achieved via the path A, C, F, H, I, K. We assume that the agent can sense the marker's position, the paths, and the objects but doesn't know *a priori* whether the marker will hit a nearby object as it slides along a path. Only the lower right Y is far enough from the path so that the marker doesn't hit it; all of the other objects are close enough to be hit.

12.3.2   Structure of Agent
The agent begins with the following procedural knowledge, encoded as rules:

• An operator-proposal rule for the task operator of moving the marker from a location along a path to a next location. This rule proposes two operators at each of the locations 1, 4, and 7, but only one operator at each of the remaining locations. At location 1, it proposes move(A-2) and move(B-3).
• An operator application rule that initiates the appropriate action in the external environment to move the marker.
• General task-independent knowledge for responding to impasses. This builds on the selection space described earlier, and includes knowledge for using different methods for action modeling, including retrieving episodic knowledge and semantic knowledge as well as using mental imagery.

The agent doesn't have any action model knowledge encoded as rules to internally simulate the effects of the operator.

12.3.3 Initial Task Performance

The agent starts at position 1, and is faced with making a decision whether to take path A or path B. To make this decision, the agent uses a look-ahead search to attempt to predict the result of each possible move and then pick the move with the best result. As was noted in chapters 5 and 9, this leads to the state structure illustrated in figure 12.9, which is an adaptation of figure 5.14 to the board game. As the figure shows, the critical point for using an action model is when the agent is applying the move operator to an internal copy of the environment as it attempts to evaluate one of the possible operators.

Because the agent lacks a procedural action model and begins with an empty episodic memory, it employs mental imagery to imagine moving the marker along path A. As shown in the figure, mental imagery predicts that if the agent moves the marker along A it will intersect object X. Mental imagery takes advantage of the spatial representation and maps the action to be modeled onto imagery operations. Making the connection between the action and mental imagery operations can involve accessing knowledge in semantic memory, or such knowledge can be encoded in rules. In our example, the agent knows that it should imagine the marker sliding along the path

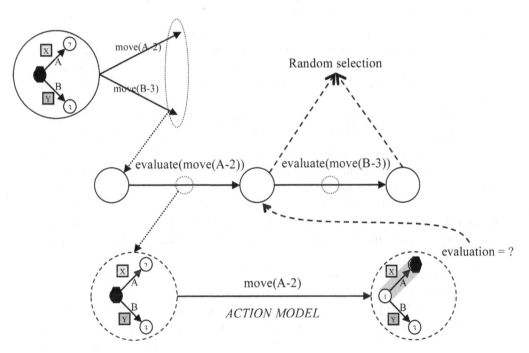

Figure 12.9
Graphical depiction of processing using an action model.

until it is centered on top of the destination location. While the perceptual memory is changing, relevant predicates are extracted, such as the intersection with object X. These predicates provide a symbolic description of the situation that serves as the resulting state.

When evaluating moving to 3 (not shown), the agent imagines moving along B and detects that the marker will intersect Y. In both cases, it attempts to access any semantic or episodic memories related to these situations, but it fails in both cases because it doesn't know how encountering those objects will affect its score. As a default, it chooses at random. In this case, we assume that it picks path B. It executes that action, encountering Y and getting 5 points.

Once at 3, the agent picks path D to get to 4. Here, the decision is between going along path E or path F. This time, after it uses mental imagery to detect that it will encounter object Y, the agent attempts a retrieval from semantic memory, which fails, then attempts a retrieval from episodic memory to recall the last time it encountered object Y. That retrieval succeeds, and the agent remembers that it received 5 points.

When it considers path F, the agent uses imagery to predict that it will encounter object $. It attempts a retrieval from semantic memory, which succeeds, and it predicts that it will receive 20 points. On the basis of these evaluations, it chooses path F. It receives 20 points, moves to 6, then moves to 7. At that point, it uses a combination of mental imagery and episodic memory to predict the result of moving to 8 (10 points). In imagining moving to 9, imagery shows that the agent will not encounter Y, so it will get a score of 0. It selects moving to 8 and finishes by moving to 10, getting a total score of 35.

In performing the task, the agent acquires additional knowledge. Episodic memory adds new memories that can be used to model complete actions (as demonstrated in chapter 9), and chunking learns selection rules as well as action modeling rules. However, mental imagery involves processing that cannot be analyzed by chunking because the results of the processing are not uniquely determined by the symbolic structures available in working memory. Therefore, chunking doesn't create rules that summarize mental imagery processing. This is similar to the policy in ACT-R of not composing rules which involve processing over external interactions (Anderson 2007).

12.3.4 Repeated Task Performance

The second time the agent plays the game, it uses episodic memory to predict the results of the paths it took the first time (B, F, and I). Since it has no episodic memories of moving on paths A, E, and J, and because it did not chunk over earlier mental-imagery processing, it must continue to use imagery for those paths. Thus, in its second attempt it will use imagery and episodic memory to predict a score of 10 for A, whereas it will use only episodic memory to predict a score of 5 for B. Similar use

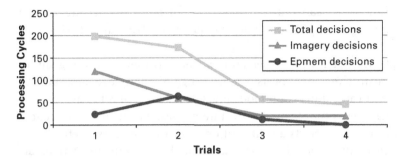

Figure 12.10
Number of processing cycles required over multiple trials.

of imagery and episodic memory will be used at nodes 4 and 7. As a result, the optimal path is taken, resulting in a score of 40.

Figure 12.10 shows the progression of how the agent's decisions are distributed across imagery and episodic memory over multiple trials. The highest line represents the total number of internal reasoning steps. The other two lines represent the number of decisions that involve imagery decisions and episodic-memory decisions. In the first trial, imagery dominates, as the agent has no experiences to draw on. In the second run, the agent must still use imagery for those cases in which it has not taken a path, but it uses episodic memory for those cases in which it has experience. Although this isn't evident in the figure, chunking creates a rule that replaces the use of semantic memory. For the third run, chunking decreases the total number of steps by eliminating the use of episodic memory. In the final trial, some imagery is still required for paths the agent never actually tried; episodic memory is no longer used, having been replaced by rules learned through chunking.

12.3.5 Discussion

The major claim of this section is that intelligent agents have available various mechanisms that can be used to predict the results of their actions in service of decision making. A related claim is that internal prediction doesn't occur in any specific architectural module but instead results from a combination of characteristics of the domain, the agent's background knowledge, experience, and the agent's available memories and processing elements. An important component of Soar's ability to support these methods is its employment of impasses when knowledge is incomplete. Impasses determine when action modeling is necessary (when there is a tie among competing actions) and provide a context for invoking alternative approaches when rule-based action-modeling knowledge is missing. In addition, substates provide the representational structures needed to support retrieving and combining knowledge without disrupting the state of the problem being attempted. These components appear to be missing, or at least difficult to achieve, in other architectures, and it would be informative to attempt to duplicate the qualitative structure achieved here in other cognitive architectures.

In this example, the agent's use of semantic memory is limited to using simple facts. However, semantic memory covers a broad range of knowledge, and one can imagine other ways it can aid in action modeling. One alternative is to have declarative instructions that specify how to modify the internal task state to model the action. In that approach, the agent selects an internal operator that initiates a retrieval for instructions related to the action being evaluated. If the relevant instructions are retrieved, task-independent knowledge selects an "interpret" operator, the purpose of which is to apply the instructions to the copy of the task state. The "interpret" operator leads to a substate where operators are selected and applied for each of the instructions. The processing in the substate allows for arbitrarily complex implementations of instructions, and is similar in spirit to how declarative instructions are used in ACT-R (Anderson 2007; Best and Lebiere 2003); however, in those cases the instructions are interpreted to control the execution of a task, whereas here they are used to model the execution of an action. We do not include a specific demonstration of this approach here, but it has been successfully used in a Blocks World agent. The format of declarative instructions is like that of an imperative programming language.

We can make some predictions about the behavior of an agent with the capabilities we described. In a spatial environment, an agent initially relies on mental imagery for action modeling (and semantic knowledge if it is available). As the agent gains experience, it switches to using episodic memory when it can. With further experience, rules learned via chunking replace episodic memory; eventually, rules are learned that choose actions directly, eliminating action modeling.

Concurrent with learning, the agent's ability to report on its internal reasoning changes as different structures become available in working memory (which is the basis for our predictions about reporting). Initially, for spatial problems, the agent can report imagining spatial situations, which then transitions to reports of using episodic memory (things it "remembers"). When using semantic memory, it can report on the instructions and facts it is using (things it "knows"). With practice, the agent loses the ability to report on its reasoning as intermediate structures are no longer generated in working memory and processing is done purely with rules without the creation of a declarative trace that the agent can report.

12.4   Analysis of Requirements

In this chapter, we examined three Soar agents that demonstrate Soar's ability to achieve many of the architectural requirements identified in chapter 2. Since each agent is a unitary demonstration, these agents don't "prove" that these requirements are achieved in the general case; however, they demonstrate that achieving these requirements is at least possible within Soar.

R0: Fixed architecture. The same architecture is used in all of the agents in this chapter without modification, and it is the same architecture used for all the agents described in earlier chapters. The difference between agents is in the input and output systems and in the knowledge encoded in procedural, semantic, and episodic memories.

R1: Realize a symbol system. Symbolic processing is used throughout all the agents.

R2: Modality-specific knowledge. The video-game-playing agent uses mental imagery, and that imagery is crucial to the success of that agent.

R3: Use large bodies of knowledge. During learning, these agents build up moderate bodies of knowledge, including episodic memory, semantic memory, RL rules, and chunks.

R4: Use knowledge at different levels of generality. In the work on action modeling, general knowledge is compiled via chunking into rules for making decisions in specific situations.

R5: Diverse levels of knowledge. The examples in section 12.3 showed how an agent can use action knowledge in different forms.

R6: Distinct internal representations. All of the agents create state representations that are independent of the current situation. In the Well World agent, the agent retrieves earlier states from episodic memory and bases its decisions on those states. The video-game agents generate alternative hypothetical states using look-ahead, as does the action-modeling agent.

R11: Levels of deliberation. All of the agents used multiple levels of deliberation.

R12: Comprehensive learning. The Well World agent demonstrates learning to use episodic memory. The video-game agent is yet another example of the use of reinforcement learning. The action-modeling agent demonstrates that chunking can be applied to many types of internal action modeling.

R13: Incremental learning. All learning in the agents is incremental and occurs in tandem with performing the task at hand.

13 Soar Applications

with Robert E. Wray III

The previous chapters focused on pedagogical domains to explain and demonstrate the structure and function of Soar. This chapter focuses on real-world applications of Soar. Section 13.1 provides an overview of the different types of applications and real-world tasks to which Soar has been applied. Section 13.2 describes TacAir-Soar, a model of pilots flying tactical aircraft. TacAir-Soar was developed in the 1990s using an earlier version of Soar; it shows what is possible using the capabilities of Soar described in chapters 4 and 5. Moreover, it is the largest Soar system developed to date, and lessons learned from its development motivated the architecture research and development that led to the extensions described in chapters 6–11. In section 13.3, we speculate as to what would be possible if we were to re-implement TacAir-Soar in the most recent version of Soar.

13.1 Applications

One coarse indication of the breadth of Soar applications is the many environments to which it has been interfaced. Soar agents have been developed in each of these environments. Although only a few of them have been fielded in real-world applications, they demonstrate that Soar supports the development of a wide variety of agents. Table 13.1 provides a partial list.

In this section, we give an overview of the different categories and relevant Soar systems and describe ways in which the problem-space computational model and the Soar realization of it guide and constrain these applications. Applying Soar to a range of applications has been important to the continuing development of Soar as a general cognitive architecture. Recall from chapter 1 that the goal of developing a cognitive architecture is to provide a general processing and representation substrate that can support a very large class of problem domains. By applying Soar to many domains, Soar researchers explore its utility and its generality. As limits or failures of the PSCM or the architecture are recognized, the theory and the implementation are adjusted to address them. In chapter 1 we discussed an example in which the move to external

Table 13.1
Software and robotic environments in which Soar has been integrated.

Category	Examples
Commercial and game-based environment simulations	SGI Flight Simulator, Descent 3, Quake II, Quake III, Unreal Tournament, Unreal 3, Crystal Space, LithTech, ORTS, FreeCiv, Gamebryo, OGRE, Torque, WildMagic, Empire, Zenilib, Planet Wars, Full Spectrum Command, Atari 2600 emulator
Military simulation environments	ModSAF, JSAF, OneSAF Testbed, OneSAF, VR Forces™, STAGE, simJr, JCATS
Robot simulation environments	Player/Stage, USARSIM, Microsoft Robotic Studio
Robot platforms	Early versions of Soar: Hero mobile robot, a PUMA robot arm, LEGO Mindstorms
	Recent versions of Soar: iRobot Create, Pioneer II robot platform, Splinterbot, iRobot's Packbot
Enterprise-software middleware	Soar has been interfaced to other software platforms via many different communication and interface protocols, including static libraries, shared object libraries, dynamically linked libraries, sockets, the Common Object Model, the Common Object Request Broker Architecture, the Distributed Interactive Simulation standard, High-Level Architecture (HLA), the Control of Agent-based Systems Grid, Apache Active MQ, and Java Message Service.
Academic research environments	General Game Playing server (Genesereth and Love 2005), RL-Glue (Tanner and White 2009), Robo-Cup soccer simulation (Marsella et al. 2001)

domains prompted refinements of the PSCM. An important requirement for these changes is that they not be specialized for a particular problem or class of problems. Meeting this requirement ensures that the evolution of Soar is "progressive" (Lakatos 1970); that is, that Soar continues to offer comparable capability for addressing previously explored applications as well as for new applications.

Soar systems have tended to cluster into four application groups: expert systems, knowledge-intensive cognitive models, human behavior models, and autonomous agents. These application groups are listed roughly in the chronological order in which Soar researchers first pursued them, and we consider them in this order in this chapter. Because of the number and the range of applications that have been created within each of these classes, there is strong empirical evidence to suggest that Soar is an appropriate and sufficient substrate for many of the aspects of general intelligence required in each of these classes. To explore the limits of the PSCM and the architectural implementation, we will apply Soar to new tasks that stretch the boundaries of these classes, and to new classes of domain applications. This approach should identify new capabilities and associated requirements for cognitive architecture and should lead to investigations into whether or how Soar meets the requirements of those capabilities.

13.1.1 Expert Systems

We use the term "expert system" to describe a program that attempts to capture and use knowledge acquired from human experts in a narrow domain that is primarily an internal human reasoning task. Thus, the domains to which an expert system is applied are largely static, such as diagnosing a disease. A chess-playing program might be conceived of as an expert system, especially if the knowledge it uses is derived from analyses of expert human chess players. However, we do not classify a program that plays a first-person-shooter computer game as an expert system, even if its encoded knowledge came directly from human game players.

The first large-scale demonstration of Soar was a reimplementation of a computer-configuration expert system called R1. R1-Soar (Rosenbloom et al. 1985) could apply shallow but efficient expert knowledge as well as very general, deep domain knowledge when it lacked directly available expert knowledge (via the PSCM operations discussed previously). Using the deep knowledge required search, which was orders of magnitude more time-intensive than using expert knowledge. However, R1-Soar compiled the deep reasoning into rules using Soar's chunking mechanism, and it underwent a transition from a deep and slow system to a shallow and fast one.

R1-Soar led to the development of many expert-system-like Soar systems. Examples include medical diagnosis (Washington and Rosenbloom 1993), algorithm design (Steier and Newell 1988), antibody identification in immunohematology (Amra et al. 1992), and others described and referenced in *The Soar Papers* (Rosenbloom et al. 1993).

A more recent example of a Soar expert system is LG-Soar (Lonsdale et al. 2006), an information-extraction system that integrates a link grammar for parsing free text with domain-specific knowledge for understanding and making operational the information within a text document (such as a Web page). LG-Soar has been used for a number of information-extraction applications. For example, it is used to process advertisements for potential participants for clinical trials. It determines the relevant criteria for a trial from the text in individual advertisements, and then forms a query to send to databases of medical records to identify patients that might be eligible for the trial(s). Because it is integrated within a complex software environment (the Web, databases, etc.), LG-Soar doesn't look like a traditional expert system. However, for a given advertisement, it is performing the expert task of identifying the criteria required for participation and then using the identified criteria to create a query to a database to find records relevant to the advertisement.

13.1.2 Cognitive Models

Originally, Soar was developed to be a general architecture that would support many different problem-solving methods and could be used on many different problems. During its early years, it became clear that Soar had many characteristics that were consistent with modeling human behavior, and research on cognitive modeling using Soar flourished. In 1989, preparing his William James Lectures, Allen Newell and his students pushed forward many research projects on Soar that related to cognitive modeling. Those lectures became the basis for Newell's 1990 book *Unified Theories of Cognition*, in which he advocated using cognitive architectures as the basis for general models of cognition. The goal of a unified theory of cognition (UTC) is to integrate functionally and descriptively the thousands of psychological regularities that have been observed in empirical psychology. To support his argument, Newell described a wide variety of cognitive modeling work using Soar. In parallel, John Anderson had been developing the ACT cognitive architecture, and in the late 1980s and the early 1990s there was a friendly competition between Soar and ACT as architectures to support psychological modeling.

The hypothesis that Soar might be a good starting point as a general theory for human cognition led to a decade of intense research in which Soar was used to create cognitive models. The most important feature of a cognitive model is that it provides detailed descriptions and predictions of psychological phenomena in a computational form. One of the distinguishing features of most Soar cognitive modeling research is that the community treats the architecture as a fixed, functional substrate. This view has two implications. First, changes at the architecture level are discouraged for the purposes of building a specific model. This is consistent with the overall Soar approach that one should not introduce any architecture-level changes to accommodate a specific task. Second, only new functional requirements should motivate changes in the architecture, rather than some solely phenomenological observation. In practice, this philosophy is conservative and somewhat constraining. However, from the point of view of Soar as a candidate UTC, this approach ensures that different models built within it derive identical constraints and computational properties from the architecture.

Newell (1990) details the cognitive modeling approach to Soar research and describes a number of cognitive models built within Soar. More recently, Soar has played a central role in the development of accounts of natural language comprehension (Lehman, Lewis, and Newell 1998), human memory limitations and coping mechanisms (Young and Lewis 1999), modeling learning in human computer interaction (Howes and Young 1997), and the integration of psychologically realistic descriptions of perception and motor control (Chong and Laird 1997). There have also been many models developed to help explain human performance of real-world tasks, including simplified versions of air-traffic control (Chong and Wray 2005;

John and Lallement 1997), hypertext browsing (Peck and John 1992), and decision making under time pressure (John, Vera, and Newell 1994; Nelson, Lehman, and John 1994). Research on cognitive modeling in Soar slowed significantly after Allen Newell's death in 1992. Research on cognitive modeling in Soar has continued throughout the years, but it has not been the major focus as it was in the early 1990s, and without Newell's passion and intellect it has waned. The recent extensions to Soar have the potential to revive research in cognitive modeling using Soar—especially for tasks that take tens of seconds to minutes or longer and for tasks that require multiple types of learning. In addition, planned extensions to episodic and semantic memory promise further improvements in Soar's ability to model human behavior at shorter time scales as insights from ACT-R's declarative memory are incorporated into Soar.

13.1.3 Human Behavior Models
Human behavior models (HBMs) capture and encode the knowledge that humans use to perform a task, then perform that task, usually in a simulated environment. There are contrasting views as to whether HBMs are a subclass of cognitive models (Jones and Laird 1997) or a distinct category (Wray and Chong 2007). Cognitive models and HBMs both seek to produce behavior that is comparable to human behavior. However, in general, HBMs express theories and commitments at a higher level of abstraction, and thus with more general and weaker predictive claims. Cognitive models tend to make precise predictions of human psychological effects (e.g., characteristics of memory retrieval) at a time scale of 50 milliseconds or less. HBMs tend to model second-to-second behavior, in which low-level psychological phenomena are typically less apparent.

HBMs mostly focus on behavior generation and the observable properties of behavior in a realistic task environment. For example, a practiced action such as a coordinated hand-eye movement (e.g., using a computer mouse to move a cursor to a new window) might be treated as a primitive action in an HBM, whereas in a cognitive model it would be decomposed into individual hand and eye movements. Similarly, HBMs usually would use a simple model of visual perception, rather than a more psychologically accurate model of the different acuities available in different parts of the visual field.

HBMs generally also require real-time generation of complex behavior at longer time scales. Real-time performance allows HBMs to be employed in simulation and training environments as replacements for human participants. Because Soar combines functional constraints motivated by psychology and real-time performance, it has proved to be especially well suited for HBM applications. Examples of Soar HBMs include models of the pilots of tactical combat aircraft and helicopters (Hill et al. 1997; Jones et al. 1999), of ground forces (Stensrud, Taylor, and Crossman 2006; Taylor, Koss, and Nielsen 2001; Wray, Laird, et al. 2005), and of air-traffic controllers (Taylor et al. 2007). HBMs also have been developed to allow conversational interactions with virtual characters in immersive simulation environments (Sims and Taylor 2009; Swartout et al. 2006). TacAir-Soar, the combat-pilot HBM, is the largest and most successful application of Soar.

13.1.4 Autonomous Agents

Historically in AI, different research communities have arisen around different approaches to building agents that interact with external environments. Soar's flexible, efficient, scalable approach to reasoning provides a good foundation for research and applications that are not meant to model human behavior explicitly. For example, Soar has been used as a plan-execution architecture (Laird et al. 1996) using methods and representations comparable to other systems including RAPS (Firby 1987),the sequencing layer of the 3T(iered)-family of robotic control architectures (Bonasso et al. 1997), and the behavior generation components in 4D/RCS (Albus 2002). Other examples of Soar applications for intelligent control and plan execution include mobile robotic control (Newell et al. 1991), stick control of a simulated aircraft (Pearson et al. 1993), simulated soccer teams (Marsella et al. 2001), and the control of individual players ("bots") in first-person-shooter computer games (Laird 2001).

Soar is also often used as an intelligent-agent architecture (Wray and Jones 2005), comparable to the belief-desire-intention (BDI) family of architectures (Wooldridge 2000). In these applications, there are usually many interacting agents operating without scripted or prescribed interaction patterns. Examples of using Soar in this manner include a decision-theoretic model of teamwork applied to platoons of helicopter pilots (Tambe 1997), intelligent user interfaces for military decision making (Lisse, Wray, and Huber 2007; Stensrud et al. 2008; Wood et al. 2003; Zaientz and Beard 2006), and high-level controllers for computer games and game-based learning environments (Magerko 2007; Wintermute, Xu, and Laird 2007; Wray, van Lent, et al. 2005).

In all these applications, Soar provides a consistent platform for integrating the breadth and depth of knowledge required in knowledge-rich systems. For example, the TacAir-Soar HBM was integrated with a Soar natural-language cognitive model to demonstrate a system that could converse with other entities in the simulation (and within the bounds of the tactical flight domain) more realistically and flexibly than with the pre-defined communication protocols of the base TacAir-Soar (Lehman, Dyke, and Rubinoff 1995). Simple physics models were also integrated with TacAir-Soar to illustrate how a model of an expert pilot could be supplemented with general common-sense knowledge for recovery in situations in which its expert knowledge was not sufficient for some situation (Nielsen et al. 2002). In another example, tools originally developed to facilitate using ontologies in applications in which Soar is used as an intelligent agent architecture have demonstrated utility across the spectrum of Soar application domains (Wray, Lisse, and Beard 2004). Thus, although it is useful to understand the requirements and properties of different application domains, Soar's generality has made it is a useful foundation for developing agents across all these classes.

13.2 TacAir-Soar

The PSCM informs and constrains Soar development. Here, to illustrate, and to introduce some of the practical challenges one faces when building a Soar system, we discuss the TacAir-Soar Human Behavior Model in more detail, describing some of the interactions between the PSCM theory and the actual implementation and reviewing some of the development challenges.

TacAir-Soar (Jones et al. 1999) was built in combination with RWA-Soar (Hill et al. 1997) in a research project, the goal of which was to determine whether it was possible to replace human controllers with human behavior models for large-scale distributed training exercises. They were the first HBMs built with Soar. With more than 8,000 rules, TacAir-Soar is the largest Soar system. TacAir-Soar models pilots and crew members of fixed-wing military airplanes; RWA-Soar models pilots and crew members of military helicopters. They are distinguished from earlier HBMs by their depth of doctrine, tactics, and mission knowledge for executing a wide variety of tactical missions, and for their ability to coordinate their behavior with other agents. They were first developed for use in large-scale, distributed real-time simulations, and used for training human controllers and commanders in managing battlefield operations. TacAir-Soar continues to be used in large-scale exercises and in training systems for pilots and ground controllers, working either in coordination with or in opposition to human users.

Each TacAir-Soar agent can perform any of the missions flown by the U.S. military, including combat air patrols, close air support, suppression of enemy air defense, and strike missions. Within a mission, an agent can take on any of the mission roles, such as flying either as the leader or as a wingman, in a two-ship formation, or in a four-ship formation. Figure 13.1 shows an example of one of the simpler missions, in which two aircraft (eagle1 and eagle2) are flying a combat air patrol. They patrol around the point labeled "Spin" in the figure. The leader (eagle1) organizes the patrol (direction, speed, etc.) around the expected ingress locations of enemy aircraft. The wingman follows the leader, maintaining formation and responding to the leader's actions. For example, the leader doesn't communicate that he will turn, but simply initiates a turn; the wingman's responsibility is to observe these actions and to maintain the formation.

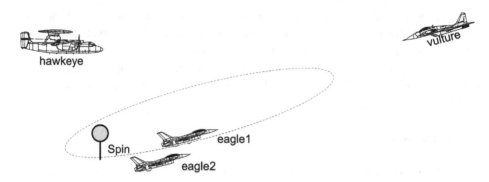

Figure 13.1
Example of a patrol mission in TacAir-Soar.

Before a mission, the aircraft are given specific instructions (rules of engagement) for intercepting enemy aircraft. In the example, the position of an enemy aircraft (vulture) is communicated by another TacAir-Soar agent (hawkeye, in a radar observation aircraft), and the leader determines that vulture is in their patrol area and evaluates its intentions according to the rules of engagement.

TacAir-Soar's knowledge is organized as a hierarchy of problem spaces and operators. Not only does this organization dynamically lead to goals and subgoals, it also provides a modular organization that allows developers to work independently on the multiple capabilities that the agent needs to perform a pilot's function. Figure 13.2 shows a subset of the hierarchical structure of the operators in TacAir-Soar, which is similar to the operator hierarchy for the Rooms World agent depicted in figure 5.7. The figure includes only descriptions of the actions associated with the operators, not the conditions under which they are selected. Asterisks indicate complex operators that are implemented in additional problem spaces not shown in the figure; underscores indicate primitive operators. In all, there are approximately 65 abstract operators and goals and 285 primitive operators in TacAir-Soar.

Assume that in the situation represented in figure 13.1 the agent decides to intercept the intruding aircraft. The leader then decomposes the intercept into the set of situation-dependent subtasks listed in figure 13.2, which are implemented as operators with substates in Soar. For example, once the agent has decided to intercept the enemy, it must decide how to perform the intercept in the current situation. Usually the first step will be to achieve-proximity and then once within radar range, search for the enemy. Figure 13.2 shows the operator decomposition after the agent has found the enemy, has determined that it should be attacked (employ-weapons), has selected a missile (select-missile), has achieved a position from which it is possible launch the missile (via get-missile-LAR and get-steering-circle), and is attempting to launch

Operator Name	Description of operator functionality
execute-mission	[perform all aspects of the current mission]
fly-wing*	[fly as a wingman in relation to the lead]
fly-route*	[fly along a pre-specific route according to a set of waypoints]
ground-attack*	[perform tactics for air-to-ground attack]
patrol*	[patrol an area, search for enemy aircraft]
intercept	[intercept enemy planes]
achieve-proximity*	[get close to enemy plane so other tactics can be engaged]
search*	[search for enemy plane]
scram*	[leave area quickly]
execute-tactic*	[execute a pre-defined tactic to attack the enemy]
employ-weapons	[use weapons against enemy]
select-missile	[select missile most appropriate for situation]
get-missile-LAR*	[attempt to achieve the launch acceptability region of missile]
get-steering-circle*	[attempt to get enemy in the steering circle]
sort-group*	[determine which enemy will be attacked]
launch-missile	[launch a missile at the enemy]
lock-radar	[obtain a lock for a radar guided missile]
lock-IR	[obtain a lock for an infrared missile]
fire-missile	[fire the missile]
wait-for-missile-clear	[wait for the missile to clear before maneuvering]
...	

Figure 13.2
Partial operator hierarchy for TacAir-Soar Agent.

the missile (launch-missile). To launch a missile, it then chooses the appropriate primitive operators listed below launch-missile.

This organization also provides a convenient mechanism for minimizing the interactions among the various components of behavior. The developers of TacAir-Soar observed that similar functionality was needed in multiple problem spaces. For example, the achieve-proximity operator was designed to help a pilot steer an aircraft toward some other object in space. With such a general formulation, the achieve-proximity operator is appropriately included in the three problem spaces listed below:

fly-flight-plan, where it steers the aircraft toward a specified point on its route
intercept, where it steers the aircraft toward an enemy aircraft's anticipated future location, as in figure 13.1
fly-formation, where it steers a wingman's aircraft to get close to the leader when it needs to form up for flying in formation.

As was pointed out in chapter 5, because Soar separates the proposal conditions for an operator from its applications, it is simple to support many different activities with a single operator. Further, because achieve-proximity is further decomposed into lower-level actions, all these operators are dependent only on achieve-proximity, rather than on the problem space from which the achieve-proximity operator was initiated. Thus, not only does the PSCM as implemented in Soar provide necessary intermediate structures for building stable, complex systems; the same structures also have the practical benefit of enabling ready reuse of subcomponents when such reuse is functionally appropriate.

TacAir-Soar uses the elaboration process in the decision cycle to develop and maintain its situational awareness—that is, its interpretation or understanding of the current situation (Endsley 2000). In TacAir-Soar, sensory inputs and remembered or hypothesized data (such as the path an enemy aircraft might take) are combined and elaborated to form hierarchical internal models of the situation, called *situation hierarchies* (Jones et al. 1999). The operators that are selected in the state stack create a context that determines which elaborations are necessary. For example, until the launch-missile problem space is entered, there is no need for the agent to elaborate the best missile it has available in the situation, the determination of which is a function in part of the target's heading and range. Soar's justification-based reason maintenance in the elaboration cycle ensures that the system is responsive to the changing situation. For example, the desired heading for a missile launch is elaborated directly from the bearing and heading of a target aircraft and is automatically re-computed whenever either of these values changes. Because rule firings are individually inexpensive, and because only elaborations that are potentially useful in the context are computed, TacAir-Soar is able to maintain a robust interpretation of the situation with minimal computational cost.

Beyond agent development, the developers of TacAir-Soar identified the following needs of users:

to specify missions for the aircraft, resulting in the creation of an Exercise Editor (Coulter and Laird 1996)

to communicate directly and naturally with agents, resulting in the creation of natural language and voice-to-text and text-to-voice interfaces (Nielsen et al. 2000)

to be given insight into the operation of the agents, resulting in the creation of graphical interfaces that present real-time information about an agent's goals and decisions (Taylor et al. 2002) and agents' ability to explain the rationales behind their actions (Johnson 1994; Taylor, Knudsen, and Holt 2006).

None of the resulting tools was strictly necessary from the point of view of creating agents that behaved as pilots do. However, meeting these user-interaction requirements proved necessary for effective operation of the various systems that use TacAir-Soar agents as components.

13.3   Imagining TacAir-Soar 2.0

The original TacAir-Soar and RWA-Soar demonstrate that it is technologically feasible to create real-time computer models of pilots that have extensive knowledge of doctrine and tactics and that perform complex missions involving large numbers of planes with minimal human supervision. These systems set a high bar for future synthetic forces. Even though they were developed in the late 1990s, there have been few follow-on systems that match the breadth and depth of their capabilities.

These systems were implemented in earlier versions of Soar, which didn't include the latest features of the current architecture (described in chapters 6–11). We expect the latest version of Soar to enable application developers to make greater autonomy and greater robustness possible, and potentially to reduce the engineering cost of building and fielding applications.

This section offers a preliminary examination of this hypothesis. To illustrate, we envision a next-generation TacAir-Soar (TacAir-Soar 2.0) that extends and augments the function and role of TacAir-Soar for integration into training and experimentation simulations and that is easier to build, customize, and maintain, reducing lifecycle costs.

The capabilities we anticipate are not uniquely enabled by the latest version of Soar. In fact, the list is inspired in part by research efforts that derived directly and indirectly from the development of TacAir-Soar and RWA-Soar. For example, TacAir-Soar and RWA-Soar directly inspired computational approaches to modeling the joint intentions of a team (Tambe 1997), opponent tracking (Tambe and Rosenbloom 1995), establishing expectations for monitoring team-specific goals (Kaminka, Pynadath, and Tambe 2002), and interleaving planning and execution (Gratch 1996, 1998; Laird et al. 1996). Less directly, some of the knowledge-acquisition challenges of developing TacAir-Soar led to attempts to develop or extend agent knowledge from instruction (Huffman and Laird 1995; Pearson and Laird 2005), via repairing incomplete or underspecified action representations (Pearson and Laird 1998), and from observation (Könik and Laird 2006; van Lent and Laird 2001). When these capabilities are more directly supported by the architecture, it becomes easier to integrate disparate knowledge-level capabilities and to maintain them, which lessens the need for developer conventions to ensure compatibility (Jones and Wray 2006).

As one simple example, consider the role of semantic memory in simplifying the maintenance of TacAir-Soar agents. TacAir-Soar maintains all declarative data in working memory. Semantic memory provides a better repository for large bodies of stable declarative knowledge, which should decrease the memory footprint of an individual agent and improve long-term maintainability. Information that might be shared includes characteristics of friendly and enemy vehicles, airframes, sensors, and weapons, and possibly declarative representations of tactics and doctrine. Semantic memory can also provide storage for large bodies of mission knowledge that could be pre-loaded during agent initialization or built up dynamically during execution. Examples of this type of information include mission briefs, maps, waypoint locations, and friendly call signs. These uses of semantic memory in TacAir-Soar 2.0 would simplify agent development and maintenance and reduce working-memory requirements, even with extremely large declarative knowledge bases, although they would not extend the capabilities of agents directly.

In the remainder of this section, we discuss ways in which Soar's architectural representations and processes (individually and in combination) can be used to extend TacAir-Soar's capabilities. We focus on the following:

internal models (which increase robustness and generality, and which support planning and expectations)
techniques for adapting existing knowledge
learning a domain through different types of semi-autonomous knowledge acquisition.

These capabilities aren't new—other AI agents and applications incorporate similar capabilities on real-world problems. What is new is the incorporation of these capabilities within an agent that has TacAir-Soar's broad and deep knowledge of a domain and has the power of the latest version of Soar to enable representation and integration of these different capabilities in a deployable real-time software implementation.

13.3.1 Models and Modeling

TacAir-Soar has expertise across many tactical missions and has the knowledge required to execute those missions. Robust across variations in missions and situations, it achieves its generality and its robustness by means of the methods described in section 13.2. It dynamically decomposes different missions into their component, common parts; it elaborates the current situation with abstract relations and properties so that different situations are processed in similar manner; and it has large bodies of knowledge, encoded as rules, for handling many different situations. All these approaches contribute to generality and robustness; however, at its core TacAir-Soar is a reactive system, one that is always trying to pick the best operator (which can be either an action or a goal) on the basis of the current situation. This approach leads to fast and efficient decision making, but requires knowledge that is specific to an operator and to the (abstract) situation.

TacAir-Soar is missing the ability to make decisions that are based not only on a direct interpretation of the current situation but also on a deeper, more "first principles" understanding of that situation. Models provide one method for providing such a deeper understanding of a domain. Models represent the dynamics of an environment and how various aspects of the environment interact, and they are often important foundations for interpretation of events, for the planning of new courses of action, and for the creation of expectations. For example, a model of a team's shared goals can lead to expectations that members of the team will take certain kinds of actions. A model of an individual's ability to take action can support an internal or "mental" simulation of that action in some imagined context. The implemented version of TacAir-Soar implicitly contains a model of the agent's actions by including reactions to many different situations. For example, an agent can commit to be at a certain location at a particular time so that an aircraft can be refueled in the air. Subsequent actions implicitly anticipate that a tanker will be present when the aircraft arrives to refuel, but TacAir-Soar doesn't explicitly create a mental representation of the future event or of the participants and conditions that define refueling.

Agents with implicit models can be brittle when they find themselves in situations not anticipated by their developers. For example, if the refueling tanker aircraft is diverted, the agent will still fly to the rendezvous unless there is programmed knowledge for reacting to that situation.

Production rules provide one means of encoding models, as was demonstrated in chapter 5; however, Soar's newest architectural mechanisms have greatly expanded the types of models that can be created in Soar. As was demonstrated in subsection 9.2.4 and in section 12.3, episodic memory makes it possible to use past experiences as approximations of how the world will change in similar future situations. SVS provides the basis for representing and reasoning about spatial information, as was demonstrated in chapter 10 and also in section 12.2 (where it was used to predict the results of actions in arcade games). Mental imagery provides a general capability for representing and reasoning about space that was completely missing from the version of Soar used to develop TacAir-Soar. Moreover, SVS supports motion simulations to model the complex behavior of objects in the world (subsection 10.3.7). These representations make it possible to create internal models of the spatial relations inherent to tactical situations (above, below, ahead, behind, etc.) and to simulate possible outcomes.

Planning

One of the most obvious uses of a model is for planning, where the agent uses the model to evaluate alternative actions. This use of a model leads to simple one-step look-ahead searches, or, more generally, to planning of future courses of actions. An action model, which invariably is more general than pre-programmed operator-selection knowledge, allows the agent to determine actions in situations in which it doesn't have pre-programmed responses. Moreover, a motion model allows an agent to generate low-level actions, as was demonstrated in subsection 10.3.7. Thus, this approach could decrease the amount of knowledge that has to be encoded in the agent, and it could increase the fidelity and robustness of the agent's behavior. Below we consider three examples in which planning could benefit TacAir-Soar 2.0.

Re-planning missions and behaviors
When flying a mission, the original TacAir-Soar could respond to externally specified changes, such as a change in the target, as well as changes in its own state, such as the need to abandon the mission because of low fuel. However, it lacked the capability to re-plan a mission, such as determining new waypoints to which to fly while taking into consideration fuel, enemy units, and mission timing. In TacAir-Soar 2.0, the agent would be capable of considering relevant spatial and temporal constraints as it planned a mission. This planning would require an internal representation of the airspace (and perhaps, depending on mission, ground terrain too) in SVS and internal action models, as discussed above. The planning would be constrained by background knowledge that encodes standard tactics, techniques, and procedures (which might include receiving permission for such changes from a higher authority). That information could be encoded in semantic memory and retrieved when appropriate during the planning process.

Tactical engagements, responding to unexpected behavior
TacAir-Soar uses its existing knowledge to classify the situation and pick a response. There is always some response that applies, even if it is a general response included to ensure that there is always at least a default action. In TacAir-Soar 2.0, the agent's reactive knowledge would be designed to cover standard situations, using appropriate doctrine and tactics. When the agent encountered an unexpected situation, such as when an enemy did something that wasn't covered by standard doctrine, none of the reactive knowledge would apply, and an impasse would arise. In the impasse, the agent would evaluate alternative actions by internally simulating them on a model of its environment, evaluating the result of those actions (and possibly additional follow on actions if the immediate result could not be evaluated), and picking the action that leads to the best result. Recall that TacAir-Soar is designed so that the execution a specific tactic or even a mission is dynamically decomposed as a hierarchy of problem spaces. Therefore, when something is "unexpected," it is unexpected within the context of a specific problem space, and the planning will occur at an appropriate level of the hierarchy.

Flight maneuvering
TacAir-Soar controls an aircraft by setting the desired altitude, speed, and heading. An underlying control system translates those desired settings into actual maneuvering. This is sufficient for the tactics and behaviors in TacAir-Soar, which dealt with beyond-visual-range engagements, but insufficient for complex tactical maneuvering required

in within-visual-range engagements and for other detailed maneuvering, such as required for take-offs and landings. The motion models in SVS would provide a means for increasing the fidelity of behavior by allowing TacAir-Soar to control its airframe at a level similar to the controls used by humans.

Creating and monitoring expectations

In TacAir-Soar, the agent never has expectations as to what will happen in the future. It responds to a wide variety of situations, and can detect specific cases of plan or mission failure, but it has no general sense of evaluating situations as to whether they are consistent with its plans, or whether a plan has to be modified. In TacAir-Soar 2.0, as a by-product of planning, the agent could create expectations of future events. Expectations could be used as the basis for appraisals, so that the agent not only reacts to situations but also attempts to evaluate its progress. Expectations, when violated, can serve as a signal to the agent that the world is not what it believes it to be. For the long term, detecting such discrepancies could help the agent learn to refine its action models so that its future planning better predicts future situations. In the short term, a discrepancy could be treated as a signal that something unexpected has happened and that the current plan might have to be modified or abandoned.

Noticing that the current plan is failing is critical to robust behavior. For example, imagine the intended rendezvous with a refueling aircraft. An obvious expectation for this situation is that the refueling aircraft will be present at the time of the rendezvous. However, if the agent doesn't observe the refueling aircraft in the vicinity (or observes it at a location too far away to meet the rendezvous constraints) then the TacAir-Soar 2.0 agent would recognize this plan failure. Failure expectations could then lead it to consider alternative actions, such as returning to its base (because it is too low on fuel to continue the mission), or to plan "repair" actions, such as sending a radio message to confirm or disconfirm rendezvous status or vectoring in the direction of the refueling aircraft. Although all these specific situations can be encoded in an agent (and were encoded in TacAir-Soar), this requirement makes development tedious and prone to mistakes. It is more efficient and robust to create and monitor expectations than to pre-program all possible mission-failure situations.

To date, we have not implemented agents that perform this type of expectation generation and self-monitoring of expectation achievement. However, it seems within reach of our current capabilities. Planning in Soar generates descriptions of future states, which could be captured by episodic memory or explicitly stored in semantic memory. During execution, the agent could periodically access episodic or semantic memory to compute the appropriate appraisals and determine whether its expectations are being satisfied. If its expectations aren't being satisfied, the agent can engage in deliberate reasoning in order to recover.

Opponent and teammate modeling

Opponent and teammate modeling is an important example of how modeling can combine with planning and expectations to provide qualitative improvements in TacAir-Soar. In TacAir-Soar, the agent represents both opponents and teammates and has knowledge to support complex responses to their actions. However, that knowledge is reactive and doesn't involve internal simulation of the other agents' internal processing. As we have demonstrated in other systems (Laird 2001b), it is possible in Soar to use models of other agents to predict their behavior. For TacAir-Soar 2.0, adding opponent modeling could improve the agent's ability to handle tactical situations, as it will anticipate an opponent's actions instead of just reacting. Models of both opponents and teammates would draw heavily on the ability of Soar agents to plan and to use mental imagery for spatial representations and reasoning (as above). Anticipation is implicit in some of the existing tactical knowledge derived from the experts who were consulted in the development of TacAir-Soar. Adding explicit anticipation, however, would make the agents more robust, and would enable them to dynamically derive high-quality behavior instead of being reliant on pre-encoded knowledge.

The ability to model teammates would also increase TacAir-Soar 2.0's robustness and generality. Consider a simple example of a wingman agent flying with a lead aircraft. The wingman must not only follow the leader, but must also maintain its own awareness of progress in executing a mission. Because communication must be kept to a minimum, the leader doesn't communicate information about the mission's progress; it expects the wingman to maintain its own mission awareness using a model of the leader. In the original TacAir-Soar, we included knowledge for all the situations that could arise if a wingman had to update its own mission awareness. Although this works, it required significant knowledge engineering and is potentially brittle—if new missions are added, or even if existing mission types are modified, additional knowledge engineering is required. A better alternative is for the wingman to have a model of the leader and to use that model in combination with its own situational awareness.

Modeling of teammates and opponents could be based on knowledge encoded in rules, in semantic memory, or in episodic memory. An agent could use its own knowledge as a baseline for modeling the behavior of other agents, and could refine it with more specific knowledge. In cases requiring an agent to model the behaviors of very different agents, some of the knowledge could be encoded in rules, but it could also be stored declaratively in semantic memory and then recalled and interpreted when needed. Episodic memory could provide a history of other agents' actions that could specialize and refine the model knowledge stored in rules and in semantic memory. Reinforcement learning could also tune general models to the specific actions of individuals. Episodic memory can store teammates' goals as communicated through shared plans or explicit communications.

Modeling summary

Agents with models will have a greater ability to overcome gaps in their execution knowledge, whether a gap derives from omissions in developer-encoded knowledge or from evolutionary changes in the domain. In effect, models enable an agent to catch "exceptions," evaluate the problem, and then generate alternative responses. Another benefit of models is that an agent could use them to reflect on some past or hypothetical situation and explain its own actions. Although different methods for generating explanations have been used in TacAir-Soar (Johnson 1994; Taylor, Knudsen, and Holt 2006), it is likely that models would lead to a deeper level of generative explanation than has been available previously.

13.3.2 Adapting Expert Behavior on the Basis of Experience

In TacAir-Soar, all tactics are pre-coded with when they are to be used and how they are to be executed. However, even in applications where a fully competent or "expert" pilot is desired, it may be advantageous for the agent to adapt that expert behavior to meet new application requirements. For example, new aircraft with performance characteristics somewhat different from those of existing aircraft could be introduced. A new weapon or radar system might be introduced, requiring adaptation of existing tactics to address the new system. In TacAir-Soar, these kinds of changes require that a developer make changes in rules and test the tuned or modified behaviors that result. Consequently, the update process is sometimes costly and requires the direct intercession of a developer, which is often inconvenient for a deployed application.

Reinforcement learning, which can automatically use feedback from performance to tune low-level control behaviors and tactics, could tune TacAir-Soar maneuver parameters to the flight dynamics of different aircraft. From a development perspective, we expect reinforcement learning to allow Soar agents to find acceptable performance solutions for boundary conditions where different control priorities intersect. Because ensuring that all boundary conditions are covered tends to be a time-intensive aspect of agent development, this approach has the potential to reduce development costs substantially.

Adapting expert behavior need not be limited to tuning, however. Acquiring and refining the action models discussed above would also enable an expert-level agent to extend and adapt its capability. Initially, as was demonstrated in section 12.3, the action models of the agent may be learned using episodic memory, with the agent using past experience to predict what will happen in a similar situation in the future. Chunking can then convert the use of episodic memory into rules that provide an efficient means for action modeling for use in the application. This approach has been shown to be feasible (see chapter 12) but has not yet been demonstrated in a fielded application.

Enabling an agent to extend and refine its expert ability in these ways can provide substantial benefits. Adaptation enables the agent to be more autonomous. It provides greater robustness, especially as application requirements and deployment contexts evolve. And it reduces software life-cycle costs, both because initial model development is simpler and because many of the changes in requirements that will occur over the lifetime of the application don't require an agent developer.

13.3.3 Learning a Domain

A great deal of effort—both knowledge acquisition and, usually to a lesser extent, knowledge encoding—goes into building agents like TacAir-Soar. Currently, Soar agents are built by a combination of writing rules, encoding knowledge in semantic memory, and using existing knowledge bases to augment semantic memory. Previously we created agents that learn from instructions (Huffman and Laird 1995); however, at that time, Soar had only rule memory for long-term knowledge representation and only chunking for learning. With the addition of the new memory and learning modules, it should be possible to extend earlier research on instruction so that we can use instruction to create agents such TacAir-Soar that require large knowledge bases. Significant research still is required in this area, but instruction has the potential to make it possible to create agents much faster and, once built, to be modified without direct coding by a developer.

Even if *de novo* creation of a TacAir-Soar-level agent is a long-term research goal, learning from instruction might be useful for adapting TacAir-Soar for different uses and tasks in the near term. TacAir-Soar has been used for multiple applications, such as training pilots to be wingmen, training air-traffic controllers, and training forward air controllers (people on the ground who guide military aircraft to targets). For each of these different applications, variations and emphases in behavior for the application had to be developed by hand. For example, it may sometimes be important for an agent to perform an action that, although incorrect from the point of view of doctrine, gives the trainee the ability to recognize and respond to the pilot's error. RL tuning in combination with learning from instruction might be used to enable an agent to adapt its doctrinal behavior to support learning goals or application goals that interact with the requirement for doctrine-defined behaviors.

14 Conclusion

In *Unified Theories of Cognition,* Allen Newell used an earlier version of Soar as an illustrative example of a general cognitive architecture. Although the present book diverges from Newell's by emphasizing functionality and artificial intelligence instead of cognitive modeling and natural intelligence, the books share two ideas. The first is that cognitive architecture is a important component of understanding intelligence, be it natural or artificial. The second is that progress in cognitive architecture requires building architectures and creating agents within them, then experimenting with them and evaluating them on a wide variety of tasks.

Throughout the previous thirteen chapters, Soar was described as a candidate cognitive architecture for supporting human-level intelligence, and we have evaluated it relative to the requirements presented in chapter 2. Although Soar falls short of achieving all those requirements, it makes substantial progress on each of them. Perhaps more important, it provides a coherent design of an end-to-end cognitive architecture based on the problem-space computational model that has the potential for meeting all the requirements. It is this overall coverage that distinguishes Soar, and obtaining this overall coverage is the most challenging aspect of research in cognitive architecture.

In the remainder of this chapter, I review and reflect on Soar from multiple perspectives. After reviewing the structure of Soar, I review how that structure supports the PSCM. These abstract characterizations of overall structure and function are the essence of what Soar is. The flow of data and the types of primitive memories and processes, the representations supported by these memories, and the processing cycle are the most important commitments in Soar. I am less firmly committed to the exact details of each memory's operation, and I expect that research in other areas of cognitive architecture, cognitive science, and AI will lead to improvements and even significant revisions in these modules.

After reviewing the structure and functionality of Soar, I analyze Soar from the perspective of the architectural requirements proposed in chapter 2 for achieving human-level behavior. I use that analysis and its accompanying identification of Soar's shortcomings to propose an agenda for future research in Soar. I then discuss which components are responsible for meeting the various requirements, and reflect on the status of Soar as a cognitive architecture in support of human-level intelligence.

14.1 Soar from a Structural Perspective

Chapter 4 presented the foundations of the structure of Soar, and chapters 5–11 presented extensions, adding impasse-driven substates, learning mechanisms, long-term memories, mental imagery, and an appraisal component that supports reinforcement learning. Further extensions are possible, but here I take stock of the current structure of Soar and the major architectural commitments.

Figure 14.1 shows the overall structure of Soar as originally presented in figure 1.4. The major feature of the architectural design is the integration of independent memory and processing units that communicate via a shared symbolic working memory populated with relational structures. Each of the long-term symbolic memory modules (procedural, semantic, and episodic) is cued via structures in working memory and

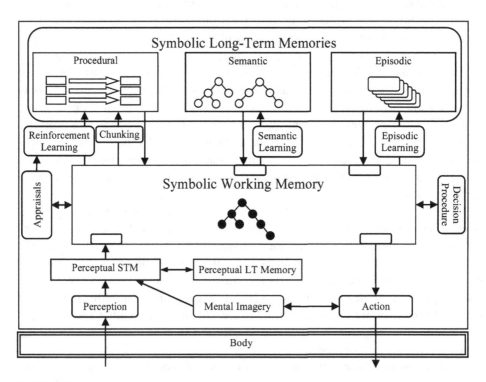

Figure 14.1
Block diagram of Soar.

creates structures in working memory. Learning is based on the structures in working memory, except for the storage of long-term visual memory. There is no direct storage from one long-term memory to another. New rules are created via chunking, where a chunk is based on the working-memory elements that are tested and created within a substate. Tuning of operator-evaluation rules by reinforcement learning is based on operator selections, rule firings, reward structures in working memory, and appraisals. Creation of new episodes is based on the contents of working memory, as are creation and modification of structures in semantic memory.

At an abstract level, Soar is similar in structure to classic Blackboard Systems (Corkill 1991), in which independent knowledge sources communicate by means of a shared global blackboard. However, the knowledge sources of a Blackboard System correspond to task-dependent functional processing elements. Hearsay II (Erman and Lesser 1980), a Blackboard System for speech understanding, had many separate knowledge sources, including some for segmenting the speech signal, processing syntax, and processing sentences. In contrast, the modules in Soar are task-neutral, providing primitive support for long-term memory, for decision making, and for learning. Task knowledge is organized as problem spaces, which are not organized as separate structural components, but which are collections of knowledge spread across the long-term memories. The memories are distinguished by the type of knowledge (procedural, semantic, episodic, and perceptual) rather than by the content of the knowledge. In contrast to Blackboard Systems, in which new modules are developed for each task, the same set of modules is used for all tasks in Soar. As was mentioned in chapter 1, many current cognitive architectures have task-neutral structural components similar to those in Soar.

The independence of the individual task-independent modules has simplified the development of Soar. Instead of having to create information channels between all of the processing and memory modules, each module connects only to working memory. As we have added new modules, existing modules have remained unchanged except to take advantage of new capabilities, and interactions between modules occur through information in working memory. Thus, adding new long-term memories and processing modules has not required redesign of the overall architecture or the individual modules. As evidence of this, the algorithm (and code) for matching production rules has not changed since the conversion of Soar from Lisp to C in the early 1990s (Doorenbos 1994). Since then, we have gone through multiple approaches for integrating Soar to external environments, added reinforcement learning, episodic memory, semantic memory, mental imagery, and appraisal processing.

The presentations throughout the book have emphasized the structure (and function) of the modules individually and within the context of working memory, procedural memory, and the decision procedure. One of the unique aspects of Soar is that it combines all the modules in figure 14.1 in a single implemented architecture.

Recently that combination has allowed us to study some of the interactions and synergies that are possible when these modules are used together in a single agent. For examples, see chapters 8, 9, and 12, where a variety of interactions among chunking, reinforcement learning, semantic memory, episodic memory, and mental imagery were demonstrated.

14.2   Soar from a Functional Perspective

As was noted in chapter 3, the functional perspective of Soar begins with the problem-space computational model. The structures in figure 14.1 are in service of a computational implementation of the PSCM in which knowledge performs the PSCM functions for elaborating the current state and proposing, evaluating, and applying operators to it. What may be surprising is that the structure of Soar doesn't map directly onto the PSCM functions. There are no operator modules in a structural view of Soar, nor are there any proposal, evaluation, or application processes. Instead, Soar is a diverse collection of memories and processes that on the surface seem unrelated to operators and states.

At the most abstract level, the functionality of the PSCM breaks down into problem-space search and knowledge search, which are brought together by the processing cycle and the decision procedure. The purpose of knowledge search is to bring knowledge to bear to perform the individual PSCM functions that support problem search. In Soar, procedural memory provides direct support for all PSCM functions, including state elaboration, operator proposal, operator evaluation, and operator application. However, there is no guarantee that the knowledge in procedural memory is sufficient for direct execution of a PSCM function. In these situations, Soar provides the ability for problem-space search to be invoked recursively within a substate in service of a PSCM function. It is usually within a substate that the other long-term memories (semantic and episodic) are accessed, in which case they provide the knowledge needed to perform PSCM functions for impassed states when procedural knowledge is insufficient. Within the substate, they are deliberately queried via operator application, where part of the operator application is performed by a rule that creates an appropriate query. Once the query has been created, the retrieval is performed; then additional rules use the result to modify the state. In such cases, performing the operator application involves knowledge search in both procedural memory (to initiate the query and use the result) and either episodic or semantic memory. Thus, these memories enhance the set of available primitive problem-space operators that can be used either directly in a task or in a substate in support of other PSCM functions. Examples of these uses are provided in chapters 8, 9, and 12.

The SVS component of Soar can be decomposed into two separate functions. SVS supports the extraction of predicates from perception, and thus provides a means of

- State Elaboration
  - ○ Procedural Knowledge
  - ○ *Problem Search in Substate*
- Operator Proposal
  - ○ Procedural Knowledge
  - ○ *Problem Search in Substate*
- Operator Evaluation
  - ○ Procedural Knowledge
  - ○ *Problem Search in Substate*
- Operator Selection
  - ○ Decision Procedure
- Operator Elaboration
  - ○ Procedural Knowledge
  - ○ *Problem Search in Substate*
- Operator Application
  - ○ Procedural Knowledge
  - ○ *Problem Search in Substate*
  - ○ Motor Actions
  - ○ Episodic Memory Retrieval
  - ○ Semantic Storage
  - ○ Semantic Memory Retrieval
  - ○ Mental Imagery Actions

Figure 14.2
PSCM Functions and their underlying implementations in Soar.

obtaining symbolic information from the environment or mental imagery. SVS also supports direct modifications to the mental imagery system, allowing an agent to imagine objects or manipulate objects in the mental imagery system. Together these provide an innate problem space with operators for modifying and extracting structures from the mental imagery system.

Figure 14.2 shows how all these components work together to support the PSCM functions. All the PSCM functions are listed (including operator elaboration for completeness), along with the knowledge and processes available for supplying the knowledge required for performing that function. For all but operator selection and operator application, there are two possibilities. One possibility is procedural knowledge encoded as rules; the other is problem search in a substate after an impasse. Operator selection is implemented by a fixed decision procedure that analyzes the preferences created in the operator-proposal and operator-evaluation functions and either selects a new operator or detects an impasse and generates a substate. In

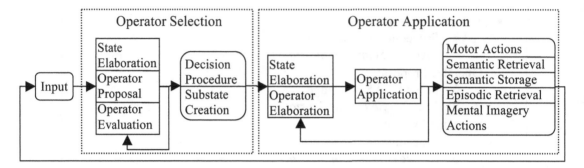

Figure 14.3
Expanded Soar processing cycle.

operator application, procedural knowledge and processing in a substate are available as in the other PSCM functions. However, operator application is distinguished by the fact that it is where the agent can initiate actions in its external environment or in mental imagery, and it is where the agent can retrieve structures from semantic memory or episodic memory as well as store structures to semantic memory (Laird, Xu, and Wintermute 2010). The types of processing that are available through operator application are also available for all other PSCM functions through substate processing. For example, an operator can be evaluated in part by retrieving a memory from episodic memory using operator application within a substate.

Soar's processing cycle implements these functions as illustrated in figure 14.3. This figure (an expansion of the processing cycle shown in figure 4.7) includes the processing and memories systems in Soar, but not the learning mechanisms. In the figure, all the rectangular boxes are PSCM functions that are performed directly by procedural knowledge. The other boxes include additional types of processing. These include input through perception (and the results of mental imagery actions), the decision procedure (which can either select an operator or create a substate if there is an impasse), and output (which supports the processing necessary for motor actions, retrievals from semantic memory, storage to semantic memory, retrievals from episodic memory, and mental imagery actions). In the current implementation, the processing cycle runs as a single thread on a single processor, although it simulates parallelism in rule firing and in the processing within a phase (such as output). In theory, processing can be further parallelized so that each module initiates its processing in a separate thread when the data needed for it to run are available. For example, when a cue for an episodic retrieval is created, the search through episodic memory could be initiated immediately, and could run in parallel with other components of the processing cycle.

In Soar, procedural knowledge, encoded as production rules, drives behavior. It is responsible for selecting and initiating the application of operators. Other types of knowledge, such as semantic, episodic, and mental imagery, have roles to play in determining and producing behavior; however, access to them is initiated by procedural knowledge. Moreover, procedural knowledge is responsible for converting those other forms of knowledge into preferences for selecting operators or into changes in the state for applying operators. Thus, Soar requires some primitive set of procedural knowledge, and we have developed the selection problem space and its extensions to support task-independent reasoning about operator selection; however, additional task-independent support for the complete PSCM is still needed.

Missing from the discussion of functionality is the role of the learning mechanisms, which include chunking, reinforcement learning, and the mechanisms for storing knowledge in episodic and semantic memory. These learning mechanisms are crucial to the operation of an agent; however, the PSCM focuses on performance and not on learning, so they play only an indirect role. Also missing is any discussion of the role of emotions and appraisal processing. At present emotions only influence reinforcement learning. Their influence on the other components of the architecture has yet to be considered.

14.3   Evaluating Soar on Architectural Requirements

In chapter 2, a set of requirements for cognitive architectures for supporting human-level agents was presented. Throughout the book, the individual components of Soar have been evaluated with respect to those requirements, but in isolation. In this section, I review the requirements in relation to the complete architecture, reviewing the contributions and shortcomings of individual architectural components as well as their integration. Where there is a shortcoming, I present it as a topic for future research, and I identify the most important Future Soar Research (FSR) items. In general, the emphasis here is on architecture; however, because behavior is a product of architecture and knowledge, the research agenda includes both architectural extensions and the development of task-independent knowledge.

R0:   Fixed for all tasks.

A cognitive architecture captures regularities in the structure of an agent that exist across all tasks and across the agent's lifetime. These regularities are reflected in the fixed memories, data structures, and algorithms embodied in the architecture. The actual behavior of an agent is determined by the combination of the architecture and its knowledge, so defining the architecture also defines the space of possible knowledge and the ways in which knowledge leads to action.

In Soar, there is a "hard" separation between the agent and the architecture. An agent's behavior can be modified only through the addition of knowledge to a long-term memory: procedural memory, semantic memory, and episodic memory, as well as the memories associated with mental imagery. Thus, the only difference between one agent and the next is in the contents of these memories, and the specific perceptual and motor systems that connect the agent to its external environment. Thus, all examples in this book use exactly the same architecture. There are no modifications to the underlying C++ code. The only exceptions are that SVS and the appraisal-based emotion modules were included in the architecture only for the demonstrations in chapters 10–12. There are some architectural parameters tied to specific modules, such as the learning rate used in reinforcement learning; however, as was mentioned at the end of chapter 7, our goal is eliminate such parameters in the near future.

R1: Realize a symbol system.

In order to support universal computation, a cognitive architecture must be a symbol system. One of the most distinctive aspects of symbolic processing is that it provides general composability, both of representations and of behavior. Soar has memories that support symbolic representations (working, semantic, and episodic) and associated processes (applying procedural knowledge and the decision procedure) for general symbolic computation.

R2: Represent and effectively use modality-specific knowledge.

For tasks that require interaction with external environments, non-symbolic representations can provide significant computational advantages. As was noted in chapter 13, many of the Soar systems inhabited real and simulated worlds in which spatial reasoning was important. Those systems relied on a combination of symbolic and numeric representations of space in working memory, along with task-specific procedural knowledge encoded in rules to reason over those representations. Because it wasn't possible to do complex numeric calculations directly in rules, such calculations were done by special-purpose modules external to Soar. Thus, we were able to develop systems in Soar that represented and reasoned about space, but only by adding special-purpose modules. These modules had some, but not all, of the capabilities of an imagery system. With the addition of mental imagery, as described in chapter 10, Soar has a general capability that supports spatial and visual imagery representations and reasoning.

Soar doesn't support representations for other sensory modalities, such as audition; however, it should be possible to add imagery modules for these modalities to Soar using methods analogous to those used in SVS. Probably more important than adding new modules is refining and extending SVS and connecting it to real sensors of the physical world. Other integrations of cognitive architectures with external sensors have lacked a true mental-imagery component, so there are many research questions related to the transformation of images to symbolic structures, as well as top-down feedback to direct image processing.

FSR1:   Extend Soar's mental imagery component so that it interfaces with real sensors.

R3:   Represent, effectively use, and efficiently access large bodies of diverse knowledge.
This requirement incorporates three intertwined issues: whether the architecture supports sufficiently diverse representations of knowledge, whether an agent can effectively use the encoded knowledge, and whether the architecture can efficiently access large bodies of all those representations of knowledge. Although effective use of knowledge implies that it can be used efficiently, we break efficiency out as a separate item because there are special issues that arise when attempting to develop systems that support efficient access to large bodies of knowledge.

R3.1:   Represent diverse knowledge.
Soar supports a range of types of representations of knowledge, including symbolic information as a graph structure in working memory, in semantic memory, and in episodic memory; procedural knowledge as operators and the supporting production rules; and modality-specific representations such as are employed for mental imagery. These have proved sufficient for the diverse set of tasks pursued in Soar to date.

One class of representations that needs additional analysis is the representation of probabilistic and uncertain information. Soar does represent uncertainty for operator selection and it uses reinforcement learning to automatically adjust the associated expected values. But Soar doesn't represent conditional belief about state structures. There are not probabilities associated with individual working-memory elements, nor are probabilities used in matching rules or in rule actions; thus, Soar doesn't support probabilistic representations of inference or action. Soar can make use of external computational aids that perform probability calculations. In one sense, Soar currently tests the hypothesis that probabilities need not be considered throughout all cognition, but only in specific areas, such as in perception processing (Wang and Laird 2010) and decision making. If this approach fails to be sufficient, subsection 4.5.4 discusses other approaches to integrate probabilistic representations in Soar.

R3.2:   Effectively use large bodies of knowledge.
The second part of requirement 3 is that agents be able to make effective use of large bodies of knowledge. Our experience with large bodies of procedural knowledge comes from real-world applications described in chapter 13, such as in TacAir-Soar; our experience with large bodies of semantic and episodic knowledge is described in chapters 8 and 9. Even with these demonstrations, there is still much more we need to learn

about creating agents that make extensive use of semantic and episodic memory. Exploring these memories leads to two different research issues.

First, we need to refine and extend the implementations of semantic memory and episodic memory. Our current implementations emphasize basic functionality and efficiency. As was discussed at the ends of chapters 8 and 9, there are many dimensions along which the implementations could be improved to increase their functionality. For semantic memory, these include developing an automatic storage mechanism, supporting multiple views of objects, and developing a retrieval mechanism that is biased by the context in working memory. For episodic memory, the improvements include adding appraisal activation in episodes to bias retrieval, expanding the mechanisms for accessing episodic memory, and including visual and spatial information in episodes.

FSR2: Expand functionality of semantic and episodic memories.

A second shortcoming of our current implementations is that the procedural knowledge for accessing and using knowledge stored in those components is task specific. We have yet to develop general task-independent problem spaces (sets of operators and the associated procedural knowledge) for using large bodies of episodic and semantic knowledge on complex problems. Even though we have demonstrated that Soar can access knowledge encoded in knowledge bases, such as WordNet, we have yet to develop general procedural knowledge for accessing that knowledge across a wide range of tasks. The goal is to have general problem spaces that support general cognitive capabilities, similar in spirit to what we developed for look-ahead planning with the selection and evaluation problem spaces in chapter 5. Cognitive capabilities are general problem-solving, reasoning, or learning techniques that can be used in many different situations, that draw on multiple architectural mechanisms, and that often are specialized with domain knowledge for a certain problem. In describing episodic memory, we listed a variety of cognitive capabilities that it might support. Other examples of cognitive capabilities could include different types of planning and reasoning, language processing, complex learning strategies, such as retrospective learning, analogy, and self-explanation. This sets an agenda for incorporating research from other subfields of AI into a cognitive architecture. Our hypothesis is that these capabilities can be achieved by using knowledge encoded within the architecture and that they do not require new architectural modules or mechanisms. This is the approach originally taken for incorporating natural-language processing in Soar (NL-Soar; Lehman, Lewis, and Newell 1998; Lonsdale and Rytting 2001), and has proved successful; however, whether this strategy will work across all these capabilities remains an open question.

Achieving these cognitive capabilities would have a significant effect on the usefulness and generality of agents developed in Soar, so that as an agent encounters new tasks it is able to take advantage of the knowledge it has acquired and of its architectural capabilities. Research on this problem would surely uncover problems that arise when a general agent uses large bodies of knowledge. Few of the existing agent-based systems based on cognitive architectures make use of large bodies of knowledge. One noteworthy exception is Companions (Forbus and Hinrichs 2006).

FSR3: Develop procedural knowledge to support using large bodies of semantic and episodic knowledge.

R3.3: Efficiently access large bodies of knowledge.
The third part of requirement 3 arises because knowledge is useful only if an agent can access it efficiently. Knowledge may come from learning, but we also want to support agents that come pre-programmed with large bodies of procedural knowledge (such as in TacAir-Soar) and large bodies of semantic knowledge (such as available in systems like Cyc and WordNet). Providing efficient access depends on the underlying implementation technology, but also on the expressiveness of how that knowledge can be accessed. The memories in Soar have been designed to provide a balance. Evaluations of these memories are presented at the ends of chapters 4, 8 and 9. As we expand the functionality of these mechanisms in FSR2, we must maintain efficient access.

R4: Represent and effectively use knowledge with different levels of generality.
In order to respond to environment regularities at different levels, an agent must be able to represent knowledge across a spectrum of generality. Symbol systems provide this capability by supporting the representation of hierarchies of concepts, so that the agent isn't forced to reason with only the data it receives from perception, but can create abstract concepts and categories. Thus, satisfying this requirement comes in part through the satisfaction of R1. For example, semantic memory can contain hierarchical representations and the agent can access both specific and general information about an object or a concept. Moreover, production rules, through testing different subsets of structures in working memory, provide a representational medium in which procedural knowledge can be encoded at different levels of generality, analogous to coarse coding. Rules can contain many conditions (so that they test very specific situations) or only a few conditions (so that they test general situations). Soar's imagery component also provides an additional mechanism for representing and reasoning about specific aspects of spatial knowledge, which would otherwise be difficult to capture in a purely symbolic architecture (Wintermute 2010).

R5: Represent and effectively use diverse amounts of knowledge.
An agent will have varied experiences and different levels of pre-programmed knowledge for the tasks it pursues. For tasks that occur often, it will have extensive and detailed knowledge, so that it is effectively an expert; for novel tasks, it will have only limited knowledge. Whatever level of knowledge the agent has, it must use it

effectively. Soar's declarative memories build up incrementally, supporting different amounts of knowledge. The challenge in achieving this requirement usually has to do with procedural memory: the agent must be able to make progress even when its knowledge of a domain is limited, while being able to take full advantage of its knowledge of a domain when it is extensive. Soar supports multiple levels of procedural knowledge, and through its support of a universal weak method it can use whatever method is appropriate to the knowledge. In contrast, many planners and problem solvers have specific requirements for task knowledge and have difficulty exploiting additional forms of knowledge or getting by with limited procedural knowledge. Moreover, when sufficient rule-based knowledge is available for a PSCM function, it is used; however, if it is missing, a substate arises in which the agent can deliberately attempt to find and use other relevant knowledge—either by accessing other long-term memories, by acting in the world, or through additional internal reasoning.

R6: *Represent and effectively use beliefs independent of current perception.*
An agent must be able to represent situations beyond what it is currently experiencing so as to maintain transient perceptual information, plan for future hypothetical situations, consider a situation from the perspective of another agent, and learn from the past through retrospective analysis. Perception is available in Soar's working memory, and operators can create persistent structures to maintain perceptual information indefinitely, as well as create arbitrary interpretations of the current situation. Substates provide an additional mechanism by which the agent can create internal representations that are distinct from perception but have the same syntactic structure as perceptual input as well as the agent's derived representations of the situation. Being able to create the same syntactic structure in a substate makes it possible to apply the agent's long-term knowledge for reasoning and acting in the world (encoded as rules as well as in semantic and episodic memories) directly, without reinterpretation or analogy. Thus, an agent can use the same long-term knowledge to determine what the agent would do (or what another agent would do) in a hypothetical situation, as was demonstrated in the planning examples in chapter 5. Substates also allow the agent to reason about alternatives without disrupting the agent's representation of the current situation. The imagery system provides another way for the agent to reason about situations it is not directly experiencing by imagining structures and detecting their interactions.

R7: *Represent and effectively use rich, hierarchical control knowledge.*
A human-level agent must be able to reason about and use complex actions, and must have the knowledge it needs to control those actions. Invariably, hierarchical representations are needed to overcome the complexity of interacting with a complex world (Simon 1969), as well as to organize internal reasoning. The PSCM provides a structure

for organizing and using hierarchical control knowledge for executing external actions and for internal reasoning. Production rules support parallel conditional actions; substates support the dynamic decomposition of hierarchical actions. Motion models (Wintermute 2009) provide an additional mechanism for controlling actions that require tight coupling of external actions with perception.

R8: Incorporate innate utilities.

Depending on an agent's goals and needs, different situations will have different utilities for the agent. Some of those utilities will be inherent to the agent's structure, the environment, and any life-long tasks that agent must pursue. Having the ability to detect the utilities of those situations helps the agent survive, pursue its tasks, and learn. As was noted in chapter 11, appraisals provide one possible subset of innate utilities, and reinforcement learning provides a mechanism for learning from them. Utilities related to survival, such as detecting low resources (thirst and hunger) and damage (pain), have been incorporated in some agents (such as "pain" for collisions in the robot agent in Rooms World).

R9: Represent and manage goals at multiple time scales.

Goals provide direction for an agent, and the agent must be able to internally represent and manage its goals. When Soar selects an operator for which it does not have operator-application knowledge encoded as rules, the ensuing substate is essentially a goal to apply that operator. As was noted in chapter 5, Soar provides the necessary mechanisms for representing and managing such goals. This mechanism is most appropriate for immediate goals that the agent is actively pursuing.

Soar lacks an architectural mechanism for managing longer-term goals (also called delayed intentions) that arise when an agent decides to pursue a goal that will influence behavior sometime in the future, such as deciding in the morning to pick up milk at the store on the way home from work that evening. One option is to store such goals as data structures in working memory. For example, in TacAir-Soar agents, all information about missions is represented in working memory, and progress on those missions is maintained and updated in working memory. Although convenient, this approach requires that these structures be maintained in working memory indefinitely. An alternative is to store longer-term goals in semantic or episodic memory, often called *prospective memory* (McDaniel and Einstein 2007); however, there must also be associated procedural knowledge that retrieves these goals when they are relevant to the current situation. Whether this will be sufficient, or whether additional architectural mechanisms will be needed to support the maintenance and retrieval of active longer-term goals, is an open question.

FSR4: Explore approaches to representing and managing longer-term goals.

R10: Access, represent, and effectively use meta-cognitive knowledge.
In order to reason about its own knowledge and the knowledge of others, an agent must be able to represent and use meta-cognitive knowledge. Soar doesn't have a separate meta-cognitive component, nor does the architecture provide direct access to the operations of the memory or processing modules, so it isn't possible to include rules that match rules, semantic memories, or episodic memories. Although this approach is technically feasible, the computational overhead of matching rules to such large memories has led us to partition memory so that knowledge retrieval is conditioned only on the contents of working memory.

In Soar, meta-cognitive reasoning is available only by exception. If everything is going smoothly, the agent never encounters an impasse and never initiates meta-cognitive reasoning. When there is an impasse, a substate is created, which indicates that the agent cannot make progress on the current problem. The substate provides a context in which the agent can reason about its own knowledge (or lack of knowledge), or even about the knowledge of others, without disrupting its representation of its current task. Semantic memory and episodic memory also provide limited meta-knowledge about the results of their retrievals, including information on retrieval failures and the quality of the match. Whether or not this level of meta-information is sufficient for human-level intelligence is an open question.

Although Soar provides limited access to meta-information about the architecture, the full PSCM, identical to what is available in task-level reasoning, is available for meta-reasoning. This is in contrast to alternatives that use special purpose reasoning modules for meta-cognition. The advantage of Soar's approach is that all the mechanisms and capabilities that are available for task-level reasoning (including meta-reasoning) are available for meta-reasoning. Thus, if knowledge is acquired during task-level problem solving, such as episodic memories of the agent's own behavior, it can be used in meta-reasoning either to predict its own behavior, or possibly the behavior of others. Moreover, within a substate, an agent can probe its own memory by creating hypothetical situations and retrieving what is stored in any of its long-term memories.

R11: Support a spectrum of bounded and unbounded deliberation.
During its lifetime, an agent experiences situations that make different demands on the time it has to respond, and on the knowledge it has available to bring to bear to make decisions. At one extreme, when there is time pressure arising from the dynamics of the environment, an agent must respond quickly, using basic knowledge. At the other extreme, when there is little or no time pressure, an agent should be able plan and analyze a situation, potentially spending almost unlimited amounts of time preparing for the future.

Soar's PSCM supports a spectrum of deliberation, including reactive procedural knowledge, sequential decisions, and unbounded reasoning in substates. At the lowest level, Soar uses parallel production rules that do not involve deliberation or integration of knowledge from multiple sources. Each rule independently determines whether its conditions match the current situation. At the next level, operator selection and operator application provides deliberation, where alternative proposed operators are explicitly represented and the choice of an operator is based on integrating knowledge retrieved from long-term memory. The final level of deliberation arises dynamically when the other two levels fail. In the substate, as was noted in chapter 5, unbounded deliberation is possible, including access to semantic and episodic memories, and mental imagery. Although in theory this processing is unbounded, it is decomposed into individual decisions and thus is interruptible at the temporal scale of an individual processing cycle whenever the agent's internal state (including its perception of the environment) evokes a response.

R12: Support diverse, comprehensive learning.

As an agent experiences the world, varieties of types of information are available to it; therefore, an intelligent agent must have sufficient learning mechanisms for capturing that information and making it available in the future to direct behavior. Soar has a variety of learning mechanisms that acquire procedural, episodic, semantic, and visual data. These learning mechanisms have been used to demonstrate a wide variety of learning strategies and methods. In some cases there has been synergy between the mechanisms so that one mechanism, such as reinforcement learning, can be used to aid in the use of knowledge acquired by another mechanism, such as episodic memory (as demonstrated in chapter 12). However, there are still many areas where we do not see the effervescence of learning that is a hallmark of humans. Important types of learning that have been demonstrated in isolated cases, such as learning new operators from instruction, must be ubiquitous in a general agent.

To delve further into this issue, we now attempt to analyze the completeness of learning from both a structural perspective and a functional perspective. The first dimension of our analysis is whether a learning mechanism exists for each of the different types of structures stored in long-term memories. In Soar, the four types of long-term knowledge are production rules (stored in procedural memory), episodes (stored in episodic memory), object structures (stored in semantic memory), and images (stored in perceptual memory). For procedural memory, production rules are created by chunking, whereas RL rules, a subset of all production rules related to operator evaluation, are tuned by reinforcement learning. For episodic memory, episodes are automatically stored by the architecture. For semantic memory, an agent can deliberately store object structures, but it isn't automatic. For perceptual memory, there are long-term memories in SVS that contain images and motion models, but there are no associated learning mechanisms. At this level, the lack of automatic learning mechanisms for semantic memory and SVS are serious omissions. The current approach requires procedural knowledge to initiate the storage of semantic knowledge, and that could significantly limit the breadth of semantic knowledge that an agent acquires.

FSR5: Develop learning mechanisms for semantic memory and long-term visual memory.

The need to develop a learning mechanism for semantic memory was identified earlier in the discussion of semantic memory and included in FSR2; however, it is important enough to be included specifically in FSR5.

The second dimension of our analysis is in terms of the PSCM functions: Does Soar have learning mechanisms that can acquire knowledge for all of the PSCM functions? At the surface level, the answer is Yes. Chunking can create rules for all PSCM functions. However, chunking depends on the existence of problem spaces and associated operators in substates to perform the reasoning necessary to produce the results, which then lead to the rules for the various PSCM functions. Thus, an important question is whether there are task-independent problem spaces available to support learning each of the PSCM functions.

In regard to operator evaluation and operator application, it was demonstrated in chapters 5, 9, and 12 that agents in Soar, using task-independent problem spaces and episodic memory, can learn both operator application knowledge (action models) and operator-evaluation knowledge (Laird, Xu, and Wintermute 2010). In other research, we have demonstrated agents that can learn to correct operator-evaluation knowledge (Laird 1998) and to correct operator-application knowledge for existing operators (Xu and Laird 2010; Pearson and Laird 2005). Most recently we have demonstrated that it is possible to learn continuous action models and discrete action models (Xu and Laird 2010). Together, these demonstrations suggest that it is possible to learn these PSCM functions, although additional research on how to make these types of learning ubiquitous for all Soar agents is required.

State elaborations are typically used to expand the set of symbolic structures used to describe a situation, whereas operator application rules generally manipulate those structures. We have examples of systems that learn state-elaboration rules, but there are no general task-independent problem spaces that create new symbolic structures that can in turn be learned over to create elaboration rules. We developed Soar systems that learned new symbolic structures and representations. However, the new structures were learned for limited tasks, and we weren't able to generalize that approach to broader situations (Miller and Laird 1996). In preliminary research we have agents that learn new concepts from perceptual processing (Wang and Laird 2010); however, it appears that new learning mechanisms (and possibly new representations of knowledge) are required to automatically derive new symbol structures from an agent's sensory experiences.

FSR6:   Develop learning mechanisms that generate new symbolic structures.

The final PSCM function is operator proposals. It makes sense that an agent has some initial primitive set of operators that it can use to initiate action in its environment. However, as was demonstrated in chapters 5 and 7, it is useful for an agent to have a hierarchy of operators, with multiple problem spaces, where some of the operators do not correspond directly to external actions, and where some operators are purely internal, modifying structures on the state. There are examples of constructing new operators, but these rely on instruction by an external agent (Huffman and Laird 1995). Although it might be possible to learn new operator proposals through a combination of chunking, episodic memory, semantic memory, and task-independent problem spaces, it is also possible that this requires new learning mechanisms, or modifications to existing mechanisms.

FSR7:   Develop learning mechanisms that create new operators and thus new problem spaces.

This discussion raises an important point about learning: It is often possible to demonstrate that an agent can learn some type of knowledge under controlled conditions for a specific task, with a set of prior knowledge to direct the learning, but that isn't the same as having that ability available for all tasks, all the time. Thus, an important challenge is to extend our research on learning new operators, extending and correcting existing operators, and learning new symbolic structures, so that it applies to every agent developed in Soar, without pre-encoded, task-dependent knowledge.

Beyond developing architectural mechanisms for expanding the coverage of learning, an important research problem is developing agents that use these mechanisms to build up large knowledge bases so that they can perform a wide variety of tasks, and can perform them at high levels of expertise. Although much of that learning may happen through unguided exploration, it may be more efficient to create agents with the ability to acquire knowledge through instruction. Instruction, especially when it is interactive and situated within a task, can be an effective method for an AI agent to acquire knowledge quickly. Our previous research in this area (Huffman and Laird 1995) was done before the recent architectural additions, and relied solely on chunking. We expect that the new architectural learning mechanisms and memories will enhance our ability to create instructable agents (Mohan and Laird 2011).

R13:   Support incremental, online learning.

An agent cannot stop the world to consolidate the information it encounters. It must learn as it behaves, and it must be able to use what it learns immediately. All of Soar's learning mechanisms are incremental. In order to be incremental, they are also relatively simple, and do not involve analysis of the entirety of agent's existing knowledge.

Reinforcement learning bases its learning on the selection and the application of operators and any ensuing reward. Chunking bases its learning on local activity in a substate. Episodic memory bases its learning on activity in working memory. Once new information has been acquired, these learning mechanisms immediately integrate it into existing long-term memories without significant generalization or post-processing. Reinforcement learning modifies the actions of existing rules by examining sequential selection and proposal of operators. Chunking adds new rules to rule memory without searching through all of rule memory, and episodic learning adds new structures without analyzing existing memories. Limited generalization and analysis is done for chunking, but there is no automatic generalization mechanism that combines knowledge learned at different times. The philosophy behind our approach is that generalization is done deliberately by operators that recall, analyze, combine, and manipulate relevant knowledge. Whatever is learned through such processing is stored by means of the existing "cheap and simple" learning mechanisms. Thus, Soar attempts to achieve this requirement by means of a combination of simple architectural learning mechanisms and more complex knowledge-based deliberation. A challenge is to develop general problem spaces that can perform the necessary generalization.

14.3.2 Potential Additional Requirements

In chapter 2 we created a list of requirements. It is possible, even likely, that we missed some important requirements. We may have missed them because we missed important characteristics of environments, tasks, and agents (C1–C8) that would give rise to the missing requirements. Alternatively, we may have missed requirements because the connections to those characteristics weren't obvious to us.

In the search for additional requirements, one of the uncertainties is whether a property we associate with human-level intelligence is really a requirement, or whether it happens to be a property of humans that, though useful, isn't necessary for achieving the breadth and depth of intelligence found in humans. A further complication is that we are most concerned about requirements related to architecture. It is possible that a capability we identify as important for human-level behavior is not an architecture requirement, but can be achieved via knowledge using other architectural mechanisms.

Below is a short list of possible missing requirements. There may be many more. Proposing and exploring such requirements is an important research problem for the cognitive architecture community.

Attention

In view of the flood of data that comes from perception and the information that can be recalled from long-term memories, one possibility is that there is a attention mechanism that focuses cognitive resources on a subset of the available information. Other cognitive architectures, such as LIDA (Franklin et al. 2006), have an explicit attention mechanism that selects a subset of an agent's internal state for further processing; others, such as ACT-R, do not. Soar doesn't have an attention mechanism for internal structures in working memory. However, perceptual attention mechanisms have been developed for Soar agents, first in the course of research on covert visual attention (Wiesmeyer and Laird 1990) and then in the course of research on overt visual attention in RWA-Soar (Hill 1999). In these approaches, attention filters and aggregates sensory data before they get into working memory. In Soar, once the sensory data are in working memory, the selection of a single operator focuses the agent's reasoning. We have not found a need for additional internal mechanisms that in some way select a subset of working memory for differential processing.

Sense of time

It is clear that humans have a sense of the passage of time, though not a perfect one. The need for this sense can be motivated by the dynamics of the environment (C2), the regularities of tasks across multiple time scales (C3), and the need for coordination of behavior with other agents (C5). At present there is no inherent sense of time in a Soar agent, although there are some temporal aspects to episodic memory. In the past, when Soar agents needed a sense of time, we added a timer as input to the agent (Jones et al. 1999), and included procedural knowledge encoded as rules that would reason about time. A similar approach has been used in ACT-R (Taatgen, Van Rijn, and Anderson 2007), although with an approach that more accurately models how human perceive and reason about time. Although the Soar approach has been adequate for the tasks implemented in the past, a more architectural approach may be necessary to support representing and reasoning about time in a general agent (Allen 1983) and its connections to memory. A temporal reasoning system has been implemented in ICARUS by Stracuzzi et al. (2009); however, it is not clear whether the approach they implemented scales up to large knowledge bases.

Sense of self

As was mentioned in requirement R6, an agent must be able to create representations of hypothetical situations as well as representations from the perspectives of others. So far, agents developed in Soar implicitly believe that all situations and knowledge as referring to themselves, without any explicit designation in working memory. However, by taking advantage of the meta-cognitive representational capabilities of substates, we have successfully developed agents that reason about the actions of others (Laird 2001b). These agents explicitly create internal representations of the agents' beliefs about other agent's beliefs. Samsonovich and Nadel (2005) have suggested that explicit designations of self are a requirement for human-level intelligence.

Even if an explicit designation is required, it isn't clear whether this needs direct architectural support, or whether it is achieved via knowledge.

Language

One of the obvious characteristics of humans is the ubiquitous use of language. In research using Soar for language processing (Lehman, Lewis, and Newell 1991; Lonsdale and Rytting; 2001), the approach has been to treat language as a skill that requires large bodies of procedural and semantic knowledge but doesn't require any special architectural mechanisms. This has also been the approach in ACT-R (Ball, Rodgers, and Gluck 2004). An important item for future research is to integrate the research described in this book with the ongoing research on language processing in Soar.

Emotion and motivation

In our research on emotion and appraisal theories, we explored only one interaction between appraisals and the rest of cognition: generating intrinsic reward for reinforcement learning. Many research results (see, e.g., Damasio 1994) indicate that emotion and mood influence other aspects of cognition not explored in our research. For example, the intensity of an emotion appears to have a significant effect on the accessibility of an episodic memory (Philippot and Schaefer 2001), and there are well-documented interactions among emotion, feeling, mood, and decision making (Lewis, Haviland-Jones, and Barret 2008). Understanding these interactions and their functional benefit could have an important effect on future designs of the architecture.

14.3.3 Summary of Analysis of Requirements

Although Soar responds in part to each of the requirements R0–R13, there are shortcomings. A significant amount of research lies ahead of us as we strive to fully meet all of these requirements. Table 14.1 is an attempt to identify which of the components of Soar are responsible for meeting each of the requirements. This is an approximation, since often multiple components, integrated within the architecture as a whole, are responsible for achieving any specific requirement. The rightmost column lists the future Soar research items associated with each of the requirements.

Some observations about connections between the components of Soar and the requirements follow.

• Requirement R0 is achieved not by any single component, but because there is a strong boundary between knowledge and architecture throughout the design of Soar.
• Requirement R1 is achieved through the combination of a symbolic working memory, associative procedural memory, and the PSCM. Those three components are sufficient to realize a symbol system.

Table 14.1

The components of Soar that directly contribute to achieving each requirement.

	Symbolic working memory	Associative procedural memory	Operator-based PSCM	Impasse-driven substates	Chunking	RL	Episodic memory	Semantic memory	Mental imagery	Appraisal-based emotions	Future Soar Research
R0 (fixed structure)											
R1 (symbol system)	X	X	X								
R2 (modality-specific knowledge)									X		1
R3 (large bodies of knowledge)		X					X	X			2, 3
R4 (levels of generality)	X	X					X	X			
R5 (amount of knowledge)		X	X	X			X	X			
R6 (non-perceptual representations)	X			X							
R7 (rich action representations)		X		X							
R8 (innate utilities)						X				X	
R9 (goals across multiple time scales)				X							4
R10 (meta-cognitive knowledge)				X							
R11 (spectrum of deliberation)		X	X	X		X					
R12 (comprehensive learning)	X	X		X	X	X	X	X		X	5, 6, 7
R13 (incremental learning)		X			X	X		X			

• The use of an associative representation (production rules) for procedural memory contributes to a large number of requirements, as does the availability of impasse-driven substates. Together with the PSCM, these components defined the early versions of Soar and continue to be distinctive characteristics of Soar's design.

• Although Soar's PSCM supports only three requirements (R1, R5, R11); it is potentially one of the most important components because it defines the reasoning cycle for an agent, and without it an agent would be unable to use any of the other components.

I conclude with reflections on our research agenda as defined by the FSRs.

Ensuring that agents can effectively employ (R3) and learn (R12) large bodies of sufficiently diverse types of knowledge covers five of the seven areas of future research (FSRs 2, 3, 5, 6, and 7). Although Soar has significant learning mechanisms, they do not yet provide the completeness that is necessary for achieving human-level intelligence. In future research, we plan to extend the current learning mechanisms and perhaps add some yet to be determined new ones. The emphasis on learning is a reflection of the centrality of the acquisition and the use of knowledge in intelligent behavior.

Extending mental imagery so that it supports input from machine vision is an important area for future research, as it is one more step in providing full sensing abilities for Soar agents. Soar agents have used vision systems in the past, but not integrated with mental imagery, and our mental imagery component has received input from low-level sensors. Although it is on our agenda, achieving this item in full will require significant advances in machine vision, and in this case we will be consumers of research results rather than a producer. Our role will be in interfacing SVS to vision systems, and exploring how imagery can provide top-down direction to vision.

The remaining item for future research (FSR4) involves the agent's creating and managing longer-term goals that cannot be pursued when they arise. To date, we have concentrated our research on autonomous agents that exist for minutes to at most a few hours, working on tasks with goals that can be pursued immediately. We plan to study how an agent can use the different long-term memory systems in Soar to maintain, recall, pursue, and possibly put aside long-term goals.

References

Albus, J. S. 2002. 4D/RCS: A reference model architecture for intelligent unmanned ground vehicles. In Proceedings of the SPIE 16th Annual International Symposium on Aerospace/Defense Sensing, Simulation and Controls, Orlando.

Allen, J. F. 1983. Maintaining knowledge about temporal intervals. *Communications of the ACM* 26 (11): 832–843.

Amra, N. K., Smith, J. W., Johnson, K. A., and Johnson, T. R. 1992. An approach to evaluating heuristics in abduction: A case study using Redsoar—An abductive system for red blood cell antibody identification. In *Proceedings of the Sixteenth Annual Symposium on Computer Applications in Medical Care*. McGraw-Hill.

Anderson, J. R. 1976. *Language, Memory, and Thought*. Erlbaum.

Anderson, J. R. 1983. *The Architecture of Cognition*. Harvard University Press.

Anderson, J. R. 1990. *The Adaptive Character of Thought*. Erlbaum.

Anderson, J. R. 1993. *Rules of the Mind*. Erlbaum.

Anderson, J. R. 2007. *How Can the Human Mind Exist in the Physical Universe?* Oxford University Press.

Anderson, J. R., Bothell, D., Lebiere, C., and Matessa, M. 1998. An integrated theory of list memory. *Journal of Memory and Language* 38, 341–380.

Anderson, J. R., Bothell, D., Byrne, M. D., Douglass, S., Lebiere, C., and Qin, Y. 2004. An integrated theory of the mind. *Psychological Review* 111, 1036–1060.

Anderson, J. R., and Lebiere, C. L. 2003. The Newell test for a theory of cognition. *Behavioral and Brain Sciences* 26, 587–637.

Anderson, J. R., and Reder, L. M. 1999. The fan effect: New results and new theories. *Journal of Experimental Psychology. General* 128 (2): 186–197.

Anderson, J. R., and Schooler, L. J. 1991. Reflections of the environment in memory. *Psychological Science* 2, 396–408.

Baars, B. J. 1988. *A Cognitive Theory of Consciousness*. Cambridge University Press.

Ball, J., Rodgers, S., and Gluck, K. 2004. Integrating ACT-R and CYC in a large-scale model of language comprehension for use in intelligent agents. In *Papers from the AAAI Workshop*. AAAI Press.

Barkowsky, T. 2007. Modeling mental spatial knowledge processing: An AI perspective. In *Spatial Processing in Navigation, Imagery, and Perception*, ed. F.Mast and L. Jäncke. Springer.

Barrett, L. F. 2006. Are emotions natural kinds? *Perspectives on Psychological Science* 1 (1): 28–58.

Barsalou, L. W. 2005. Abstraction as dynamic interpretation in perceptual symbol systems. In *Building Object Categories*, ed. L. Gershkoff-Stowe and D. Rakison. Erlbaum.

Barsalou, L. W. 2008. Grounded cognition. *Annual Review of Psychology* 59, 617–645.

Baylor, G. W. 1971. A Treatise on the Mind's Eye: An Empirical Investigation of Visual Mental Imagery. Ph.D. thesis, Carnegie Mellon University.

Benjamin, P., Lyons, D., and Lonsdale, D. 2004. ADAPT: A cognitive architecture for robotics. In Proceedings of the Sixth International Conference on Cognitive Modeling.

Benjamin, P., Lyons, D., and Lonsdale, D. 2006. Embodying a cognitive model in a mobile robot. In Proceedings of the SPIE Conference on Intelligent Robots and Computer Vision.

Best, B. J., and Lebiere, C. 2003. Teamwork, communication, and planning in ACT-R agents engaging in urban combat in virtual environments. In Proceedings of the International Joint Conference on Artificial Intelligence.

Bianchi, R. A. C., Ribeiro, C. H. C., and Costa, A. H. R. 2008. Accelerating autonomous learning by using heuristic selection of actions. *Journal of Heuristics* 14 (2): 135–168.

Black, H. S. 1953. *Modulation Theory*. Van Nostrand.

Bloch, M. K. 2009. *Hierarchical Reinforcement Learning in the Taxicab Domain*. Technical Report CCA-TR-2009-02, Center for Cognitive Architecture, University of Michigan.

Bonasso, R. P., Firby, R. J., Gat, E., Kortenkamp, D., and Slack, M. 1997. A proven three-tiered architecture for programming autonomous robots. *Journal of Experimental & Theoretical Artificial Intelligence* 9, 171–215.

Bonasso, R. P., Firby, R. J., Gat, E., Kortenkamp, D., Miller, D. P., and Slack, M. G. 1997. Experiences with an architecture for intelligent, reactive agents. *Journal of Experimental & Theoretical Artificial Intelligence* 9, 237–256.

Bratman, M. E. 1987. *Intention, Plans, and Practical Reason*. Harvard University Press.

Brooks, R. A. 1999. *Cambrian Intelligence*. MIT Press.

Brown, J. S., and VanLehn, K. A. 1980. Repair theory: A generative theory of bugs in procedural skills. *Cognitive Science* 4, 379–426.

Brownston, L., Farrell, R., Kant, E., and Martin, N. 1985. *Programming Expert Systems in OPS5: An Introduction to Rule-Based Programming.* Addison-Wesley.

Campbell, M., Hoane, A. J., and Hsu, F. 2002. Deep Blue. *Artificial Intelligence* 134 (1–2): 57–83.

Card, S., Moran, T. P., and Newell, A. 1983. *The Psychology of Human Computer Interaction.* Erlbaum.

Carpenter, P. A., Just, M. A., and Shell, P. 1990. What one intelligence test measures: A theoretical account of the processing in the Raven Progressive Matrices Test. *Psychological Review* 97 (3): 404–431.

Cassimatis, N. L. 2002. Polyscheme: A Cognitive Architecture for Integrating Multiple Representation and Inference Schemes. Ph.D. thesis, Massachusetts Institute of Technology.

Cassimatis, N. L. 2006. A cognitive substrate for human-level intelligence. *AI Magazine* 27 (2): 45–56.

Cassimatis, N. L., Bello, P., and Langley, P. 2008. Ability, parsimony and breadth in models of higher-order cognition. *Cognitive Science* 33 (8): 1304–1322.

Chen, W., and Fahlman, S. E. 2008. Modeling mental contexts and their interactions. In *AAAI Fall Symposium on Biologically Inspired Cognitive Architectures.* AAAI Press.

Chi, M. T. H., and VanLehn, K. A. 1991. The content of physics self-explanations. *Journal of the Learning Sciences* 1, 69–105.

Chong, R. S. 2003. The Addition of an Activation and Decay Mechanism to the Soar Architecture. In Proceedings of the Fifth International Conference on Cognitive Modeling, Bamberg, Germany.

Chong, R. S., and Laird, J. E. 1997. Identifying dual-task executive process knowledge using EPIC-Soar. In *Proceedings of the 19th Annual Conference of the Cognitive Science Society.* Erlbaum.

Chong, R. S., and Wray, R. E. 2005. Constraints on architectural models: Elements of ACT-R, Soar and EPIC in human learning and performance. In *Modeling Human Behavior with Integrated Cognitive Architectures: Comparison, Evaluation, and Validation,* ed. K. Gluck and R. Pew. Erlbaum.

Cohen, P. R. 1995. *Empirical Methods for Artificial Intelligence.* MIT Press.

Corkill, D. D. 1991. Blackboard systems. *AI Expert* 6 (9): 40–47.

Corkin, S. 2002. What's new with the amnesic patient H.M.? *Nature Reviews. Neuroscience* 3 (2): 153–160.

Coulter, K., and Laird, J. E. 1996. A briefing-based graphical interface for exercise specification. In Proceedings of the Sixth Conference on Computer Generated Forces and Behavioral Representation, Orlando.

Covrigaru, A., and Lindsay, R. 1991. Deterministic autonomous systems. *AI Magazine* 12 (3): 110–117.

Cutumisu, M., Szafron, D., Bowling, M., and Sutton, R. S. 2008. Agent learning using action-dependent learning rates in computer role-playing games. In Proceedings of the Fourth AIIDE Conference, Stanford.

Damasio, A. 1994. *Descartes' Error: Emotion, Reason, and the Human Brain*. Avon Books.

DeJong, G. F., and Mooney, R. J. 1986. Explanation-based learning: An alternative view. *Machine Learning* 1 (2): 145–176.

Derbinsky, N., and Laird, J. E. 2009. Efficiently implementing episodic memory. In Proceedings of the International Conference on Case-Based Reasoning.

Derbinsky, N., and Laird, J. E. 2011. Effective and efficient management of Soar's working memory via base-level activation. In *Papers from the 2011 AAAI Fall Symposium Series: Advances in Cognitive Systems*. AAAI Press.

Derbinsky, N., Laird, J. E., and Smith, B. 2010. Towards efficiently supporting large symbolic declarative memories. In Proceedings of the Tenth International Conference on Cognitive Modeling, Philadelphia.

Derbinsky, N., and Laird, J. E. 2011. A functional analysis of historical memory retrieval bias in the word sense disambiguation task. In Proceedings of the Twenty-Fifth Conference on Artificial Intelligence.

Dietterich, T. G. 1998. The MAXQ method for hierarchical reinforcement learning. In Proceedings of the Fifteenth International Conference on Machine Learning.

Dietterich, T. G. 2000. Hierarchical reinforcement learning with the MAXQ value function decomposition. *Journal of Artificial Intelligence Research* 13, 227–303.

Doorenbos, B. 1994. Combining left and right unlinking for matching a large number of rules. In Proceedings of the Twelfth National Conference on Artificial Intelligence.

Douglass, S. A., Ball, J., and Rodgers, S. 2009. Large declarative memories in ACT-R. In Proceedings of the Ninth International Conference of Cognitive Modeling, Manchester.

Douglass, S. A., and Myers, C. W. 2010. Concurrent knowledge activation calculation in large declarative memories. In Proceedings of the Tenth International Conference of Cognitive Modeling, Philadelphia.

Doyle, J. 1979. A truth maintenance system. *Artificial Intelligence* 12 (3): 251–272.

Emond, B. 2006. WN-LEXICAL: An ACT-R module built from the WordNet lexical database. In Proceedings of the Seventh International Conference on Cognitive Modeling, Trieste.

Endsley, M. 2000. Theoretical underpinnings of situation awareness: A critical review. In *Situation Awareness Analysis and Measurement*, ed. M. Endsley and D. Garland. Erlbaum.

Englemore, R., and Morgan, T, eds. 1988. *Blackboard Systems*. Addison-Wesley.

Epstein, S. L. 1994. For the right reasons: The FORR architecture for learning in a skill domain. *Cognitive Science* 18 (3): 479–511.

Erman, L. D., and Lesser, V. R. 1980. The HEARSAY-II speech understanding system: Integrating knowledge to resolve uncertainty. *Computing Surveys* 12, 213–253.

Ernst, G., and Newell, A. 1969. *GPS: A Case Study in Generality and Problem Solving*. Academic Press.

Erol, K., Hendler, J., and Nau, D. 1994. HTN planning: Complexity and expressivity. In Proceedings of the National Conference on Artificial Intelligence.

Ferrucci, D., Brown, E., Chu-Carroll, J., Fan, J., Gondek, D., Kalyanpur, A., et al. 2010. Building Watson: An overview of the DeepQA project. *AI Magazine* 31 (3): 59–79.

Fikes, R., Hart, P. E., and Nilsson, N. J. 1972. Learning and executing generalized robot plans. *Artificial Intelligence* 3, 251–288.

Fikes, R., and Nilsson, N. 1971. STRIPS: A new approach in the application of theorem proving to problem solving. *Artificial Intelligence* 2, 189–208.

Finke, R. A. 1989. *Principles of Mental Imagery*. MIT Press.

Firby, J. R. 1987. An investigation into reactive planning in complex domains. In Proceedings of the Twelfth National Conference on Artificial Intelligence, Seattle.

Forbus, K., and Gentner, D. 1997. Qualitative mental models: Simulations or memories? In Proceedings of the Eleventh International Workshop on Qualitative Reasoning, Cortona.

Forbus, K. D., and Hinrichs, T. R. 2006. Companion cognitive systems: A step toward human-level AI. *AI Magazine* 27 (2): 83–95.

Forbus, K. D., Neilsen, P., and Faltings, B. 1991. Qualitative spatial reasoning: The Clock Project. *Artificial Intelligence* 51 (1–3): 417–471.

Forgy, C. L. 1981. *OPS5 User's Manual*. Technical Report CMU-CS-81-135, Carnegie Mellon University.

Forgy, C. L. 1982. Rete: a fast algorithm for the many pattern/many object pattern match problem. *Artificial Intelligence* 19, 17–37.

Franklin, S., Kelemen, A., and McCauley, L. 1998. IDA: A cognitive agent architecture. In *Proceedings of the IEEE Conference on Systems, Man and Cybernetics*. IEEE Press.

Franklin, S., and Patterson, F. G., Jr. 2006. *The LIDA Architecture: Adding New Modes Of Learning to an Intelligent, Autonomous, Software Agent. Integrated Design and Process Technology, IDPT-2006*. Society for Design and Process Science.

Freed, M. 1998. Managing multiple tasks in complex, dynamic environments. In *Proceedings of the Fifteenth National Conference on Artificial Intelligence*. AAAI Press.

Friedman-Hill, E. 2003. *JESS in Action: Java Rule-Based Systems*. Manning Publications.

Funt, B. V. 1976. WHISPER: A Computer Implementation using Analogues in Reasoning. Ph.D. dissertation. Available from ProQuest Dissertations and Theses database.

Furnas, G., Qu, Y., Shrivastava, S., and Peters, G. 2000. The use of intermediate graphical constructions in problem solving with dynamic, pixel-level diagrams. In Proceedings of the First International Conference on the Theory and Application of Diagrams, Edinburgh.

Gardner, M. 1994. *My Best Mathematical and Logic Puzzles*, Dover.

Gat, E. 1991. Integrating planning and reacting in a heterogeneous asynchronous architecture for mobile robots. *SIGART Bulletin* 2, 17–74.

Gelernter, H. 1959. Realization of a geometry theorem-proving machine. In Proceedings of the International Conference on Information Processing, Paris.

Genesereth, M., Love, N., and Pell, B. 2005. General game playing: Overview of the AAAI competition. *AI Magazine* 26 (2): 62–72.

Georgeff, M., and Lansky, A. 1986. Procedural knowledge. *Proceedings of the IEEE Special Issue on Knowledge Representation* 74 (10): 1383–1398.

Ghallab, M., Nau, D., and Traverso, P. 2004. *Automated Planning: Theory and Practice*. Morgan Kaufmann.

Giarratano, J., and Riley, G. 2004. *Expert Systems: Principles and Programming*, fourth edition. Course Technology.

Gilhooly, K. J., Logie, R. H., and Wynn, V. 1999. Syllogistic reasoning tasks, working memory and skill. *European Journal of Cognitive Psychology* 11, 473–498.

Glasgow, J., and Papadias, D. 1992. Computational imagery. *Cognitive Science* 16, 355–394.

Gluck, K., and Pew, R, eds. 2005. *Modeling Human Behavior with Integrated Cognitive Architectures: Comparison, Evaluation, and Validation*. Erlbaum.

Goldman, A. 1989. Interpretation psychologized. *Mind & Language* 4, 161–185.

Gorski, N. A., and Laird, J. E. 2011. Learning to use episodic memory. *Cognitive Systems Research* 12 (2): 144–153.

Gratch, J. 1996. Task-decomposition planning for command decision making. In Proceedings of the Sixth Conference on Computer Generated Forces and Behavioral Representation, Orlando.

Gratch, J. 1998. Reasoning about multiple plans in dynamic multi-agent environments. Presented at AAAI Fall Symposium on Distributed Continual Planning, Orlando.

Gratch, J., and Marsella, M. 2004. A domain-independent framework for modeling emotion. *Cognitive Systems Research* 5, 269–306.

Gratch, J., Marsella, S., and Mao, W. 2006. Towards a validated model of "emotional intelligence." In Proceedings of the 21st Conference on Artificial Intelligence, Boston.

Gratch, J., Marsella, S., and Petta, P. 2009. Modeling the antecedents and consequences of emotion. *Journal of Cognitive Systems Research* 10 (1): 1–5.

Grush, R. 2004. The emulation theory of representation: Motor control, imagery, and perception. *Behavioral and Brain Sciences* 27 (3): 377–396.

Gunzelmann, G., and Lyon, D. R. 2007. Cognitive architectures: Valid control mechanisms for spatial information processing. In *Technical Report #SS07–01: AAAI Spring Symposium Series: Control Mechanisms for Spatial Knowledge Processing in Cognitive/Intelligent Systems*, ed. H. Schultheis et al. AAAI Press.

Harrison, A. M., and Schunn, C. D. 2002. ACT-R/S: A computational and neurologically inspired model of spatial reasoning. In Proceedings of the 24th Annual Meeting of the Cognitive Science Society.

Hayes-Roth, B. 1995. An architecture for adaptive intelligent systems. *Artificial Intelligence* 72 (1–2): 329–365.

Hayes-Roth, B., and Hewett, M. 1988. BB1: An implementation of the blackboard control architecture. In *Blackboard Systems*, ed. R. Engelmore and T. Morgan. Addison-Wesley.

Hernández, D. 1994. *Qualitative Representation of Spatial Knowledge*. Springer-Verlag.

Hill, R. 1999. Modeling perceptual attention in virtual humans. In Proceedings of the Eighth Conference on Computer Generated Forces and Behavioral Representation, Orlando.

Hill, R. W., Chen, J., Gratch, J., Rosenbloom, P., and Tambe, M. 1997. Intelligent agents for the synthetic battlefield: A company of rotary wing aircraft. In *Proceedings of the Ninth Conference on Innovative Applications of Artificial Intelligence*. AAAI Press.

Ho, W. C., Dautenhahn, K., and Nehaniv, C. L. 2003. Comparing different control architectures for autobiographic agents in static virtual environments. In *Intelligent Virtual Agents*, ed. Z. Ruttkay et al. Springer.

Hogewoning, E., Broekens, J., Eggermont, J., and Bovenkamp, E. 2007. Strategies for affect-controlled action-selection in Soar RL. In *IWINAC 2007 Part II*, ed. J. Mira and J. Alvarez. Springer.

Howes, A., and Young, R. M. 1997. The role of cognitive architecture in modeling the user: Soar's learning mechanism. *Human-Computer Interaction* 12 (4): 311–343.

Hsu, W., Prietula, M., and Steier, D. M. 1989, Merl-Soar: Scheduling within a general architecture for intelligence. In Proceedings of the Third International Conference on Expert Systems and the Leading Edge in Production and Operations Management, Columbia.

Hudlicka, E. 2004. Beyond cognition: Modeling emotion in cognitive architectures. In *Proceedings of the Sixth International Conference on Cognitive Modeling*. Erlbaum.

Huffman, S. B., and Laird, J. E. 1992. Using concrete, perceptually-based representations to avoid the frame problem. In Proceedings of the AAAI Spring Symposium on Reasoning with Diagrammatic Representations.

Huffman, S. B., and Laird, J. E. 1995. Flexibly instructable agents. *Journal of Artificial Intelligence Research* 3, 271–324.

Jilk, D. J., Lebiere, C., O'Reilly, R. C., and Anderson, J. R. 2008. SAL: An explicitly pluralistic cognitive architecture. *Journal of Experimental & Theoretical Artificial Intelligence* 20, 197–218.

John, B. E., and Lallement, Y. 1997. Strategy use while learning to perform the Kanfer-Ackerman air traffic controller task. In Proceedings of the Nineteenth Annual Conference of the Cognitive Science Society.

John, B. E., Vera, A. H., and Newell, A. 1994. Towards real time GOMS: A model of expert behavior in a highly interactive task. *Behaviour & Information Technology* 13, 255–267.

Johnson, W. L. 1994. Agents that learn to explain themselves. In *Proceedings of the Twelfth National Conference on Artificial Intelligence*. AAAI Press.

Jones, R. M., Furtwangler, S., and van Lent, M. 2011. Characterizing the performance of applied intelligent agents in Soar. In Proceedings of BRIMS 2011, Sundance.

Jones, R. M., and Laird, J. E. 1997. Constraints on the design of a high-level model of cognition. In Proceedings of the Nineteenth Annual Conference of the Cognitive Science Society.

Jones, R. M., Laird, J. E., Nielsen, P. E., Coulter, K. J., Kenny, P., and Koss, F. V. 1999. Automated intelligent agents for combat flight simulation. *AI Magazine* 20 (1): 27–42.

Jones, R. M., and Wray, R. E. 2006. Comparative analysis of frameworks for knowledge-intensive intelligent agents. *AI Magazine* 27 (3): 57–70.

Just, M. A., Carpenter, P. A., and Varma, S. 1999. Computational modeling of high-level cognition and brain function. *Human Brain Mapping* 8, 128–136.

Just, M. A., and Varma, S. 2007. The organization of thinking: What functional brain imaging reveals about the neuroarchitecture of complex cognition. *Cognitive, Affective & Behavioral Neuroscience* 7, 153–191.

Kaminka, G. A., Pynadath, D. V., and Tambe, M. 2002. Monitoring teams by overhearing: A multi-agent plan recognition approach. *Journal of Artificial Intelligence Research* 17, 83–135.

Kieras, D. E., and Meyer, D. E. 1997. An overview of the EPIC architecture for cognition and performance with application to human-computer interaction. *Human-Computer Interaction* 12, 391–438.

Kim, J., and Rosenbloom, P. S. 2000. Bounding the cost of learned rules. *Artificial Intelligence* 120, 43–80.

Kolodner, J. 1993. *Case-Based Reasoning*. Morgan Kaufmann Publishers.

Könik, T., and Laird, J. 2006. Learning goal hierarchies from structured observations and expert annotations. *Machine Learning* 64, 263–287.

Korf, R. E. 1985. Depth-first iterative-deepening: An optimal admissible tree search. *Artificial Intelligence* 27 (1): 97–109.

Kosslyn, S. M., Chabris, C. F., Marsolek, C. M., and Koenig, O. 1992. Categorical versus coordinate spatial representations: Computational analyses and computer simulations. *Journal of Experimental Psychology. Human Perception and Performance* 18, 562–577.

Kosslyn, S. M., Thompson, W. L., and Ganis, G. 2006. *The Case for Mental Imagery.* Oxford University Press.

Kuokka, D. R. 1991. MAX: A meta-reasoning architecture for "X." *SIGART Bulletin* 2 (4): 93–97.

Kurup, U., and Chandrasekaran, B. 2006. Multi-modal cognitive architectures: A partial solution to the frame problem. In Proceedings of the 28th Annual Conference of the Cognitive Science Society, Vancouver.

Laird, J. E. 1983. Universal Subgoaling. Ph.D. dissertation, Carnegie Mellon University.

Laird, J. E. 1988. Recovery from incorrect knowledge. In Proceedings of the National Conference on Artificial Intelligence.

Laird, J. E. 1991a. Soar. In *Encyclopedia of Artificial Intelligence,* ed. S. Shapiro. Wiley.

Laird, J. E. 1991b. Preface for special section on integrated cognitive architectures. *SIGART Bulletin* 2 (12): 123.

Laird, J. E. 2001a. Using a computer game to develop advanced AI. *Computer* 34, 70–75.

Laird, J. E. 2001b. It knows what you're going to do: Adding anticipation to a Quakebot. In Proceedings of the Fifth International Conference on Autonomous Agents, Montreal.

Laird, J. E. 2008. Extending the Soar cognitive architecture. In Proceedings of the Artificial General Intelligence Conference, Memphis.

Laird, J. E. 2009. Towards cognitive robotics. In Proceedings of the SPIE Defense and Sensing Conferences, Orlando.

Laird, J. E. 2010. *Soar Tutorial, 9.2.* Technical Report CCA-TR-2010-1, Center for Cognitive Architecture, University of Michigan.

Laird, J. E., and Congdon, C. B. 2010. *Soar User's Manual, Version 9.2,* Technical Report CCA-TR-2010-1, Center for Cognitive Architecture, University of Michigan.

Laird, J. E., Derbinsky, N., and Tinkerhess, M. 2011. A case study in integrating probabilistic decision making and learning in a symbolic cognitive architecture: Soar plays dice. In *Papers from the 2011 AAAI Fall Symposium Series: Advances in Cognitive Systems.* AAAI Press.

Laird, J. E., Derbinsky, N., and Voigt, J. 2011. Performance evaluation of declarative memory systems in Soar. In Proceedings of BRIMS 2011, Sundance.

Laird, J. E., Hucka, M., Yager, E., and Tucker, C. 1991. Robo-Soar: An integration of external interaction, planning, and learning, using Soar. *Robotics and Autonomous Systems* 8 (1–2): 113–129.

Laird, J. E., and Newell, A. 1983. A universal weak method: Summary of results. In *Proceedings of the Eighth International Joint Conference on Artificial Intelligence,* ed. A. Bundy. William Kaufmann.

Laird, J. E., Newell, A., and Rosenbloom, P. S. 1987. Soar: An architecture for general intelligence. *Artificial Intelligence* 33 (3): 1–64.

Laird, J. E., Pearson, D. J., Jones, R. M., and Wray, R. E., III. 1996. Dynamic knowledge integration during plan execution. In *Papers from the 1996 AAAI Fall Symposium on Plan Execution: Problems and Issues*. AAAI Press.

Laird, J. E., Pearson, D. J., and Huffman, S. B. 1997. Knowledge-directed adaptation in intelligent agents. *Journal of Intelligent Information Systems* 9, 261–275.

Laird, J. E., and Rosenbloom, P. S. 1990. Integrating execution, planning, and learning in Soar for external environments. In Proceedings of the National Conference of Artificial Intelligence, Boston.

Laird, J. E., and Rosenbloom, P. S. 1996. The evolution of the Soar cognitive architecture. In *Mind Matters: A Tribute to Allen Newell*, ed. D. Steier and T. Mitchell. Erlbaum.

Laird, J. E., Rosenbloom, P. S., and Newell, A. 1986. *Universal Subgoaling and Chunking: The Automatic Generation and Learning of Goal Hierarchies*. Kluwer.

Laird, J. E., Wray, R. E., III, Marinier, R. P., III, and Langley, P. 2009. Claims and challenges in evaluating human-level intelligent systems. In Proceedings of the Second Conference on Artificial General Intelligence.

Laird, J. E., Xu, J. Z., and Wintermute, S. 2010. Using diverse cognitive mechanisms for action modeling. In Proceedings of the Tenth International Conference on Cognitive Modeling, Philadelphia.

Lakatos, I. 1970. Falsification and the Methodology of Scientific Research Programmes. In *Criticism and the Growth of Knowledge*, ed. I. Lakatos and A. Musgrave. Cambridge University Press.

Langley, P., and Choi, D. 2006. A unified cognitive architecture for physical agents. In *Proceedings of the Twenty-First National Conference on Artificial Intelligence*. AAAI Press.

Langley, P., Laird, J. E., and Rogers, S. 2009. Cognitive architectures: Research issues and challenges. *Cognitive Systems Research* 10 (2): 141–160.

Langley, P., McKusick, K., and Allen, J. 1991. A design for the Icarus architecture. *SIGART Bulletin* 2: 104–109.

Larkin, J. H., and Simon, H. A. 1987. Why a diagram is (sometimes) worth ten thousand words. *Cognitive Science* 11, 65–99.

Lathrop, S. D. 2008. Extending Cognitive Architectures with Spatial and Visual Imagery Mechanisms. Ph.D. dissertation, University of Michigan.

Lathrop, S. D., and Laird, J. E. 2007. Towards incorporating visual imagery into a cognitive architecture. In *Proceedings of the Eighth International Conference on Cognitive Modeling*. Taylor and Francis/Psychology Press.

Lathrop, S. D., and Laird, J. E. 2009. Extending cognitive architectures with mental imagery. In Proceedings of the Second Conference on Artificial General Intelligence, Arlington.

Legg, S., and Hutter, M. 2007. Universal intelligence: A definition of machine intelligence. *Minds and Machines* 17 (4): 391–444.

Lehman, J. F., Dyke, J. V., and Rubinoff, R. 1995. Natural language processing for intelligent forces (IFORs): Comprehension and generation in the air combat domain. In Proceedings of the Fifth Conference on Computer Generated Forces and Behavioral Representation, Orlando.

Lehman, J. F., Lewis, R. L., and Newell, A. 1991. Integrating knowledge sources in language comprehension. In Proceedings of the Thirteenth Annual Conference of the Cognitive Science Society.

Lehman, J. F., Lewis, R. L., and Newell, A. 1998. Architectural influences on language comprehension. In *Cognitive Architecture*, ed. Z. Pylyshyn. Ablex.

Lenat, D. 1995. CYC: A large-scale investment in knowledge infrastructure. *Communications of the ACM* 38 (11): 33–38.

Lenat, D., and Guha. R. V. 1990. *Building Large Knowledge-Based Systems: Representation and Inference in the CYC Project*. Addison-Wesley.

Levine, M., Jankovic, I. M., and Palij, M. 1982. Principles of spatial problem solving. *Journal of Experimental Psychology. General* 111, 157–185.

Lewis, C. 1987. Composition of production. In *Production System Models of Learning and Development*, ed. D. Klahr, P. Langley, and R. Neches. MIT Press.

Lewis, M., Haviland-Jones, J. M., and Barret, L. F. 2008. Handbook of Emotions, third edition. Guilford.

Lewis, R. L. 1996. Interference in short-term memory: The magical number two (or three) in sentence processing. *Journal of Psycholinguistic Research* 25, 93–115.

Lisse, S., Wray, R. E., and Huber, M. 2007. Beyond the ad-hoc and the impractically formal: Lessons from the implementation of formalisms of intention. Presented at AAAI Spring Symposium on Intentions in Intelligent Systems, Stanford.

Lonsdale, D., and Rytting, C. A. 2001. Integrating WordNet with NL-Soar; WordNet and other lexical resources: Applications, extensions, and customizations. In Proceedings of NAACL-2001, Association for Computational Linguistics.

Lonsdale, D., Tustison, C., Parker, C., and Embley, D. W. 2006. Formulating queries for assessing clinical trial eligibility. In *Proceedings of the Eleventh International Conference on Applications of Natural Language to Information Systems*. Springer.

Looks, M., Goertzel, B., and Pennachin, C. 2004. Novamente: An integrative architecture for general intelligence. In *Achieving Human-Level Intelligence Through Integrated Systems and Research*. AAAI Press.

Loyall, A. B., Neal Reilly, W. S., Bates, J., and Weyhrauch, P. 2004. System for authoring highly interactive, personality-rich interactive characters. In Proceedings of Eurographics/ACM SIGGRAPH Symposium on Computer Animation.

Lyon, D. R., Gunzelmann, G., and Gluck, K. 2008. A computational model of spatial visualization capacity. *Cognitive Psychology* 57, 122–152.

McCarthy, S. 2004. *Becoming a Tiger.* Harper Collins.

McDaniel, M. A., and Einstein, G. O. 2007. *Prospective Memory: An Overview and Synthesis of an Emerging Field.* Sage.

McDermott, J. 1980. R1: An expert in the computer systems domain. In Proceedings of the First Annual National Conference on Artificial Intelligence, Stanford University.

Magerko, B. 2007. Evaluating preemptive story direction in the interactive drama architecture. *Journal of Game Development* 3.

Magerko, B., Laird, J. E., Assanie, M., Kerfoot, A., and Stokes, D. 2004. AI characters and directors for interactive computer games. In *Proceedings of the 2004 Innovative Applications of Artificial Intelligence Conference.* AAAI Press.

Marinier, R. 2008. A Computational Unification of Cognitive Control, Emotion, and Learning. Ph.D. dissertation, University of Michigan, Ann Arbor.

Marinier, R., Laird, J., and Lewis, R. 2009. A computational unification of cognitive behavior and emotion. *Journal of Cognitive Systems Research* 10 (1): 48–69.

Marr, D. 1982. *Vision.* Freeman.

Marsella, C. S., Adibi, J., Al-Onaizan, Y., Kaminka, G. A., Muslea, I., Tallis, M., et al. 2001. On being a teammate: Experiences acquired in the design of RoboCup teams. *Journal of Autonomous Agents and Multi-Agent Systems* 4 (1–2).

Marsella, S., and Gratch, J. 2009. EMA: A model of emotional dynamics. *Journal of Cognitive Systems Research* 10 (1): 70–90.

Meyer, D. E., and Kieras, D. E. 1997. A computational theory of executive control processes and human multiple-task performance: Part 1. Basic mechanisms. *Psychological Review* 104, 3–65.

Miller, G. A. 1995. WordNet: A lexical database for English. *Communications of the ACM* 38 (11): 39–41.

Miller, C. S., and Laird, J. E. 1996. Accounting for graded performance within a discrete search framework. *Cognitive Science* 20 (4): 499–537.

Minton, S. N. 1985. Selectively generalizing plans for problem-solving. In Proceedings of the Ninth International Joint Conference on Artificial intelligence.

Minton, S. N., Carbonell, J., Knoblock, C., Kuokka, D. R., Etzioni, O., and Gil, Y. 1989. Explanation-based learning: A problem-solving perspective. *Artificial Intelligence* 40 (1): 63–118.

Mitchell, T. M., Allen, J., Chalasani, P., Cheng, J., Etzoni, O., Ringuette, M., et al. 1991. Theo: A framework for self-improving systems. In *Architectures for Intelligence*, ed. K. VanLehn. Erlbaum.

Mitchell, T. M., Keller, R. M., and Kedar-Cabelli, S. T. 1986. Explanation-based generalization: A unifying view. *Machine Learning* 1 (1): 47–80.

Mohan, S., and Laird, J. E. 2011. An object-oriented approach to reinforcement learning in an action game. In Proceedings of the Seventh AIIDE Conference, Stanford.

Moran, T. P. 1973. The Symbolic Imagery Hypothesis: An Empirical Investigation via a Production System Simulation of Human Behavior in a Visualization Task. Ph.D. thesis, Carnegie Mellon University.

Musliner, D. J., Durfee, E. H., and Shin, K. G. 1993. CIRCA: A cooperative intelligent real-time control architecture. *IEEE Transactions on Systems, Man, and Cybernetics* 23 (6): 1561–1574.

Nason, S., and Laird, J. 2005. Soar-RL, integration reinforcement learning with Soar. *Cognitive Systems Research* 6, 51–59.

Neal Reilly, W. S. 1996. *Believable Social and Emotional Agents*. Technical Report CMU-CS-96-138, Carnegie Mellon University.

Neal Reilly, W. S. 2006. Modeling what happens between emotional antecedents and emotional consequents. In *Proceedings of the Eighteenth European Meeting on Cybernetics and Systems Research*. Austrian Society for Cybernetic Studies.

Nelson, G., Lehman, J. F., and John, B. 1994. Integrating cognitive capabilities in a real-time task. In Proceedings of the Sixteenth Annual Conference of the Cognitive Science Society.

Newell, A. 1968. Heuristic programming: Ill-structured problems. In *Progress in Operations Research III*, ed. J. Arofonsky. Wiley.

Newell, A. 1973. Production systems: Models of control structures. In *Visual Information Processing*, ed. W. Chase. Academic Press.

Newell, A. 1982. The knowledge level. *Artificial Intelligence* 18, 87–127.

Newell, A. 1990. *Unified Theories of Cognition: The William James Lectures 1987*. Harvard University Press.

Newell, A. 1991. Reasoning, problem solving and decision processes: The problem space as a fundamental category. In *Attention and Performance VIII*, ed. N. Nickerson. Erlbaum.

Newell, A., and Rosenbloom, P. S. 1981. Mechanisms of skill acquisition and the law of practice. In *Learning and Cognition*, ed. J. Anderson. Erlbaum.

Newell, A., and Simon, H. A. 1956. The logic theory machine: A complex information processing system. *Institute of Radio Engineers Transactions on Information Theory* 2 (3): 61–79.

Newell, A., and Simon, H. A. 1972. *Human Problem Solving*. Prentice-Hall.

Newell, A., and Steier, D. M. 1993. Intelligent control of external software systems. *Artificial Intelligence in Engineering* 8 (1): 3–21.

Newell, A., Yost, G. R., Laird, J. E., Rosenbloom, P. S., and Altmann, E. M. 1991. Formulating the problem space computational model. In *CMU Computer Science: A 25th Anniversary Commemorative*, ed. R. Rashid. ACM Press/Addison-Wesley.

Nielsen, P., Beard, J., Kiessel, J., and Beisaw, J. 2002. Robust behavior modeling. In Proceedings of the Eleventh Computer Generated Forces Conference.

Nielsen, P., Koss, F., Taylor, G., and Jones, R. M. 2000. Communication with intelligent agents. In Proceedings of the 2000 Interservice/Industry Training Simulation, and Education Conference, Orlando.

Norman, J. 2000. Differentiating diagrams: A new approach. In *Theory and Application of Diagrams*, ed. M. Anderson, P. Cheng, P., and V. Haarslev. Springer.

Nuxoll, A. M. 2007. Enhancing intelligent agents with episodic memory. Ph.D. thesis, University of Michigan.

Nuxoll, A. M., and Laird, J. 2004. A cognitive model of episodic memory integrated with a general cognitive architecture. In Proceedings of the International Conference on Cognitive Modeling.

Nuxoll, A. M., and Laird, J. E. 2007. Extending cognitive architecture with episodic memory. In Proceedings of the 22nd National Conference on Artificial Intelligence.

Nuxoll, A. M., and Laird, J. E., and James, M. 2004. Comprehensive working memory activation in Soar. In Proceedings of the International Conference on Cognitive Modeling.

Nuxoll, A. M., Tecuci, D., Ho, W. C., and Wang, N. 2010. Comparing forgetting algorithms for artificial episodic memory systems. In Proceedings of the Symposium on Human Memory for Artificial Agents.

O'Reilly, R. C., and Munakata, Y. 2000. *Computational Explorations in Cognitive Neuroscience*. MIT Press.

Pearson, D. J. 1996. Learning Procedural Planning Knowledge in Complex Environments, Ph.D. thesis, University of Michigan.

Pearson, D. J., Huffman, S. B., Willis, M. B., Laird, J. E., and Jones, R. M. 1993. A symbolic solution to intelligent real-time control. *IEEE Robotics and Autonomous Systems* 11, 279–291.

Pearson, D. J., and Laird, J. E. 1998. Toward incremental knowledge correction for agents in complex environments. *Machine Intelligence* 15: 185–204.

Pearson, D. J., and Laird, J. E. 2004. Redux: Example-driven diagrammatic tools for rapid knowledge acquisition. In Proceedings of the Conference on Behavior Representation in Modeling and Simulation, Washington.

Pearson, D. J., and Laird, J. E. 2005. Incremental learning of procedural planning knowledge in challenging environments. *Computational Intelligence* 21 (4): 414.

Peck, V. A., and John, B. E. 1992. Browser-Soar: A computational model of a highly interactive task. In *Proceedings of the ACM SIGCHI Conference on Human Factors in Computing Systems*. ACM Press.

Pollock, J. L. 1999. Rational cognition in OSCAR. In *Proceedings of Agent Theories, Architectures, and Languages*. Springer.

Post, E. 1943. Formal reductions of the general combinatorical problem. *American Journal of Mathematics* 65, 197–268.

Pylyshyn, Z. W. 1986. *Computation and Cognition: Toward a Foundation for Cognitive Science*. MIT Press.

Pylyshyn, Z. W. 2001. Visual indexes, preconceptual objects, and situated vision. *Cognition* 80 (1–2): 127–158.

Ram, A., and Santamaría, J. C. 1997. Continuous case-based reasoning. *Artificial Intelligence* 90 (1–2): 25–77.

Richardson, M., and Domingos, P. 2006. Markov logic networks. *Machine Learning* 62, 107–136.

Roseman, I., and Smith, C. 2001. Appraisal theory: Overview, assumptions, varieties, controversies. In *Appraisal Processes in Emotion: Theory, Methods, Research*, ed. K. Scherer, A. Schorr, and T. Johnstone. Oxford University Press.

Rosenbloom, P. S. 2006. A cognitive odyssey: From the power law of practice to a general learning mechanism and beyond. *Tutorials in Quantitative Methods for Psychology* 2 (2): 38–42.

Rosenbloom, P. S. 2011. Rethinking cognitive architecture via graphical models. *Cognitive Systems Research* 12 (2): 198–209.

Rosenbloom, P. S., Laird, J. E., McDermott, J., Newell, A., and Oruich, E. 1985. R1-Soar: An experiment in knowledge intensive programming in a problem-solving architecture. *IEEE Transactions on Pattern Analysis and Machine Intelligence* 7 (5): 561–569.

Rosenbloom, P. S., Laird, J. E., and Newell, A. 1986. Meta-levels in Soar. In Proceedings of the Workshop on Meta-level Architecture and Reflection, Sardinia.

Rosenbloom, P. S., Laird, J. E., and Newell, A. 1993. *The Soar Papers: Research on Integrated Intelligence*. MIT Press.

Rosenbloom, P. S., Laird, J. E., Newell, A., and McCarl, R. 1991. A preliminary analysis of the foundations of Soar. *Artificial Intelligence* 47 (1–3): 289–325.

Rummery, G. A., and Niranjan, M. 1994. *On-Line Q-Learning Using Connectionist Systems*. Technical Report CUED/F-INFENG/TR 166, Engineering Department, Cambridge University.

Sacerdoti, E. D. 1977. *A Structure for Plans and Behavior*. Elsevier.

Salichs, M., and Malfaz, M. 2006. Using emotions on autonomous agents: The role of happiness, sadness, and fear. In *Adaptation in Artificial and Biological Systems*. University of Bristol.

Samsonovich, A. V., and Nadel, L. 2005. Fundamental principles and mechanisms of the conscious self. *Cortex* 41 (5): 669–689.

Scherer, K. 2001. Appraisal considered as a process of multi-level sequential checking. In *Appraisal Processes in Emotion: Theory, Methods, Research*, ed. K. Scherer, A. Schorr, A., and T. Johnstone. Oxford University Press.

Scherer, K., Schorr, A., and Johnstone, T, eds. 2001. *Appraisal Processes in Emotion: Theory, Methods, Research*. Oxford University Press.

Schmidhuber, J. 1991. A possibility for implementing curiosity and boredom in model-building neural controllers. In *From Animals to Animats: Proceedings of the First International Conference on Simulation of Adaptive Behavior*, ed. J.-A. Meyer and S. Wilson. MIT Press.

Shapiro, D., and Langley, P. 1999. Controlling physical agents through reactive logic programming. In *Proceedings of the Third International Conference on Autonomous Agents*. ACM Press.

Simon, H. A. 1969. *The Sciences of the Artificial*, first edition. MIT Press.

Simon, H. A., and Newell, A. 1958. Heuristic problem solving: The next advance in operations research. *Operations Research* 6 (1): 1–10.

Sims, E., and Taylor, G. 2009. Modeling believable virtual humans for interpersonal communication. Presented at Interservice/Industry Training, Simulation and Education Conference, Orlando.

Singh, S., Barto, A, and Chentanez, N. 2004. Intrinsically motivated reinforcement learning. *Proceedings of Advances in Neural Information Processing Systems* 17.

Singh, S., Jaakkola, T., Littman, M. L., and Szepesvári, C. 2000. Convergence results for single-step on-policy reinforcement-learning algorithms. *Machine Learning* 38, 287–308.

Smith, C. A., and Kirby, L. A. 2001. Toward delivering on the promise of appraisal theory. In *Appraisal Processes in Emotion: Theory, Methods, Research*, ed. K. Scherer, A. Schorr, and T. Johnstone. Oxford University Press.

Steier, D. M. 1987. CYPRESS-Soar: A case study in search and learning in algorithm design. In Proceedings of the Tenth International Joint Conference on Artificial Intelligence.

Steier, D. M., Laird, J. E., Newell, A., Rosenbloom, P. S., Flynn, R., Golding, A., et al. 1987. Varieties of learning in Soar: 1987. In Proceedings of the Fourth International Machine Learning Workshop, Irvine.

Steier, D. M., and Newell, A. 1988. Integrating multiple sources of knowledge into Designer-Soar, an automatic algorithm designer. In *Proceedings of the Seventh National Conference on Artificial Intelligence*. AAAI Press.

Stensrud, B., Taylor, G., and Crossman, J. 2006. IF-Soar: A virtual, speech-enabled agent for indirect fire training. Presented at 25th Army Science Conference, Orlando.

Stensrud, B., Taylor, G., Schricker, B., Montefusco, J., and Maddox, J. 2008. An intelligent user interface for enhancing computer generated forces. Presented at Simulation Interoperability Workshop, Orlando.

Stracuzzi, D. J., Li, N., Cleveland, G., and Langley, P. 2009. Representing and reasoning over time in a cognitive architecture. In Proceedings of Thirty-First Annual Meeting of Cognitive Science Society, Amsterdam.

Strosnider, J., and Paul, C. 1994. A structured view of real-time problem solving. *AI Magazine* 15 (2): 45–66.

Sun, R. 1997. Learning, action, and consciousness: A hybrid approach towards modeling consciousness. *Neural Networks* 10 (7): 1317–1331.

Sun, R. 2004. Desiderata for cognitive architecture. *Philosophical Psychology* 17 (3): 341–373.

Sun, R. 2006. The CLARION cognitive architecture: extending cognitive modeling to social simulation. In *Cognition and Multi-Agent Interaction*, ed. R. Sun. Cambridge University Press.

Sussman, G. J. 1975. *A Computer Model of Skill Acquisition*. Elsevier Science Inc.

Sutton, R. S., and Barto, A. G. 1998. *Reinforcement Learning: An Introduction*. MIT Press.

Swartout, W., Gratch, J., Hill, R., Hovy, E., Marsella, S., Rickel, J., et al. 2006. Toward virtual humans. *AI Magazine* 27 (1): 96–108.

Taatgen, N., Van Rijn, H., and Anderson, J. R. 2007. An integrated theory of prospective time interval estimation: The role of cognition, attention, and learning. *Psychological Review* 114 (3): 577–598.

Tabachneck-Schijf, H. J. M., Leonardo, A. M., and Simon, H. A. 1997. CaMeRa: A computational model of multiple representations. *Cognitive Science* 21 (3): 305–350.

Tambe, M. 1997. Towards flexible teamwork. *Journal of Artificial Intelligence Research* 7, 83–124.

Tambe, M., Johnson, W. L., Jones, R. M., Koss, F., Laird, J. E., Rosenbloom, P. S., et al. 1995. Intelligent agents for interactive simulation environments. *AI Magazine* 16 (1): 15–40.

Tambe, M., Newell, A., and Rosenbloom, P. S. 1990. The problem of expensive chunks and its solution by restricting expressiveness. *Machine Learning* 5 (3): 299–348.

Tambe, M., and Rosenbloom, P. S. 1995. RESC: An approach for real-time, dynamic agent tracking. Presented at 14th International Joint Conference on Artificial Intelligence.

Tanner, B., and White, A. 2009. RL-Glue: Language-independent software for reinforcement-learning experiments. *Journal of Machine Learning Research* 10, 2133–2136.

Tate, A. 1977. Generating project networks. In Proceedings of IJCAI-1977.

Taylor, G., Jones, R. M., Goldstein, M., Fredericksen, R., and Wray, R. E. 2002. VISTA: A generic toolkit for agent visualization. In Proceedings of the Eleventh Conference on Computer Generated Forces and Behavioral Representation, University of Central Florida.

Taylor, G., Koss, F., and Nielsen, P. E. 2001. Special Operations Forces IFORS. Presented at Tenth Conference on Computer Generated Forces and Behavioral Representation.

Taylor, G., Knudsen, K., and Holt, L. 2006. Explaining agent behavior. In Proceedings of the Fourteenth Behavior Representation in Modeling and Simulation, Baltimore.

Taylor, G., Quist, M., Furtwangler, S., and Knudsen, K. 2007. Toward a hybrid cultural cognitive architecture. Presented at Cognitive Science Workshop on Culture and Cognition, Nashville.

Taylor, G., Stensrud, B., Eitelman, S., Durham, C., and Harger, E. 2007. *Toward Automating Airspace Management. Computational Intelligence for Security and Defense Applications (CISDA)*. IEEE Press.

Thibadeau, R., Just, M. A., and Carpenter, P. A. 1982. A model of the time course and content of reading. *Cognitive Science* 6, 157–203.

Thorndike, E. 1932. *The Fundamentals of Learning*. Teachers College Press.

Tulving, E. 1983. *Elements of Episodic Memory*. Clarendon.

van Lent, M., and Laird, J. E. 2001. Learning procedural knowledge through observation. In *International Conference on Knowledge Capture*. ACM Press.

Veloso, M. M., Carbonell, J. G., P'erez, M., Borrajo, D., Fink, E., and Blythe, J. 1995. Integrating planning and learning: The Prodigy architecture. *Journal of Experimental & Theoretical Artificial Intelligence* 7 (1): 81–120.

Vere, S. A., and Bickmore, T. W. 1990. A basic agent. *Computational Intelligence* 6, 41–60.

Walsh, M. M., and Anderson, J. R. 2010. Neural correlates of temporal credit assignment. In Proceedings of the Tenth International Conference on Cognitive Modeling. Philadelphia.

Wang, Y., and Laird, J. E. 2007. The importance of action history in decision making and reinforcement learning. In Proceedings of the Eighth International Conference on Cognitive Modeling. Ann Arbor.

Wang, Y., and Laird, J. E. 2010. A computational model of functional category learning in a cognitive architecture. In Proceedings of the Tenth International Conference on Cognitive Modeling, Philadelphia.

Washington, R., and Rosenbloom, P. S. 1993. Applying problem solving and learning to diagnosis. In *The Soar Papers: Research on Integrated Intelligence*, ed. P. Rosenbloom, J. Laird, and A. Newell. MIT Press.

Watkins, C. J. C. H. 1989. Learning from Delayed Rewards. Ph.D. thesis, University of Cambridge.

Wiesmeyer, M. D., and Laird, J. E. 1990. A computer model of visual attention. Presented at Twelfth Annual Conference of the Cognitive Science Society, Boston.

Wintermute, S. 2009a. Integrating reasoning and action through simulation. In Proceedings of the Second Conference on Artificial General Intelligence, Arlington.

Wintermute, S. 2009b. *An Overview of Spatial Processing in Soar/SVS*. Technical Report CCA-TR-2009-01, Center for Cognitive Architecture, University of Michigan.

Wintermute, S. 2009c. Representing problems (and plans) using imagery. In *Papers from the 2009 AAAI Fall Symposium Series: Multi-Representational Architectures for Human-Level Intelligence*. AAAI Press.

Wintermute, S. 2010. Abstraction, Imagery, and Control in Cognitive Architecture. Ph.D. thesis, University of Michigan, Ann Arbor.

Wintermute, S., and Laird, J. E. 2007. Predicate projection in a bimodal spatial reasoning system. In Proceedings of the 22nd AAAI Conference on Artificial Intelligence. Vancouver.

Wintermute, S., and Laird, J. E. 2008. Bimodal spatial reasoning with continuous motion. In Proceedings of the 23rd AAAI Conference on Artificial Intelligence, Chicago.

Wintermute, S., and Laird, J. E. 2009. Imagery as compensation for an imperfect abstract problem representation. In Proceedings of the 31st Annual Conference of the Cognitive Science Society.

Wintermute, S., Xu, J., and Laird, J. E. 2007. SORTS: A human-level approach to real-time strategy AI. In *Proceedings of the Third Artificial Intelligence and Interactive Digital Entertainment Conference*. AAAI Press.

Wood, S., Zaientz, J., Beard, J., Frederiksen, R., and Huber, M. 2003. CIANC3: An agent-based intelligent interface for the future combat system. In Proceedings of the 2003 Conference on Behavior Representation in Modeling and Simulation, Scottsdale.

Wooldridge, M. J. 2000. *Reasoning about Rational Agents*. MIT Press.

Wray, R. E., and Chong, R. S. 2007. Comparing cognitive models and human behavior models: Two computational tools for expressing human behavior. *Journal of Aerospace Computing, Information, and Communication* 4, 836–852.

Wray, R. E., Chong, R. S., Phillips, J., Rogers, S., and Walsh, B. 1992. A Survey of Cognitive and Agent Architectures. Available at http://ai.eecs.umich.edu/cogarch0/.

Wray, R. E., and Jones, R. M. 2005. An introduction to Soar as an agent architecture. In *Cognition and Multi-Agent Interaction: From Cognitive Modeling to Social Interaction*, ed. R. Sun. Cambridge University Press.

Wray, R. E., and Laird, J. E. 2003. An architectural approach to consistency in hierarchical execution. *Journal of Artificial Intelligence Research* 19, 355–398.

Wray, R. E., Laird, J. E., Nuxoll, A., Stokes, D., and Kerfoot, A. 2005. Synthetic adversaries for urban combat training. *AI Magazine* 26 (3): 82–92.

Wray, R. E., Lisse, S., and Beard, J. 2004. Investigating ontology infrastructures for execution-oriented autonomous agents. *Robotics and Autonomous Systems* 49, 113–122.

Wray, R. E., van Lent, M., Beard, J. T., and Brobst, P. 2005. The design space of control options for AIs in computer games. In *Proceedings of the IJCAI 2005 Workshop on Reasoning, Representation, and Learning in Computer Games*. US Naval Research Laboratory, Edinburgh.

Xu, J., and Laird, J. E. 2010. Instance-based online learning of deterministic relational action models. In Proceedings of the 24th Conference on Artificial Intelligence, Atlanta.

Xu, J., and Laird, J. E. 2011.Combining learned discrete and continuous action models. In Proceedings of the Twenty-Fifth Conference on Artificial Intelligence.

Yik, M., Russell, J., and Barrett, L. 1999. Structure of self-reported current affect: Integration and beyond. *Journal of Personality and Social Psychology* 77 (3): 600–619.

Young, R., and Lewis, R. L. 1999. The Soar cognitive architecture and human working memory. In *Models of Working Memory: Mechanisms of Active Maintenance and Executive Control*, ed. A. Miyake, and P. Shah. Cambridge University Press.

Zaientz, J. D., and Beard, J. 2006. Using knowledge-based interface design techniques to support visual analytics. In Proceedings of the International Conference on Intelligent User Interfaces, Sydney.

Zwaan, R., and Radvansky, G. 1998. Situation models in language comprehension and memory. *Psychological Bulletin* 123, 162–185.

Index

Printed in the United States
by Baker & Taylor Publisher Services

Printed in the United States
by Baker & Taylor Publisher Services